Lecture Notes in Economics and Mathematical Systems

Managing Editors: M. Beckmann and H. P. Künzi

Systems Theory

101

W. Murray Wonham

Linear Multivariable Control

A Geometric Approach

Springer-Verlag
Berlin · Heidelberg · New York 1974

Dr. Walter Murray Wonham
Department of Electrical
Engineering
University of Toronto
Toronto/Canada M5S 1A4

Library of Congress Cataloging in Publication Data

Wonham, W M 1934-
Linear multivariable control.

(Lecture notes in economics and mathematical systems ; 101 : Operations research)
Bibliography: p.
Includes index.
1. Control theory. 2. Algebras, Linear. I. Title. II. Series: Lecture notes in economics and mathematical systems ; 101. III. Series: Operations research (Berlin).
QA402.3.W59 629.8'312 74-19470

AMS Subject Classifications (1970): 93B25

ISBN 3-540-06956-9 Springer-Verlag Berlin · Heidelberg · New York
ISBN 0-387-06956-9 Springer-Verlag New York · Heidelberg · Berlin

Offsetprinting and bookbinding: Julius Beltz, Hemsbach/Bergstr.

To Anne

PREFACE

In writing this monograph my objective is to present a recent, 'geometric' approach to the structural synthesis of multivariable control systems that are linear, time-invariant, and of finite dynamic order. The book is addressed to graduate students specializing in control, to engineering scientists engaged in control systems research and development, and to mathematicians with some previous acquaintance with control problems.

The label 'geometric' is applied for several reasons. First and obviously, the setting is linear state space and the mathematics chiefly linear algebra in abstract (geometric) style. The basic ideas are the familiar system concepts of controllability and observability, thought of as geometric properties of distinguished state subspaces. Indeed, the geometry was first brought in out of revulsion against the orgy of matrix manipulation which linear control theory mainly consisted of, not so long ago. But secondly and of greater interest, the geometric setting rather quickly suggested new methods of attacking synthesis which have proved to be intuitive and economical; they are also easily reduced to matrix arithmetic as soon as you want to compute. The essence of the 'geometric' approach is just this: instead of looking directly for a feedback law (say $u = Fx$) which would solve your synthesis problem if a solution exists, first characterize solvability as a verifiable property of some constructible state subspace, say $\mathscr{S}$. Then, if all is well, you may calculate F from $\mathscr{S}$ quite easily. When it works, the method converts what is usually an intractable nonlinear problem in F, to a straightforward quasilinear one in $\mathscr{S}$.

By this means the first reasonably complete structure theory has been given for two control problems of longstanding interest: regulation, and noninteraction. Of course, no claim is made that the methods employed are the best, and I leave the reader to judge whether one sort of orgy has just been replaced by another.

The book is organized as follows. Chapter 0 is a quick review of linear algebra and selected rudiments of linear systems. It is assumed that the reader already has some working knowledge in these areas. Chapters 1 - 3 cover mainly standard material on controllability and observability, although sometimes in a more 'geometric' style than has been customary, and at times with greater completeness than in the literature to date. The essentially new concepts are (A, B)-invariant subspaces and (A, B)-controllability subspaces: these are introduced in Chapters 4 and 5, along with a few primitive applications by way of motivation and illustration. The first major application – to tracking and regulation – is developed in leisurely style through Chapters 6 – 8. In Chapters 6 and 7 purely algebraic conditions are investigated, for output regulation alone and then for regulation along with internal stability. Chapter 8 attacks the problem of qualitative insensitivity to small parameter variations. The result is a simplified, 'generic' version of the general algebraic setup, leading finally to a structurally stable synthesis, as required in any practical implementation. A similar plan is followed in treating the second main topic, noninteracting control: first the algebraic development, in Chapters 9 and 10, then generic solvability in Chapter 11. No description is attempted of structurally stable synthesis of noninteracting controllers, as this is seen to require adaptive control, at a level of complexity beyond the domain of strictly linear structures; but its feasibility in principle should be clear. The two closing Chapters 12 and 13 deal with quadratic optimization. While not strongly dependent on the preceding geometric ideas the presentation, via dynamic programming, is perhaps a little more complete than what is available in this style in current textbooks. In any event the topic is standard in most courses on linear control.

The framework throughout is state space, only casual use being made of frequency domain representations and procedures. It would be a highly worthwhile project to link the 'geometric approach' with some of the recent synthesis techniques based on transfer matrices. Again for the future, intriguing possibilities exist for the use of geometric methods in exploring other major problems of multivariable system structure: for instance, the contrasting philosophies of hierarchical and decentralized control. I hope the book may be seminal in these respects.

A word on pedagogy. The main text is devoted to the theoretical development. To minimize clutter, nearly all routine numerical examples have been placed among the exercises at the end of each chapter. With these as guide the reader should easily learn to translate the relatively abstract language of the theory, with its stress on the qualitative and geometric, into the computational language of everyday matrix arithmetic. While the book is not primarily a design manual, the computational procedures sketched out have all been programmed in APL and successfully run on systems of (modest) dynamic order 10 to 15. But much worthwhile and interesting work can and should be done on numerical aspects which are here entirely ignored.

More than half this book is based on published research coauthored with several colleagues and graduate students, and it is a pleasure to re-affirm my considerable debt to them: Steve Morse, Boyd Pearson, Ellis Fabian, Bruce Francis and Omar Sebakhy. In addition I owe much to conversations with Ted Davison, Mike Sain, Harold Smith, Jakov Snyders, Shi-Ho Wang, Ming Chan, Witold Gesing, Jan Van den Kieboom and Joe Yuan. Finally, thanks are due to Professor A.V. Balakrishnan for his editorial encouragement to publish this work in the Springer-Verlag 'Lecture Notes' series; and to Mrs. Rita de Clercq Zubli for her expert preparation of the typescript.

Toronto
June, 1974

W.M. Wonham

CONTENTS

CHAPTER 13. QUADRATIC OPTIMIZATION II: DYNAMIC RESPONSE (cont'd)

LIST OF FIGURES

CHAPTER 0

MATHEMATICAL PRELIMINARIES

We quickly review linear algebra and the rudiments of linear dynamic systems. Almost nothing is proved: detailed developments can be found in the textbooks listed at the end of the chapter. The reader unfamiliar with this material is advised to sample Ex. 0.1 before going further.

0.1 Notation

If k is a positive integer, $\underline{k}$ denotes the set of integers $\{1, 2, \ldots, k\}$. If Λ is a finite set, $|\Lambda|$ denotes the number of its elements. The real and imaginary parts of a complex number, vector, etc. are written $\mathcal{R}e$, $\mathcal{I}m$, respectively.

0.2 Linear Spaces

The definition of a linear (vector) space is assumed known. We consider only spaces over the field of real numbers $\mathbb{R}$ or complex numbers $\mathbb{C}$. The symbol $\mathbb{F}$ will be used for either field. Linear spaces are denoted by script capitals $\mathcal{X}$, $\mathcal{Y}, \ldots$; their elements (vectors) by lower case Roman letters, x, y, ...; and field elements by lower case Roman or Greek letters. The symbol 0 stands for anything which is zero (a number, vector, map, or subspace), according to context.

Let $x_1, \ldots, x_k \in \mathcal{X}$, defined over $\mathbb{F}$. Their span, written

$$\mathrm{Span}_{\mathbb{F}}\{x_1, \ldots, x_k\} \quad \text{or} \quad \mathrm{Span}_{\mathbb{F}}\{x_i,\ i \in \underline{k}\}$$

is the set of all linear combinations of the x_i, with coefficients in $\mathbb{F}$. The subscript $\mathbb{F}$ will be dropped if the field is clear from context. $\mathcal{X}$ is finite-dimensional if there exist a (finite) k and a set $\{x_i,\ i \in \underline{k};\ x_i \in \mathcal{X}\}$ whose span is $\mathcal{X}$. The least k for which this happens is the dimension of $\mathcal{X}$, written $d(\mathcal{X})$. If $k = d(\mathcal{X})$, a spanning set $\{x_i,\ i \in \underline{k}\}$ is a basis for $\mathcal{X}$.

Unless otherwise stated, all linear spaces are finite dimensional; the rare exceptions will be some common function spaces, to be introduced only when needed.

A set $\{x_i \in \mathcal{X},\ i \in \underline{m}\}$ is (linearly) independent (over $\mathbb{F}$) if for all sets $\{c_i \in \mathbb{F},\ i \in \underline{m}\}$, the relation

$$\sum_{i=1}^{m} c_i x_i = 0 \tag{1}$$

implies $c_i = 0$ (all $i \in \underline{m}$). If the x_i ($i \in \underline{m}$) are independent, and if $x \in \text{Span}\{x_i, i \in \underline{m}\}$, then the representation

$$x = c_1 x_1 + \cdots + c_m x_m$$

is unique. The vectors of a basis are necessarily independent. If $m > d(\mathcal{X})$, the set $\{x_i, i \in \underline{m}\}$ must be dependent, i.e., there exist $c_i \in \mathbf{F}$ ($i \in \underline{m}$) not all zero, such that (1) is true.

Let $d(\mathcal{X}) = n$ and fix a basis $\{x_i, i \in \underline{n}\}$. If $x \in \mathcal{X}$ then $x = c_1 x_1 + \cdots + c_n x_n$ for unique $c_i \in \mathbf{F}$. For computational purposes x will be represented, as usual, by the $n \times 1$ column vector $\text{col}(c_1, \ldots, c_n)$. As usual, vector addition, and scalar multiplication by elements in $\mathbf{F}$, are done componentwise on the representative column vectors.

In most of our applications, linear spaces $\mathcal{X}$, etc. will be defined initially over $\mathbb{R}$. It is then sometimes convenient to introduce the complexification of $\mathcal{X}$, written $\mathcal{X}_{\mathbb{C}}$ and defined, over the field $\mathbb{C}$, as the set of formal sums

$$\mathcal{X}_{\mathbb{C}} = \{x_1 + i x_2 : x_1, x_2 \in \mathcal{X}\},$$

i being the imaginary unit. Addition and scalar multiplication in $\mathcal{X}_{\mathbb{C}}$ are done in the obvious way. In this notation if $x = x_1 + i x_2 \in \mathcal{X}_{\mathbb{C}}$ then $\mathcal{Re}\, x \triangleq x_1$ and $\mathcal{Im}\, x \triangleq x_2$. Note that $d(\mathcal{X}_{\mathbb{C}}) = d(\mathcal{X})$, because if $\{x_i, i \in \underline{n}\}$ is a basis for $\mathcal{X}$, so that

$$\mathcal{X} = \text{Span}_{\mathbb{R}}\{x_i, i \in \underline{n}\}$$

then

$$\mathcal{X}_{\mathbb{C}} = \text{Span}_{\mathbb{C}}\{x_i, i \in \underline{n}\},$$

and clearly $x_1, \ldots, x_n$ are independent over $\mathbb{C}$.

0.3 Subspaces

A (linear) subspace $\mathcal{S}$ of the linear space $\mathcal{X}$ is a subset of $\mathcal{X}$ which is a linear space under the operations of vector addition and scalar multiplication inherited from $\mathcal{X}$: namely $\mathcal{S} \subset \mathcal{X}$ (as a set) and for all $x_1, x_2 \in \mathcal{S}$ and $c_1, c_2 \in \mathbf{F}$ we have $c_1 x_1 + c_2 x_2 \in \mathcal{S}$. The notation $\mathcal{S} \subset \mathcal{X}$ (with $\mathcal{S}$ a script capital) will henceforth mean that $\mathcal{S}$ is a subspace of $\mathcal{X}$. If $x_i \in \mathcal{X}$ ($i \in \underline{k}$), then $\text{Span}\{x_i, i \in \underline{k}\}$ is a subspace of $\mathcal{X}$. Geometrically, a subspace is a hyperplane passing through the origin of $\mathcal{X}$. We have $0 \le d(\mathcal{S}) \le d(\mathcal{X})$, with $d(\mathcal{S}) = 0$ (resp. $d(\mathcal{X})$) if and only if $\mathcal{S} = 0$ (resp. $\mathcal{X}$).

If $\mathcal{R}, \mathcal{S} \subset \mathcal{X}$ we define subspaces $\mathcal{R} + \mathcal{S} \subset \mathcal{X}$ and $\mathcal{R} \cap \mathcal{S} \subset \mathcal{X}$ according to

$$\mathcal{R} + \mathcal{S} \triangleq \{r + s : r \in \mathcal{R}, s \in \mathcal{S}\},$$
$$\mathcal{R} \cap \mathcal{S} \triangleq \{x : x \in \mathcal{R}, x \in \mathcal{S}\}.$$

These definitions are extended in the obvious way to finite collections of subspaces.

The family of all subspaces of $\mathcal{X}$ is partially ordered by subspace inclusion ($\subset$), and under the operations + and $\cap$ is easily seen to form a <u>lattice</u>: namely, $\mathcal{R} + \mathcal{S}$ is the smallest subspace containing both $\mathcal{R}$ and $\mathcal{S}$, while $\mathcal{R} \cap \mathcal{S}$ is the largest subspace contained in both $\mathcal{R}$ and $\mathcal{S}$.

Inclusion relations among subspaces may be pictured by a <u>lattice diagram</u>, in which the nodes represent subspaces, and a rising branch from $\mathcal{R}$ to $\mathcal{S}$ means $\mathcal{R} \subset \mathcal{S}$. Thus, for arbitrary $\mathcal{R}, \mathcal{S} \subset \mathcal{X}$, we have the diagram shown below.

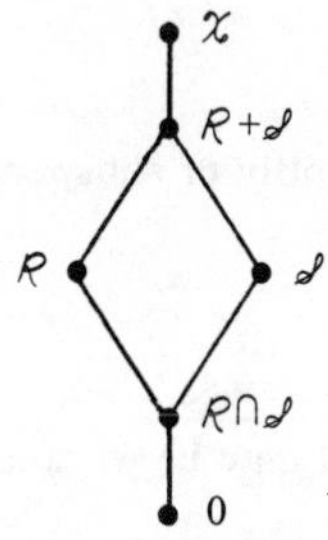

If $\mathcal{R}, \mathcal{S}, \mathcal{T} \subset \mathcal{X}$ with $\mathcal{R} \supset \mathcal{S}$, then

$$\mathcal{R} \cap (\mathcal{S} + \mathcal{T}) = \mathcal{R} \cap \mathcal{S} + \mathcal{R} \cap \mathcal{T} = \mathcal{S} + \mathcal{R} \cap \mathcal{T}. \tag{2}$$

Equation (2) is the <u>modular distributive rule</u>; a lattice in which it holds is called <u>modular</u>. For details, and the standard technique of proof for such identities, see Ex. 0.2.

For arbitrary $\mathcal{R}, \mathcal{S}, \mathcal{T} \subset \mathcal{X}$, with no inclusion relation postulated, the equality

$$\mathcal{R} \cap (\mathcal{S} + \mathcal{T}) = \mathcal{R} \cap \mathcal{S} + \mathcal{R} \cap \mathcal{T} \tag{3}$$

implies both

$$\mathcal{S} \cap (\mathcal{R} + \mathcal{T}) = \mathcal{R} \cap \mathcal{S} + \mathcal{S} \cap \mathcal{T} \tag{4a}$$

and (by symmetry)

$$\mathcal{T} \cap (\mathcal{R} + \mathcal{S}) = \mathcal{R} \cap \mathcal{T} + \mathcal{S} \cap \mathcal{T}. \tag{4b}$$

Two subspaces $\mathcal{R}, \mathcal{S} \subset \mathcal{X}$ are <u>(linearly) independent</u> if $\mathcal{R} \cap \mathcal{S} = 0$. A family of k subspaces $\mathcal{R}_1, \ldots, \mathcal{R}_k$ is <u>independent</u> if

$$\mathcal{R}_i \cap (\mathcal{R}_1 + \cdots + \mathcal{R}_{i-1} + \mathcal{R}_{i+1} + \cdots + \mathcal{R}_k) = 0$$

for all $i \in \underline{k}$. Note that an independent set of vectors cannot include the zero vector, but any independent family of subspaces remains independent if we adjoin one or more zero subspaces. The following statements are equivalent:

(i) The family $\{\mathcal{R}_i, i \in \underline{k}\}$ is independent.

(ii) $$\sum_{i=1}^{k}\left(\mathcal{R}_i \cap \sum_{j\neq i}\mathcal{R}_j\right) = 0 .$$

(iii) $$\sum_{i=2}^{k}\left(\mathcal{R}_i \cap \sum_{j=1}^{i-1}\mathcal{R}_j\right) = 0 .$$

(iv) Every vector $x \in \mathcal{R}_1 + \cdots + \mathcal{R}_k$ has a unique representation $x = r_1 + \cdots + r_k$ with $r_i \in \mathcal{R}_i$.

If $\{\mathcal{R}_i,\ i \in \underline{k}\}$ is an independent family of subspaces of $\mathcal{X}$, the sum

$$\mathcal{R} \triangleq \mathcal{R}_1 + \cdots + \mathcal{R}_k$$

is called an internal direct sum, and may be written

$$\mathcal{R} = \mathcal{R}_1 \oplus \cdots \oplus \mathcal{R}_k = \bigoplus_{i=1}^{k} \mathcal{R}_i .$$

In general the symbol $\oplus$ indicates that the subspaces being added are known, or claimed, to be independent.

If $\mathcal{R}, \mathcal{S} \subset \mathcal{X}$ there exist $\hat{\mathcal{R}} \subset \mathcal{R}$ and $\hat{\mathcal{S}} \subset \mathcal{S}$ such that

$$\mathcal{R} + \mathcal{S} = \hat{\mathcal{R}} \oplus \mathcal{R} \cap \mathcal{S} \oplus \hat{\mathcal{S}} . \tag{5}$$

In general $\hat{\mathcal{R}}$ and $\hat{\mathcal{S}}$ are by no means unique. The decomposition (5) does not have a natural extension to three or more subspaces.

If $\mathcal{R}$ and $\mathcal{S}$ are independent, clearly

$$d(\mathcal{R} \oplus \mathcal{S}) = d(\mathcal{R}) + d(\mathcal{S}) ;$$

and from (5) we have for arbitrary $\mathcal{R}$ and $\mathcal{S}$,

$$d(\mathcal{R} + \mathcal{S}) = d(\mathcal{R}) + d(\mathcal{S}) - d(\mathcal{R} \cap \mathcal{S}) .$$

Let $\mathcal{X}_1$ and $\mathcal{X}_2$ be arbitrary linear spaces over $\mathbf{F}$. The external direct sum of $\mathcal{X}_1$ and $\mathcal{X}_2$, written (temporarily) $\mathcal{X}_1 \tilde{\oplus} \mathcal{X}_2$, is the linear space of all ordered pairs $\{(x_1, x_2):\ x_1 \in \mathcal{X}_1,\ x_2 \in \mathcal{X}_2\}$, under componentwise addition and scalar multiplication. Writing $\approx$ for isomorphism (i.e., dimensional equality of linear spaces), we have

$$\mathcal{X}_1 \approx \{(x_1, 0):\ x_1 \in \mathcal{X}_1\} \subset \mathcal{X}_1 \tilde{\oplus} \mathcal{X}_2 ,$$

and we shall identify $\mathcal{X}_1$ with its isomorphic image. The construction extends to a finite collection of $\mathcal{X}_i$ in the obvious way. Evidently the definition makes $\mathcal{X}_1$ and $\mathcal{X}_2$ independent subspaces of $\mathcal{X}_1 \tilde{\oplus} \mathcal{X}_2$, and in this sense we have

$$\mathcal{X}_1 \tilde{\oplus} \mathcal{X}_2 = \mathcal{X}_1 \oplus \mathcal{X}_2 ,$$

where $\oplus$ denotes the internal direct sum defined earlier. Conversely, if we start with independent subspaces $\mathcal{X}_1, \mathcal{X}_2$ of a parent space $\mathcal{X}$, then clearly

$$\mathcal{X}_1 \tilde{\oplus} \mathcal{X}_2 \approx \mathcal{X}_1 \oplus \mathcal{X}_2$$

in a natural way. So we shall usually not distinguish the two types of direct sum, writing $\oplus$ for either, when context makes it clear which is meant. When the distinction matters we shall be explicit.

0.4 Maps and Matrices

Let $\mathcal{X}$ and $\mathcal{Y}$ be linear spaces over $\mathbf{F}$. A function $\varphi: \mathcal{X} \to \mathcal{Y}$ is a linear transformation (or map, for short) if

$$\varphi(c_1 x_1 + c_2 x_2) = c_1 \varphi(x_1) + c_2 \varphi(x_2) \tag{6}$$

for all $x_1, x_2 \in \mathcal{X}$ and $c_1, c_2 \in \mathbf{F}$. Of course, the sum and scalar multiplications on the left (or right) of (6) refer to the corresponding operations in $\mathcal{X}$ (or $\mathcal{Y}$). Maps will usually be denoted by Roman capitals A, B, ... An exception may occur when $d(\mathcal{Y}) = 1$, as we may then identify $\mathcal{Y} = \mathbf{F}$ and call φ a linear functional f' (see Section 0.12, below).

Let $\{x_i,\ i \in \underline{n}\}$ be a basis for $\mathcal{X}$ and $\{y_j,\ j \in \underline{p}\}$ a basis for $\mathcal{Y}$. If $C: \mathcal{X} \to \mathcal{Y}$ is a map, we have

$$C x_i = c_{1i} y_1 + c_{2i} y_2 + \cdots + c_{pi} y_p , \qquad i \in \underline{n} ,$$

for uniquely determined elements $c_{ji} \in \mathbf{F}$. Thus a map is completely determined by its action on a basis: linearity does the rest.

The array

$$\text{Mat } C = \begin{bmatrix} c_{11} & \cdots & c_{1n} \\ \vdots & & \vdots \\ c_{p1} & \cdots & c_{pn} \end{bmatrix}$$

is the matrix of C relative to the given basis pair. We assume that the rules of matrix algebra are known. Matrices are handy in computing the action of maps, but we shall not often need them in developing the theory. Sometimes we do not distinguish sharply between C and

Mat C, writing C ~ Mat C, or even C = Mat C, where an array is exhibited in place of Mat C on the right.

More fundamentally, one can think of Mat C as a function $\underline{p} \times \underline{n} \to \mathbf{F}$. The symbol $\mathbf{F}^{p \times n}$ denotes the class of all $p \times n$ matrices with elements in $\mathbf{F}$. It is turned into a linear space over $\mathbf{F}$, of dimension pn, by the usual operations of matrix addition and scalar multiplication.

Let $C: \mathcal{X} \to \mathcal{Y}$ be a map. $\mathcal{X}$ is the domain of C and $\mathcal{Y}$ is the codomain; the size of Mat C is thus $d(\mathcal{Y}) \times d(\mathcal{X})$. The kernel (or null space) of C is the subspace

$$\operatorname{Ker} C \triangleq \{x : x \in \mathcal{X} \quad \& \quad Cx = 0\} \subset \mathcal{X},$$

while the image (or range) of C is the subspace

$$\operatorname{Im} C \triangleq \{y : y \in \mathcal{Y} \quad \& \quad \exists x \in \mathcal{X},\ y = Cx\} \subset \mathcal{Y}.$$

Note the distinction between image and codomain.

If $\mathcal{R} \subset \mathcal{X}$, we write

$$C\mathcal{R} \triangleq \{y : y \in \mathcal{Y} \quad \& \quad \exists x \in \mathcal{R},\ y = Cx\} ;$$

and if $\mathcal{S} \subset \mathcal{Y}$,

$$C^{-1}\mathcal{S} \triangleq \{x : x \in \mathcal{X} \quad \& \quad Cx \in \mathcal{S}\} .$$

Both $C\mathcal{R} \subset \mathcal{Y}$ and $C^{-1}\mathcal{S} \subset \mathcal{X}$ are subspaces. Observe that C^{-1} is the functional inverse of the map C (regarded simply as a function), and as such it is a function from the subspaces of $\mathcal{Y}$ to those of $\mathcal{X}$. In this usage C^{-1} does not denote a map from $\mathcal{Y}$ to $\mathcal{X}$. In the special case where $d(\mathcal{X}) = d(\mathcal{Y})$ and the ordinary inverse of C exists as a map $\mathcal{Y} \to \mathcal{X}$, this map will also be written, as usual, C^{-1}, and clearly the two usages are then consistent.

As easy consequences of the definitions, we have

$$d(C\mathcal{R}) = d(\mathcal{R}) - d(\mathcal{R} \cap \operatorname{Ker} C) ,$$

$$d(C^{-1}\mathcal{S}) = d(\operatorname{Ker} C) + d(\mathcal{S} \cap \operatorname{Im} C) ,$$

and in particular, as $\operatorname{Im} C = C\mathcal{X}$,

$$d(\mathcal{X}) = d(\operatorname{Ker} C) + d(\operatorname{Im} C) .$$

Also, for $\mathcal{S} \subset \mathcal{Y}$ there exists $\mathcal{R} \subset \mathcal{X}$, in general not unique, such that

$$d(\mathcal{R}) = d(\mathcal{S} \cap \operatorname{Im} C)$$

and

$$\mathcal{R} \oplus \operatorname{Ker} C = C^{-1}\mathcal{S} .$$

If $C: \mathcal{X} \to \mathcal{Y}$ and $\mathcal{R}_1, \mathcal{R}_2 \subset \mathcal{X}$ we have

$$C(\mathcal{R}_1 + \mathcal{R}_2) = C\mathcal{R}_1 + C\mathcal{R}_2 ;$$

but in general

$$C(\mathcal{R}_1 \cap \mathcal{R}_2) \subset (C\mathcal{R}_1) \cap (C\mathcal{R}_2) , \tag{7}$$

with equality if and only if

$$(\mathcal{R}_1 + \mathcal{R}_2) \cap \operatorname{Ker} C = \mathcal{R}_1 \cap \operatorname{Ker} C + \mathcal{R}_2 \cap \operatorname{Ker} C . \tag{8}$$

Dually, if $\mathcal{S}_1, \mathcal{S}_2 \subset \mathcal{Y}$ we have

$$C^{-1}(\mathcal{S}_1 \cap \mathcal{S}_2) = C^{-1}\mathcal{S}_1 \cap C^{-1}\mathcal{S}_2 ;$$

but

$$C^{-1}(\mathcal{S}_1 + \mathcal{S}_2) \supset C^{-1}\mathcal{S}_1 + C^{-1}\mathcal{S}_2 ,$$

with equality if and only if

$$(\mathcal{S}_1 + \mathcal{S}_2) \cap \operatorname{Im} C = \mathcal{S}_1 \cap \operatorname{Im} C + \mathcal{S}_2 \cap \operatorname{Im} C .$$

If $\mathcal{R}_1 \cap \mathcal{R}_2 = 0$, in general

$$C(\mathcal{R}_1 \oplus \mathcal{R}_2) \neq C\mathcal{R}_1 \oplus C\mathcal{R}_2 ,$$

because the subspaces on the right need not be independent; they are independent if and only if

$$(\mathcal{R}_1 \oplus \mathcal{R}_2) \cap \operatorname{Ker} C = \mathcal{R}_1 \cap \operatorname{Ker} C \oplus \mathcal{R}_2 \cap \operatorname{Ker} C .$$

Essential to any grasp of algebra is a command of Greek adverbs. A map $C: \mathcal{X} \to \mathcal{Y}$ is an <u>epimorphism</u> (or C is <u>epic</u>) if $\operatorname{Im} C = \mathcal{Y}$. C is a <u>monomorphism</u> (or C is <u>monic</u>) if $\operatorname{Ker} C = 0$. If C is epic there is a map $C_r^{-1}: \mathcal{Y} \to \mathcal{X}$, a <u>right inverse</u> of C, such that

$$C C_r^{-1} = 1_{\mathcal{Y}} , \tag{9}$$

the identity map on $\mathcal{Y}$. If C is monic there is a map $C_\ell^{-1}: \mathcal{Y} \to \mathcal{X}$, a <u>left inverse</u> of C, such that

$$C_\ell^{-1} C = 1_{\mathcal{X}} ,$$

the identity on $\mathcal{X}$. If C is both epic and monic, C is an isomorphism, and this can happen only if $d(\mathcal{X}) = d(\mathcal{Y})$. Then we write $\mathcal{X} \approx \mathcal{Y}$ and $C: \mathcal{X} \approx \mathcal{Y}$. Conversely if $d(\mathcal{X}) = d(\mathcal{Y})$, and if $\{x_i, i \in \underline{n}\}$, $\{y_j, j \in \underline{n}\}$ are bases for $\mathcal{X}$ and $\mathcal{Y}$, respectively, we can manufacture an isomorphism $C: \mathcal{X} \approx \mathcal{Y}$ by defining $Cx_i \triangleq y_i$ $(i \in \underline{n})$.

An arbitrary map $A: \mathcal{X} \to \mathcal{X}$ is an endomorphism of $\mathcal{X}$. A is an automorphism of $\mathcal{X}$ if A is an isomorphism.

Let $\mathcal{V} \subset \mathcal{X}$. The map $V: \mathcal{V} \to \mathcal{X}$, defined by $Vx = x$ for $x \in \mathcal{V}$, is the insertion map of $\mathcal{V}$ in $\mathcal{X}$. Clearly V is monic and $\mathcal{V} = \operatorname{Im} V$. Let $\{x_i, i \in \underline{n}\}$ be a basis for $\mathcal{X}$. If $\{v_i, i \in \underline{k}\}$ is a basis for $\mathcal{V}$ we can write for suitable $\alpha_{ji} \in \mathbf{F}$,

$$v_i = \alpha_{1i} x_1 + \cdots + \alpha_{ni} x_n , \qquad i \in \underline{k} ,$$

so that

$$\operatorname{Mat} V = \begin{bmatrix} \alpha_{11} & \cdots & \alpha_{1k} \\ \vdots & & \vdots \\ \alpha_{n1} & \cdots & \alpha_{nk} \end{bmatrix} .$$

Thus the insertion map is represented by any matrix whose column vectors form a basis for $\mathcal{V}$ relative to the given basis for $\mathcal{X}$. This is a standard device for the numerical representation of a subspace.

Let $\mathcal{X} = \mathcal{R} \oplus \mathcal{S}$. Since the representation $x = r + s$ $(r \in \mathcal{R}, s \in \mathcal{S})$ is unique for each $x \in \mathcal{X}$, there is a function $x \mapsto r$, called the projection on $\mathcal{R}$ along $\mathcal{S}$. It is easy to see that the projection is a (linear) map $Q: \mathcal{X} \to \mathcal{X}$ such that

$$\mathcal{X} = Q\mathcal{X} \oplus (1 - Q)\mathcal{X} .$$

Note that $1 - Q$ is the projection on $\mathcal{S}$ along $\mathcal{R}$, so that $Q(1 - Q) = 0$, or $Q^2 = Q$. Conversely if $Q: \mathcal{X} \to \mathcal{X}$ is a map such that $Q^2 = Q$ (the property of idempotence) it is easy to show that

$$\mathcal{X} = \operatorname{Im} Q \oplus \operatorname{Ker} Q ,$$

i.e., Q is the projection on Im Q along Ker Q.

For computational purposes it is also useful to employ the natural projection $\tilde{Q}: \mathcal{X} \to \mathcal{R}$, again defined as the map $x = r + s \mapsto r$, but with $\mathcal{R}$ rather than $\mathcal{X}$ as codomain. These seemingly fussy distinctions are essential both for conceptual clarity and for consistency in performing matrix calculations.

0.5 Factor Spaces

Let $\mathcal{S} \subset \mathcal{X}$. Call vectors $x, y \in \mathcal{X}$ equivalent mod $\mathcal{S}$ if $x - y \in \mathcal{S}$. We define the factor space (or quotient space) $\mathcal{X}/\mathcal{S}$ as the set of all equivalence classes

$$\bar{x} \triangleq \{y : y \in \mathcal{X}, y - x \in \mathcal{S}\} , \qquad x \in \mathcal{X} .$$

In $\mathcal{X}/\mathcal{S}$ define

$$\bar{x}_1 + \bar{x}_2 \triangleq \overline{x_1 + x_2}, \qquad x_1, x_2 \in \mathcal{X}$$

and

$$c\bar{x} \triangleq \overline{cx}, \qquad x \in \mathcal{X},\ c \in \mathbf{F}.$$

It is a standard exercise to show that these definitions of sum and scalar multiplication in $\mathcal{X}/\mathcal{S}$ are unambiguous, and turn $\mathcal{X}/\mathcal{S}$ into a linear space over $\mathbf{F}$. One easily sees that

$$d\left(\frac{\mathcal{X}}{\mathcal{S}}\right) = d(\mathcal{X}) - d(\mathcal{S}).$$

Indeed if $\mathcal{R} \subset \mathcal{X}$ is any subspace such that $\mathcal{R} \oplus \mathcal{S} = \mathcal{X}$, and if $\{r_1, \ldots, r_\rho\}$ is a basis for $\mathcal{R}$, then $\{\bar{r}_1, \ldots, \bar{r}_\rho\}$ is a basis for $\mathcal{X}/\mathcal{S}$, so that $d(\mathcal{X}/\mathcal{S}) = \rho$.

As an application of these ideas we see that if $C: \mathcal{X} \to \mathcal{Y}$ then

$$\operatorname{Im} C = C\mathcal{X} \approx \frac{\mathcal{X}}{\operatorname{Ker} C}.$$

In particular, if C is monic, $\mathcal{X} \approx C\mathcal{X}$; and if C is epic,

$$\mathcal{Y} \approx \frac{\mathcal{X}}{\operatorname{Ker} C}.$$

For $x \in \mathcal{X}$ the element $\bar{x} \in \mathcal{X}/\mathcal{S}$ is the <u>coset of</u> $\mathcal{X}$ <u>mod</u> $\mathcal{S}$. The function $x \mapsto \bar{x}$ is a map P: $\mathcal{X} \to \mathcal{X}/\mathcal{S}$ called the <u>canonical projection of</u> $\mathcal{X}$ <u>on</u> $\mathcal{X}/\mathcal{S}$. Clearly P is epic, and $\operatorname{Ker} P = \mathcal{S}$.

This terminology sharply distinguishes P from the projections Q and $\tilde{Q}$ defined earlier: note that $\mathcal{X}/\mathcal{S}$ is <u>not</u> a subspace of $\mathcal{X}$, and if $\mathcal{S} \neq 0$, Q is not epic. Concretely, let $\mathcal{R} \oplus \mathcal{S} = \mathcal{X}$ for some $\mathcal{R}$. Make up a basis for $\mathcal{X}$ by taking the union of a basis $\{x_1, \ldots, x_\rho\}$ for $\mathcal{R}$ and of one for $\mathcal{S}$, in that order, and take $\{\bar{x}_1, \ldots, \bar{x}_\rho\}$ as a basis for $\mathcal{X}/\mathcal{S}$. If Q (resp. $\tilde{Q}$) is the projection (resp. natural projection) on $\mathcal{R}$ along $\mathcal{S}$, we have

$$\operatorname{Mat} Q = \begin{bmatrix} I^{\rho\times\rho} & 0^{\rho\times\sigma} \\ 0^{\sigma\times\rho} & 0^{\sigma\times\sigma} \end{bmatrix},$$

$$\operatorname{Mat} \tilde{Q} = \begin{bmatrix} I^{\rho\times\rho} & 0^{\rho\times\sigma} \end{bmatrix},$$

and

$$\operatorname{Mat} P = \begin{bmatrix} I^{\rho\times\rho} & 0^{\rho\times\sigma} \end{bmatrix},$$

where superscripts indicate matrix dimensions.

If $\mathcal{S} \subset \mathcal{T} \subset \mathcal{X}$ and P: $\mathcal{X} \to \mathcal{X}/\mathcal{S}$ is canonical, we define

$$\frac{\mathcal{T}}{\mathcal{S}} \triangleq P\mathcal{T};$$

thus $\mathcal{T}/\mathcal{S}$ is a subspace of $\mathcal{X}/\mathcal{S}$. If $\mathcal{T}\subset\mathcal{X}$ is arbitrary, we have

$$P\mathcal{T} = \frac{\mathcal{T}+\mathcal{S}}{\mathcal{S}}.$$

If $\bar{\mathcal{T}}$ is a subspace of $\mathcal{X}/\mathcal{S}$, then $\mathcal{T} \triangleq P^{-1}\bar{\mathcal{T}}$ is the largest subspace of $\mathcal{X}$ with the properties: (i) $\mathcal{T}\supset\mathcal{S}$ and (ii) $P\mathcal{T} = \bar{\mathcal{T}}$. Thus P^{-1} determines a bijection between the family of subspaces of $\mathcal{X}/\mathcal{S}$ and the family of subspaces $\mathcal{T}\subset\mathcal{X}$ such that $\mathcal{T}\supset\mathcal{S}$.

If $\mathcal{S}\subset\mathcal{U}\cap\mathcal{V}$, then

$$\frac{\mathcal{U}}{\mathcal{S}}+\frac{\mathcal{V}}{\mathcal{S}}=\frac{\mathcal{U}+\mathcal{V}}{\mathcal{S}}$$

and

$$\frac{\mathcal{U}}{\mathcal{S}}\cap\frac{\mathcal{V}}{\mathcal{S}}=\frac{\mathcal{U}\cap\mathcal{V}}{\mathcal{S}}.$$

Finally if $\mathcal{S}\subset\mathcal{T}\subset\mathcal{X}$,

$$\frac{(\mathcal{X}/\mathcal{S})}{(\mathcal{T}/\mathcal{S})}\approx\frac{\mathcal{X}}{\mathcal{T}};$$

and if $\mathcal{T}$ is arbitrary,

$$\frac{\mathcal{T}+\mathcal{S}}{\mathcal{S}}\approx\frac{\mathcal{T}}{\mathcal{T}\cap\mathcal{S}}.$$

Now let $C: \mathcal{X}\to\mathcal{Y}$ be a map and let $\operatorname{Ker} C\supset\mathcal{S}$. If $P: \mathcal{X}\to\mathcal{X}/\mathcal{S}$ is the canonical projection we claim there is a unique map $\bar{C}: \mathcal{X}/\mathcal{S}\to\mathcal{Y}$ such that

$$C = \bar{C}P. \tag{10}$$

Thus C 'factors through' $\mathcal{X}/\mathcal{S}$. To see this let $\mathcal{X} = \mathcal{R}\oplus\mathcal{S}$, with $\{r_1, \dots, r_\rho\}$, $\{\bar{r}_1, \dots, \bar{r}_\rho\}$ bases for $\mathcal{R}$ and $\mathcal{X}/\mathcal{S}$, respectively. Define

$$\bar{C}\bar{r}_i = Cr_i, \qquad i\in\underline{\rho}. \tag{11}$$

As $C\mathcal{S}= 0$, the definition is unambiguous. If $x = r+s$,

$$Cx = C(r+s) = Cr = \bar{C}\bar{r} = \bar{C}Px$$

which verifies (10). On the other hand (10) implies (11), which shows that $\bar{C}$ is unique.

0.6 Commutative Diagrams

Relations between maps and spaces are often displayed by an 'arrow diagram'; thus

$$\mathcal{X}\xrightarrow{C}\mathcal{Y}$$

displays the map C: $\mathscr{X} \to \mathscr{Y}$. A diagram with several connecting arrows, as in

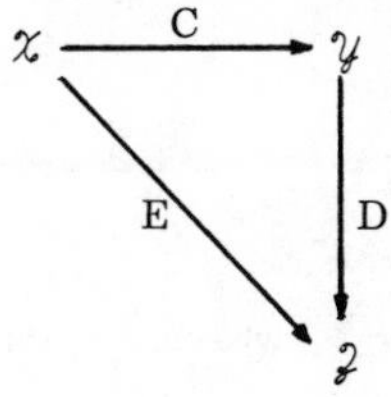

is said to <u>commute</u> if the maps composed by following different paths between the same end points are equal, i.e., $DC = E$. A dotted arrow indicates that the corresponding map is asserted to exist and to make the diagram commute. Thus the result (10) on factor spaces can be displayed as

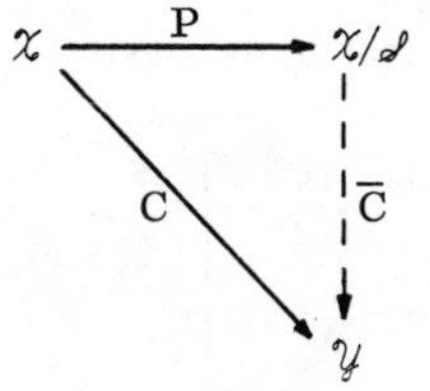

$\operatorname{Ker} C \supset \mathscr{S}$.

Commutative diagrams are helpful mnemonic and heuristic devices, and the reader is urged to draw one when the occasion arises.

A sequence of maps B: $\mathscr{U} \to \mathscr{X}$, C: $\mathscr{X} \to \mathscr{Y}$ is <u>exact at</u> $\mathscr{X}$ if $\operatorname{Im} B = \operatorname{Ker} C$. Thus B is monic if the sequence (or diagram)

$$0 \longrightarrow \mathscr{U} \xrightarrow{B} \mathscr{X}$$

is exact at $\mathscr{U}$ (the first arrow represents the map with image $0 \subset \mathscr{U}$), while C is epic if the sequence

$$\mathscr{X} \xrightarrow{C} \mathscr{Y} \longrightarrow 0$$

is exact at $\mathscr{Y}$ (the second arrow represents the map with image 0, i.e., the zero map).

0.7 <u>Invariant Subspaces. Induced Maps</u>

Let A: $\mathscr{X} \to \mathscr{X}$ and let $\mathscr{S} \subset \mathscr{X}$ have the property $A\mathscr{S} \subset \mathscr{S}$. $\mathscr{S}$ is said to be A-<u>invariant</u>. Write $\bar{\mathscr{X}} = \mathscr{X}/\mathscr{S}$ and let P: $\mathscr{X} \to \bar{\mathscr{X}}$ be the canonical projection. We claim that there exists a unique map $\bar{A}$: $\bar{\mathscr{X}} \to \bar{\mathscr{X}}$ such that $\bar{A}P = PA$, i.e., the diagram (12) commutes.

$$\begin{array}{ccc} \mathcal{X} & \xrightarrow{\ A\ } & \mathcal{X} \\ {\scriptstyle P}\downarrow & & \downarrow{\scriptstyle P} \\ \bar{\mathcal{X}} & \xrightarrow{\ \bar{A}\ } & \bar{\mathcal{X}} \end{array} \tag{12}$$

Indeed let $\{\bar{x}_i,\ i \in \underline{\rho}\}$ be a basis for $\bar{\mathcal{X}}$, where $\bar{x}_i = Px_i$. If (12) commutes then

$$\bar{A}\bar{x}_i = \bar{A}Px_i = PAx_i, \qquad i \in \underline{\rho}. \tag{13}$$

On the other hand, since $A\mathcal{S} \subset \mathcal{S}$ and $P\mathcal{S} = 0$, the definition of $\bar{A}\bar{x}_i$ by (13) is unambiguous and so actually determines a map $\bar{A}$ with the stated property. $\bar{A}$ is the *map induced in* $\bar{\mathcal{X}}$ *by* A.

Let $\mathcal{R}$ be any subspace such that $\mathcal{S} \oplus \mathcal{R} = \mathcal{X}$, and let $\{r_i,\ i \in \underline{\rho}\}$ be a basis for $\mathcal{R}$. Choosing a basis $\{s_j,\ j \in \sigma\}$ for $\mathcal{S}$, we see that in the basis $\{s_1, \ldots, r_\rho\}$ for $\mathcal{X}$,

$$\text{Mat}\,A = \begin{bmatrix} A_1^{\sigma\times\sigma} & A_3^{\sigma\times\rho} \\ 0^{\rho\times\sigma} & A_2^{\rho\times\rho} \end{bmatrix}. \tag{14}$$

The matrix of $\bar{A}$ in the basis $\{\bar{r}_i,\ i \in \underline{\rho}\}$ is simply $A_2^{\rho\times\rho}$.

If $A\mathcal{S} \subset \mathcal{S}$ we denote the *restriction of* A *to* $\mathcal{S}$ by $A|\mathcal{S}$. In the basis $\{s_j,\ j \in \underline{\sigma}\}$, $A|\mathcal{S}$ has the matrix $A_1^{\sigma\times\sigma}$.

Let $A\mathcal{S} \subset \mathcal{S}$. If there exists a subspace $\mathcal{T} \subset \mathcal{X}$ such that $A\mathcal{T} \subset \mathcal{T}$ and $\mathcal{S} \oplus \mathcal{T} = \mathcal{X}$, then $\mathcal{S}$ is said to *decompose* $\mathcal{X}$ (*relative to* A). In this case, choosing $\mathcal{T}$ for $\mathcal{R}$ above, we have that Mat A in (14) is block diagonal, and $A_2 = \text{Mat}(A|\mathcal{T})$.

0.8 Characteristic Polynomial. Spectrum.

Let $\mathcal{X}$ be a linear space over $\mathbb{F}$, with $d(\mathcal{X}) = n$, and let $A: \mathcal{X} \to \mathcal{X}$ be an arbitrary endomorphism. The *characteristic polynomial* (ch.p.) of A is the $n^{\underline{th}}$ degree monic polynomial

$$\pi(\lambda) \triangleq \det(\lambda 1 - A).$$

Here det means determinant, the definition and properties of which we assume known. Henceforth we omit writing the identity map in $\lambda 1 - A$. Whether $\mathbb{F}$ is $\mathbb{R}$ or $\mathbb{C}$ we define the *spectrum* of A, written $\sigma(A)$, to be the set of n complex zeros of $\pi(\lambda)$, listed according to multiplicity. The elements of $\sigma(A)$ are the *eigenvalues* of A: $\lambda \in \sigma(A)$ if and only if there exists a nonzero vector $x \in \mathcal{X}_{\mathbb{C}}$ such that $Ax = \lambda x$. Then x is an *eigenvector of* A *corresponding to* λ.

If $\mathbb{F} = \mathbb{R}$, the elements of Mat A are real, so $\sigma(A)$ has the general form

$$\sigma(A) = \{\alpha_1, \alpha_2, \ldots;\ \beta_1, \beta_1^*;\ \beta_2, \beta_2^*;\ \cdots\},$$

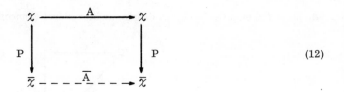

where $\alpha_i \in \mathbb{R}$, $\beta_j \in \mathbb{C}$, and * denotes complex conjugate. Such a set of complex numbers will be called symmetric (about the real axis).

As an example of spectrum calculation, we note that the block triangular structure of Mat A in (14) implies, via the characteristic polynomial,

$$\sigma(A) = \sigma(A|\mathscr{S}) \mathbin{\dot{\cup}} \sigma(\bar{A}) \ ,$$

where $\dot{\cup}$ denotes union with any common elements repeated.

0.9 Polynomial Rings

In the sequel, certain polynomials associated with linear transformations play an important role. The set of all polynomials in a single 'indeterminate' λ, and with coefficients in a field $\mathbf{F}$, has the structure of a ring, in particular of a principal ideal domain, under the usual rules of polynomial addition and multiplication. This ring is denoted by $\mathbf{F}[\lambda]$. For our purposes it is enough to recall a few of the basic facts. A polynomial is monic if its leading coefficient (i.e., the coefficient of its highest power of λ) is 1. Associated with any finite set of nonzero polynomials $\rho_1(\lambda), \ldots, \rho_k(\lambda) \in \mathbf{F}[\lambda]$ is their least common multiple (LCM) defined as the unique monic polynomial $\mu(\lambda)$ of least degree such that $\rho_i(\lambda) | \mu(\lambda)$ [i.e., $\rho_i(\lambda)$ divides $\mu(\lambda)$] for $i \in \underline{k}$. Similarly there exists a unique monic polynomial $\delta(\lambda)$, the greatest common divisor (GCD) of the $\rho_i(\lambda)$, defined as the monic polynomial of greatest degree such that $\delta(\lambda) | \rho_i(\lambda)$, $i \in \underline{k}$. If

$$\delta(\lambda) = \mathrm{GCD}[\rho_1(\lambda), \ldots, \rho_k(\lambda)] \ ,$$

there exist polynomials $\sigma_1(\lambda), \ldots, \sigma_k(\lambda)$ (not unique, or necessarily monic) such that

$$\sigma_1(\lambda)\,\rho_1(\lambda) + \cdots + \sigma_k(\lambda)\,\rho_k(\lambda) = \delta(\lambda) \ . \tag{15}$$

The set $\{\rho_i(\lambda), i \in \underline{k}\}$ is coprime if $\delta(\lambda) = 1$. Both δ and a suitable set σ_i can be calculated by the well known Euclidean algorithm.

An irreducible element $\pi(\lambda) \in \mathbf{F}[\lambda]$ is a polynomial which cannot be factored as a product of polynomials of lower degree. If $\mathbf{F} = \mathbb{C}$, the irreducible polynomials are those of form $c_1\lambda + c_2$; if $\mathbf{F} = \mathbb{R}$ the irreducible polynomials are of form

$$r_1\lambda + r_2 \quad \text{or} \quad r_3\lambda^2 + r_4\lambda + r_5$$

with $r_i \in \mathbb{R}$ and $r_4^2 - 4r_3r_5 < 0$. Finally, any polynomial in $\mathbf{F}[\lambda]$ of degree ≥ 1 can be factored as a product of powers of pairwise coprime irreducible polynomials of degree ≥ 1, and such a prime factorization is unique up to the order of factors and the selection of (nonzero) leading coefficients in the polynomials involved.

Occasionally we need the ring of polynomials in N indeterminates, denoted by $\mathbf{F}[\underline{\lambda}]$, where $\underline{\lambda} \triangleq (\lambda_1, \ldots, \lambda_N)$. Finally, we recall that $\mathbf{F}[\underline{\lambda}]$ can be imbedded in the fraction field of rational expressions in $\underline{\lambda}$, denoted by $\mathbf{F}(\underline{\lambda})$.

0.10 Rational Canonical Structure

Let $\mathcal{X}$ be a linear space over $\mathbf{F}$ with $d(\mathcal{X}) = n$, and let $A: \mathcal{X} \to \mathcal{X}$ be an arbitrary endomorphism. Write $\pi(\lambda)$ for the ch.p. of A. The Hamilton-Cayley Theorem states that $\pi(A) = 0$. The minimal polynomial (m.p.) of A is the monic polynomial $\alpha(\lambda)$ of least degree such that $\alpha(A) = 0$. The m.p. of A is unique, and divides every nonzero polynomial $\beta(\lambda)$ such that $\beta(A) = 0$; in particular, $\alpha(\lambda) | \pi(\lambda)$, so that $\deg \alpha \le n$. Let $x \in \mathcal{X}$. The minimal polynomial of x (relative to A) is the unique monic polynomial $\xi_x(\lambda)$ of least degree such that $\xi_x(A)x = 0$. We have $\xi_x(\lambda) | \alpha(\lambda)$ for all x; furthermore

$$\alpha(\lambda) = \text{LCM}\{\xi_x(\lambda) : x \in \mathcal{X}\} .$$

We shall need the important

PROPOSITION 0.1. *If $A: \mathcal{X} \to \mathcal{X}$ and the m.p. of A is $\alpha(\lambda)$, there exists $x \in \mathcal{X}$ such that $\alpha(\lambda)$ is the m.p. of x relative to A, i.e., $\xi_x(\lambda) = \alpha(\lambda)$.*

If $\alpha(\lambda) = \pi(\lambda)$, i.e., $\deg \alpha = n$, A is said to be cyclic, and there exists $g \in \mathcal{X}$ such that the vectors

$$g, Ag, \ldots, A^{n-1}g$$

form a basis for $\mathcal{X}$. Such g is a (cyclic) generator for $\mathcal{X}$ (relative to A). If g is a generator the set of all generators coincides with the set of vectors $\gamma(A)g$, where $\gamma(\lambda) \in \mathbf{F}[\lambda]$ is coprime with $\alpha(\lambda)$.

Let A be cyclic with generator g and let

$$\alpha(\lambda) \triangleq \lambda^n - \left(a_1 + a_2\lambda + \cdots + a_n\lambda^{n-1}\right) .$$

Define auxiliary polynomials

$$\left.\begin{aligned} \alpha^{(0)}(\lambda) &\triangleq \alpha(\lambda) \\ \alpha^{(1)}(\lambda) &\triangleq \lambda^{n-1} - \left(a_2 + a_3\lambda + \cdots + a_n\lambda^{n-2}\right) \\ \alpha^{(n-1)}(\lambda) &\triangleq \lambda - a_n \\ \alpha^{(n)}(\lambda) &\triangleq 1 . \end{aligned}\right\} \qquad (16)$$

The $\alpha^{(i)}$ satisfy the recursion relation

$$\lambda\alpha^{(i)}(\lambda) = \alpha^{(i-1)}(\lambda) + a_i\alpha^{(n)}(\lambda)\,, \qquad i \in \underline{n}\,. \tag{17}$$

Now introduce the vectors

$$e_i \triangleq \alpha^{(i)}(A)g\,, \qquad i \in \underline{n}\,,$$

with $e_0 \triangleq 0$. The e_i ($i \in \underline{n}$) are clearly a basis for $\mathcal{X}$. Replacing λ by A in (17) and operating on g, we get

$$Ae_i = e_{i-1} + a_i e_n\,, \qquad i \in \underline{n}\,. \tag{18}$$

By (18), in this basis

$$\text{Mat}\,A = \begin{bmatrix} 0 & 1 & 0 & \cdot & \cdot & \cdot & 0 \\ 0 & 0 & 1 & 0 & \cdot & \cdot & 0 \\ \cdot & \cdot & \cdot & \cdot & \cdot & \cdot & \cdot \\ 0 & \cdot & \cdot & \cdot & \cdot & 0 & 1 \\ a_1 & a_2 & \cdot & \cdot & \cdot & \cdot & a_n \end{bmatrix}.$$

This is the companion form of Mat A.

Now let A: $\mathcal{X} \to \mathcal{X}$ be arbitrary. A subspace $\mathcal{S} \subset \mathcal{X}$ with $A\mathcal{S} \subset \mathcal{S}$ is A-cyclic if $A|\mathcal{S}$ is cyclic. Let A have m.p. $\alpha(\lambda)$ and, by Proposition 0.1, choose $x \in \mathcal{X}$ with m.p. $\alpha(\lambda)$. If $\deg\alpha = m$, the vectors

$$x,\ Ax,\ \ldots,\ A^{m-1}x$$

span an m-dimensional A-cyclic subspace with cyclic generator x. In general, we call $\mathcal{S} \subset \mathcal{X}$ maximal cyclic (relative to A) if $\mathcal{S}$ is A-cyclic and $A|\mathcal{S}$ has m.p. $\alpha(\lambda)$. Our next result states that such $\mathcal{S}$ can be 'split off' from $\mathcal{X}$.

PROPOSITION 0.2. *If* A: $\mathcal{X} \to \mathcal{X}$ *and* $\mathcal{S} \subset \mathcal{X}$ *is maximal cyclic relative to* A, *then* $\mathcal{S}$ *decomposes* $\mathcal{X}$ *relative to* A.

By successive application of Propositions 0.1 and 0.2, $\mathcal{X}$ can be decomposed into a minimal number of A-cyclic direct summands, in an essentially unique way. This is the main result in linear algebra; the precise statement follows.

THEOREM 0.1. (Rational Canonical Structure). Let A: $\mathcal{X} \to \mathcal{X}$ be an endomorphism of $\mathcal{X}$. There exist a positive integer k and subspaces $\mathcal{X}_i \subset \mathcal{X}$ ($i \in \mathbf{k}$) with the properties:

(i) $\mathcal{X} = \mathcal{X}_1 \oplus \cdots \oplus \mathcal{X}_k$. (19)

(ii) For $i \in \mathbf{k}$, $A\mathcal{X}_i \subset \mathcal{X}_i$ and $A|\mathcal{X}_i$ is cyclic.

(iii) If $\alpha_i(\lambda)$ is the m.p. of $A|\mathcal{X}_i$ then α_1 is the m.p. of A, and

$$\alpha_2|\alpha_1,\ \alpha_3|\alpha_2, \ldots, \alpha_k|\alpha_{k-1}.$$

(iv) There are exactly one integer k and one list of monic polynomials $\alpha_1, \ldots, \alpha_k$ such that a family of subspaces $\mathcal{X}_1, \ldots, \mathcal{X}_k$ exists with the properties (i) - (iii).

We shall apply this theorem only when $\mathbb{F} = \mathbb{R}$; then, of course, the $\alpha_i \in \mathbb{R}[\lambda]$. The integer k will be called the cyclic index of A. The polynomials $\alpha_1, \ldots, \alpha_k$ are the invariant factors of A, and characterize Mat A to within a transformation of form $T^{-1}AT$ (similarity transformation). Note that the theorem does not claim that the $\mathcal{X}_i$ themselves are unique; in general they are not.

If $A_i = A|\mathcal{X}_i$, a basis in $\mathcal{X}_i$ can be chosen as above such that Mat A_i is a companion matrix with ch.p. $\alpha_i(\lambda)$. Then

$$\text{Mat } A = \text{diag}[\text{Mat } A_1, \ldots, \text{Mat } A_k],$$

the rational canonical form of Mat A.

The following generalization of Proposition 0.2 states that an A-invariant subspace $\mathcal{S}$ decomposes $\mathcal{X}$ (relative to A) if the rational canonical structure of $A|\mathcal{S}$ is 'maximal.'

PROPOSITION 0.3. Let A: $\mathcal{X} \to \mathcal{X}$ and $A\mathcal{S} \subset \mathcal{S} \subset \mathcal{X}$. Suppose

$$\mathcal{S} = \mathcal{S}_1 \oplus \cdots \oplus \mathcal{S}_j,$$

where $A\mathcal{S}_i \subset \mathcal{S}_i$ ($i \in \mathbf{j}$) and $A|\mathcal{S}_i$ is cyclic with m.p. equal to the ith invariant factor α_i of A. Then there exists $\mathcal{T} \subset \mathcal{X}$ such that $A\mathcal{T} \subset \mathcal{T}$, $\mathcal{S} \oplus \mathcal{T} = \mathcal{X}$, and

$$\mathcal{T} = \mathcal{T}_{j+1} \oplus \cdots \oplus \mathcal{T}_k,$$

where the $\mathcal{T}_i$ are A-invariant and A-cyclic, and the m.p. of $A|\mathcal{T}_i$ is α_i ($i = j+1, \ldots, k$).

Two maps A: $\mathcal{X} \to \mathcal{X}$ and $\hat{A}$: $\hat{\mathcal{X}} \to \hat{\mathcal{X}}$ are similar if they are related by a similarity transformation: namely, there is an isomorphism T: $\mathcal{X} \approx \hat{\mathcal{X}}$ such that $\hat{A}T = TA$, i.e., the diagram below commutes.

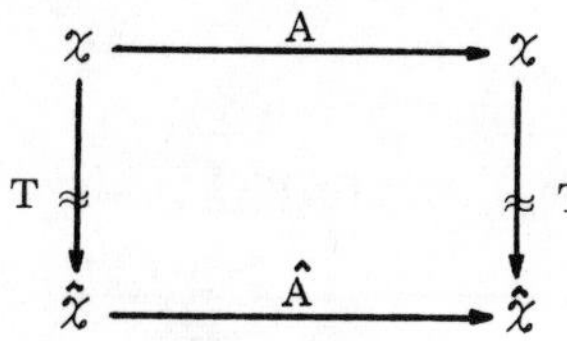

We write in this case $A \approx \hat{A}$. It is clear that two maps are similar if and only if they have the same rational canonical structure.

0.11 Jordan Decomposition

In the notation of Section 0.10 let $\mathbf{F} = \mathbb{R}$, and

$$\alpha(\lambda) = \gamma_1(\lambda)\,\gamma_2(\lambda) \cdots \gamma_p(\lambda)\,, \tag{20}$$

where the $\gamma_i(\lambda) \in \mathbb{R}[\lambda]$ are pairwise coprime. Define

$$\tilde{\mathcal{X}}_i \triangleq \operatorname{Ker} \gamma_i(A)\,, \qquad i \in \underline{p}\,. \tag{21}$$

By use of (15) it is easy to check that

$$\mathcal{X} = \tilde{\mathcal{X}}_1 \oplus \cdots \oplus \tilde{\mathcal{X}}_p\,, \tag{22}$$

$$A\tilde{\mathcal{X}}_i \subset \tilde{\mathcal{X}}_i\,, \qquad i \in \underline{p}\,, \tag{23}$$

and the m.p. of $A|\tilde{\mathcal{X}}_i$ is γ_i. If (20) is actually a prime factorization of $\alpha(\lambda)$ over $\mathbb{R}[\lambda]$, then (22) provides a 'modal' decomposition of $\mathcal{X}$, relative to A, which is unique. Of course, $A|\tilde{\mathcal{X}}_i$ need not be cyclic.

The foregoing modal decomposition applied to each map $A|\mathcal{X}_i$, with the $\mathcal{X}_i$ as in (19), yields

$$\mathcal{X}_i = \tilde{\mathcal{X}}_{i1} \oplus \cdots \oplus \tilde{\mathcal{X}}_{ip_i}\,, \qquad i \in \underline{k}\,.$$

Since $A|\mathcal{X}_i$ is cyclic, so is $A|\tilde{\mathcal{X}}_{ij}$, and we obtain a decomposition of $\mathcal{X}$ into cyclic subspaces on each of which the m.p. $\alpha_{ij}(\lambda)$ of A is of form $q(\lambda)^\nu$, where $q(\lambda)$ is an irreducible polynomial, of first or second degree, and ν is a positive integer. This is the (real) Jordan decomposition of $\mathcal{X}$. The polynomials $\alpha_{ij}(\lambda)$ ($j \in \underline{p}_i$, $i \in \underline{k}$) are the elementary divisors of A.

The corresponding canonical form of Mat A is obtained as follows. Let the m.p. of $A|\tilde{\mathcal{X}}_{ij}$ be $\theta(\lambda)$ (where i, j are fixed). First suppose $\theta(\lambda) = (\lambda - \mu)^\nu$, where μ is real. Let g be a generator for $\tilde{\mathcal{X}}_{ij}$, and define a basis $\{e_1, \ldots, e_\nu\}$ for $\tilde{\mathcal{X}}_{ij}$ according to

$$e_t = (A - \mu 1)^{\nu - t} g\,, \qquad t \in \underline{\nu}\,.$$

Then

$$(A - \mu 1)e_1 = 0 ,$$

$$(A - \mu 1)e_{t+1} = e_t , \qquad t \in \underline{\nu - 1} ,$$

so in this basis

$$\mathrm{Mat}(A|\mathcal{X}_{ij}) = \begin{bmatrix} \mu & 1 & 0 & \cdot & \cdot & \cdot & \cdot \\ 0 & \mu & 1 & 0 & \cdot & \cdot & \cdot \\ \cdot & \cdot & \cdot & \cdot & \cdot & \cdot & \cdot \\ 0 & \cdot & \cdot & \cdot & \cdot & \mu & 1 \\ 0 & \cdot & \cdot & \cdot & \cdot & 0 & \mu \end{bmatrix} . \tag{24}$$

Next suppose $\theta(\lambda) = \left[(\lambda - \mu_1)^2 + \mu_2^2\right]^\nu$ with μ_1, μ_2 real and $\mu_2 \neq 0$. To find a convenient real basis, factor $\theta(\lambda) = \varphi(\lambda)\varphi^*(\lambda)$ over $\mathbb{C}$, where

$$\varphi(\lambda) \triangleq (\lambda - \mu_1 - i\mu_2)^\nu ,$$

$$\varphi^*(\lambda) \triangleq (\lambda - \mu_1 + i\mu_2)^\nu .$$

Writing $\mathcal{X}$ for $\mathcal{X}_{ij}$ and A for $A|\mathcal{X}_{ij}$, let $\mathcal{X}_{\mathbb{C}}$ be the complexification of $\mathcal{X}$, and note that

$$\mathcal{X}_{\mathbb{C}} = \mathrm{Ker}\,\varphi(A) \oplus \mathrm{Ker}\,\varphi^*(A) = \mathcal{X}_0 \oplus \mathcal{X}_0^* ,$$

say, where $\mathcal{X}_0$ (resp. $\mathcal{X}_0^*$) is cyclic with m.p. $\varphi(\lambda)$ (resp. $\varphi^*(\lambda)$). Let $\mathcal{X}_0$ have a cyclic generator $g = g_1 + ig_2$, where $g_1 = \mathcal{R}e\, g$, $g_2 = \mathcal{I}m\, g$, so that

$$\mathcal{X}_0 = \mathrm{Span}_{\mathbb{C}}\left\{(A - \mu_1 - i\mu_2)^{t-1}(g_1 + ig_2) , \quad t \in \underline{\nu}\right\}.$$

Define

$$e_{2\nu} = g_2 , \qquad e_{2\nu-1} = g_1$$

and

$$\begin{aligned} e_{2t} &= \mathcal{I}m(A - \mu_1 - i\mu_2)(e_{2t+1} + ie_{2t+2}) \\ e_{2t-1} &= \mathcal{R}e(A - \mu_1 - i\mu_2)(e_{2t+1} + ie_{2t+2}) \end{aligned} \tag{25}$$

for $t \in \underline{\nu - 1}$. Then

$$\mathcal{X}_0 = \mathrm{Span}_{\mathbb{C}}\{e_1 + ie_2, \ldots, e_{2\nu-1} + ie_{2\nu}\} ;$$

furthermore

$$(A - \mu_1 - i\mu_2)(e_1 + ie_2) = 0$$

so that

$$Ae_1 = \mu_1 e_1 - \mu_2 e_2$$
$$Ae_2 = \mu_2 e_1 + \mu_1 e_2\ ; \tag{26}$$

and from (25),

$$Ae_{2t-1} = \mu_1 e_{2t-1} - \mu_2 e_{2t} + e_{2t-3}$$
$$Ae_{2t} = \mu_2 e_{2t-1} + \mu_1 e_{2t} + e_{2t-2} \tag{27}$$

for $t = 2, \ldots, \nu$. Now if $\varphi(A)x = 0$ and

$$x_1 = \mathcal{R}e\ x\ , \qquad x_2 = \mathcal{I}m\ x$$

then clearly $\varphi^*(A)x^* = 0$, where $x^* = x_1 - ix_2$; and the reverse is true. It follows that

$$\mathcal{X}_0^* = \mathrm{Span}_{\mathbb{C}}\{e_1 - ie_2, \ldots, e_{2\nu-1} - ie_{2\nu}\}\ .$$

Therefore the 2ν vectors

$$e_1 \pm ie_2, \ldots, e_{2\nu-1} \pm ie_{2\nu}$$

are linearly independent over $\mathbb{C}$, which implies that

$$e_1, e_2, \ldots, e_{2\nu-1}, e_{2\nu} \tag{28}$$

are linearly independent over $\mathbb{R}$. We can now take the set (28) as a basis for the (real) space $\mathcal{X} = \mathcal{X}_{ij}$: by (26) and (27),

$$\mathrm{Mat}\,A = \mathrm{Mat}(A\,|\,\mathcal{X}_{ij}) = \begin{bmatrix} M & I_2 & 0 & \cdot & \cdot & \cdot & \cdot \\ 0 & M & I_2 & 0 & \cdot & \cdot & \cdot \\ \cdot & \cdot & \cdot & \cdot & \cdot & \cdot & \cdot \\ 0 & \cdot & \cdot & \cdot & \cdot & M & I_2 \\ 0 & \cdot & \cdot & \cdot & \cdot & 0 & M \end{bmatrix}_{2\nu \times 2\nu}, \tag{29}$$

where

$$M = \begin{bmatrix} \mu_1 & \mu_2 \\ -\mu_2 & \mu_1 \end{bmatrix}, \qquad I_2 = \begin{bmatrix} 1 & 0 \\ 0 & 1 \end{bmatrix}.$$

Thus the complete real Jordan form of Mat A will be the appropriate diagonal array of blocks of type (24) and (29).

For the case $\mathbb{F} = \mathbb{C}$, the (complex) Jordan form is even simpler, each $\theta(\lambda)$ being of form $(\lambda - \mu)^{\nu}$ with $\mu \in \mathbb{C}$.

The following is a useful decomposition property of arbitrary invariant subspaces.

PROPOSITION 0.4. Let the m.p. of A be $\alpha = \gamma_1 \gamma_2 \cdots \gamma_p$, where the γ_i are pairwise coprime, and let $\tilde{\mathcal{X}}_i = \mathrm{Ker}\, \gamma_i(A)$, $i \in \mathbf{p}$. Then (as already noted)

$$\mathcal{X} = \tilde{\mathcal{X}}_1 \oplus \cdots \oplus \tilde{\mathcal{X}}_p ;$$

and if $\mathcal{R} \subset \mathcal{X}$ is A-invariant,

$$\mathcal{R} = \mathcal{R} \cap \tilde{\mathcal{X}}_1 \oplus \cdots \oplus \mathcal{R} \cap \tilde{\mathcal{X}}_p .$$

To conclude our discussion of canonical structure we shall give a criterion for an invariant subspace to decompose $\mathcal{X}$, and relate this result to the solvability of Sylvester's matrix equation. We assume that a subspace $\mathcal{R} \subset \mathcal{X}$ is given, with $A\mathcal{R} \subset \mathcal{R}$. Let $J: \mathcal{R} \to \mathcal{X}$ be the insertion of $\mathcal{R}$ in $\mathcal{X}$, $1_{\mathcal{R}}$ the identity on $\mathcal{R}$, and $A_1 = A|\mathcal{R}$. It is easily seen that $\mathcal{R}$ decomposes $\mathcal{X}$ relative to A if and only if there exists a map $Q: \mathcal{X} \to \mathcal{R}$ such that

$$QJ = 1_{\mathcal{R}} \tag{30}$$
$$QA = A_1 Q . \tag{31}$$

Indeed if (30) and (31) hold, set $\mathcal{S} = \mathrm{Ker}\, Q$. Then if $x \in \mathcal{X}$,

$$x = JQx + (1 - JQ)x ;$$

since $Q(1 - JQ)x = 0$, we have $x \in \mathcal{R} + \mathcal{S}$, so that $\mathcal{R} + \mathcal{S} = \mathcal{X}$. Also, $x \in \mathcal{R} \cap \mathcal{S}$ implies $x = 1_{\mathcal{R}} x = QJx = 0$, hence $\mathcal{R} \cap \mathcal{S} = 0$. Finally, $Qx = 0$ implies $QAx = A_1 Qx = 0$, so $A\mathcal{S} \subset \mathcal{S}$. Conversely if $\mathcal{R} \oplus \mathcal{S} = \mathcal{X}$ with $A\mathcal{S} \subset \mathcal{S}$, let Q be the natural projection $\mathcal{R} \oplus \mathcal{S} \to \mathcal{R}$.

Now let $\mathcal{R} \oplus \tilde{\mathcal{S}} = \mathcal{X}$, where $\tilde{\mathcal{S}}$ is an arbitrary complement of $\mathcal{R}$ in $\mathcal{X}$. In a compatible basis A and J have matrices

$$A \sim \begin{bmatrix} A_1 & A_3 \\ 0 & A_2 \end{bmatrix}, \qquad J \sim \begin{bmatrix} I \\ 0 \end{bmatrix}. \tag{32}$$

By (32), the relations (30) and (31) are equivalent to

$$Q \sim [I \quad Q_2]$$

and

$$A_1 Q_2 - Q_2 A_2 - A_3 = 0 . \tag{33}$$

Thus to check whether $\mathcal{R}$ decomposes $\mathcal{X}$ it is enough to verify that the linear matrix equation (33) (Sylvester's equation) has a solution Q_2. This computational problem is in principle straightforward.

Of greater theoretical interest is the following result, which can be obtained from the structure theory already presented.

PROPOSITION 0.5. $\mathcal{R}$ decomposes $\mathcal{X}$ if and only if the elementary divisors of $A|\mathcal{R}$, with those of the induced map $\bar{A}$ in $\mathcal{X}/\mathcal{R}$, together give all the elementary divisors of A.

In (32), A_1 is the matrix of $A|\mathcal{R}$ and A_2 that of $\bar{A}$. Proposition 0.5 thus solves the existence problem for (33) in a style which respects the role of A_1 and A_2 as endomorphisms in their own right. As a special case (and already a consequence of (20)–(23)), (33) has a solution which is even unique, if the spectra of A_1 and A_2 are disjoint. So, in this case the (linear) map

$$L: \mathbf{F}^{n_1 \times n_2} \to \mathbf{F}^{n_1 \times n_2},$$

given by

$$L(Q) \triangleq A_1 Q - Q A_2,$$

is an isomorphism.

0.12 Dual Spaces

Let $\mathcal{X}$ be a linear vector space over $\mathbf{F}$. The set of all linear functionals $x': \mathcal{X} \to \mathbf{F}$ is denoted by $\mathcal{X}'$. $\mathcal{X}'$ is turned into a linear vector space by the definitions

$$(x_1' + x_2')x \triangleq x_1'x + x_2'x\ ; \qquad x_i' \in \mathcal{X}',\ x \in \mathcal{X}$$

$$(kx_1')x \triangleq k(x_1'x)\ ; \qquad x_1' \in \mathcal{X}',\ x \in \mathcal{X}, \qquad k \in \mathbf{F}.$$

If $\{x_1, \ldots, x_n\}$ is a basis for $\mathcal{X}$, the corresponding dual basis for $\mathcal{X}'$ is the unique set $\{x_1', \ldots, x_n'\} \subset \mathcal{X}'$ such that $x_i'x_j = \delta_{ij}$ $(i, j \in \underline{n})$.

If $C: \mathcal{X} \to \mathcal{Y}$, its dual map $C': \mathcal{Y}' \to \mathcal{X}'$ is defined as follows. Temporarily write $C'(y')$ for the value in $\mathcal{X}'$ of C' at y' and let C' be determined by the requirement

$$[C'(y')]x = y'(Cx) \tag{34}$$

for all $x \in \mathcal{X}$ and $y' \in \mathcal{Y}'$. By choosing arbitrary bases in $\mathcal{X}$ and $\mathcal{Y}$, and their duals in $\mathcal{X}'$ and $\mathcal{Y}'$, it is easily verified that C' exists and is unique. In these bases, if

$$\text{Mat}\, C = [c_{ij}]$$

then

$$\text{Mat}\, C' = [c_{ji}] ,$$

the transpose of Mat C. It is usually convenient to denote the action of C' by writing the argument y' to the left of the (unprimed) symbol C:

$$C'(y') = y'C ,$$

so that (34) takes the symmetric form

$$(y'C)x = y'(Cx) .$$

This notation matches the matrix convention that $x \in \mathcal{X}$ is represented as a column vector and $y' \in \mathcal{Y}'$ as a row vector.

A nice consequence of (34) is that every commutative diagram has a dual commutative diagram obtained by replacing all maps and spaces by their duals and reversing all the arrows. Under dualization exact sequences remain exact. Thus the sequence

$$0 \longrightarrow \mathcal{X} \xrightarrow{C} \mathcal{Y} ,$$

expressing the fact that $C: \mathcal{X} \to \mathcal{Y}$ is monic, has the dual

$$0 \longleftarrow \mathcal{X}' \xleftarrow{C'} \mathcal{Y}' ,$$

which states that $C': \mathcal{Y}' \to \mathcal{X}'$ is epic. Similarly C epic implies C' monic.

Let $\mathcal{S} \subset \mathcal{X}$. The annihilator of $\mathcal{S}$, written $\mathcal{S}^\perp$, is the set of all $x' \in \mathcal{X}'$ such that $x'\mathcal{S} = 0$. Clearly $\mathcal{S}^\perp$ is a subspace of $\mathcal{X}'$. Thus $0^\perp = \mathcal{X}'$, $\mathcal{X}^\perp = 0$, and in general $\mathcal{S}^\perp \approx \mathcal{X}/\mathcal{S}$.

If $\mathcal{R} \subset \mathcal{X}$ and $\mathcal{S} \subset \mathcal{X}$ then

$$(\mathcal{R} + \mathcal{S})^\perp = \mathcal{R}^\perp \cap \mathcal{S}^\perp ,$$
$$(\mathcal{R} \cap \mathcal{S})^\perp = \mathcal{R}^\perp + \mathcal{S}^\perp ,$$

and $\mathcal{R} \subset \mathcal{S}$ implies $\mathcal{R}^\perp \supset \mathcal{S}^\perp$.

Fix $x \in \mathcal{X}$, and in $\tilde{\mathcal{X}} \triangleq (\mathcal{X}')'$ define $\tilde{x}$ by

$$\tilde{x}(x') = x'(x) , \qquad x' \in \mathcal{X}' . \tag{35}$$

On the other hand, if $\tilde{x} \in \tilde{\mathcal{X}}$ let $\{x_i', \ i \in \underline{n}\}$ be a basis for $\mathcal{X}'$ and define $x \in \mathcal{X}$ (uniquely) by the requirement

$$x_i' x = \tilde{x}(x_i') , \qquad i \in \underline{n} . \tag{36}$$

Equations (35) and (36) provide a natural isomorphism $\tilde{\tilde{\mathcal{X}}} \approx \mathcal{X}$, and from now on we identify $(\mathcal{X}')' = \mathcal{X}$. Thus if $\mathcal{R} \subset \mathcal{X}$ then $(\mathcal{R}^\perp)^\perp = \mathcal{R}$.

If $C: \mathcal{X} \to \mathcal{Y}$ then

$$(\operatorname{Im} C)^\perp = \operatorname{Ker} C'$$

and

$$(\operatorname{Ker} C)^\perp = \operatorname{Im} C' .$$

Finally if $\mathcal{R} \subset \mathcal{X}$ and $\mathcal{S} \subset \mathcal{Y}$,

$$(C\mathcal{R})^\perp = (C')^{-1}\mathcal{R}^\perp$$

and

$$(C^{-1}\mathcal{S})^\perp = C'\mathcal{S}^\perp .$$

0.13 Inner Product Spaces

It is sometimes useful to regard $\mathcal{X}$ as an inner product space and thereby identify $\mathcal{X}$ with its dual $\mathcal{X}'$. Assume $\mathbb{F} = \mathbb{C}$; the results for $\mathbb{R}$ are immediate by specialization. Let $\{x_1, \ldots, x_n\}$ be a fixed basis for $\mathcal{X}$. If $x, y \in \mathcal{X}$ with

$$x = \sum_{i=1}^{n} c_i x_i , \qquad y = \sum_{i=1}^{n} d_i x_i ,$$

we define the inner product of x and y as

$$\langle x, y \rangle \triangleq \sum_{i=1}^{n} c_i d_i^* .$$

The inner product is linear in x, and antilinear (i.e., linear within conjugation of scalar multiples) in y.

With the basis $\{x_i, i \in \underline{n}\}$ fixed, an isomorphism $\mathcal{X}' \approx \mathcal{X}: x' \mapsto x$ is induced as follows: define x (uniquely) by the requirement

$$\langle x, x_i \rangle = x' x_i , \qquad i \in \underline{n} .$$

Explicitly, if $\{x_i', i \in \underline{n}\}$ is the dual basis in $\mathcal{X}'$, and

$$x' = c_1 x_1' + \cdots + c_n x_n'$$

then

$$x = c_1 x_1 + \cdots + c_n x_n .$$

Under this isomorphism it is often convenient to identify $\mathcal{X}'$ with $\mathcal{X}$, and write the inner product $\langle x, z\rangle$ as $x'z^*$. Here, if

$$z = d_1 x_1 + \cdots + d_n x_n , \qquad d_i \in \mathbb{C}$$

then, of course,

$$z^* = d_1^* x_1 + \cdots + d_n^* x_n .$$

The Euclidean norm of $x \in \mathcal{X}$, written $|x|$, is

$$|x| \triangleq +\sqrt{\langle x, x\rangle} = +\sqrt{(x^*)' x} = + \sqrt{\sum_{i=1}^{n} |c_i|^2} .$$

0.14 Hermitian and Symmetric Maps

Let $\mathcal{X}$ be an inner product space over $\mathbb{C}$; the results for $\mathbb{R}$ follow by specialization. A map $P: \mathcal{X} \to \mathcal{X}$ is Hermitian if $\langle x, Py\rangle = \langle Px, y\rangle$ for all $x, y \in \mathcal{X}$. Equivalently, if the inner product is related to a basis $\{x_i,\ i \in \underline{n}\}$ as in Section 0.13, we have

$$x'(Py)^* = (Px)' y^* = x'P'y^* .$$

This implies that $P' = P^*$, where P^* is defined by

$$P^* x_i \triangleq (Px_i)^* , \qquad i \in \underline{n} .$$

Thus P is Hermitian if and only if $P = (P')^*$: in matrices, P coincides with its conjugate transpose. The main result on Hermitian maps is the following.

THEOREM 0.2 (Spectral Theorem). *Let $P: \mathcal{X} \to \mathcal{X}$ be Hermitian. Then the eigenvalues of P are all real. Furthermore, if the distinct eigenvalues $\lambda_1, \ldots, \lambda_k$ occur with multiplicity n_i $(i \in \underline{k})$, there exist unique subspaces $\mathcal{X}_i$ $(i \in \underline{k})$ with the properties*

(i) $\mathcal{X} = \mathcal{X}_1 \oplus \cdots \oplus \mathcal{X}_k , \qquad d(\mathcal{X}_i) = n_i .$

(ii) $P\mathcal{X}_i \subset \mathcal{X}_i , \qquad i \in \underline{k} .$

(iii) $P|\mathcal{X}_i = \lambda_i 1_{\mathcal{X}_i} , \qquad i \in \underline{k} .$

(iv) *The $\mathcal{X}_i$ are orthogonal, in the sense that $\langle x_i, x_j\rangle = 0$ for all $x_i \in \mathcal{X}_i$, $x_j \in \mathcal{X}_j$ with $j \neq i$.*

As a simple consequence, if $x^{*\prime} Px = 0$ for all x, then $P = 0$.

We shall mainly need Theorem 0.2 when $\mathcal{X}$ is defined over $\mathbb{R}$. Then 'Hermitian' is replaced by 'symmetric': P is symmetric if $P' = P$. In the complexification $\mathcal{X}_{\mathbb{C}}$ one has that $P^* = P$, and 'symmetric' does mean 'Hermitian'. Keeping $\mathbb{F} = \mathbb{R}$, we call R: $\mathcal{X} \to \mathcal{X}$ orthogonal if R is invertible and $R^{-1} = R'$. Thus $(Rx)' Ry = x'y$ for all $x, y \in \mathcal{X}$. In matrices, Theorem 0.2 states that, for suitable orthogonal R,

$$R'PR = \operatorname{diag}\left[\lambda_1 I_{n_1}, \ldots, \lambda_k I_{n_k}\right].$$

A Hermitian map P is positive definite, written $P > 0$ (or positive semidefinite, written $P \geq 0$) if $\langle x, Px \rangle > 0$ (or ≥ 0) for all $x \in \mathcal{X}$. By Theorem 0.2, $P \geq 0$ and $\langle x, Px \rangle = 0$ imply $x \in \operatorname{Ker} P$. With Q also Hermitian, write $P \geq Q$ if $P - Q \geq 0$. Observe that $P \geq Q$ and $Q \geq P$ imply $P = Q$. Thus the class of Hermitian maps on $\mathcal{X}$ is partially ordered by inequality ($\geq$), although if $d(\mathcal{X}) > 1$ it does not form a lattice.

The norm of P is the number

$$|P| \triangleq \max\{\langle x, Px \rangle: |x|^2 = 1\} = \max\{x^{*\prime} Px: |x|^2 = 1\}$$
$$= \max\{|\lambda|: \lambda \in \sigma(P)\}.$$

In the remainder of this section we take $\mathbb{F} = \mathbb{R}$. In the sense of the partial ordering of symmetric maps we may speak of monotone nondecreasing sequences $\{P_k\}$, written $P_k \uparrow$ (or nonincreasing, written $P_k \downarrow$), such that $P_{k+1} \geq P_k$ (or $P_{k+1} \leq P_k$). We have

PROPOSITION 0.6. If P_k, Q are symmetric maps such that $P_k \geq Q$ ($k = 1, 2, \ldots$) and $P_k \downarrow$, then

$$P \triangleq \lim P_k, \qquad k \to \infty,$$

exists.

Here the limit means

$$y'Px = \lim y' P_k x, \qquad k \to \infty,$$

for all $x, y \in \mathcal{X}$. A similar result holds for monotone nondecreasing sequences which are bounded above.

0.15 Well-Posedness and Genericity

Let A, B, ... be matrices with elements in $\mathbb{R}$ and suppose $\Pi(A, B, \ldots)$ is some property which may be asserted about them. In applications where A, B, ... represent the data of a physical problem, it is often important to know various topological features of Π. For instance, if Π is true at a nominal parameter set $\underline{p}_0 = (A_0, B_0, \ldots)$ it may be desirable or natural that Π be true at points $\underline{p}$ in a neighborhood of $\underline{p}_0$, corresponding to small deviations of the parameters from their nominal values.

Most of the properties of interest to us will turn out to hold true for all sets of parameter values except possibly those which correspond to points $\underline{p}$ which lie on some algebraic hypersurface in a suitable parameter space, and which are thus, in an intuitive sense, atypical. To make this idea precise, we borrow some terminology from algebraic geometry. Let

$$\underline{p} = (\underline{p}_1, \ldots, \underline{p}_N) \in \mathbb{R}^N ,$$

and consider polynomials $\varphi(\lambda_1, \ldots, \lambda_N)$ with coefficients in $\mathbb{R}$. A <u>variety</u> $\underline{V} \subset \mathbb{R}^N$ is defined to be the set of common zeros of a finite number of polynomials $\varphi_1, \ldots, \varphi_k$:

$$\underline{V} = \{\underline{p}: \ \varphi_i(\underline{p}_1, \ldots, \underline{p}_N) = 0 , \qquad i \in \underline{k}\} .$$

$\underline{V}$ is <u>proper</u> if $\underline{V} \neq \mathbb{R}^N$ and <u>nontrivial</u> if $\underline{V} \neq \emptyset$. A parameter point $\underline{p} \in \mathbb{R}^N$ is <u>typical</u> (relative to $\underline{V}$) if $\underline{p} \in \underline{V}^c$, the complement of $\underline{V}$. In this setup, a <u>property</u> Π is merely a function Π: $\mathbb{R}^N \to \{0, 1\}$, where $\Pi(\underline{p}) = 1$ (or 0) means Π holds (or fails) at $\underline{p}$. Let $\underline{V}$ be a proper variety. We shall say that Π is <u>generic relative to</u> $\underline{V}$ provided $\Pi(\underline{p}) = 0$ only if $\underline{p} \in \underline{V}$; and that Π is <u>generic</u> provided such a $\underline{V}$ exists. If Π is generic, we sometimes write

$$\Pi = 1 \ \text{(g)} .$$

Assign to $\mathbb{R}^N$ the usual Euclidean topology. If $\underline{V}$ is any variety it is clear from the continuity of its defining polynomials that $\underline{V}$ is closed. Thus if Π is generic relative to $\underline{V}$ and if Π holds at $\underline{p} \in \underline{V}^c$, Π also holds in a sufficiently small neighborhood of $\underline{p}$. In this sense the property Π is <u>well-posed</u> at points $\underline{p} \in \underline{V}^c$. Let $\underline{p}_0 \in \underline{V}$, with $\underline{V}$ nontrivial and proper. It is clear that every neighborhood of $\underline{p}_0$ contains points $\underline{p} \notin \underline{V}$; otherwise, each defining polynomial φ of $\underline{V}$ vanishes identically in some neighborhood of $\underline{p}_0$, hence vanishes on $\mathbb{R}^N$, and therefore $\underline{V} = \mathbb{R}^N$, in contradiction to the assumption that $\underline{V}$ is proper. Thus if Π is generic relative to $\underline{V}$ and if Π fails at $\underline{p}_0$, Π can be made to hold if $\underline{p}_0$ is shifted by a suitable perturbation, arbitrarily small. We may summarize by saying that the set of points $\underline{p}$, where a generic property is well-posed, is both open and dense in $\mathbb{R}^N$. On the other hand, not too much should be made of the feature 'open and dense' by itself: there exist in $\mathbb{R}^N$ open dense sets of arbitrarily small positive 'probability' (Lebesgue measure).* A generic property has the strong feature that it is well-posed in an open set whose complement has zero 'probability'.

---

* Well-order the rational points in $\mathbb{R}^N$, around the $n^{\underline{th}}$ place an open ball of volume $\epsilon/2^n$, and take the union.

As a primitive illustration of these ideas, let $C \in \mathbb{R}^{m\times n}$, $y \in \mathbb{R}^{m\times 1}$ and consider the assertion: there exists $x \in \mathbb{R}^{n\times 1}$ such that $y = Cx$. Say that $\underline{p} \triangleq (C, y)$ has property Π (i.e., $\Pi(\underline{p}) = 1$) if and only if our assertion is true. By listing the elements of C and y in arbitrary order, regard $\underline{p}$ as a data point in $\mathbb{R}^N$, $N = mn + m$. Now $\Pi(\underline{p}) = 1$ if and only if $y \in \operatorname{Im} C$, i.e.,

$$\operatorname{Rank}[C, y] = \operatorname{Rank} C . \tag{37}$$

It follows easily that Π is well-posed at $\underline{p}$ if and only if $\operatorname{Rank} C = m$, and Π is generic if and only if $m \le n$.

To verify these statements note first that (37) fails only if

$$\operatorname{Rank} C = d(\operatorname{Im} C) < m . \tag{38}$$

But (38) implies that all $m \times m$ minors of C vanish: let $\underline{V} \subset \mathbb{R}^N$ be the variety so determined. If $m \le n$, $\underline{V}$ is clearly proper, hence Π is generic, as claimed. On the other hand, if $m \ge n+1$, (37) holds only if all $(n+1) \times (n+1)$ minors of $[C, y]$ vanish. The variety $\underline{W}$ so defined is proper, and $\Pi(\underline{p}) = 0$ for $\underline{p} \in \underline{W}^c$, hence Π cannot be generic. Finally, if $\operatorname{Rank} C = m$ at $\underline{p}$ then (equivalently) at least one $m \times m$ minor of C is nonzero at $\underline{p}$, hence nonzero in a neighborhood of $\underline{p}$, so Π is well-posed at $\underline{p}$. Conversely if $\operatorname{Rank} C < m$ at $\underline{p}$ then a suitable $\tilde{y}$, with $|\tilde{y} - y|$ arbitrarily small, will make

$$\operatorname{Rank}[C, \tilde{y}] = \operatorname{Rank} C + 1 ;$$

namely, if $\tilde{p} \triangleq (C, \tilde{y})$, then $\Pi(\tilde{p}) = 0$, hence Π is not well-posed at $\underline{p}$.

0.16 Linear Systems

We consider mainly finite-dimensional, constant-parameter (i.e., time-invariant) linear systems, modelled by equations of form

$$\begin{aligned} \dot{x}(t) &= Ax(t) + Bu(t) \\ y(t) &= Cx(t) \end{aligned} \tag{39}$$

for $t \ge 0$. The vectors x, y, u belong to real linear spaces $\mathcal{X}, \mathcal{Y}, \mathcal{U}$, respectively, with

$$d(\mathcal{X}) = n, \qquad d(\mathcal{Y}) = p, \qquad d(\mathcal{U}) = m .$$

Here $\mathcal{X}$ is the <u>state space</u>, $\mathcal{Y}$ the <u>output space</u>, and $\mathcal{U}$ the <u>input space</u>. For our purposes it is sufficient to assume that $u(.)$ is piecewise continuous.

In some applications one encounters output equations of more general form

$$y(t) = C_1 x(t) + C_2 u(t) . \tag{40}$$

We shall, however, make the assumption that a model of this type is well enough approximated by adjoining to (39) the auxiliary $m^{\underline{th}}$ order system

$$\epsilon \dot{v}(t) = -v(t) + u(t) ,$$

where $\epsilon > 0$ is taken small compared to the dominant time constants of interest; and then by replacing (40) with

$$y(t) = C_1 x(t) + C_2 v(t) .$$

If $x(0) = x_0$ then (39) implies

$$x(t) = e^{tA} x_0 + \int_0^t e^{(t-\tau) A} Bu(\tau)\, d\tau , \qquad t \geq 0 ,$$

or more generally

$$x(t) = e^{(t-t_0) A} x(t_0) + \int_{t_0}^t e^{(t-\tau) A} Bu(\tau)\, d\tau$$

for $t_0 \geq 0$, $t \geq 0$.

It is sometimes convenient to know e^{tA} explicitly. For this let $\pi(\lambda)$ be the ch.p. of A:

$$\pi(\lambda) = \lambda^n - \left(p_1 + p_2 \lambda + \cdots + p_n \lambda^{n-1}\right) .$$

Define auxiliary polynomials (cf. (16))

$$\pi^{(r)}(\lambda) = \lambda^{n-r} - \left(p_{r+1} + p_{r+2} \lambda + \cdots + p_n \lambda^{n-r-1}\right)$$

for $r \in \underline{n}$. A short calculation verifies that

$$\pi(\lambda)(\lambda - A)^{-1} = \sum_{r=1}^{n} \pi^{(r)}(\lambda)\, A^{r-1} .$$

Then if $\mathfrak{G}$ is any Jordan contour enclosing $\sigma(A)$ in the complex plane, we have by Cauchy's theorem

$$e^{tA} = \frac{1}{2\pi i}\oint_{\mathfrak{C}} (zI - A)^{-1} e^{tz}\, dz = \sum_{r=1}^{n} \psi_r(t) A^{r-1}, \tag{41}$$

where

$$\psi_r(t) \triangleq \frac{1}{2\pi i}\oint_{\mathfrak{C}} \frac{\pi^{(r)}(z)}{\pi(z)} e^{tz}\, dz, \qquad r \in \underline{n}.$$

Instead of the characteristic polynomial π, any multiple of the m.p. of A could be used in this calculation, if the auxiliary polynomials are defined accordingly.

0.17 Transfer Matrices. Signal Flow Graphs

If in (39), $x(0) = 0$, and $|u(.)|$ grows at most exponentially fast as $t \uparrow \infty$, then $y(.)$ has the Laplace transform

$$\hat{y}(s) \triangleq \int_0^\infty e^{-st} y(t)\, dt = \int_0^\infty e^{-st}\left[C\int_0^t e^{(t-\tau)A} Bu(\tau)\, d\tau\right] dt$$

$$= C\int_0^\infty e^{-st}\left[\int_0^t e^{(t-\tau)A} Bu(\tau)\, d\tau\right] dt = C(sI - A)^{-1} B\hat{u}(s),$$

defined for $\mathcal{R}e\, s$ sufficiently large. The matrix

$$H(s) \triangleq C(sI - A)^{-1} B$$

is the transfer matrix of the triple of matrices (C, A, B), and is defined for $s \in \mathbb{C} - \sigma(A)$. For such s, $H(s)$ can be viewed as the matrix of a map $\mathcal{U} \to \mathcal{Y}$, taken as linear spaces over $\mathbb{C}$.

While transfer matrices play no role in the synthesis procedures of this book, they will be useful for casual descriptive purposes. In this regard, a complex system comprising interconnected subsystems can be represented by its signal flow graph. Informally, this is a directed graph in which the nodes are variables (like $u, x, y, \ldots$) and the branches are the transfer matrices relating them. A node variable is the weighted sum of node variables at the tail of entering branches, the weights being the branch transfer matrices; if no branch enters a node, its variable is an 'input'; if no branch leaves a node, it is an 'output'. The signal flow graph is drawn after taking formal Laplace transforms of everything in sight. Thus the system equations

$$\dot{x} = Ax + Bu, \qquad x(0) = x_0$$
$$u = Fx + v, \qquad y = Cx$$

yield

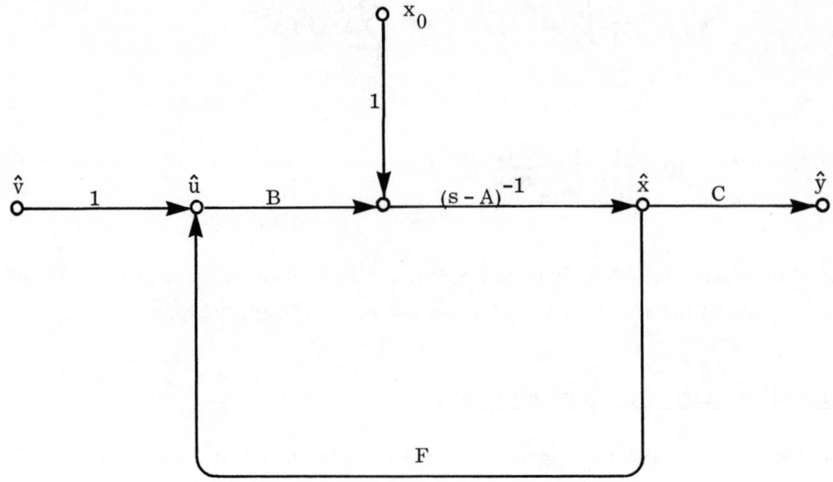

Fig. 0.1.

Signal Flow Graph for the System:

$$\hat{x}(s) = (s - A)^{-1}\left[x_0 + B\,\hat{u}(s)\right]$$

$$\hat{u}(s) = F\,\hat{x}(s) + \hat{v}(s)$$

$$\hat{y}(s) = C\,\hat{x}(s)$$

$$\hat{x}(s) = (s-A)^{-1}\left(x_0 + B\hat{u}(s)\right),$$

$$\hat{u}(s) = F\hat{x}(s) + \hat{v}(s), \qquad \hat{y}(s) = C\hat{x}(s),$$

whence the graph, Fig. 0.1. From now on we drop the (^) on node variables in graphs; and frequently leave off the initial values x_0, with their corresponding branches.

0.18 Rouché's Theorem

This well known result from complex function theory will find applications to 'root loci'.

THEOREM 0.3. *If* $f(z)$ *and* $g(z)$ *are analytic inside and on a closed contour* $\mathfrak{C}$, *and* $|g(z)| < |f(z)|$ *for* z *on* $\mathfrak{C}$ *then* $f(z)$ *and* $f(z)+g(z)$ *have the same number of zeros inside* $\mathfrak{C}$.

0.19 Exercises

0.1 Prove, or look up the proofs of, all the unproved assertions in this chapter. The next six exercises provide hints for the easier items; the hard structural results of Section 0.10 are amply covered in the textbooks referenced in Section 0.20.

0.2 Prove the modular distributive rule (2). HINT: This and the remaining identities among subspaces in this chapter are all provable by the standard technique of establishing the inclusions LHS $\subset$ RHS and RHS $\subset$ LHS by direct computation. Thus, for (2), note that $x \in \mathcal{R}\cap\mathcal{S} + \mathcal{R}\cap\mathcal{T}$ means $x = r_1 + r_2$, say, where $r_1 \in \mathcal{R}\cap\mathcal{S}$ and $r_2 \in \mathcal{R}\cap\mathcal{T}$. Thus $r_1, r_2 \in \mathcal{R}$, hence $r_1 + r_2 \in \mathcal{R}$ (since $\mathcal{R}$ is a subspace); similarly, $r_1 + r_2 \in \mathcal{S}+\mathcal{T}$, by definition of subspace addition; so $r_1 + r_2 \in \mathcal{R}\cap(\mathcal{S}+\mathcal{T})$, as claimed. For the reverse inclusion, $x \in \mathcal{R}\cap(\mathcal{S}+\mathcal{T})$ means, in obvious notation, $x = r = s+t$, say; but $\mathcal{R}\supset\mathcal{S}$ implies $s \in \mathcal{R}$, hence $s \in \mathcal{R}\cap\mathcal{S}$; then $t = r - s \in \mathcal{R}$ implies $t \in \mathcal{R}\cap\mathcal{T}$; therefore

$$x = s+t \in \mathcal{R}\cap\mathcal{S} + \mathcal{R}\cap\mathcal{T}$$

as claimed, and the proof is complete.

0.3 Prove (5). HINT: Note that if $\mathcal{T}\subset\mathcal{R}$, one can always write $\mathcal{R} = \hat{\mathcal{R}} \oplus \mathcal{T}$ for suitable $\hat{\mathcal{R}}\subset\mathcal{R}$: simply take a basis $\{t_1, \dots, t_k\}$ for $\mathcal{T}$, extend it to a basis $\{t_1, \dots, t_k, \hat{r}_1, \dots, \hat{r}_\ell\}$ for $\mathcal{R}$, and set $\hat{\mathcal{R}} \triangleq \mathrm{Span}\{\hat{r}_1, \dots, \hat{r}_\ell\}$. Of course, $\hat{\mathcal{R}}$ is not unique, as one sees by simple pictures in $\mathbb{R}^2$ or $\mathbb{R}^3$.

0.4 Given $C: \mathcal{X}\to\mathcal{Y}$ epic, prove the existence of a right inverse C_r^{-1} as in (9). HINT: The technique is to define a map C_r^{-1} by specifying its action on a basis. Let $\{y_i, i \in \underline{p}\}$ be a basis for $\mathcal{Y}$. C being epic, there are $x_i \in \mathcal{X}$ $(i \in \underline{p})$ such that $Cx_i = y_i$ $(i \in \underline{p})$, so define $C_r^{-1} y_i \triangleq x_i$ ($i \in \mathbf{p}$). In general the x_i are not unique, hence C_r^{-1} is not unique either.

0.5 Prove (22). HINT: First suppose $p = 2$. By coprimeness (cf. (15)) one has

$$1 = \sigma_1(\lambda)\gamma_1(\lambda) + \sigma_2(\lambda)\gamma_2(\lambda)$$

for suitable $\sigma_i(\lambda)$ ($i \in \mathbf{p}$). Replacing λ by A and operating on $x \in \mathcal{X}$ yield the representation

$$x = \sigma_1(A)\gamma_1(A)x + \sigma_2(A)\gamma_2(A)x,$$

which is clearly of the form required. The proof is finished by induction on p.

0.6 Prove the second statement of Proposition 0.4. HINT: Factor the m.p. of $A|\mathcal{R}$.

0.7 Prove Proposition 0.6. HINT: Use the polarization identity

$$2x'Py = (x+y)'P(x+y) - x'Px - y'Py,$$

plus the fact that the numerical sequences $\{x'P_k x\}$ are monotone and bounded.

0.8 Let $P \geq 0$ be a symmetric map on $\mathcal{X}$ (over $\mathbb{R}$). Show that P has a unique, nonnegative, symmetric square root: i.e., there exists $Q \geq 0$ symmetric, with $Q^2 = P$, and these properties determine Q uniquely. HINT: First prove the assertion for $P = 0$ and $P = 1$, then exploit Theorem 0.3.

0.9 Let $A: \mathcal{X} \to \mathcal{X}$. Show that the family of A-invariant subspaces of $\mathcal{X}$ is a lattice, relative to $\subset$, $+$, and $\cap$, hence is a sublattice of the lattice of all subspaces of $\mathcal{X}$. HINT: It is enough to show that if $\mathcal{R}$ and $\mathcal{S}$ are A-invariant, so are $\mathcal{R} + \mathcal{S}$ and $\mathcal{R} \cap \mathcal{S}$.

0.10 Let $A: \mathcal{X} \to \mathcal{X}$, $A\mathcal{N} \subset \mathcal{N}$, $A\mathcal{S} \subset \mathcal{S}$, and $\mathcal{S} \supset \mathcal{N}$. Let $P_1: \mathcal{X} \to \mathcal{X}/\mathcal{N}$ and $Q: \mathcal{X} \to \mathcal{X}/\mathcal{S}$ be the respective canonical projections, and let $\bar{A}$, $\bar{\bar{A}}$ be the maps induced by A in respectively $\mathcal{X}/\mathcal{N}$ and $\mathcal{X}/\mathcal{S}$. Prove the existence of a map $P_2: \mathcal{X}/\mathcal{N} \to \mathcal{X}/\mathcal{S}$ such that the diagram below commutes.

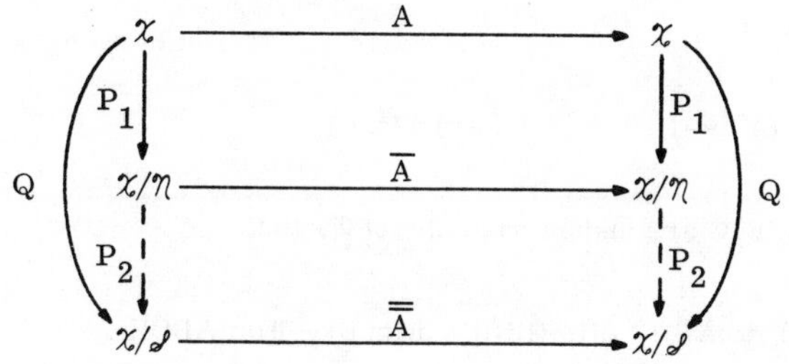

HINT: Note that $\mathcal{X}/\mathcal{S} \approx (\mathcal{X}/\mathcal{N})/(\mathcal{S}/\mathcal{N})$ in a natural way, and consider the canonical projection from $\mathcal{X}/\mathcal{N}$ to its indicated factor space.

0.11 Develop matrix algorithms for the computation of $\mathcal{R} + \mathcal{S}$, $\mathcal{R} \cap \mathcal{S}$, and $A^{-1}\mathcal{R}$. HINT: If R and S are insertion maps for $\mathcal{R}$ and $\mathcal{S}$, consider the corresponding matrix $[R, S]$. The span of its columns is $\mathcal{R} + \mathcal{S}$. To get an insertion map for $\mathcal{R} + \mathcal{S}$ simply eliminate redundant columns: e.g., working from left to right, eliminate columns which are linearly dependent on their predecessors. For the intersection, represent the elements of the dual space $\mathcal{X}'$ as row vectors, and let $R^{\perp}: \mathcal{R}^{\perp} \to \mathcal{X}'$ be an insertion map for $\mathcal{R}^{\perp}$, with a similar definition for $S^{\perp}$. Thus $R^{\perp}$ can be any matrix with independent rows, such that $R^{\perp}x = 0$ if and only if $x \in \mathcal{R}$. Noting that $(\mathcal{R} \cap \mathcal{S})^{\perp} = \mathcal{R}^{\perp} + \mathcal{S}^{\perp}$, conclude that

$$\mathcal{R} \cap \mathcal{S} = \mathrm{Ker} \begin{bmatrix} R^{\perp} \\ S^{\perp} \end{bmatrix}.$$

Elimination of redundant rows will give an insertion map for $(\mathcal{R} \cap \mathcal{S})^{\perp}$. As an immediate result of the definitions, one now has

$$A^{-1}\mathcal{R} = \mathrm{Ker}[R^{\perp}A] \; .$$

0.12 The following miscellaneous facts are sometimes useful; the proofs are straightforward.

(i) $C(C^{-1}\mathcal{S}) = \mathcal{S} \cap \mathrm{Im}\, C$.

(ii) $C^{-1}(C\mathcal{R}) = \mathcal{R} + \mathrm{Ker}\, C$.

(iii) $C\mathcal{R} \subset \mathcal{S}$ if and only if $\mathcal{R} \subset C^{-1}\mathcal{S}$.

(iv) In general $C^{-1}\mathcal{S} \subset \mathcal{R}$ does not imply, and is not implied by, $\mathcal{S} \subset C\mathcal{R}$.

(v) If $A: \mathcal{X} \to \mathcal{X}$ and $\mathcal{B}, \mathcal{R}, \mathcal{S} \subset \mathcal{X}$, then $A\mathcal{R} \subset A\mathcal{S} + \mathcal{B}$ if and only if $\mathcal{R} \subset \mathcal{S} + A^{-1}\mathcal{B}$.

(vi) If $\mathcal{R} \subset \mathcal{X}$ and $A: \mathcal{X} \to \mathcal{X}$ then for $j = 0, 1, 2, \ldots$, define

$$A^{-j}\mathcal{R} \triangleq A^{-1}(\cdots(A^{-1}(A^{-1}\mathcal{R}))\cdots) \qquad \text{(j-fold)};$$

and prove:

$$\left((A')^j \mathcal{R}^\perp\right)^\perp = A^{-j}\mathcal{R} = \left(A^j\right)^{-1}\mathcal{R}.$$

(vii) If A, B, C are endomorphisms of $\mathcal{X}$, then

$$d[\mathrm{Im}(AB)] + d[\mathrm{Im}(BC)] \le d(\mathrm{Im}\, B) + d[\mathrm{Im}(ABC)] .$$

(viii) If A: $\mathcal{X} \to \mathcal{X}$ and $\mathcal{B}, \mathcal{R} \subset \mathcal{X}$, then

$$\frac{A\mathcal{R} + \mathcal{B}}{\mathcal{B}} \approx \frac{\mathcal{R}}{\mathcal{R} \cap A^{-1}\mathcal{B}} .$$

(ix) If $\mathcal{R}, \mathcal{S} \subset \mathcal{X}$ and C: $\mathcal{X} \to \mathcal{Y}$, then

$$\frac{C\mathcal{R} \cap C\mathcal{S}}{C(\mathcal{R} \cap \mathcal{S})} \approx \frac{(\mathcal{R} + \mathcal{S}) \cap \mathrm{Ker}\, C}{\mathcal{R} \cap \mathrm{Ker}\, C + \mathcal{S} \cap \mathrm{Ker}\, C} .$$

(x) If $\mathcal{R}, \mathcal{S} \subset \mathcal{Y}$ and C: $\mathcal{X} \to \mathcal{Y}$, then

$$\frac{C^{-1}(\mathcal{R} + \mathcal{S})}{C^{-1}\mathcal{R} + C^{-1}\mathcal{S}} \approx \frac{(\mathcal{R} + \mathcal{S}) \cap \mathrm{Im}\, C}{\mathcal{R} \cap \mathrm{Im}\, C + \mathcal{S} \cap \mathrm{Im}\, C} .$$

0.20 Notes and References

The material in this chapter is standard. For coverage of linear algebra at the level required, see Gantmakher [1], Greub [1], Jacobson [1], or MacLane and Birkhoff [1]. Of these, and for our requirements, the most useful all-round text is probably Gantmakher's. For an introduction to algebraic geometry see e.g. Ch. 16 of Van der Waerden [1]. The elementary results needed on linear differential equations are amply covered by Gantmakher [1], Lefschetz [1] or Hale [1]. Rouché's Theorem is proved in Titchmarsh [1]. For the general background in systems theory desirable as a prerequisite for this book, see especially Desoer [1]; also helpful are Porter [1] and Ch. 2 of Kalman, Falb and Arbib [1].

CHAPTER 1

INTRODUCTION TO CONTROLLABILITY

It is natural to say that a dynamic system is 'controllable' if, by suitable manipulation of its inputs, the system outputs can be made to behave in some desirable way. In this chapter one version of this concept will be made precise, and some of its implications explored, for the system of Section 0.16:

$$\dot{x}(t) = Ax(t) + Bu(t) , \qquad t \geq 0 . \tag{1}$$

We start by examining those states which, roughly speaking, the control u(.) in (1) is able to influence.

1.1 Reachability

Let $\underline{U}$ denote the linear space of piecewise continuous controls $t \mapsto u(t) \in \mathcal{U}$, defined for $t \geq 0$; and denote by $\varphi(t;\ x_0, u)$ the corresponding solution of (1) with $x(0) = x_0$; i.e.,

$$\varphi(t;\ x_0, u) = e^{tA} x_0 + \int_0^t e^{(t-s)A} Bu(s)\, ds . \tag{2}$$

A state $x \in \mathcal{X}$ is reachable from x_0 if there exist t and u, with $0 < t < \infty$ and $u \in \underline{U}$, such that $\varphi(t;\ x_0, u) = x$. Let $\mathcal{R}_0$ be the set of states reachable from $x_0 = 0$. It is readily checked from (2), and the admissibility of piecewise continuous controls, that $\mathcal{R}_0$ is a linear subspace of $\mathcal{X}$. We now describe $\mathcal{R}_0$ directly in terms of A and B. For this, let $\mathcal{B} \triangleq \operatorname{Im} B$ and

$$\langle A | \mathcal{B} \rangle \triangleq \mathcal{B} + A\mathcal{B} + \cdots + A^{n-1}\mathcal{B} . \tag{3}$$

THEOREM 1.1. $\mathcal{R}_0 = \langle A | \mathcal{B} \rangle$.

PROOF: If $x \in \mathcal{R}_0$ then for suitable t and u,

$$x = \int_0^t e^{(t-s)A} Bu(s)\, ds = \sum_{i=1}^{n} A^{i-1} B \int_0^t \psi_i(t-s)\, u(s)\, ds \qquad \text{by } (0.41)$$

$$\in \langle A | \mathcal{B} \rangle .$$

For the reverse inclusion, we show first that

$$\langle A|\mathcal{B}\rangle = \operatorname{Im} W_t , \qquad t > 0 , \tag{4}$$

where

$$W_t \triangleq \int_0^t e^{sA} BB' e^{sA'} ds .$$

As in Section 0.13 we here identify $\mathcal{X}' = \mathcal{X}$, $\mathcal{U}' = \mathcal{U}$, and regard W_t as a map in $\mathcal{X}$. As W_t is symmetric, (4) is equivalent to

$$\langle A|\mathcal{B}\rangle^{\perp} = \operatorname{Ker} W_t , \qquad t > 0 .$$

If $x \in \operatorname{Ker} W_t$ then $x' W_t x = 0$, i.e.,

$$\int_0^t \left| B' e^{sA'} x \right|^2 ds = 0 ,$$

and so

$$B' e^{sA'} x = 0 , \qquad 0 \le s \le t.$$

Repeated differentiation at $s = 0$ yields

$$B' A'^{i-1} x = 0 , \qquad i \in \underline{n} ,$$

so that

$$x \in \bigcap_{i=1}^{n} \operatorname{Ker}(B' A'^{i-1}) = \bigcap_{i=1}^{n} \left[\operatorname{Im}(A^{i-1} B)\right]^{\perp} = \left[\sum_{i=1}^{n} \operatorname{Im}(A^{i-1} B)\right]^{\perp} = \langle A|\mathcal{B}\rangle^{\perp} .$$

If $x \in \langle A|\mathcal{B}\rangle^{\perp}$, reversing the argument yields $x' W_t x = 0$, and $W_t \ge 0$ implies $x \in \operatorname{Ker} W_t$.

Now let $x \in \langle A|\mathcal{B}\rangle$ and fix $t > 0$. Then $x = W_t z$ for some $z \in \mathcal{X}$. Setting

$$u(s) = B' e^{(t-s) A'} z , \qquad 0 \le s \le t ,$$

we see that

$$W_t z = \varphi(t;\ 0, u) \in \mathcal{R}_0 . \ \blacksquare$$

By the construction in the proof of Theorem 1.1, $x \in \mathcal{R}_0$ implies that for every $t > 0$ there exists $u \in \underline{U}$ such that $x = \varphi(t;\ 0, u)$. From (2) it now follows that $x \in \mathcal{X}$ is reachable from x_0 if and only if $x - e^{tA} x_0 \in \mathcal{R}_0$ for some t, $0 < t < \infty$.

1.2 Controllability

The subspace $\mathcal{R}_0 = \langle A|\mathcal{B}\rangle \subset \mathcal{X}$ is the controllable subspace of the pair (A, B). From (3) (and Cayley-Hamilton) it is clear that $A\mathcal{R}_0 \subset \mathcal{R}_0$, i.e., $\mathcal{R}_0$ is A-invariant. Let $\bar{\mathcal{X}} \triangleq \mathcal{X}/\mathcal{R}_0$, $P: \mathcal{X} \to \bar{\mathcal{X}}$ be the canonical projection, $\bar{A}$ the map induced in $\bar{\mathcal{X}}$ by A; and write $\bar{x} \triangleq Px$. Since $PB = 0$ we have from (1),

$$\dot{\bar{x}}(t) = \bar{A}\bar{x}(t) .$$

Thus the control u(.) has no influence on the coset of x mod $\mathcal{R}_0$. In this notation, Theorem 1.1 says that all states can be reached from 0 when $\bar{\mathcal{X}} = \bar{0}$, i.e., $\mathcal{R}_0 = \mathcal{X}$. Thus we are led to the definition: the pair (A, B) is <u>controllable</u> if its controllable subspace is the whole space, i.e., $\langle A|\mathcal{B}\rangle = \mathcal{X}$.

With (A, B) controllable, we have that

$$W_t = \int_0^t e^{sA} BB' e^{sA'} ds$$

is positive definite for every $t > 0$. With $t > 0$ fixed, set

$$u(s) \triangleq B' e^{(t-s)A'} W_t^{-1}\left(x - e^{tA} x_0\right), \qquad 0 \le s \le t .$$

Then it is clear that $\varphi(t;\ x_0, u) = x$. That is, every state x can be reached from any state x_0 in a time interval of arbitrary positive length.

Next we note that controllability of (A, B) is preserved under arbitrary automorphisms of $\mathcal{X}$ and $\mathcal{U}$.

PROPOSITION 1.1. *Let* $T: \mathcal{X} \approx \mathcal{X}$ *and* $G: \mathcal{U} \approx \mathcal{U}$, *and let* (A, B) *be controllable. Then* $(T^{-1}AT, T^{-1}BG)$ *is controllable.*

PROOF:

$$\sum_{i=1}^{n} \left(T^{-1}AT\right)^{i-1} \operatorname{Im}(T^{-1}BG) = \sum_{i=1}^{n} \left(T^{-1}AT\right)^{i-1} T^{-1} \operatorname{Im}(BG)$$

$$= T^{-1} \sum_{i=1}^{n} A^{i-1} \mathcal{B} = T^{-1}\mathcal{X} = \mathcal{X}. \quad \blacksquare$$

The next two propositions state that controllability of (A, B) implies controllability in factor spaces, and in subspaces which decompose A.

PROPOSITION 1.2. *Let* $\langle A|\mathcal{B}\rangle = \mathcal{X}$ *and* $A\mathcal{V} \subset \mathcal{V} \subset \mathcal{X}$. *Write* $\bar{\mathcal{X}} = \mathcal{X}/\mathcal{V}$, $\bar{\mathcal{B}} = (\mathcal{B} + \mathcal{V})/\mathcal{V}$ *and let* $\bar{A}$ *be the map induced by* A *in* $\bar{\mathcal{X}}$. *Then*

$$\langle \bar{A}|\bar{\mathcal{B}}\rangle = \bar{\mathcal{X}}.$$

PROOF: Let $P: \mathcal{X} \to \overline{\mathcal{X}}$ be the canonical projection; thus $\overline{\mathcal{B}} = P\mathcal{B}$ and $\overline{A}P = PA$. Then

$$\overline{\mathcal{X}} = P\langle A|\mathcal{B}\rangle = P(\mathcal{B} + A\mathcal{B} + \cdots + A^{n-1}\mathcal{B}) = \overline{\mathcal{B}} + \overline{A}\overline{\mathcal{B}} + \cdots + \overline{A}^{n-1}\overline{\mathcal{B}} = \langle \overline{A}|\overline{\mathcal{B}}\rangle . \blacksquare$$

The geometric relationships in Proposition 1.2 are exhibited in the commutative diagram below.

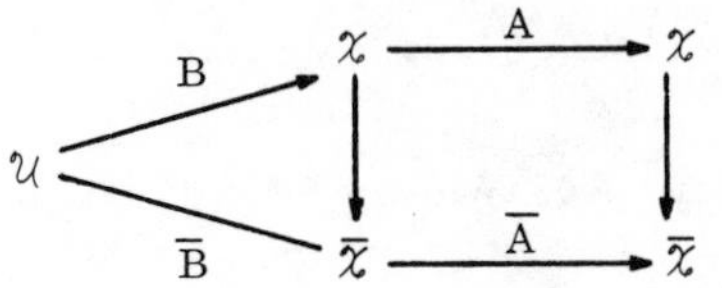

The pair $(\overline{A}, \overline{B})$ constitutes a 'lower-order model' of the pair (A, B) from which the structure of $A|\mathcal{V}$ has been excluded. The lemma states that the model is controllable if the original pair (A, B) is.

PROPOSITION 1.3. <u>Let</u> $\langle A|\mathcal{B}\rangle = \mathcal{X}$ <u>and let</u> $\mathcal{R} \subset \mathcal{X}$ <u>decompose</u> A: <u>i.e.,</u> $A\mathcal{R} \subset \mathcal{R}$ <u>and there exists</u> $\mathcal{J} \subset \mathcal{X}$ <u>with</u> $A\mathcal{J} \subset \mathcal{J}$ <u>and</u> $\mathcal{R} \oplus \mathcal{J} = \mathcal{X}$. <u>If</u> Q <u>is the projection on</u> $\mathcal{R}$ <u>along</u> $\mathcal{J}$ <u>then</u>

$$\mathcal{R} = \langle A|Q\mathcal{B}\rangle .$$

PROOF: Clearly $QA = AQ$. Therefore,

$$\begin{aligned} \mathcal{R} = Q\mathcal{X} &= Q(\mathcal{B} + A\mathcal{B} + \cdots + A^{n-1}\mathcal{B}) \\ &= Q\mathcal{B} + AQ\mathcal{B} + \cdots + A^{n-1}Q\mathcal{B} = \langle A|Q\mathcal{B}\rangle . \blacksquare \end{aligned}$$

1.3 <u>Single-Input Systems</u>

Let $d(\mathcal{B}) = 1$ and write $\mathcal{B} = \text{Span}\{b\} = \mathcal{b}$ for some $b \in \mathcal{X}$. The corresponding system equation is $\dot{x} = Ax + bu$, where $u(.)$ is scalar-valued, i.e., the system has a single control input. Suppose (A, b) is controllable. Since $\langle A|\mathcal{b}\rangle = \mathcal{X}$ it follows that the vectors $\{b, Ab, \ldots, A^{n-1}b\}$ are a basis for $\mathcal{X}$; thus A is cyclic, and b is a generator.

Let the minimal polynomial (m.p.) of A be

$$\alpha(\lambda) = \lambda^n - \left(a_1 + a_2\lambda + \cdots + a_n\lambda^{n-1}\right) .$$

Introduce the auxiliary polynomials $\alpha^{(i)}(\lambda)$ defined in (0.16) and the corresponding basis

$$e_i \triangleq \alpha^{(i)}(A)\,b\,, \qquad i \in \underline{n}\,. \tag{6}$$

Then $b = e_n$, and the matrices of A and b are

$$A \sim \begin{bmatrix} 0 & 1 & 0 & 0 & \cdot & \cdot & 0 & 0 \\ 0 & 0 & 1 & 0 & \cdot & \cdot & 0 & 0 \\ \cdot & \cdot & \cdot & \cdot & \cdot & \cdot & \cdot & \cdot \\ 0 & \cdot & \cdot & \cdot & \cdot & \cdot & 0 & 1 \\ a_1 & a_2 & \cdot & \cdot & \cdot & \cdot & \cdot & a_n \end{bmatrix}, \qquad b \sim \begin{bmatrix} 0 \\ \cdot \\ \cdot \\ 0 \\ 1 \end{bmatrix}. \tag{7}$$

We refer to (7) as the <u>standard canonical form</u> of the controllable (matrix) pair (A, b).

Call (A, b) and (A_1, b_1) <u>similar</u> if for some T: $\mathcal{X} \approx \mathcal{X}$,

$$A_1 = T^{-1}AT\,, \qquad b_1 = T^{-1}b\,.$$

Similarity is an equivalence relation on (A, b) pairs. Since similarity leaves invariant the characteristic polynomial of A, hence the a_i ($i \in \underline{n}$), our discussion shows that every controllable pair is similar to exactly one pair of form (7). It is even true that the basis in which the matrices of (A, b) have standard canonical form is unique: for if $T^{-1}AT = A$ and $Tb = b$ then by (6), $Te_i = e_i$ ($i \in \underline{n}$) and therefore $T = 1$.

1.4 Multi-Input Systems

Let $\langle A|\mathcal{B}\rangle = \mathcal{X}$, with $d(\mathcal{B}) = m$. Since each vector $b \in \mathcal{B}$ generates a cyclic subspace $\langle A|b\rangle$ it is plausible that we must have $m \geq k$, where k is the cyclic index of A. This is true, and more: it is possible to select independent vectors $b_i \in \mathcal{B}$ ($i \in \underline{k}$) such that the subspaces $\langle A|b_i\rangle$ span $\mathcal{X}$; unfortunately, however, these subspaces cannot in general be made independent.

THEOREM 1.2. <u>Let</u> $\langle A|\mathcal{B}\rangle = \mathcal{X}$, <u>with</u> $d(\mathcal{B}) = m$; <u>and let</u> k <u>be the cyclic index of</u> A. <u>Then</u> $m \geq k$. <u>Let the invariant factors of</u> A <u>be</u> $\alpha_1, \ldots, \alpha_k$. <u>There exist</u> A-<u>invariant subspaces</u> $\mathcal{X}_i \subset \mathcal{X}$ <u>and vectors</u> $b_i \in \mathcal{B}$ ($i \in \underline{k}$) <u>with the properties:</u>

(i) $\mathcal{X} = \mathcal{X}_1 \oplus \cdots \oplus \mathcal{X}_k$.

(ii) $A|\mathcal{X}_i$ <u>is cyclic with m.p.</u> α_i, $\qquad i \in \underline{k}$.

(iii) $\langle A|b_1 + \cdots + b_i\rangle = \mathcal{X}_1 \oplus \cdots \oplus \mathcal{X}_i$, $\qquad i \in \underline{k}$.

Briefly, the theorem says that $\mathscr{X}$ has a rational canonical decomposition having the special property (iii) with respect to $\mathscr{B}$. The proof depends on simple properties of polynomials in $\mathbb{R}[\lambda]$ and on controllability of subspaces.

LEMMA 1.1. Let $\alpha, \gamma_1, \dots, \gamma_m$ belong to $\mathbb{R}^m[\lambda]$. Then

$$\underset{i \in \underline{m}}{\mathrm{LCM}} \left[\frac{\alpha}{\mathrm{GCD}(\alpha, \gamma_i)} \right] = \frac{\alpha}{\mathrm{GCD}(\alpha, \gamma_1, \dots, \gamma_m)} .$$

PROOF: If π^{μ} is a prime factor of α and $\mathrm{GCD}(\alpha, \gamma_i)$ has the corresponding factor π^{μ_i} then

$$\underset{i \in \underline{m}}{\mathrm{LCM}} \left(\frac{\pi^{\mu}}{\pi^{\mu_i}} \right) = \pi^{\max_i(\mu - \mu_i)},$$

and

$$\frac{\pi^{\mu}}{\mathrm{GCD}\left(\pi^{\mu}, \pi^{\mu_1}, \dots, \pi^{\mu_m}\right)} = \frac{\pi^{\mu}}{\pi^{\min_i \mu_i}} = \pi^{\mu - \min_i \mu_i} .$$

Since $\max_i(\mu - \mu_i) = \mu - \min_i \mu_i$, the assertion follows. ∎

LEMMA 1.2. Let $\mathscr{B} \subset \mathscr{X}$ be an arbitrary subspace of $\mathscr{X}$, having minimal polynomial β with respect to A. There exists a vector $b \in \mathscr{B}$ with minimal polynomial β.

Note that $\mathscr{B}$ is not assumed to be A-invariant.

PROOF: Let

$$\mathscr{X} = \bigoplus_{i=1}^{k} \mathscr{X}_i$$

be any decomposition of $\mathscr{X}$ such that $A | \mathscr{X}_i$ is cyclic with minimal polynomial α_i. Let $\mathscr{X}_i = \langle A | g_i \rangle$ ($i \in \underline{k}$) and let $\mathscr{B} = \mathrm{Span}\{b_1, \dots, b_m\}$. We have

$$b_i = \gamma_{i1}(A) g_1 + \cdots + \gamma_{ik}(A) g_k , \qquad i \in \underline{m} ,$$

for suitable $\gamma_{ij} \in \mathbb{R}[\lambda]$; and we may arrange that $\deg \gamma_{ij} < \deg \alpha_j$. Let β_i ($i \in \underline{m}$) be the m.p. of b_i:

$$\beta_i = \underset{j \in \underline{k}}{\mathrm{LCM}} \left[\frac{\alpha_j}{\mathrm{GCD}(\alpha_j, \gamma_{ij})} \right] .$$

Then

$$\beta = \mathrm{LCM}(\beta_1, \dots, \beta_m) = \underset{j \in \underline{k}}{\mathrm{LCM}} \; \underset{i \in \underline{m}}{\mathrm{LCM}} \left[\frac{\alpha_j}{\mathrm{GCD}(\alpha_j, \gamma_{ij})} \right]$$

$$= \underset{j \in \underline{k}}{\mathrm{LCM}} \left[\frac{\alpha_j}{\mathrm{GCD}(\alpha_j, \gamma_{1j}, \dots, \gamma_{mj})} \right]$$

by application of Lemma 1.1. Now define

$$b = r_1 b_1 + \cdots + r_m b_m ,$$

where the $r_i \in \mathbb{R}$ $(i \in \underline{m})$ are to be determined. Then

$$b = \sum_{j=1}^{k} \sum_{i=1}^{m} r_i \gamma_{ij}(A) g_j ,$$

and if β_0 is the m.p. of b,

$$\beta_0 = \underset{j \in \underline{k}}{\mathrm{LCM}} \left[\frac{\alpha_j}{\mathrm{GCD}\left(\alpha_j, \sum_{i=1}^{m} r_i \gamma_{ij}\right)} \right] .$$

We wish to choose the r_i so that $\beta_0 = \beta$, and for this it is clearly sufficient that

$$\mathrm{GCD}\left(\alpha_j, \sum_{i=1}^{m} r_i \gamma_{ij}\right) = \mathrm{GCD}(\alpha_j, \gamma_{1j}, \dots, \gamma_{mj}) , \qquad j \in \underline{k} .$$

Denote the GCD on the right by γ_j and let $\gamma_{ij} = \hat{\gamma}_{ij} \gamma_j$ $(i \in \underline{m},\ j \in \underline{k})$. It is enough to choose the r_i so that

$$\mathrm{GCD}\left(\alpha_j, \sum_{i=1}^{m} r_i \hat{\gamma}_{ij}\right) = 1 , \qquad j \in \underline{k} . \tag{8}$$

For this, let $\lambda_{i1}, \dots, \lambda_{i\nu(i)}$ be the roots of $\alpha_i(\lambda)$ over $\mathbb{C}$. Then (8) holds provided

$$\sum_{i=1}^{m} r_i \hat{\gamma}_{ij}(\lambda_{j\mu}) \neq 0 ; \qquad \mu \in \underline{\nu}_i, \ j \in \underline{k} . \tag{9}$$

Observe that not all $\hat{\gamma}_{ij}(\lambda_{j\mu})$ can vanish in any sum; otherwise, for some j, μ and all $i \in \underline{m}$, $\hat{\gamma}_{ij}$ has the factor $\lambda - \lambda_{j\mu}$ in common with α_j, a contradiction. It follows that $r_i \in \mathbb{R}$ exist such that (9) is true: indeed, for each μ, j either the real or imaginary part of the sum in (9) does not vanish identically; writing $r' = (r_1, \ldots, r_m)$ we see that (9) is equivalent to $r'v_\nu \neq 0$ for a finite number of real, nonzero m-vectors v_ν; and so it is required merely to choose a point $r \in \mathbb{R}^m$ in the complement of a finite union of (m - 1)-dimensional hyperplanes. ▌

The proof shows that roughly speaking, a vector $b \in \mathcal{B}$ is almost certain to have the property required, if it is chosen at random. Indeed, the result depends on the existence of plenty of vectors in the space, and is false if the underlying field is finite (Ex. 1.4).

COROLLARY 1.1. If A is cyclic and (A, B) is controllable, there exists a vector $b \in \mathcal{B}$ such that (A, b) is controllable.

PROOF (of Theorem 1.2): Observe that the m.p. of a vector $b \in \mathcal{X}$ coincides with the m.p. of $\langle A | b \rangle$. Since $\langle A | \mathcal{B} \rangle = \mathcal{X}$, Lemma 1.2 provides an element $b_1 \in \mathcal{B}$ whose m.p. coincides with the m.p. of A, which we denote by α_1. Define $\mathcal{X}_1 \triangleq \langle A | b_1 \rangle$. Since $\mathcal{X}_1 \subset \mathcal{X}$ is maximal cyclic, there exists, by Proposition 0.2, a subspace $\mathcal{Z} \subset \mathcal{X}$ such that

$$\langle A | b_1 \rangle \oplus \mathcal{Z} = \mathcal{X}$$

and

$$A\mathcal{Z} \subset \mathcal{Z} .$$

Let Q be the projection on $\mathcal{Z}$ along $\mathcal{X}_1$. By Proposition 1.3,

$$\langle A | Q\mathcal{B} \rangle = \mathcal{Z} .$$

If $\hat{\alpha}_2$ is the m.p. of $A|\mathcal{Z}$ there exists, again by Lemma 1.2, a vector $b_2 \in \mathcal{B}$ such that the m.p. of Qb_2 is $\hat{\alpha}_2$. Define $\mathcal{X}_2 \triangleq \langle A | Q b_2 \rangle$. Then $b_2 \in \mathcal{X}_1 \oplus \mathcal{X}_2$ and

$$\langle A | b_1 + b_2 \rangle = \mathcal{X}_1 \oplus \mathcal{X}_2 .$$

Continuing in this way, we obtain eventually, for some r,

$$\mathcal{X} = \mathcal{X}_1 \oplus \cdots \oplus \mathcal{X}_r ,$$

with $A|\mathcal{X}_i$ cyclic with m.p. $\hat{\alpha}_i$. Since the subspace $\mathcal{X}_i$ split off at the $i^{\underline{th}}$ stage is maximal cyclic,

$$\hat{\alpha}_2 | \alpha_1, \ldots, \hat{\alpha}_r | \hat{\alpha}_{r-1} ;$$

and by the uniqueness of the rational canonical decomposition (Theorem 0.1) it follows that $r = k$ and $\hat{\alpha}_i = \alpha_i$ $(i \in \underline{k})$. Again by the construction we have

$$\langle A \mid \mathcal{B}_1 + \cdots + \mathcal{B}_i \rangle = \mathcal{X}_i , \qquad i \in \underline{k} ,$$

as required. ▮

1.5 Controllability is Generic

On the basis of the discussion of genericity in Section 0.15, we can easily show the following.

THEOREM 1.3. Let (A, B) be a matrix pair with $A \in \mathbb{R}^{n \times n}$, $B \in \mathbb{R}^{n \times m}$. The property that (A, B) be controllable is generic, and is well-posed at every point (A, B) where it holds.

PROOF: By listing the entries of A and B, we regard $\underline{p} = (A, B)$ as a point in $\mathbb{R}^N$, where $N = n^2 + nm$. It is easily seen (Ex. 1.2) that (A, B) is controllable if and only if the $n \times nm$ matrix

$$X \triangleq [B, AB, \dots, A^{n-1}B]$$

has rank n. Write $x_1, \dots, x_{nm}$ for the columns of X. Then controllability of (A, B) fails if and only if every determinant formed by selecting n columns x_i vanishes; that is

$$\varphi_i(\underline{p}) = \det \left[x_{i_1}, \dots, x_{i_n} \right] = 0 ,$$

where i ranges over all multi-indices $i = (i_1, \dots, i_n)$ with $1 \le i_1 < i_2 < \cdots < i_n \le nm$. Let $\underline{V} \subset \mathbb{R}^N$ be the set of common zeros of the φ_i. Clearly $\underline{V}$ is a variety in $\mathbb{R}^N$. Also, choosing an (A, B) pair with A and the first column of B in the standard canonical form (7), we see that controllable pairs exist, hence $\underline{V}$ is proper. It is now obvious that controllability is generic relative to $\underline{V}$, and well-posedness at $\underline{p} \in \underline{V}^c$ is clear. ▮

The foregoing discussion suggests that it is 'easy' for a pair (A, B) to be controllable. However, it should be borne in mind that we have defined controllability in a purely qualitative, algebraic way. In practice it could well turn out that the controllability matrix X introduced in the proof is poorly conditioned (typically, if n is large and $m = 1$). But apart from pointing out their existence, we shall not attempt to discuss these important numerical problems here.

1.6 Exercises

1.1 Show that there is a basis for $\mathcal{X}$ in which A and B have matrices of form

$$A \sim \begin{bmatrix} A_1 & A_3 \\ & \\ 0 & A_2 \end{bmatrix}, \qquad B \sim \begin{bmatrix} B_1 \\ \\ 0 \end{bmatrix}.$$

Describe $\langle A|\mathcal{B}\rangle$ in this basis.

1.2 (A, B) is a controllable matrix pair if and only if

$$\operatorname{Rank}[B, AB, \dots, A^{n-1}B] = n .$$

This $n \times nm$ block matrix is the controllability matrix of (A, B).

1.3 Discuss the behavior of u(.), defined in the proof of Theorem 1.1, as $t \downarrow 0$.

1.4 Lemma 1.2 is false in general, if A and B are matrices over a finite field. For a counterexample consider the binary field GF(2), i.e., the integers (mod 2), let A be cyclic with m.p. $\alpha(\lambda)$ and generator g, and let $B = [b_1, b_2]$ with $b_i = \alpha_i(A)g$. Show that (A, B) is controllable, yet (A, b) is not controllable for any $b \in \mathcal{B}$, if and only if

$$\mathrm{GCD}(\alpha_1, \alpha_2, \alpha) = 1 ,$$
$$\mathrm{GCD}(\alpha_1 + \alpha_2, \alpha) \neq 1 ,$$

and $$\mathrm{GCD}(\alpha_i, \alpha) \neq 1 , \qquad i \in \underline{2} .$$

Concretely choose, for instance,

$$\alpha_1(\lambda) = \lambda , \qquad \alpha_2(\lambda) = \lambda^2 + 1$$

$$\alpha(\lambda) = \alpha_1(\lambda)\, \alpha_2(\lambda) \left(\alpha_1(\lambda) + \alpha_2(\lambda)\right) = \lambda^5 + \lambda^4 + \lambda^2 + \lambda ,$$

and verify directly that (A, B) provides the counterexample required. Here one may take

$$A = \begin{bmatrix} 0 & 1 & 0 & 0 & 0 \\ 0 & 0 & 1 & 0 & 0 \\ 0 & 0 & 0 & 1 & 0 \\ 0 & 0 & 0 & 0 & 1 \\ 0 & 1 & 1 & 0 & 1 \end{bmatrix}, \qquad B = \begin{bmatrix} 0 & 0 \\ 0 & 0 \\ 0 & 1 \\ 1 & 1 \\ 1 & 0 \end{bmatrix}.$$

1.5 Show by an example that the subspaces $\langle A|\mathcal{b}_i\rangle$ in Theorem 1.2 cannot in general be chosen to be independent.

1.6 Develop a matrix representation of (A, B) which exhibits the properties stated in Theorem 1.2.

1.7 Suppose $\mathcal{X} = \mathcal{X}_1 \oplus \cdots \oplus \mathcal{X}_\ell$ and $A\mathcal{X}_i \subset \mathcal{X}_i$, $i \in \underline{\ell}$. Write $A_i = A|\mathcal{X}_i$, P_i: $\mathcal{X} \to \mathcal{X}_i$ for the natural projection on $\mathcal{X}_i$, and $B_i = P_iB$, $i \in \underline{\ell}$. Assuming the m.p. of the A_i are coprime in pairs, show that (A, B) is controllable if and only if (A_i, B_i) is controllable for each $i \in \underline{\ell}$. HINT: Apply Proposition 0.4.

1.8 Regard $\mathcal{U}, \mathcal{X}$ as linear vector spaces over $\mathbb{C}$. Show that (A, B) is controllable if and only if the $n \times (n+m)$ matrix $[A - \lambda I, B]$ has rank n for every eigenvalue λ of A. HINT: consider

$$\text{Ker}\begin{bmatrix} A' - \lambda I \\ B' \end{bmatrix}$$

where the matrix is regarded as a map from $\mathcal{X}'$ to $\mathcal{X}' \oplus \mathcal{U}'$.

1.7 Notes and References

The definition of controllability used here, and the identification of this concept as one of fundamental importance, are due to Kalman [1], [2]; see also Gilbert [1]. The standard canonical form for a single-input controllable pair was discovered independently by several workers around 1961, but apparently first published by Popov [1]. Corollary 1.1 is due to Wonham [1] and its subsequent generalization in the form of Theorem 1.2 to Heymann [2]; see also Guidorzi [1]. The proof given here is new. The fact that the set of controllable pairs is open and dense was pointed out by Lee and Markus [1]: their elegant proof of denseness appeals to a Hamel basis, while the proof given here is quite elementary. The result in Ex. 8 is due to Hautus [1].

CHAPTER 2

CONTROLLABILITY, FEEDBACK AND POLE ASSIGNMENT

Consider as usual the system

$$\dot{x}(t) = Ax(t) + Bu(t) , \qquad t \geq 0 . \tag{1}$$

Suppose we are free to modify (1) by setting

$$u(t) = Fx(t) + v(t) , \qquad t \geq 0 ,$$

where v(.) is a new external input, and F: $\mathcal{X} \to \mathcal{U}$ is a constant map. We refer to F as the state feedback. The obvious result of introducing state feedback is to change the pair (A, B) in (1) into the pair (A + BF, B). We shall explore the effect of such a transformation of pairs on controllability and on the spectrum of A + BF. Our main result is that if (A, B) is controllable then $\sigma(A + BF)$ can be assigned arbitrarily by suitable choice of F, and this property in turn implies controllability.

2.1 Controllability and Feedback

We first prove the simple and gratifying result that controllability is not affected by state feedback. The following statement goes a little further.

LEMMA 2.1. For any state feedback F: $\mathcal{X} \to \mathcal{U}$,

$$\langle A + BF \,|\, \mathcal{B} \rangle = \langle A \,|\, \mathcal{B} \rangle .$$

In particular, if (A, B) is controllable, so is (A + BF, B).

PROOF: Observe that $(A + BF)\mathcal{R} \subset A\mathcal{R} + \mathcal{B}$ for all $\mathcal{R} \subset \mathcal{X}$. Writing $\hat{A} = A + BF$, we have

$$\langle A + BF \,|\, \mathcal{B} \rangle = \mathcal{B} + \hat{A}\mathcal{B} + \cdots + \hat{A}^{n-1}\mathcal{B} = \mathcal{B} + \hat{A}(\mathcal{B} + \hat{A}(\cdots(\mathcal{B} + \hat{A}\mathcal{B}))\cdots)$$

$$\subset \mathcal{B} + A\mathcal{B} + \cdots + A^{n-1}\mathcal{B} = \langle A \,|\, \mathcal{B} \rangle . \tag{2}$$

Since (2) holds for all A, B, F there results, on replacing first F by -F and then A by A + BF, that $\langle A|\mathcal{B}\rangle \subset \langle A+BF|\mathcal{B}\rangle$. ▮

Our next observation is that state feedback can be used to replace a multi-input controllable system ($d(\mathcal{B}) > 1$) by a single-input controllable system. Furthermore, the single controlling input can enter via any nonzero vector $b \in \mathcal{B}$, if feedback is chosen accordingly.

LEMMA 2.2. Let $0 \neq b \in \mathcal{B}$. If (A, B) is controllable, there exists $F: \mathcal{X} \to \mathcal{U}$ such that (A + BF, b) is controllable.

PROOF: Let $b_1 = b$, and let $n_1 = d(\langle A|\mathcal{b}_1\rangle)$. Put $x_1 = b_1$ and $x_j = Ax_{j-1} + b_1$ $(j = 2, \ldots, n_1)$. Then the x_j $(j \in \underline{n_1})$ are a basis for $\langle A|\mathcal{b}_1\rangle$. If $n_1 < n$ choose $b_2 \in \mathcal{B}$ such that $b_2 \notin \langle A|\mathcal{b}_1\rangle$; such a b_2 exists by controllability. Let n_2 be the dimension of $\langle A|\mathcal{b}_2\rangle$ mod $\langle A|\mathcal{b}_1\rangle$, i.e., the largest integer such that the vectors

$$x_1, \ldots, x_{n(1)}, b_2, Ab_2, \ldots, A^{n_2-1} b_2, \qquad n(1) \triangleq n_1,$$

are independent; and define

$$x_{n(1)+i} = Ax_{n(1)+i-1} + b_2, \qquad i \in \underline{n_2}.$$

Then $\{x_1, \ldots, x_{n(1)+n(2)}\}$ is a basis for $\langle A|\mathcal{b}_1 + \mathcal{b}_2\rangle$. Continuing thus, we obtain eventually $x_1, \ldots, x_n$ independent, and x_{i+1} has the form

$$x_{i+1} = Ax_i + \tilde{b}_i, \qquad i \in \underline{n-1},$$

where $\tilde{b}_i \in \mathcal{B}$. Choose F such that

$$BFx_i = \tilde{b}_i, \qquad i \in \underline{n},$$

where $\tilde{b}_n \in \mathcal{B}$ is arbitrary: since $\tilde{b}_i = Bu_i$ for suitable $u_i \in \mathcal{U}$, and the x_i are independent, F certainly exists. Then

$$(A+BF)x_i = x_{i+1}, \qquad i \in \underline{n-1},$$

so that

$$x_i = (A+BF)^{i-1} b, \qquad i \in \underline{n},$$

and therefore

$$\mathcal{X} = \langle A+BF|\mathcal{b}\rangle. \; ▮$$

2.2 Pole Assignment

In applications state feedback is introduced to change the dynamic behavior of the free, uncontrolled system $\dot{x} = Ax$ in some desirable way: to achieve stability, say, or to speed up response. Such criteria can sometimes be expressed as conditions on the spectrum of the modified system matrix $A + BF$. Thus

$$\max\{\mathcal{R}e\,\lambda:\ \lambda \in \sigma(A+BF)\} < 0$$

for stability; and, with suitable $\alpha > 0$, $\beta \geq 0$,

$$\max\{\mathcal{R}e\,\lambda:\ \lambda \in \sigma(A+BF)\} \leq -\alpha$$

$$\max\{|\mathcal{I}m\,\lambda|:\ \lambda \in \sigma(A+BF)\} \leq \beta$$

for rapid response with limited frequency of oscillation. It is an important fact that any spectral criterion can be met by state feedback, provided (A, B) is controllable. Conversely, this property of (A, B) characterizes controllability. For a single-input system the result is virtually obvious by inspection of the standard canonical form (1.7), and we exploit this observation in the proof.

THEOREM 2.1. <u>The pair</u> (A, B) <u>is controllable if and only if, for every symmetric set</u> Λ <u>of</u> n <u>complex numbers, there exists a map</u> $F: \mathcal{X} \to \mathcal{U}$ <u>such that</u> $\sigma(A+BF) = \Lambda$.

PROOF: (Only if) First suppose $d(\mathcal{B}) = 1$, $\mathcal{B} = b$. It was shown in Section 1.3 that there is a basis for $\mathcal{X}$ in which A, b have the standard canonical matrices (1.7); there A has the characteristic polynomial

$$\lambda^n - \left(a_1 + a_2\lambda + \cdots + a_n\lambda^{n-1}\right).$$

Let $\Lambda = \{\lambda_1, \ldots, \lambda_n\}$ and write

$$(\lambda-\lambda_1)\cdots(\lambda-\lambda_n) = \lambda^n - \left(\hat{a}_1 + \hat{a}_2\lambda + \cdots + \hat{a}_n\lambda^{n-1}\right).$$

Let f' be the row vector

$$f' = (\hat{a}_1 - a_1, \ldots, \hat{a}_n - a_n).$$

Then it is clear that the matrix $A + bf'$ is again of form (1.7), with a_i replaced by $\hat{a}_i$ ($i \in \underline{n}$). This completes the proof when $d(\mathcal{B}) = 1$.

For the general case choose, by Lemma 2.2, any vector $b = Bu \in \mathcal{B}$ and a map $F_1: \mathcal{X} \to \mathcal{U}$ such that $(A + BF_1, b)$ is controllable. Regard b as a map $\mathbb{R} \to \mathcal{X}$. We have just shown the existence of $f': \mathcal{X} \to \mathbb{R}$ such that $\sigma(A + BF_1 + bf') = \Lambda$. Then

$$F = F_1 + uf'$$

is a map with the property required.

(If) Let λ_i ($i \in \underline{n}$) be real and distinct, with $\lambda_i \notin \sigma(A)$ ($i \in \underline{n}$). Choose F so that $\sigma(A + BF) = \{\lambda_1, \ldots, \lambda_n\}$. Let $x_i \in \mathcal{X}$ ($i \in \underline{n}$) be the corresponding eigenvectors: that is,

$$(A + BF) x_i = \lambda_i x_i, \qquad i \in \underline{n}$$

so that

$$x_i = (\lambda_i - A)^{-1} BF x_i, \qquad i \in \underline{n}.$$

Now

$$(\lambda - A)^{-1} = \sum_{j=1}^{n} \rho_j(\lambda) A^{j-1}$$

for suitable rational functions $\rho_j(\lambda)$, defined in $\mathbb{C} - \sigma(A)$. So

$$x_i = \sum_{j=1}^{n} \rho_j(\lambda_i) A^{j-1} BF x_i \in \langle A | \mathcal{B} \rangle, \qquad i \in \underline{n}.$$

Since the x_i span $\mathcal{X}$, $\langle A | \mathcal{B} \rangle = \mathcal{X}$ as claimed. ∎

Remark 1.

The result just proved is sometimes called the 'pole assignment' theorem, in reference to the fact that the eigenvalues of $A + BF$ are the poles of the closed-loop system transfer matrix

$$(sI - A - BF)^{-1} B. \tag{3}$$

Some hints for computing $F = F(\Lambda)$ are given in Ex. 1.1.

Remark 2.

In practice the assignment of $\sigma(A + BF)$ would only partially meet typical design requirements for the closed loop transfer matrix (3). An interesting problem, largely unexplored, is how to utilize the remaining freedom of choice of F (in case $m \geq 2$, when such freedom exists) to achieve further desirable properties. These could relate, for instance, to overshoot in step response or to parameter sensitivity.

2.3 Incomplete Controllability and Pole Shifting

Suppose (A, B) is not controllable. Write $\mathcal{R} \triangleq \langle A | \mathcal{B} \rangle$, with $d(\mathcal{R}) = \rho < n$. By Lemma 2.1,

$$\langle A + BF | \mathcal{B} \rangle = \mathcal{R} \tag{4}$$

for all F: $\mathcal{X} \to \mathcal{U}$. Let P: $\mathcal{X} \to \mathcal{X}/\mathcal{R}$ be the canonical projection and denote by a bar the map induced in $\mathcal{X}/\mathcal{R}$ by a map in $\mathcal{X}$. By (4), $(A+BF)\mathcal{R} \subset \mathcal{R}$. Since $\overline{A+BF}$ is defined uniquely by the relation

$$(\overline{A+BF})\,P = P(A+BF) \;,$$

and since by (4) PB = 0, we have $\overline{A+BF} = \overline{A}$. There follows

$$\sigma(A+BF) = \sigma[(A+BF)\,|\mathcal{R}] \;\dot{\cup}\; \sigma(\overline{A+BF}) = \sigma[(A+BF)\,|\mathcal{R}] \;\dot{\cup}\; \sigma(\overline{A}) \;.$$

Thus the $n-\rho$ eigenvalues $\sigma(\overline{A}) \subset \sigma(A)$ are invariant under all transformations of A by state feedback, whereas Theorem 2.1 shows that the remaining ρ eigenvalues, corresponding to 'modes' in $\mathcal{R}$, can be assigned arbitrarily by suitable choice of F.

In applications we may wish to distinguish between 'good' (e.g., stable) eigenvalues and 'bad' eigenvalues. For this let the complex plane be partitioned as

$$\mathbb{C} = \mathbb{C}_g \cup \mathbb{C}_b \;, \qquad \mathbb{C}_g \cap \mathbb{C}_b = \emptyset \;. \tag{5}$$

[In place of (5) we often write $\mathbb{C} = \mathbb{C}_g \,\dot{\cup}\, \mathbb{C}_b$]. Choose $\mathbb{C}_g$ so that

$$\mathbb{C}_g^* = \mathbb{C}_g \qquad \text{and} \qquad \mathbb{C}_g \cap \mathbb{R} \neq \emptyset \;; \tag{6}$$

i.e., if $s \in \mathbb{C}_g$ then $s^* \in \mathbb{C}_g$, and $\mathbb{C}_g$ includes at least one point on the real axis. A partition (5) with properties (6) will be called <u>symmetric</u>. Now let the m.p. of A be $\alpha(\lambda)$, and factor

$$\alpha(\lambda) = \alpha_g(\lambda)\,\alpha_b(\lambda) \;,$$

where the zeros in $\mathbb{C}$ of α_g (resp. α_b) belong to $\mathbb{C}_g$ (resp. $\mathbb{C}_b$). Since α_g and α_b are coprime, we have by (0.22)

$$\mathcal{X} = \mathcal{X}_g(A) \oplus \mathcal{X}_b(A) \;,$$

where

$$\mathcal{X}_g(A) \triangleq \text{Ker}\, \alpha_g(A), \qquad \mathcal{X}_b(A) \triangleq \text{Ker}\, \alpha_b(A).$$

The subspaces $\mathcal{X}_g(A)$ and $\mathcal{X}_b(A)$ can be thought of as the good and bad modal subspaces of A, respectively. The criterion of Theorem 2.2, below, says that the bad eigenvalues of A can be converted to good ones by state feedback, if and only if the bad modes of A are controllable.

LEMMA 2.3. <u>If</u> $\mathbb{C} = \mathbb{C}_g \cup \mathbb{C}_b$ <u>with</u> $\mathbb{C}_g \cap \mathbb{C}_b = \emptyset$, <u>and</u> $T: \mathcal{X} \to \mathcal{X}$ <u>has m.p.</u> $\tau(\lambda) = \tau_g(\lambda)\tau_b(\lambda)$, <u>then</u> Ker $\tau_b(T) \neq 0$ <u>only if</u> $\sigma(T) \cap \mathbb{C}_b \neq \emptyset$.

PROOF: Suppose $\sigma(T) \cap \mathbb{C}_b = \emptyset$. Then $\tau(\lambda)$ can have no zeros in $\mathbb{C}_b$, i.e., $\tau_b(\lambda) = 1$. Thus $\tau_b(T) = 1_{\mathcal{X}}$ and Ker $\tau_b(T) = 0$. ∎

THEOREM 2.2. <u>Let</u> $\mathbb{C} = \mathbb{C}_g \dot{\cup} \mathbb{C}_b$ <u>be a symmetric partition of</u> $\mathbb{C}$. <u>There exists</u> $F: \mathcal{X} \to \mathcal{U}$ <u>such that</u>

$$\sigma(A + BF) \subset \mathbb{C}_g$$

<u>if and only if</u>

$$\mathcal{X}_b(A) \subset \langle A | \mathcal{B} \rangle. \tag{7}$$

PROOF: In the proof we write $\mathcal{X}_g, \mathcal{X}_b$ for $\mathcal{X}_g(A)$, $\mathcal{X}_b(A)$.

(If) The argument is summarized in the commutative diagram below.

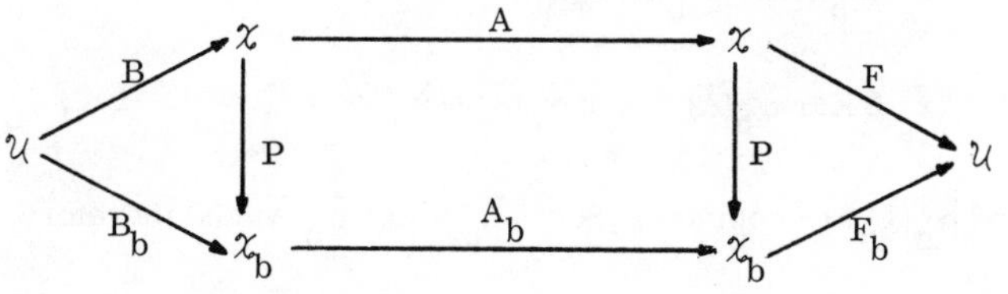

Let $P: \mathcal{X} \to \mathcal{X}_b$ be the natural projection. By (7)

$$\mathcal{X}_b = P\langle A | \mathcal{B} \rangle = \langle A_b | \mathcal{B}_b \rangle,$$

where

$$A_b = A | \mathcal{X}_b, \qquad B_b = PB.$$

Since (A_b, B_b) is controllable, there exists $F_b: \mathcal{X}_b \to \mathcal{U}$ such that[1]

---

[1] If $d(\mathcal{X}_b)$ is odd we must here use the hypothesis $\mathbb{C}_g \cap \mathbb{R} = \emptyset$.

$$\sigma(A_b + B_b F_b) \subset \mathbb{C}_g .$$

Define

$$F \triangleq F_b P , \qquad A_g \triangleq A | \mathcal{X}_g .$$

Then

$$(A + BF) | \mathcal{X}_g = A_g$$

and so

$$\sigma(A + BF) = \sigma[(A + BF) | \mathcal{X}_g] \,\dot{\cup}\, \sigma[P(A + BF) | \mathcal{X}_b]$$

$$= \sigma(A_g) \,\dot{\cup}\, \sigma(A_b + B_b F_b) \subset \mathbb{C}_g .$$

(Only if) We use the notation introduced at the beginning of this section. Let $\bar{\alpha}$ be the m.p. of $\bar{A}$. Clearly $\bar{\alpha} = \bar{\alpha}_g \bar{\alpha}_b$, where $\bar{\alpha}_g | \alpha_g$ and $\bar{\alpha}_b | \alpha_b$. Since $\bar{\alpha}_g, \bar{\alpha}_b$ must be coprime,

$$\bar{\mathcal{X}} = \operatorname{Ker} \bar{\alpha}_g(\bar{A}) \oplus \operatorname{Ker} \bar{\alpha}_b(\bar{A}) . \tag{8}$$

Now suppose $\mathcal{X}_b \not\subset \mathcal{R} \triangleq \langle A | \mathcal{B} \rangle$. There exists $x \in \mathcal{X}$ with

$$\alpha_b(A) x = 0 , \qquad x \notin \mathcal{R} .$$

Writing $\bar{x} = Px$, we have

$$\alpha_b(\bar{A}) \bar{x} = \bar{0} , \qquad \bar{x} \neq \bar{0} .$$

In accordance with (8) write $\bar{x} = \bar{x}_g + \bar{x}_b$. Then

$$\bar{0} = \alpha_b(\bar{A}) \bar{x} = \alpha_b(\bar{A}) \bar{x}_g .$$

Therefore

$$\bar{x}_g \in \operatorname{Ker} \alpha_b(\bar{A}) \cap \operatorname{Ker} \bar{\alpha}_g(\bar{A}) = \bar{0} ,$$

since $\alpha_b(\lambda)$ and $\bar{\alpha}_g(\lambda)$ are coprime. So $\bar{x} = \bar{x}_b \in \operatorname{Ker} \bar{\alpha}_b(\bar{A})$ and therefore

$$\operatorname{Ker} \bar{\alpha}_b(\bar{A}) \neq \bar{0} .$$

But $\overline{A + BF} = \bar{A}$ for all F, so Lemma 2.3 implies

$$\sigma(\overline{A + BF}) \cap \mathbb{C}_b \neq \emptyset . \quad \blacksquare$$

2.4 Stabilizability

As an application of the foregoing ideas, define the stability and instability regions.

$$\mathbb{C}^- \triangleq \{s: \mathcal{R}e\, s < 0\}, \qquad \mathbb{C}^+ \triangleq \{s: \mathcal{R}e\, s \geq 0\}.$$

We say that (A, B) is <u>stabilizable</u> if there exists F: $\mathcal{X} \to \mathcal{U}$ such that

$$\sigma(A + BF) \subset \mathbb{C}^- .$$

Let the m.p. of A be α and factor $\alpha = \alpha^- \alpha^+$, where the complex zeros of α^- (resp. α^+) belong to $\mathbb{C}^-$ (resp. $\mathbb{C}^+$). The subspace Ker $\alpha^+(A) \subset \mathcal{X}$ is the subspace of 'unstable modes' of A, and we conclude from Theorem 2.2 that (A, B) is stabilizable if and only if the unstable modes of A are controllable. This special case is important enough to state separately.

THEOREM 2.3. <u>(A, B) is stabilizable if and only if</u>

$$\text{Ker}\, \alpha^+(A) \subset \langle A | \mathcal{B} \rangle .$$

2.5 Exercises

2.1 Let

$$A = \begin{bmatrix} 1 & 0 & 0 & 0 \\ 0 & 0 & 1 & 0 \\ 0 & 0 & 0 & 0 \\ 1 & 0 & 0 & 0 \end{bmatrix}, \qquad B = \begin{bmatrix} 1 & 0 \\ 1 & 0 \\ 0 & 1 \\ 0 & 0 \end{bmatrix}.$$

Find F, such that

$$\sigma(A + BF) = \{-1, -1, -1 + i, -1 - i\}.$$

Describe as completely as you can the class of F for which the given spectrum is assigned. HINT: 1. Check that (A, B) is controllable. 2. Take a random linear combination $b \triangleq Bu$ of the columns of B and choose a random F_0: then $A_0 \triangleq A + BF_0$ almost surely has distinct eigenvalues, hence is cyclic, so by Corollary 1.1 the pair (A_0, b) is almost surely controllable: check it. 3. Follow the constructive proof of Theorem 2.1 to get f' such that $A_0 + bf'$ has the required spectrum, and 4. Set $F = F_0 + uf'$. With F selected, determine the $\tilde{F}$ for which $\sigma(A + BF + B\tilde{F}) = \sigma(A + BF)$.

2.2 Write a computer program for pole assignment: it will be needed later.

2.3 Give a matrix proof of Theorem 2.2 based on the representation of Ex. 1.1.

2.4 Consider the system pair

$$A = \begin{bmatrix} 0 & 1 & 0 & 0 & 0 \\ 0 & 0 & 0 & 0 & 0 \\ 0 & 0 & -2 & 0 & 0 \\ 0 & 0 & 0 & 0 & 1 \\ 0 & 0 & 0 & 0 & 0 \end{bmatrix}, \qquad B = \begin{bmatrix} 0 & 0 \\ 1 & 1 \\ 0 & 0 \\ 0 & 0 \\ 1 & -1 \end{bmatrix}.$$

Say an eigenvalue λ is 'good' if and only if $\mathcal{R}e\ \lambda \le -1$. Check convertibility of bad eigenvalues by state feedback, using the criterion of Theorem 2.3.

2.5 Assume (A, B) controllable and construct a basis for $\mathcal{X}$ as follows. Let B have column matrix $[b_1, \ldots, b_m]$. Let n_i be the dimension of $\langle A | \mathcal{b}_i \rangle$ mod $\langle A | \mathcal{b}_1 + \cdots + \mathcal{b}_{i-1} \rangle$ $(i \in \underline{m},\ b_0 = 0)$. By reordering the b_i if necessary we can arrange that $n_i \ne 0$ $(i \in \underline{\ell})$ and $n_1 + \cdots + n_\ell = n$ for some $\ell \le m$. Show that in the basis

$$\left\{ b_1, \ldots, A^{n_1 - 1} b_1, b_2, \ldots, A^{n_2 - 1} b_2, \ldots, b_\ell, \ldots, A^{n_\ell - 1} b_\ell \right\}$$

the matrix of A is in block upper-triangular form. Then show that F_1 can be chosen so that $A + BF_1$ has distinct eigenvalues, hence is cyclic. Using Corollary 1.1 complete the proof of the 'only if' half of Theorem 2.1.

2.6 Notes and References

Lemma 2.1 has been noted independently by various authors. Lemma 2.2 is due to Heymann [1]; the proof here follows Wonham and Morse [1]. Theorem 2.1 was proved, for complex A, B, F and arbitrary complex Λ, by Langenhop [1] and by Popov [2]. The result for real A, B, F and symmetric Λ is due to Wonham [1], who used the argument outlined in Exercise 2.5. Theorem 2.2 generalizes the criterion for stabilizability given by Wonham [1] and repeated here as Theorem 2.3. A geometric criterion for stabilizability, expressed in terms of the differential equation but equivalent to the criterion of Theorem 2.3, was introduced earlier by Krasovskii [1]; cf. also Krasovskii [2]. A computational algorithm for pole assignment is described by Davison and Chow [1].

CHAPTER 3

OBSERVABILITY AND DYNAMIC OBSERVERS

Observability is a property of a dynamic system together with its measurable inputs and outputs according to which these alone suffice to determine exactly the state of the system. A data processor which performs state determination is called an 'observer'. In an intuitive sense observability is a property dual to controllability: a system is controllable if any state can be reached by suitable choice of inputs; it is observable if (in the absence of inputs) its state can be computed by suitable processing of outputs. For linear time-invariant systems this intuitive duality translates into a precise algebraic duality.

In this chapter we discuss observability, and observers of various kinds, for our standard system. As in Chapter 1 we start with a problem description in functional terms, but move quickly to the underlying algebraic questions.

3.1 Observability

Consider the system

$$\dot{x}(t) = Ax(t) + v(t), \qquad t \geq 0, \tag{1}$$

$$y(t) = Cx(t), \qquad t \geq 0, \tag{2}$$

$$x(0) = x_0. \tag{3}$$

Our point of view is the following. The system map A and output map C are known, as are the input v(s) and output y(s) on some interval $t-\alpha \leq s \leq t$. The state $x(t-\alpha)$ is unknown, so x(t) cannot in general be computed from the data listed. The situation of interest is just when such a computation is possible.

To formalize this idea, let $\underline{V}$ (resp. $\underline{Y}$) be the set of piecewise-continuous functions $[0,\infty) \to \mathcal{X}$ (resp. $[0,\infty) \to \mathcal{Y}$); and for $t \geq \alpha > 0$ let

$$\begin{aligned} \omega_\alpha(t,s) &= 1, & t-\alpha \leq s \leq t, \\ &= 0, & \text{otherwise.} \end{aligned}$$

We define the system (1), (2) to be observable if for some $\alpha > 0$ there exists a function

$$\Omega: [\alpha,\infty) \times \underline{V} \times \underline{Y} \to \mathcal{X} \tag{4}$$

with the property

$$\Omega[t, \omega_\alpha(t,\cdot)\, v(\cdot), \omega_\alpha(t,\cdot)\, y(\cdot)] = x(t)\ , \qquad t \geq \alpha$$

for all solutions $x(\cdot), y(\cdot)$ of (1) and (2), with $v \in \underline{V}$ and $x_0 \in \mathcal{X}$.

The choice of function sets $\underline{V}$ and $\underline{Y}$ appearing in the definition is certainly not crucial, nor is the restriction that the processing interval $[t-\alpha, t]$ be of fixed length. Actually, for linear time-invariant systems all plausible definitions of observability turn out to be equivalent to the following algebraic condition:

Let $d(\mathcal{X}) = n$. The pair of maps (C, A) is <u>observable</u> if

$$\bigcap_{i=1}^{n} \mathrm{Ker}(CA^{i-1}) = 0\ . \tag{5}$$

THEOREM 3.1. <u>The system (1), (2) is observable if and only if the pair</u> (C, A) <u>is observable.</u>

The proof depends on the 'dual' of a construction already used in proving Theorem 1.1.

LEMMA 3.1. <u>The matrix pair</u> (C, A) <u>is observable if and only if the symmetric matrix</u>

$$W_\alpha \triangleq \int_0^\alpha e^{-\sigma A'} C' C\, e^{-\sigma A}\, d\sigma \tag{6}$$

<u>is positive definite for every</u> $\alpha > 0$.

The simple proof is omitted.

PROOF of Theorem 3.1 ('<u>If</u>' <u>statement</u>). Applying Lemma 3.1, define

$$\Omega[t, \omega_\alpha(t,\cdot)\, v(\cdot), \omega_\alpha(t,\cdot)\, y(\cdot)]$$
$$\triangleq W_\alpha^{-1} \int_0^\alpha e^{-\sigma A'} C' \left[y(t-\sigma) + C \int_0^\sigma e^{-\tau A} v(t-\sigma+\tau)\, d\tau \right] d\sigma\ . \tag{7}$$

It is enough to check that the right side of (7) reduces to $x(t)$ for $t \geq \alpha$. For this, note from (1) that

$$y(s) = C x(s) = C \left[e^{-(t-s)A} x(t) - \int_s^t e^{-(\tau-s)A} v(\tau)\, d\tau \right] \tag{8}$$

for $t-\alpha \leq s \leq t$. Multiply both sides of (8) by $e^{-(t-s)A'} C'$, integrate over $[t-\alpha, t]$ and use (6) to obtain the desired result. ▮

The proof of necessity in Theorem 3.1 is deferred to the next section.

3.2 Unobservable Subspace

The definition (5) suggests that the subspace $\mathcal{N} \subset \mathcal{X}$, defined as

$$\mathcal{N} \triangleq \bigcap_{i=1}^{n} \operatorname{Ker}(CA^{i-1}),$$

plays a significant role. We call $\mathcal{N}$ the unobservable subspace of (C, A). Clearly $A\mathcal{N} \subset \mathcal{N}$. Let $\overline{\mathcal{X}} = \mathcal{X}/\mathcal{N}$, P: $\mathcal{X} \to \overline{\mathcal{X}}$ be the canonical projection and $\overline{A}$: $\overline{\mathcal{X}} \to \overline{\mathcal{X}}$ the map induced in $\overline{\mathcal{X}}$ by A. Since $\operatorname{Ker} C \supset \mathcal{N}$, there exists a map $\overline{C}$: $\overline{\mathcal{X}} \to \mathcal{Y}$ such that $\overline{C}P = C$, as shown below.

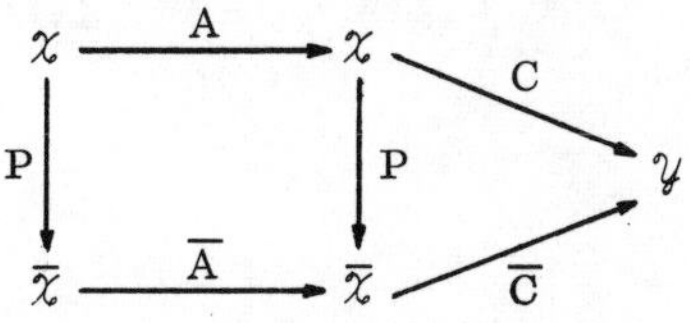

(9)

LEMMA 3.2. The pair $(\overline{C}, \overline{A})$ is observable.

PROOF: Since $n = d(\mathcal{X}) \geq d(\overline{\mathcal{X}})$ it is enough to show that

$$\overline{\mathcal{N}} = \bigcap_{i=1}^{n} \operatorname{Ker}(\overline{C}\,\overline{A}^{i-1}) = \overline{0}\,.$$

If $\overline{x} = Px \in \overline{\mathcal{N}}$ then $\overline{C}\,\overline{A}^{i-1}Px = 0$ ($i \in \underline{n}$). From (9) there results $CA^{i-1}x = 0$ ($i \in \underline{n}$), i.e., $x \in \mathcal{N}$, so $\overline{x} = Px = 0$. ▮

Since $(\overline{C}, \overline{A})$ is observable, it is possible to construct an observer for the 'factor system'

$$\dot{\overline{x}} = \overline{A}\,\overline{x} + \overline{v}$$
$$y = \overline{C}\,\overline{x}$$

just as described in Section 3.1: details of coordinatization are suggested in Ex. 3.2. Thus it is always possible to identify the coset of the system state modulo the unobservable subspace. Our next result states that this is the best one can do.

LEMMA 3.3. Let $x_1(\cdot), x_2(\cdot)$ be solutions of (1) – (3) for the same input $v(\cdot)$ but possibly different initial states x_{10}, x_{20}. If for some $t \geq 0$

$$x_1(t) - x_2(t) \in \mathcal{N}$$

then

$$y_1(s) = y_2(s)\,, \qquad s \geq 0\,.$$

PROOF: For all $s \geq 0$, and $i \in \underline{2}$,

$$y_i(s) = C\left[e^{(s-t)A}x_i(t) + \int_t^s e^{(s-\tau)A}v(\tau)\,d\tau\right]$$

so that

$$y_1(s) - y_2(s) = C\,e^{(s-t)A}[x_1(t) - x_2(t)] = \sum_{r=1}^{n} \psi_r(s-t)\,C\,A^{r-1}[x_1(t) - x_2(t)] = 0\,, \qquad s \geq 0\,,$$

by definition of $\mathcal{N}$. ▮

We can now complete the proof of Theorem 3.1.

PROOF of Theorem 3.1 ('Only if' statement). If (C, A) is not observable, i.e., $\mathcal{N} \neq 0$, let $0 \neq x_{10} - x_{20} \in \mathcal{N}$. With $v(\cdot)$ arbitrary, the corresponding solutions $x_i(\cdot)$ of (1) and (3) satisfy

$$x_1(t) - x_2(t) = e^{tA}(x_{10} - x_{20})\,,$$

and therefore $0 \neq x_1(t) - x_2(t) \in \mathcal{N}$ for $t \geq 0$. By Lemma 3.3, $y_1(s) = y_2(s)$ for $s \geq 0$, and therefore every function Ω of the type (4) yields

$$\Omega[t, v(\cdot), y_1(\cdot)] = \Omega[t, v(\cdot), y_2(\cdot)]\,, \qquad t \geq 0\,. \;▮$$

3.3 Full Order Dynamic Observer

The observer of Section 3.1 computes a running weighted average of the data on a finite time interval. A dynamic structure better matched to our theoretical setup is that of a linear differential equation: for this, the averaging interval is infinite, and in the observable case the observer error tends to zero exponentially fast as $t \to \infty$. In practice, to obtain satisfactory convergence the observer's dynamic response must be rapid, and this possibility depends on the pole assignment property of observable pairs. For the latter we need only verify that observability and controllability are algebraically dual.

LEMMA 3.4. *Let* $C: \mathcal{X} \to \mathcal{Y}$ *and* $A: \mathcal{X} \to \mathcal{X}$ *be maps with duals* $C': \mathcal{Y}' \to \mathcal{X}'$ *and* $A': \mathcal{X}' \to \mathcal{X}'$. *Then* (C, A) *is observable if and only if* (A', C') *is controllable.*

PROOF: We have

$$\mathcal{N}^{\perp} = \left[\bigcap_{i=1}^{n} \operatorname{Ker}(CA^{i-1})\right]^{\perp} = \sum_{i=1}^{n} \left[\operatorname{Ker}(CA^{i-1})\right]^{\perp}$$

$$= \sum_{i=1}^{n} \operatorname{Im}(A'^{\,i-1} C') = \langle A' \,|\, \operatorname{Im} C' \rangle ,$$

and therefore $\mathcal{N} = 0$ if and only if $\langle A' \,|\, \operatorname{Im} C' \rangle = \mathcal{X}'$. ∎

From Lemma 3.4 and Theorem 2.1 there follows immediately

THEOREM 3.2. *The pair* (C, A) *is observable if and only if, for every symmetric set* Λ *of* n *complex numbers, there exists a map* $K: \mathcal{Y} \to \mathcal{X}$ *such that*

$$\sigma(A + KC) = \Lambda .$$

We now seek an observer in the form of a differential equation

$$\dot{z}(t) = Jz(t) + Ky(t) + v(t) , \qquad t \ge 0 , \tag{10}$$
$$z(0) = z_0 ,$$

where $z(t) \in \mathcal{X}$, $y(\cdot)$ and $v(\cdot)$ are as in (1) and (2), and $J: \mathcal{X} \to \mathcal{X}$ and $K: \mathcal{Y} \to \mathcal{X}$ are to be determined. Write

$$e(t) = x(t) - z(t) , \qquad t \ge 0 . \tag{11}$$

We wish to arrange that $e(t) \to 0$ as $t \to \infty$. Applying Theorem 3.2, select K such that

$$\sigma(A - KC) = \Lambda \subset \mathbb{C}^{-}$$

and then set $J = A - KC$. From (1), (10), and (11) the result is

$$\dot{e}(t) = J e(t) , \qquad t \ge 0 ,$$

and so $e(t) \to 0$ for every pair of initial states x_0, z_0. In practice, Λ is chosen in such a way that convergence is rapid compared to the response of the system (1) which is being observed.

3.4 Minimal Order Dynamic Observer

The dynamic order of the observer (10) is n, the same as that of the observed system (1). Yet n is unnecessarily large: for if the output matrix C has rank p then from y(t) alone we can at once compute the coset of x(t) in the p-dimensional quotient space $\mathcal{X}/\text{Ker}\, C$. In this section we show what is now plausible: a dynamic observer can be constructed having the same form as (10), but of dynamic order $n-p$, to yield exactly the missing component of x(t) in the $(n-p)$-dimensional subspace Ker C. Because $v(\cdot) \in \underline{V}$ is assumed unrestricted, it is easily seen that no observer of general form (10) could have lower order than $n-p$, if z(t) is to yield, with y(t), an asymptotic identification of x(t) in the limit $t \to \infty$. In this sense an $(n-p)^{th}$ order observer is *minimal.*

To construct a minimal observer we need a rather special preliminary result on controllability which afterwards will be dualized for the application at hand.

LEMMA 3.5. *Let* (A, B) *be controllable, and* $d(\mathcal{B}) = m$. *Let* Λ *be a symmetric set of* $n-m$ *complex numbers. There exist an* $(n-m)$*-dimensional subspace* $\mathcal{V} \subset \mathcal{X}$ *and a map* $F: \mathcal{X} \to \mathcal{U}$, *such that*

$$\mathcal{B} \oplus \mathcal{V} = \mathcal{X},$$

$$(A+BF)\mathcal{V} \subset \mathcal{V},$$

and

$$\sigma[(A+BF)\,|\,\mathcal{V}] = \Lambda.$$

We emphasize that the subspace $\mathcal{V}$ in general depends on Λ.

PROOF: Choose $\mathcal{D}$ arbitrarily such that $\mathcal{B} \oplus \mathcal{D} = \mathcal{X}$ and let P: $\mathcal{X} \to \mathcal{X}$ be the projection on $\mathcal{D}$ along $\mathcal{B}$. We show first that

$$\langle PA\,|\,PA\mathcal{B}\rangle = \mathcal{D}. \tag{12}$$

For this it is enough to verify that

$$x'(\mathcal{B} \oplus \langle PA\,|\,PA\mathcal{B}\rangle) = 0$$

implies $x' = 0$, for all $x' \in \mathcal{X}'$. Now $x'\mathcal{B} = 0$ implies $x'(I-P) = 0$, or $x'P = x'$. Then $x'PA\mathcal{B} = 0$ yields $x'A\mathcal{B} = 0$. Similarly, $x'PAPA\mathcal{B} = 0$ implies $x'APA\mathcal{B} = 0$; $x'A\mathcal{B} = 0$ implies $x'AP = x'A$; and so $x'A^2\mathcal{B} = 0$. Induction on i yields

$$x' A^{i-1} \mathcal{B} = 0\,, \qquad i \in \underline{n}\,,$$

i.e., $x'\langle A \,|\, \mathcal{B}\rangle = 0$, hence $x' = 0$, as claimed.

By (12) and the pole assignment property there exists F_0: $\mathcal{X} \to \mathcal{U}$, such that

$$\sigma[(PA + PABF_0)\,|\,\mathcal{D}] = \Lambda\,.$$

Let

$$\mathcal{V} = (P + BF_0)\mathcal{D}\,.$$

Since $\mathcal{D} \cap \mathcal{B} = 0$ it is clear that $\mathcal{V} \cap \mathcal{B} = 0$ and $\mathcal{V} \approx \mathcal{D}$, so $\mathcal{B} \oplus \mathcal{V} = \mathcal{X}$. Define F: $\mathcal{X} \to \mathcal{U}$ such that

$$BF = (BF_0 P - 1 + P)\,A\,;$$

F certainly exists, since

$$\operatorname{Im}(BF_0 P - 1 + P) \subset \mathcal{B}\,.$$

A direct computation now verifies that the diagram below commutes:

$$\begin{array}{ccc} \mathcal{D} & \xrightarrow{\;PA + PABF_0\;} & \mathcal{D} \\ {\scriptstyle P + BF_0}\Big\downarrow{\scriptstyle \approx} & & {\scriptstyle \approx}\Big\downarrow{\scriptstyle P + BF_0} \\ \mathcal{V} & \xrightarrow{\;A + BF\;} & \mathcal{V} \end{array}$$

Thus $(A + BF)\mathcal{V} \subset \mathcal{V}$. Since $(P + BF_0)\,|\,\mathcal{D}$ is an isomorphism $\mathcal{D} \approx \mathcal{V}$, we have that

$$\sigma[A + BF\,|\,\mathcal{V}] = \sigma[(PA + PABF_0)\,|\,\mathcal{D}] = \Lambda\,. \;\blacksquare$$

Now assume (C, A) is observable and apply Lemma 3.5 to the controllable pair (A', C'). Write $\mathcal{C}' = \operatorname{Im} C'$: $d(\mathcal{C}') = p$. Having chosen a symmetric set $\Lambda \subset \mathbb{C}$ with $|\Lambda| = n - p$, we can find an $(n-p)$-dimensional subspace $\mathcal{V}' \subset \mathcal{X}'$, and a map K: $\mathcal{Y} \to \mathcal{X}$, such that

$$\begin{gathered} \mathcal{C}' \oplus \mathcal{V}' = \mathcal{X}'\,, \\ (A - KC)'\,\mathcal{V}' \subset \mathcal{V}'\,, \end{gathered} \tag{13}$$

and

$$\sigma[(A - KC)'\,|\,\mathcal{V}'] = \Lambda\,.$$

Let V': $\mathcal{V}' \to \mathcal{X}'$ be the insertion map. Then $V'(x') = x'$ for $x' \in \mathcal{V}'$. Define T': $\mathcal{V}' \to \mathcal{V}'$ by

$$T'(x') = (A - KC)'(x')\,, \qquad x' \in \mathcal{V}'\,,$$

so that

$$(A - KC)' V' = V'T'$$

and

$$\sigma(T') = \Lambda .$$

Thus

$$V(A - KC) = TV , \qquad \sigma(T) = \Lambda .$$

Next, taking annihilators in (13) yields

$$\mathrm{Ker}\, C \cap \mathrm{Ker}\, V = (\mathrm{Im}\, C')^{\perp} \cap (\mathrm{Im}\, V')^{\perp} = \mathcal{C}' \cap \mathcal{V}' = 0 . \tag{14}$$

Let $\mathcal{Y} \oplus \mathcal{V}$ be the external direct sum of $\mathcal{Y}$ and $\mathcal{V}$. Then (14) implies that the map

$$Q: \mathcal{X} \to \mathcal{Y} \oplus \mathcal{V} , \qquad x \mapsto Cx + Vx$$

is monic and, as $\mathcal{Y} \oplus \mathcal{V} \approx \mathcal{X}$, Q is also epic, hence an isomorphism. Summarizing, we have

THEOREM 3.3. Let (C, A) be observable, with A: $\mathcal{X} \to \mathcal{X}$, $d(\mathcal{X}) = n$, C: $\mathcal{X} \to \mathcal{Y}$, $d(\mathcal{Y}) = p$, and C epic. Let $\Lambda \subset \mathbb{C}$ be symmetric with $|\Lambda| = n - p$. There exist a subspace $\mathcal{V} \subset \mathcal{X}$ with $d(\mathcal{V}) = n - p$, and maps K: $\mathcal{Y} \to \mathcal{X}$, T: $\mathcal{V} \to \mathcal{V}$ and V: $\mathcal{X} \to \mathcal{V}$, such that

$$V(A - KC) = TV , \qquad \sigma(T) = \Lambda . \tag{15}$$

Furthermore, the map

$$Q: \mathcal{X} \to \mathcal{Y} \oplus \mathcal{V} , \qquad x \mapsto Cx + Vx \tag{16}$$

is an isomorphism.

We are now in a position to construct a minimal-order dynamic observer for the system (1) and (2). Assuming observability, consider the differential equation

$$\dot{z}(t) = Tz(t) + VKy(t) + Vv(t) , \qquad t \geq 0 , \tag{17}$$

where T, V, and K are given by Theorem 3.3. Write

$$e(t) = Vx(t) - z(t) , \qquad t \geq 0 .$$

Computing $\dot{e}$ from (1) and (17), and using (15), we find

$$\dot{e} = Te .$$

Thus if $\Lambda \subset \mathbb{C}^-$, we have that

$$z(t) = Vx(t) - e(t) , \qquad t \geq 0 ,$$

where $e(t) \to 0$ exponentially fast. By (2) and (16)

$$x(t) = Q^{-1}[y(t) + Vx(t)] \doteqdot Q^{-1}[y(t) + z(t)] , \tag{18}$$

with error exponentially small as $t \to \infty$. In practice Λ is chosen such that the identification error in (18) vanishes rapidly compared to the response time of the observed system (1).

3.5 Observers and Pole Shifting

In (1) set $v(t) = Bu(t)$, to obtain

$$\dot{x} = Ax + Bu . \tag{19}$$

Suppose it is desired to realize dynamic behavior corresponding to a control $u = Fx$. If the directly measured variable is not x but $y = Cx$, we must synthesize control by means of an observer. For the observer (10), we have

$$z(t) - x(t) \to 0 , \qquad t \to \infty ,$$

and therefore put

$$u(t) = Fz(t) , \qquad t \geq 0 . \tag{20}$$

The combined system (19), (2), (10) is now

$$\dot{x} = Ax + Bu \tag{21a}$$

$$\dot{z} = Jz + Ky + Bu , \tag{21b}$$

where $J = A - KC$. Setting $e = x - z$, and using (2) and (20), we get

$$\dot{x} = (A + BF)x - BFe \tag{22a}$$

$$\dot{e} = Je . \tag{22b}$$

Thus the spectrum of the combined system matrix in (21) coincides with that of (22), namely

$$\sigma(A + BF) \dot{\cup} \sigma(J) . \tag{23}$$

It is clear from (23) that, for instance, a stable combined system can be synthesized provided (A, B) is stabilizable and (C, A) is observable.

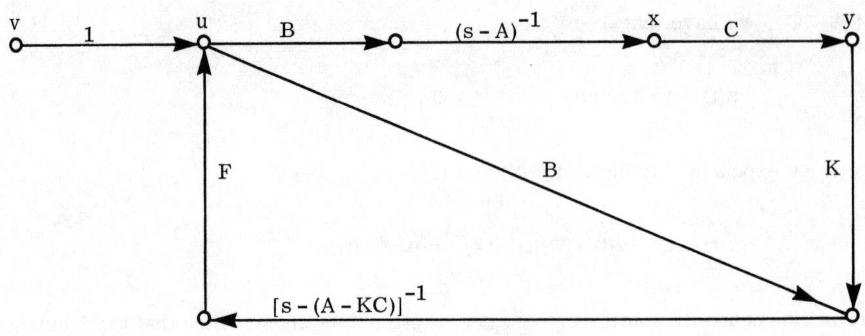

Fig. 3.1.

Signal Flow Graph for Observer-Compensator

The signal flow graph corresponding to (20) and (21) is given in Fig. 3.1. In practice it may be convenient to synthesize the combination of observer with z-feedback as a single 'compensator' with $m \times m$ transfer matrix $T(s)$ such that $\hat{u}(s) = T(s)\hat{y}(s)$. By inspection of Fig. 3.1 (with $v = 0$),

$$\hat{u} = F[s - (A - KC)]^{-1}(B\hat{u} + K\hat{y}) ,$$

and so

$$\begin{aligned} T(s) &= \left(I - F[s - (A - KC)]^{-1} B\right)^{-1} F[s - (A - KC)]^{-1} K \\ &= F[s - (A + BF - KC)]^{-1} K . \end{aligned}$$

However, there is no guarantee that $A + BF - KC$ is stable, even though $A + BF$ and $A - KC$ are stable individually.

The principle of stabilization via an observer also applies to an observer of minimal order. With the observer defined by (15) – (17) set, in (19),

$$u = FQ^{-1}(y + z) .$$

The combined system is

$$\dot{x} = Ax + Bu , \tag{24a}$$
$$\dot{z} = Tz + VKy + VBu . \tag{24b}$$

Set $z = Vx - e$; recall that

$$y = Cx , \qquad V(A - KC) = TV ;$$

and note from (16) that

$$Q^{-1}(C + V) = 1 ,$$

the identity on $\mathcal{Y} \oplus \mathcal{V}$. Then (24) yields

$$\begin{aligned} \dot{x} &= (A + BF)x - BFQ^{-1}e , \\ \dot{e} &= Te . \end{aligned} \tag{25}$$

The spectrum of the combined system matrix in (25) is, therefore,

$$\sigma(A + BF) \,\dot{\cup}\, \sigma(T) . \tag{26}$$

From Theorem 3.3 and (26) we may draw the same conclusion as before: the combined system can be stabilized if (A, B) is stabilizable and (C, A) is observable.

3.6 Detectability

A property weaker than observability, but fundamental to the quadratic optimization problem considered later, is that (at least) the subspace of unstable modes of A be observable. This property is the dual for (C, A) of the property of stabilizability for (A, B) introduced in Section 2.4. As in that section, factor the m.p. $\alpha(\lambda)$ of A in the form

$$\alpha(\lambda) = \alpha^+(\lambda)\,\alpha^-(\lambda)\,,$$

where the zeros of α^+ (resp. α^-) over $\mathbb{C}$ belong to the closed right (resp. open left) half plane, and write

$$\mathcal{X}^+(A) \triangleq \text{Ker}\,\alpha^+(A)\,, \qquad \mathcal{X}^-(A) \triangleq \text{Ker}\,\alpha^-(A)\,.$$

We say that (C, A) is <u>detectable</u> if

$$\bigcap_{i=1}^{n} \text{Ker}(CA^{i-1}) \subset \mathcal{X}^-(A)\,; \tag{27}$$

i.e., A is stable on the unobservable subspace of (C, A).

PROPOSITION 3.1. <u>The pair</u> (C, A) <u>is detectable if and only if</u> (A′, C′) <u>is stabilizable</u>.

PROOF: Note that the m.p. of A′ coincides with that of A; it is then immediately verified that

$$\text{Im}\,\alpha^-(A') = \text{Ker}\,\alpha^+(A')\,.$$

Taking annihilators in (27),

$$\sum_{i=1}^{n} \text{Im}(A'^{\,i-1}C') \supset [\text{Ker}\,\alpha^-(A)]^\perp = \text{Im}\,\alpha^-(A') = \text{Ker}\,\alpha^+(A')$$

and the result follows by Theorem 2.3. ▮

Our choice of the term 'detectable' was prompted by the following observation.

PROPOSITION 3.2. <u>Regard</u> $\mathcal{X}$ <u>and</u> $\mathcal{Y}$ <u>as inner product spaces over</u> $\mathbb{C}$, <u>and let</u> (C, A) <u>be detectable</u>. A <u>is stable if and only if the map</u>

$$W(t) \triangleq \int_0^t e^{sA'} C'Ce^{sA}\, ds$$

<u>is a norm-bounded function of</u> t <u>as</u> t $\uparrow \infty$.

PROOF: It is clear that W(•) is bounded if A is stable. For the converse assume A is unstable, and let μ be an eigenvalue of A with $\mathcal{R}e\,\mu \geq 0$ and eigenvector ξ. Then

$$\xi^{*\prime} W(t)\, \xi = \int_0^t e^{2s\mathcal{R}e\,\mu} |C\xi|^2\, ds\ .$$

Suppose the integral is bounded. Then $C\xi = 0$, i.e.,

$$CA^{i-1}\xi = \mu^{i-1} C\xi = 0\ , \qquad i \in \underline{n}\ . \tag{28}$$

By (27) and (28)

$$\xi \in \bigcap_{i=1}^{n} \operatorname{Ker}(CA^{i-1}) \subset \mathcal{X}^-(A)\ ,$$

and therefore

$$\xi \in \mathcal{X}^-(A) \cap \mathcal{X}^+(A) = 0\ ,$$

in contradiction to the assumption that ξ is an eigenvector. ▮

We conclude this section with the obvious remark that (C, A) is detectable if and only if there exists K: $\mathcal{Y} \to \mathcal{X}$ such that A + KC is stable.

3.7 <u>Detectors and Pole Shifting</u>

The dynamic observer of Section 3.5 enabled us to identify the complete state x. But if our ultimate purpose is only to stabilize the system, it is enough to identify x modulo the subspace $\mathcal{X}^-(A)$ of stable modes of A. In general, an observer for this purpose can be constructed with dynamic order smaller than d(Ker C), the dimension of the minimal observer for x. It is also intuitively clear that such a restricted observer, or <u>detector</u>, exists only if the pair (C, A) is detectable. Loosely stated, our problem is to derive a lower-order model of the system, with observable pair $(\overline{C}, \overline{A})$ which preserves the structure of A on its unstable modal subspace $\mathcal{X}^+(A)$.

To formulate the correct algebraic problem consider again (1) and (2), setting v = 0 without loss of generality. Introduce a 'model' of (1), (2) having dynamic equations

$$\begin{aligned} \dot{\overline{x}} &= \overline{A}\overline{x}\ , \\ \overline{y} &= \overline{C}\overline{x}\ . \end{aligned} \tag{29}$$

Denote the corresponding state and output spaces by $\bar{\mathscr{X}}$ and $\bar{\mathscr{Y}}$. Since (29) is to model the behavior of (1) on (at least) the invariant subspace

$$\mathscr{X}^+(A) \approx \frac{\mathscr{X}}{\mathscr{X}^-(A)},$$

we identify $\bar{\mathscr{X}}$ as some factor space $\mathscr{X}/\mathscr{S}$, where

$$A\mathscr{S} \subset \mathscr{S} \subset \mathscr{X}^-(A) .$$

Next we must guarantee that the model output $\bar{y}$ carries no more information than does the directly measured output y: realizability demands the existence of a map D: $\mathscr{Y} \rightarrow \bar{\mathscr{Y}}$ such that

$$\bar{y} = Dy . \tag{30}$$

Clearly (30) justifies the further identification $\bar{\mathscr{Y}} = \mathscr{Y}$. In this way we are led to the algebraic setup depicted in the diagram (31).

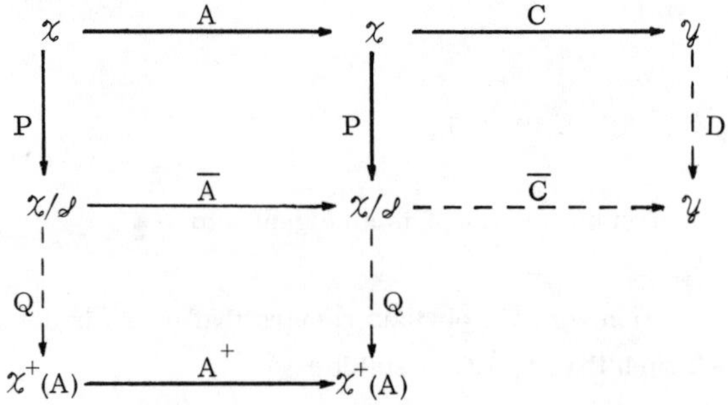

(31)

Here we may as well arrange that the pair $(\bar{C}, \bar{A})$ be observable. For if it is not, project out its unobservable subspace in accordance with the diagram (9) and Lemma 3.2, then note that the corresponding canonical projection can be composed with the projection P in (31).

The structure displayed in the diagram is summarized in

THEOREM 3.4. Let A: $\mathscr{X} \rightarrow \mathscr{X}$ and C: $\mathscr{X} \rightarrow \mathscr{Y}$ with (C, A) detectable. Let $\mathscr{K} \subset \mathscr{X}$, $\mathscr{S} \subset \mathscr{X}$ be subspaces with the properties

$$\mathscr{K} \supset \operatorname{Ker} C + \mathscr{S}, \qquad \bigcap_{i=1}^{n} A^{-i+1}\mathscr{K} \subset \mathscr{X}^-(A) \tag{32}$$

and

$$A\mathscr{S} \subset \mathscr{S} \subset \mathscr{X}^-(A) .$$

Let $\bar{A}$: $\mathscr{X}/\mathscr{S} \rightarrow \mathscr{X}/\mathscr{S}$ be the map induced by A in $\mathscr{X}/\mathscr{S}$ and write P: $\mathscr{X} \rightarrow \mathscr{X}/\mathscr{S}$ for the canonical projection. Then

(i) *there exists a map* D: $\mathscr{Y} \to \mathscr{Y}$ *such that*

$$\mathrm{Ker}\ DC = \mathscr{K}$$

and (DC, A) *is detectable*;

(ii) *there exists a map* $\overline{C}$: $\mathscr{X}/\mathscr{S} \to \mathscr{Y}$ *such that*

$$\overline{C}P = DC \; ; \tag{33}$$

(iii) $(\overline{C}, \overline{A})$ *is observable if and only if*

$$\mathscr{S} = \bigcap_{i=1}^{n} A^{-i+1}\mathscr{K},$$

i.e., $\mathscr{S}$ *is the largest* A-*invariant subspace of* $\mathscr{K}$;

(iv) *if* $A^{+} = A\,|\,\mathscr{X}^{+}(A)$, *there exists an epimorphism* Q: $\mathscr{X}/\mathscr{S} \to \mathscr{X}^{+}(A)$ *such that*

$$A^{+}Q = Q\overline{A} \, .$$

PROOF:

(i) By (32) $\mathscr{K} \supset \mathscr{S}$, and the first assertion follows easily. As for detectability

$$\bigcap_{i=1}^{n} \mathrm{Ker}(DCA^{i-1}) = \bigcap_{i=1}^{n} A^{-i+1}\mathscr{K} \subset \mathscr{X}^{-}(A) \, .$$

(ii) The existence of $\overline{C}$ is immediate from

$$\mathrm{Ker}\, P = \mathscr{S} \subset \mathscr{K} = \mathrm{Ker}(DC) \, .$$

(iii) Write

$$\mathscr{S}^{*} = \bigcap_{i=1}^{n} A^{-i+1}\mathscr{K} \, .$$

A routine application of (33) and the definitions verifies that

$$\bigcap_{i=1}^{n} \mathrm{Ker}(\overline{C}\,\overline{A}^{i-1}) = \frac{\mathscr{S}^{*}}{\mathscr{S}} \, ,$$

whence the assertion follows.

(iv) Write

$$x = x^+ + x^- , \qquad x \in \mathcal{X},\ x^\pm \in \mathcal{X}^\pm(A) ,$$

and for $\bar{x} = Px \in \mathcal{X}/\mathcal{S}$ let

$$Q\bar{x} = x^+ .$$

It is trivial to check that Q is well defined and has the stated properties. ▌

The foregoing discussion has reduced the problem of identifying x mod $\mathcal{X}^-(A)$ to that of constructing an observer (which we shall choose to be minimal in the sense of Section 3.4) for an observable model $(\overline{C}, \overline{A})$ related to (C, A) as in (31). Observability implies $\mathcal{S} = \mathcal{S}^*$, hence the possible models are completely determined by the choice of $\mathcal{K}$, and the corresponding observer has dynamic order

$$d(\text{Ker}\,\overline{C}) = d\left(\frac{\mathcal{K}}{\mathcal{S}^*}\right) .$$

With these preliminaries we can state the purely algebraic

Minimal Detector Problem (MDP):

Given A: $\mathcal{X} \to \mathcal{X}$ and C: $\mathcal{X} \to \mathcal{Y}$ with (C, A) detectable, find $\mathcal{K} \subset \mathcal{X}$ such that

$$\mathcal{K} \supset \text{Ker}\,C \tag{34}$$

$$\bigcap_{i=1}^{n} A^{-i+1}\mathcal{K} \subset \mathcal{X}^-(A) \tag{35}$$

and

$$d(\mathcal{K}) - d\left(\bigcap_{i=1}^{n} A^{-i+1}\mathcal{K}\right) = \text{minimum} . \tag{36}$$

An effective procedure for solving MDP is not currently available. However, a solution always exists, as (34) and (35) are satisfied in particular by $\mathcal{K} = \text{Ker}\,C$. In general, however, Ker C is not minimal in the sense of (36). A lower bound for this minimum is easily derived:

$$d\left(\frac{\mathcal{K}}{\mathcal{S}^*}\right) \geq d\left[\frac{(\text{Ker}\,C + \mathcal{S}^*)}{\mathcal{S}^*}\right] = d(\text{Ker}\,C) - d(\mathcal{S}^* \cap \text{Ker}\,C)$$

$$\geq d(\text{Ker}\,C) - d[\mathcal{X}^-(A) \cap \text{Ker}\,C] . \tag{37}$$

On the basis solely of (34) and (35), the bound (37) is the best possible, although it cannot always be attained, as the second of the following examples shows.

EXAMPLE 1

Suppose

$$\mathrm{Ker}\, C = \mathscr{G}^+ \oplus \mathscr{G}^- ,$$

where

$$\mathscr{G}^\pm \subset \mathcal{X}^\pm(A) .$$

Let

$$\mathcal{K} = \mathcal{X}^-(A) \oplus \mathscr{G}^+ .$$

By detectability

$$\mathscr{I}^* = \bigcap_{i=1}^{n} A^{-i+1}[\mathcal{X}^-(A) \oplus \mathscr{G}^+] = \mathcal{X}^-(A) ;$$

so that

$$d\left(\frac{\mathcal{K}}{\mathscr{I}^*}\right) = d(\mathscr{G}^+) ,$$

which is minimal by (37).

EXAMPLE 2

Consider the detectable pair

$$A = \left[\begin{array}{ccc|cc} -1 & 1 & 0 & & \\ 0 & -1 & 1 & & 0 \\ 0 & 0 & -1 & & \\ \hline & & & 0 & 1 \\ & 0 & & 0 & 0 \end{array}\right], \qquad C = \begin{bmatrix} 0 & 0 & 0 & 0 & 1 \\ 0 & 1 & 1 & 1 & 0 \end{bmatrix}. \tag{38}$$

Denoting the unit vectors by e_i ($i \in \underline{5}$) and setting $\mathcal{K} = \mathrm{Ker}\, C$, we find

$$\mathrm{Ker}\, C = \mathrm{Span}\{e_1, e_2 - e_3, e_3 - e_4\} ,$$

$$\mathscr{I}^* = \mathrm{Span}\{e_1\} ,$$

$$d\left(\frac{\mathcal{K}}{\mathscr{I}^*}\right) = 2$$

and

$$d\left[\frac{\mathrm{Ker}\, C}{\mathcal{X}^-(A) \cap \mathrm{Ker}\, C}\right] = 1 .$$

It is easy to see that no other choice of $\tilde{\mathcal{K}}$ will lead to a lower value of $d(\tilde{\mathcal{K}}/\tilde{\mathscr{I}}^*)$. Indeed as

$$\tilde{\mathscr{I}}^* \subset \mathcal{X}^-(A) = \mathrm{Span}\{e_1, e_2, e_3\}$$

and $\tilde{\mathcal{K}} \supset \mathrm{Ker}\, C = \mathcal{K}$, it follows from (38) that $\tilde{\mathscr{I}}^*$ must be one of the subspaces

$$\mathcal{J}^*, \ \mathrm{Span}\{e_1, e_2\}, \quad \text{or} \quad \mathcal{X}^-(A).$$

If $\tilde{\mathcal{J}}^* = \mathcal{J}^*$, clearly

$$d\left(\frac{\tilde{\mathcal{K}}}{\tilde{\mathcal{J}}^*}\right) \geq d\left(\frac{\mathcal{K}}{\mathcal{J}^*}\right).$$

If $\tilde{\mathcal{J}}^* = \mathcal{X}^-(A)$, then $\tilde{\mathcal{K}} \supset \mathrm{Ker}\, C + \mathcal{X}^-(A)$; but

$$e_4 \in [\mathrm{Ker}\, C + \mathcal{X}^-(A)] \cap \mathcal{X}^+(A)$$

and $Ae_4 = 0$, so that $e_4 \in \tilde{\mathcal{J}}^*$, a contradiction. Finally, if $\tilde{\mathcal{J}}^* = \mathrm{Span}\{e_1, e_2\}$ then

$$d(\tilde{\mathcal{K}}) \geq d(\mathcal{K}) + 1$$

and

$$d\left(\frac{\tilde{\mathcal{K}}}{\tilde{\mathcal{J}}^*}\right) \geq d(\mathcal{K}) + 1 - 2 = 2$$

as before.

We conclude this section with the obvious remark that the entire discussion remains valid for a general symmetric partition

$$\mathbb{C} = \mathbb{C}_g \dot{\cup} \mathbb{C}_b,$$

and corresponding modal decomposition

$$\mathcal{X} = \mathcal{X}_g(A) \oplus \mathcal{X}_b(A),$$

provided $\mathcal{X}^+(A), \mathcal{X}^-(A)$ are replaced by $\mathcal{X}_b(A), \mathcal{X}_g(A)$, respectively.

3.8 Pole Shifting by Dynamic Compensation

In this section we adopt an approach to pole shifting which, unlike that of Section 3.5, makes no explicit reliance on the observer action of the auxiliary dynamic element to be coupled to the original system. Of course, it will still be true that the observability property of the given system must be postulated if complete freedom of pole assignability is required.

Consider as usual

$$\dot{x} = Ax + Bu, \qquad y = Cx. \tag{39}$$

We shall say that (C, A, B) is complete if (C, A) is observable and (A, B) is controllable. When (C, A) is observable, we define the observability index $\varkappa_0$ of (C, A) according to

$$\varkappa_0 \triangleq \min\left\{j:\ 1 \le j \le n,\ \bigcap_{i=1}^{j} \operatorname{Ker}(CA^{i-1}) = 0\right\}.$$

Clearly $\varkappa_0$ exists and $1 \le \varkappa_0 \le n$.

Write $\nu \triangleq \varkappa_0 - 1$, and introduce an auxiliary state space $\mathcal{W}$ with $d(\mathcal{W}) = \nu$. Our problem is to find an auxiliary dynamic system

$$\dot{w} = Ww + v\ , \tag{40}$$

which, when coupled to (39) according to

$$\begin{aligned} u &= Hy + Gw \\ v &= Ky\ , \end{aligned} \tag{41}$$

will assign to the composite system a specified spectrum Λ with $|\Lambda| = n + \nu$. The system (40) is the (dynamic) compensator.

That our problem is solvable is claimed by

THEOREM 3.5. Let (C, A, B) be complete and let the observability index of (C, A) be $\nu + 1$. Introduce $\mathcal{W}$, independent of $\mathcal{X}$, with $d(\mathcal{W}) = \nu$. Then for every symmetric set Λ of $n + \nu$ complex numbers, there exist maps

$$G: \mathcal{W} \to \mathcal{U}, \quad H: \mathcal{Y} \to \mathcal{U}, \quad K: \mathcal{Y} \to \mathcal{W}, \quad \text{and} \quad W: \mathcal{W} \to \mathcal{W},$$

such that (in a basis adapted to $\mathcal{X} \oplus \mathcal{W}$)

$$\sigma\left(\begin{bmatrix} A + BHC & BG \\ KC & W \end{bmatrix}\right) = \Lambda.$$

Remarks

1. In the composite system (39) – (41) only the 'measurements' (y, w) are made directly accessible to the 'controls' (u, v).
2. If a minimal order dynamic observer were used as compensator, as in Section 3.5, its generic order, relative to the space $\mathbb{R}^{pn+n^2}$ of all pairs (C, A), would be, obviously,

$$d(\operatorname{Ker} C) = n - p \quad (g)\ .$$

One would assign the spectrum of the composite system as $\sigma = \sigma_1 \dot{\cup} \sigma_2$ with $|\sigma_1| = n$, $|\sigma_2| = n - p$. Now clearly,

$$\varkappa_0 = \min\{j:\ jp \geq n\}\ (g) = \left[\frac{n}{p}\right] + 1,$$

and so $\nu = [n/p]$ (g). Thus the compensator has dynamic order $[n/p] \ll n - p$ in 'typical' cases where n is large and p is relatively small.

3. Theorem 3.5 can be dualized in obvious fashion, to yield a dynamic compensator of order one less than the controllability index $\varkappa_c$ of (A, B), where

$$\varkappa_c \triangleq \min\left\{j:\ 1 \leq j \leq n,\ \sum_{i=1}^{j} A^{i-1}\mathcal{B} = \mathcal{X}\right\}.$$

The 'better' of the two results would be used in applications where reduction of compensator order is important.

To prove Theorem 3.5 we need five preliminary results, of some interest in their own right. The key step is achieved by Lemma 3.9, below.

LEMMA 3.6. *Suppose* $A: \mathcal{X} \to \mathcal{X}$ *and* $\mathcal{X} = \mathcal{R} \oplus \mathcal{S}$, *where* $\mathcal{R}$ *and* $\mathcal{S}$ *are* A*-invariant and* A*-cyclic, with* $\sigma(A|\mathcal{R}) \cap \sigma(A|\mathcal{S}) = \emptyset$. *Then* $\mathcal{X}$ *is* A*-cyclic, with m.p. the product of the m.p.'s of* $A|\mathcal{R}$ *and* $A|\mathcal{S}$.

The simple proof is left to the reader. Now recall from Section 0.10 the definition of cyclic index. We have

LEMMA 3.7. *Let* $\mathcal{X} = \mathcal{X}_1 \oplus \mathcal{X}_2$ *and* $A\mathcal{X}_i \subset \mathcal{X}_i$ $(i \in \underline{2})$. *Let* $A_i \triangleq A|\mathcal{X}_i$ *and let the cyclic index of* $\mathcal{X}_i$ *be* k_i. *If* $\sigma(A_1) \cap \sigma(A_2) = \emptyset$ *then the cyclic index of* A *is* $k \triangleq \max(k_1, k_2)$.

PROOF: Write $\mathcal{R} \triangleq \mathcal{X}_1$, $\mathcal{S} \triangleq \mathcal{X}_2$ and let

$$\mathcal{R} = \bigoplus_{i=1}^{k_1} \mathcal{R}_i, \qquad \mathcal{S} = \bigoplus_{i=1}^{k_2} \mathcal{S}_i$$

be rational canonical decompositions with respect to A_1, A_2. Suppose $k_1 \leq k_2$. By Lemma 3.6 the subspaces $\mathcal{R}_i \oplus \mathcal{S}_i$ $(i \in \underline{k_1})$ are cyclic, with minimal polynomials the corresponding products, hence

$$\mathcal{X} = (\mathcal{R}_1 \oplus \mathcal{S}_1) \oplus \cdots \oplus \left(\mathcal{R}_{k_1} \oplus \mathcal{S}_{k_1}\right) \oplus \mathcal{S}_{k_1+1} \oplus \cdots \oplus \mathcal{S}_{k_2}$$

is a rational canonical decomposition of $\mathcal{X}$, and has cyclic index k_2. ▌

LEMMA 3.8. Let (C, A, B) be complete and suppose A has cyclic index k. There exist $b \in \mathcal{B}$ and $c' \in \operatorname{Im} C'$ such that $(C, A + bc', B)$ is complete and has cyclic index $k - 1$.

PROOF: We observe, by Lemma 2.1 and its dual, that $(C, A + bc', B)$ is complete for any $b \in \mathcal{B}$ and $c' \in \operatorname{Im} C'$. To finish the proof choose, by Theorem 1.2, $\mathcal{R}$ and $\mathcal{S} \subset \mathcal{X}$ such that $\mathcal{X} = \mathcal{R} \oplus \mathcal{S}$, where $A\mathcal{R} \subset \mathcal{R}$, $A\mathcal{S} \subset \mathcal{S}$, $\mathcal{R}$ is maximal A-cyclic, and $\mathcal{R} = \langle A | b \rangle$ for some $b \in \mathcal{B} \cap \mathcal{R}$. Now if $A_0 \triangleq A|\mathcal{R}$ and $C_0 \triangleq C|\mathcal{R}$ then (C_0, A_0) is observable. By the obvious dual of Corollary 1.1, there exists $\tilde{c}_0' \in \operatorname{Im} C_0' \subset \mathcal{R}'$ such that $(\tilde{c}_0', A_0)$ is observable. Define $b_0: \mathbb{R} \to \mathcal{R}$ according to $b_0 t \triangleq tb$ $(t \in \mathbb{R})$. Then $b_0 \tilde{c}_0': \mathcal{R} \to \mathcal{R}$ is well-defined.

Next consider the maps

$$A_0(t) \triangleq A_0 + t b_0 \tilde{c}_0' : \mathcal{R} \to \mathcal{R}, \qquad t \in \mathbb{R} .$$

It will be shown that $\sigma[A_0(t)]$ can be separated from $\sigma(A|\mathcal{S})$. Let

$$\pi_0(\lambda) \triangleq \lambda^\rho - \left(a_1 + a_2\lambda + \cdots + a_\rho \lambda^{\rho-1}\right)$$

be the m.p. (= ch.p.) of A_0. Then

$$\pi_0(\lambda, t) \triangleq \det[\lambda - A_0(t)] = \pi_0(\lambda) - t\left(\tilde{a}_1 + \tilde{a}_2\lambda + \cdots + \tilde{a}_\rho \lambda^{\rho-1}\right)$$

for suitable $\tilde{a}_i \in \mathbb{R}$ $(i \in \underline{\rho})$, not depending on t. It is easy to see that

$$\tilde{\pi}_0(\lambda) \triangleq \tilde{a}_1 + \tilde{a}_2\lambda + \cdots + \tilde{a}_\rho \lambda^{\rho-1}$$

is coprime with $\pi_0(\lambda)$. Otherwise, there exists $\lambda_0 \in \mathbb{C}$ such that $\pi_0(\lambda_0) = \tilde{\pi}_0(\lambda_0) = 0$. Taking (say) (A_0, b_0) in the standard form (1.7), so that

$$\tilde{c}_0' = (\tilde{a}_1, \ldots, \tilde{a}_\rho) \in \mathbb{R}^{1\times\rho},$$

we see that

$$x_0 \triangleq \operatorname{col}\left(1, \lambda_0, \ldots, \lambda_0^{\rho-1}\right) \in \mathbb{C}^{\rho\times 1}$$

is an eigenvector of A_0 with $x_0 \in \operatorname{Ker} c_0'$. But this contradicts the fact that (c_0', A_0) is observable. We conclude that $\pi_0(\lambda, t)$ has no root λ_0 which is fixed for all $t \in J$, J any subinterval of $\mathbb{R}$. But the root-set of $\pi_0(\lambda, t)$ is continuous in the sense of (Rouché's) Theorem 0.3, with respect to the parameter $t \in \mathbb{R}$, and it follows easily (Ex. 3.13) that for some $t_0 \in \mathbb{R}$ we must have

$$\sigma[A_0(t_0)] \cap \sigma(A|\mathcal{S}) = \emptyset . \tag{42}$$

Let $c_0' \triangleq t_0 \tilde{c}_0'$. There is $c' \in \operatorname{Im} C'$ such that $c' | \mathcal{R} = c_0'$. Consider $A_1 \triangleq A + bc'$. We have $A_1 \mathcal{R} \subset \mathcal{R}$. If $\bar{A}_1$ is the map induced by A_1 on $\mathcal{X}/\mathcal{R}$, the diagram below commutes.

$$\begin{array}{ccc} \mathcal{S} & \xrightarrow{\quad A | \mathcal{S} \quad} & \mathcal{S} \\ \big\downarrow \approx & & \big\downarrow \approx \\ \mathcal{X}/\mathcal{R} & \xrightarrow{\quad \bar{A}_1 \quad} & \mathcal{X}/\mathcal{R} \end{array}$$

Thus

$$\sigma(A_1 | \mathcal{R}) \cap \sigma(\bar{A}_1) = \sigma(A_1 | \mathcal{R}) \cap \sigma(A | \mathcal{S}) = \emptyset .$$

Hence there exists $\mathcal{T} \subset \mathcal{X}$ with $\mathcal{X} = \mathcal{R} \oplus \mathcal{T}$, $A_1 \mathcal{T} \subset \mathcal{T}$ and

$$\sigma(A_1 | \mathcal{R}) \cap \sigma(A_1 | \mathcal{T}) = \emptyset .$$

Since $A_1 | \mathcal{T} \approx \bar{A}_1$, the cyclic index of $A_1 | \mathcal{T}$ is $k - 1$, and the result follows by Lemma 3.7. ▌

The key step is provided by

LEMMA 3.9. If (C, A, B) is complete there exists $H: \mathcal{Y} \to \mathcal{U}$ such that $A + BHC$ is cyclic.

PROOF: If the cyclic index of A is k, apply Lemma 3.8 $k - 1$ times to get that

$$A + b_1 c_1' + \cdots + b_{k-1} c_{k-1}'$$

is cyclic for suitable $b_i \in \mathcal{B}$, $c_i' \in \operatorname{Im} C'$ ($i \in \underline{k-1}$). We have $b_i = Bu_i$ and $c_i' = v_i' C$ for some $u_i \in \mathcal{U}$ and $v_i' \in \mathcal{Y}'$, so we need only set

$$H \triangleq \sum_{i=1}^{k-1} u_i v_i' . \ ▌$$

Remark

Fix (C, A, B) complete and choose H as in Lemma 3.9. Let ℓ be a cyclic generator for $A + BHC$. Then

$$\det [\ell, (A + BHC)\ell, \ldots, (A + BHC)^{n-1} \ell] \neq 0 ,$$

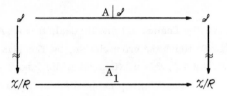

and this inequality remains true for all $H \in \mathbb{R}^{m\times p}$ except those H which, as points in $\mathbb{R}^{mp}$, belong to a proper variety $\underline{V} \subset \mathbb{R}^{mp}$. Thus A + BHC is cyclic in the complement $\underline{V}^c$, namely for 'almost all' H.

It is now clear that in proving Theorem 3.5 we can assume a priori that A is cyclic: otherwise a preliminary transformation $A \mapsto A + BH_0C$ will make it so.

The next, rather special result will provide an isomorphism needed later.

LEMMA 3.10. Let (c', A, B) be complete; let $\mathcal{T}$ be independent of $\mathcal{X}$ with $d(\mathcal{T}) = \tau \le n-1$; let $T: \mathcal{T} \to \mathcal{T}$ be cyclic with generator $g \in \mathcal{T}$; let $h' \in \mathcal{T}'$ be determined by

$$h'g = \cdots = h'T^{\tau-2}g = 0\,, \qquad h'T^{\tau-1}g = 1\,; \tag{43}$$

let $\ell \in \mathcal{X}$ be a vector such that

$$\ell \in \mathcal{B} + A\mathcal{B} + \cdots + A^{\tau}\mathcal{B}\,; \tag{44}$$

define $\mathcal{X}_e \triangleq \mathcal{X} \oplus \mathcal{T}$; and relative to $\mathcal{X}_e$ let

$$A_e \triangleq \begin{bmatrix} A & -\ell h' \\ 0 & T \end{bmatrix}, \qquad B_e \triangleq \begin{bmatrix} B \\ 0 \end{bmatrix}.$$

Then there exist a subspace $\mathcal{S} \subset \mathcal{X}_e$ and a map $F_e: \mathcal{X}_e \to \mathcal{U}$ such that

$$\mathcal{X} \oplus \mathcal{S} = \mathcal{X}_e\,,$$

$$(A_e + B_e F_e)\mathcal{S} \subset \mathcal{S}\,, \tag{45}$$

and

$$\operatorname{Ker} F_e \cap \mathcal{X} \supset \operatorname{Ker} c'\,. \tag{46}$$

Under these conditions

$$(A_e + B_e F_e)\,|\,\mathcal{S} \approx T\,. \tag{47}$$

For a systemic interpretation of the lemma see Ex. 3.14.

PROOF: We shall construct $\mathcal{S}$ in the form

$$\mathcal{S} = \operatorname{Im}\begin{bmatrix} R \\ I \end{bmatrix} \tag{48}$$

for a suitable map R: $\mathcal{T} \to \mathcal{X}$. Now by (44) there exists $b \in \mathcal{B}$, such that

$$\ell - A^{\tau} b = b_1 + Ab_2 + \cdots + A^{\tau-1} b_{\tau} \tag{49}$$

for suitable $b_i \in \mathcal{B}$ ($i \in \underline{\tau}$). Let $b = Bu$ ($u \in \mathcal{U}$) and set $F_e = [uc', G]$ for some G: $\mathcal{T} \to \mathcal{U}$, to be determined. Clearly, F_e satisfies (46), and (47) will be automatic if (45) is true. In view of (48), (45) and (47) are equivalent to

$$(A + bc')R + BG - \ell h' = RT . \tag{50}$$

To determine R subject to (50), we set

$$Rg \triangleq b \tag{51a}$$

and

$$R(T^i g) \triangleq (A + bc')R(T^{i-1} g) + (BG - \ell h')T^{i-1} g \tag{51b}$$

for $i \in \underline{\tau - 1}$. It remains only to define G on the basis $\{g, Tg, \ldots, T^{\tau-1} g\}$ so as to ensure that

$$\begin{aligned} R(T^{\tau} g) &= (A + bc')R(T^{\tau-1} g) + (BG - \ell h')T^{\tau-1} g \\ &\equiv R\left(\theta_1 1 + \theta_2 T + \cdots + \theta_{\tau} T^{\tau-1}\right) g , \end{aligned} \tag{52}$$

$\theta_i \in \mathbb{R}$ being the coefficients of the m.p. of T. For this, use (49) and (51) to eliminate R and ℓ from (52). Then define G so that vectors formally in $A^{i-1}\mathcal{B}$ ($i \in \underline{\tau}$) are matched on both sides of the equation which results. ∎

COROLLARY 3.1. Under the conditions of Lemma 3.10 and with R, b as in the proof, there follows

$$\begin{bmatrix} I & R \\ 0 & I \end{bmatrix} \begin{bmatrix} A & \ell h' \\ gc' & T \end{bmatrix} = \begin{bmatrix} A + bc' & BG \\ gc' & S \end{bmatrix} \begin{bmatrix} I & R \\ 0 & I \end{bmatrix} ,$$

where

$$S \triangleq T - gc'R .$$

By dualization of Corollary 3.1, we get

COROLLARY 3.2. Let (C, A, b) be complete in $\mathcal{X}$ and (h′, T, g) complete in $\mathcal{T}$, with h′, g conjugate in the sense of (43). Let $d(\mathcal{T}) = \tau \le n - 1$, $\ell' \in \mathcal{X}'$, and

$$\operatorname{Ker} \ell' \supset \bigcap_{i=1}^{\tau+1} \operatorname{Ker}(CA^{i-1}) .$$

<u>Then there exist maps</u> $c' \in \operatorname{Im} C'$, $K: \mathcal{Y} \to \mathcal{T}$ <u>and</u> $S: \mathcal{T} \to \mathcal{T}$ <u>such that,</u> in $\mathcal{X} \oplus \mathcal{T}$,

$$\begin{bmatrix} A & bh' \\ g\ell' & T \end{bmatrix} \approx \begin{bmatrix} A+bc' & bh' \\ KC & S \end{bmatrix}.$$

We can now deliver the <u>coup de grâce</u>.

PROOF of Theorem 3.5. As already noted we may assume that A is cyclic. There is then $b \in \mathcal{B}$ such that (C, A, b) is complete. Choose W_0: $\mathcal{W} \to \mathcal{W}$ cyclic, then $g \in \mathcal{W}$ and $h' \in \mathcal{W}'$ such that (h', W_0, g) is complete, with

$$h'T^{i-1}g = 0, \qquad i \in \underline{\nu-2}\ ; \ h'T^{\nu-1}g = 1.$$

It is now simple to check that the pair

$$\begin{bmatrix} A & bh' \\ 0 & W_0 \end{bmatrix}, \begin{bmatrix} 0 \\ g \end{bmatrix}$$

is controllable in $\mathcal{X} \oplus \mathcal{W}$, hence there exist $\ell' \in \mathcal{X}'$ and $m' \in \mathcal{W}'$ such that

$$\sigma\left(\begin{bmatrix} A & bh' \\ g\ell' & W_0+gm' \end{bmatrix}\right) = \Lambda .$$

Since

$$\bigcap_{i=1}^{\nu+1} \operatorname{Ker}(CA^{i-1}) = 0$$

the conditions of Corollary 3.2 are satisfied (with the replacement of $\mathcal{T}$ by $\mathcal{W}$, τ by ν, and T by W_0+gm'). It follows that

$$\begin{bmatrix} A & bh' \\ g\ell' & W_0+gm' \end{bmatrix} \approx \begin{bmatrix} A+bc' & bh' \\ KC & W \end{bmatrix} \tag{53}$$

for suitable c′, K, W, and the proof is finished. ▌

From the proof it is clear that the role of Corollary 3.2, and thus of Lemma 3.10, is to provide an equivalence between the physically unrealizable composite system on the left side of (53), and the realizable system on the right. Here 'realizability' is understood, of course, in the sense of respecting the processing constraint that only (y, w) can be directly measured.

A computational procedure for compensator design is summarized in Ex. 3.15.

3.9 Observer for a Single Linear Functional

As a second application of the definition of observability index we show in this section how to construct a dynamic observer of order $\nu \triangleq \varkappa_0 - 1$ which asymptotically evaluates a given functional $f'x$ on the state of the system

$$\dot{x} = Ax + v, \qquad y = Cx.$$

For this, introduce the observer equation

$$\dot{w} = Tw + Ry + Vv$$

and output functional $k'y + h'w$. The error with which this functional evaluates $f'x$ is then

$$e = f'x - k'y - h'w,$$

and it is enough to arrange that $e(t) \to 0$ as $t \to \infty$, with exponents in an assigned 'good' subset $\mathbb{C}_g \subset \mathbb{C}^- \triangleq \{s: \mathcal{R}e\, s < 0\}$.

Introduce the observer state space $\mathcal{W}$ independent of $\mathcal{X}$, with $d(\mathcal{W}) = \nu$. On $\mathcal{X} \oplus \mathcal{W}$ consider the map

$$A_e \triangleq \begin{bmatrix} A & 0 \\ RC & T \end{bmatrix}.$$

Choose $T: \mathcal{W} \to \mathcal{W}$ cyclic, with minimal polynomial

$$\theta(\lambda) \triangleq \lambda^\nu - \left(t_1 + t_2\lambda + \cdots + t_\nu \lambda^{\nu-1}\right)$$

having all its roots in $\mathbb{C}_g$; and fix h' arbitrarily such that (h', T) is observable.

Next assume that the external input $v(t) \equiv 0$. For the desired behavior of $e(\cdot)$ it clearly suffices to choose $R: \mathcal{Y} \to \mathcal{W}$ and $k' \in \mathcal{Y}'$ such that

$$[f' - k'C, -h']\,\theta(A_e) = 0. \tag{54}$$

To see that such a choice is possible, notice that

$$\theta(A_e) = \begin{bmatrix} \theta(A) & 0 \\ Q & 0 \end{bmatrix}, \tag{55}$$

where

$$Q \triangleq \sum_{i=1}^{\nu} \theta_i(T)\, RCA^{i-1} \tag{56}$$

and

$$\theta_i(\lambda) \triangleq \lambda^{\nu-i} - \left(t_{i+1} + t_{i+2}\lambda + \cdots + t_\nu \lambda^{\nu-1-i}\right). \tag{57}$$

By (57) the functionals

$$w_i' \triangleq h'\theta_i(T), \qquad i \in \underline{\nu}, \tag{58}$$

span $\mathcal{W}'$. Also, by definition of observability index, we have

$$f'\theta(A) = \sum_{i=1}^{\nu+1} e_i' C A^{i-1} \tag{59}$$

for suitable $e_i' \in \mathcal{Y}'$ ($i \in \underline{\nu+1}$). Now (55) – (59) imply that (54) will follow if

$$k' = e_{\nu+1}' \tag{60}$$

and

$$w_i' R = e_i' + t_i e_{\nu+1}', \qquad i \in \underline{\nu}.$$

With k' and R uniquely determined by (60), it is now not difficult to verify that, for arbitrary $v(\cdot)$, $e(\cdot)$ will continue to satisfy the differential equation

$$\theta\left(\frac{d}{dt}\right) e(t) = 0,$$

provided $V: \mathcal{X} \to \mathcal{W}$ is defined by

$$h'T^{i-1}V = (f' - k'C)A^{i-1} - \sum_{j=1}^{i-1} h'T^{j-1}RCA^{i-1-j}, \qquad i \in \underline{\nu}.$$

While the problem of this section admits the straightforward computational solution just provided, it may be of interest to the reader to develop a geometric treatment in the style of Section 3.4. For this, one may introduce the subspace $\mathcal{V}' \triangleq \operatorname{Im} V' \subset \mathcal{X}'$, note that

$$(\mathcal{V}')^\perp \cap \operatorname{Ker} C \subset \operatorname{Ker} f',$$

and seek $K: \mathcal{Y} \to \mathcal{X}$ such that $(A - KC)' \mathcal{V}' \subset \mathcal{V}'$.

3.10 Preservation of Observability and Detectability

It is often useful to know that 'desirable' properties like observability or detectability are preserved when the pair (C, A) is modified in various standard ways. As an obvious dual of Lemma 2.1 we have, for instance, that if (C, A) is observable (or detectable) then so is (C, A + KC) for every $K: \mathcal{Y} \to \mathcal{X}$.

In the following we regard $\mathcal{X}$ as an inner product space over $\mathbb{R}$. If $M: \mathcal{X} \to \mathcal{X}$ and $M \geq 0$, $\sqrt{M}$ denotes the positive semidefinite square root. We have

THEOREM 3.6.

(i) If $C_1'C_1 = C_2'C_2$ and (C_1, A) is observable (resp. detectable) then (C_2, A) is observable (resp. detectable).

(ii) If $M \geq 0$ and $(\sqrt{M}, A)$ is observable (resp. detectable), then for all $Q \geq 0$, $N > 0$ and all B, F, the pair $(\sqrt{M+Q+F'NF}, A+BF)$ is observable (resp. detectable).

PROOF: Write

$$\mathcal{N}(C) \triangleq \bigcap_{i=1}^{n} \operatorname{Ker}(CA^{i-1}),$$

$$W(C) \triangleq \sum_{i=1}^{n} A'^{i-1}C'CA^{i-1}.$$

Clearly $\mathcal{N}(C) = \operatorname{Ker} W(C)$ for every $C: \mathcal{X} \to \mathcal{Y}$. Then

$$\mathcal{N}(C_1) = \operatorname{Ker} W(C_1) = \operatorname{Ker} W(C_2) = \mathcal{N}(C_2),$$

proving (i). For (ii), since

$$\begin{aligned}\operatorname{Ker}\sqrt{M+Q+F'NF} &\subset \operatorname{Ker}\sqrt{M} \cap \operatorname{Ker} F \\ &\subset \operatorname{Ker}(K\sqrt{M}) \cap \operatorname{Ker}(BF) \subset \operatorname{Ker}(K\sqrt{M} - BF)\end{aligned}$$

for all K, the equation

$$\tilde{A}(\tilde{K}) \triangleq (A+BF) + \tilde{K}\sqrt{M+Q+F'NF} = A + K\sqrt{M}$$

is solvable for $\tilde{K}$, given arbitrary K. It follows that $\tilde{A}(\tilde{K})$ can be assigned an arbitrary symmetric spectrum (resp. can be stabilized) by suitable choice of $\tilde{K}$, whenever $A+K\sqrt{M}$ has the same property relative to K. ▌

It is clear that the foregoing discussion is not changed if $\mathcal{X}^+, \mathcal{X}^-$ are replaced by $\mathcal{X}_b, \mathcal{X}_g$ as defined in Section 2.3. Thus, 'the bad modes of the system (C, A) are observable' if

$$\mathcal{N}(C) \subset \mathcal{X}_g(A) ,$$

i.e., A is well-behaved on the unobservable subspace.

3.11 Exercises

3.1 Prove Lemma 3.1.

3.2 With $\mathcal{N}$ as in Section 3.2, let $\mathcal{X} = \mathcal{M} \oplus \mathcal{N}$, $x = x_1 + x_2$. Let $Q_1: \mathcal{X} \to \mathcal{M}$, $Q_2: \mathcal{X} \to \mathcal{N}$ be the natural projections, and write

$$\begin{aligned} A_1 &= Q_1 A \,|\, \mathcal{M}, & C_1 &= C \,|\, \mathcal{M}, \\ A_{21} &= Q_2 A \,|\, \mathcal{M}, & A_2 &= Q_2 A \,|\, \mathcal{N} . \end{aligned}$$

Show that (C_1, A_1) is observable and draw a signal flow graph for the system equations expressed in a basis adapted to $\mathcal{M} \oplus \mathcal{N}$. Indicate how a dynamic observer should be coupled to the system in order to yield an asymptotic identification of x_1.

3.3 Consider the dual maps $A': \mathcal{X}' \to \mathcal{X}'$ and $C': \mathcal{Y}' \to \mathcal{X}'$. The <u>observable subspace</u> of (C, A) is defined to be $\langle A' \,|\, \mathrm{Im}\, C' \rangle \subset \mathcal{X}'$. (C, A) is observable if and only if its observable subspace is all of $\mathcal{X}'$.

3.4 Verify in detail the following synthesis of the matrices of a minimal observer. Assume (C, A) observable, with C: $p \times n$ and Rank $C = p$; A: $n \times n$; and $\Lambda \subset \mathbb{C}$ symmetric, with $|\Lambda| = n - p = r$. We want T: $r \times r$, V: $r \times n$, and K: $n \times p$, with the properties

$$\mathrm{Rank} \begin{bmatrix} C \\ V \end{bmatrix} = n , \qquad V(A - KC) = TV , \qquad \sigma(T) = \Lambda .$$

1. Choose D: $r \times n$, such that

$$\mathrm{Rank} \begin{bmatrix} C \\ D \end{bmatrix} = n .$$

2. Define

$$W = \begin{bmatrix} C \\ D \end{bmatrix}$$

and transform A and C according to

$$\tilde{A} = WAW^{-1} = \begin{bmatrix} \tilde{A}_{11}^{p \times p} & \tilde{A}_{12}^{p \times r} \\ \tilde{A}_{21}^{r \times p} & \tilde{A}_{22}^{r \times r} \end{bmatrix}, \qquad \tilde{C} = CW^{-1} = \left[I^{p \times p}, 0^{p \times r} \right] .$$

The pair $(\tilde{A}_{12}, \tilde{A}_{22})$ is observable.

3. Using a pole assignment procedure, compute $\tilde{K}_0$: $r \times p$, such that

$$\sigma(\tilde{A}_{22} - \tilde{K}_0\tilde{A}_{12}) = \Lambda .$$

4. Compute

$$\tilde{T} = \tilde{A}_{22} - \tilde{K}_0\tilde{A}_{12}, \qquad \tilde{V} = \left[-\tilde{K}_0, I_r\right], \qquad \tilde{K} = \begin{bmatrix} \tilde{A}_{11} + \tilde{A}_{12}\tilde{K}_0 \\ \tilde{A}_{21} + \tilde{A}_{22}\tilde{K}_0 \end{bmatrix}.$$

5. Compute $T = \tilde{T}$, $V = \tilde{V}W$, $VK = \tilde{V}\tilde{K}$.

6. The observer is

$$\dot{z} = Tz + VKy + Vv \quad \text{and} \quad x(t) \sim \begin{bmatrix} C \\ V \end{bmatrix}^{-1} \begin{bmatrix} y(t) \\ z(t) \end{bmatrix}, \qquad t \to \infty .$$

Also

$$\begin{bmatrix} C \\ V \end{bmatrix}^{-1} = W^{-1} \begin{bmatrix} I^{p \times p} & 0 \\ \tilde{K}_0 & I^{r \times r} \end{bmatrix}.$$

3.6 For the system triple (C, A, B) as in (1), let $\mathcal{N}$ be the unobservable subspace and $\mathcal{R}$ the controllable subspace. Let

$$\mathcal{X} = \mathcal{X}_1 \oplus \mathcal{X}_2 \oplus \mathcal{X}_3 \oplus \mathcal{X}_4 ,$$

where

$$\mathcal{X}_1 = \mathcal{N} \cap \mathcal{R}, \qquad \mathcal{X}_2 \oplus \mathcal{X}_1 = \mathcal{R}$$
$$\mathcal{X}_3 \oplus \mathcal{X}_1 = \mathcal{N}, \qquad \mathcal{X}_4 \oplus (\mathcal{R} + \mathcal{N}) = \mathcal{X} .$$

Write down the system equations using a basis for $\mathcal{X}$ adapted to the $\mathcal{X}_i$. Interpret each $\mathcal{X}_i$ in terms of controllability and observability of the corresponding subsystem: e.g., $\mathcal{X}_1$ is the 'controllable but unobservable' component of the state space. Draw the signal flow graph of the composite system.

3.7 Verify in detail that if (A, B) is stabilizable and (C, A) is detectable then $x(\cdot)$ can be stabilized by feedback of the form

$$u(t) = Y[t, y(\cdot)]$$

where $Y[t, \cdot]$ is a linear operator on functions $y = y(s)$ defined for $s \le t$. Synthesize Y as a combination of detector and suitable matrix 'gains', and draw the signal flow graph of the stabilized system.

3.8 For the system $\dot{x} = Ax + Bu$, $y = Cx$, assume that $u = Fz$, where $z(\cdot)$ is the output of a dynamic observer with input $y(\cdot)$. Show that, for every choice of F, the spectrum of the closed-loop system map of the combined system always includes $\sigma(A_0) \dot{\cup} \sigma(\bar{A})$, where $A_0 = A|\mathcal{N}$, $\bar{A}$ is the map induced by A on $\mathcal{X}/(\langle A|\mathcal{B}\rangle + \mathcal{N})$, and $\mathcal{N}$ is the unobservable subspace. Briefly, 'only the controllable, observable poles can be shifted by feedback'.

3.9 For the system $\dot{x} = Ax + Bu$, $y = Cx$, show that stabilization is possible by means of dynamic compensation <u>only if</u> the unstable modes of A are controllable and observable, that is,

$$\mathcal{X}^+(A) \cap \mathcal{N} = 0 , \qquad \mathcal{X}^+(A) \subset \langle A|\mathcal{B}\rangle .$$

3.10 Consider the system

$$\dot{x} = Ax + v , \qquad y = Cx , \qquad z = Dx .$$

In the notation of Section 3.1, show that there exists a functional Ω, such that

$$\Omega[t, \omega_\alpha(t,\cdot)v(\cdot), \omega_\alpha(t,\cdot)y(\cdot)] = z(t)$$

for all $x(0) \in \mathcal{X}$ and $t \geq \alpha$, if and only if

$$\mathcal{N} \subset \text{Ker } D ,$$

where

$$\mathcal{N} \triangleq \bigcap_{i=1}^{n} \text{Ker}(CA^{i-1}) .$$

Thus, '$z(\cdot)$ is observable from $y(\cdot)$ and $v(\cdot)$ if and only if D annihilates the unobservable subspace'.

3.11 For the system $\dot{x} = Ax + Bu$, $y = Cx$, show that there exists $K: \mathcal{Y} \to \mathcal{U}$, such that $A + BKC$ is stable, if

$$\mathcal{X}^+(A) \subset \langle A|\mathcal{B}\rangle$$

and

$$\mathcal{X}^+(A) \cap \langle A|\text{Ker } C\rangle = 0 .$$

Convenient necessary and sufficient conditions for solvability of this problem are not known.

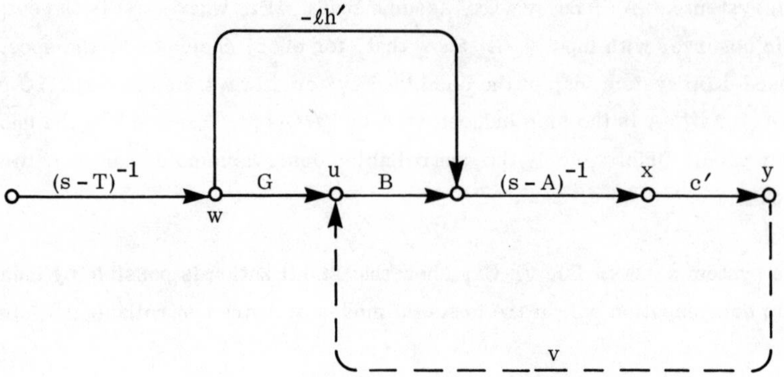

Fig. 3.2.

Composite System: Lemma 3.10

3.12 The matrix pair (C, A) is observable if and only if, with A: $n \times n$,

$$\text{Rank}_{\mathbb{C}} \begin{bmatrix} A - \lambda I \\ C \end{bmatrix} = n$$

for all $\lambda \in \sigma(A)$. What is the corresponding criterion for detectability?

3.13 Show that (42) is satisfied for some $t_0 \in \mathbb{R}$. HINT: Take any finite subset of $\mathbb{C}$, say, $z_1, \dots, z_k$, and prove the existence of a nested sequence of nonempty closed intervals $\mathbb{R} \supset J_1 \supset J_2 \supset \cdots \supset J_k$ with the property: the root set of $\pi_0(\lambda, t)$ is disjoint from $\{z_1, \dots, z_i\}$ for all $t \in J_i$. This proof even extends to a denumerable subset of $\mathbb{C}$.

3.14 Interpret Lemma 3.10 as a statement about the existence of a 'subsystem' within the composite system with flow graph in Fig. 3.2.

3.15 Develop a computational procedure for synthesizing the compensator of Section 3.8. HINT:

1. Pick H_0 'at random' to make $A_{new} \triangleq A + BH_0C$ cyclic, and set $A = A_{new}$.
2. Pick $b = Bu$ 'at random' to make (A, b) controllable.
3. Pick

$$W_0 = \begin{bmatrix} 0 & 1 & 0 & \cdot & \cdot & \cdot & \cdot & 0 \\ 0 & 0 & 1 & \cdot & \cdot & \cdot & \cdot & 0 \\ \cdot & \cdot & \cdot & \cdot & \cdot & \cdot & \cdot & \cdot \\ 0 & \cdot & \cdot & \cdot & \cdot & \cdot & 0 & 1 \\ 0 & \cdot & \cdot & \cdot & \cdot & \cdot & \cdot & 0 \end{bmatrix}_{\nu \times \nu}, \qquad g = \begin{bmatrix} 0 \\ \cdot \\ \cdot \\ \cdot \\ 0 \\ 1 \end{bmatrix}_{\nu \times 1}, \qquad h' = \begin{bmatrix} 1 & 0 & \cdot & \cdot & \cdot & 0 \end{bmatrix}_{1 \times \nu}.$$

4. By pole assignment compute ℓ': $1 \times n$, m': $1 \times \nu$, so that

$$\begin{bmatrix} A & bh' \\ 0 & W_0 \end{bmatrix} + \begin{bmatrix} 0 \\ g \end{bmatrix} [\ell' \ \ m']$$

has the desired spectrum Λ, $|\Lambda| = n + \nu$.

5. Compute $\hat{e}', \hat{e}_i'$: $1 \times p$ ($i \in \underline{\nu}$), not necessarily unique, such that

$$\ell' - \hat{e}' CA^{\nu} = \hat{e}_1' C + \hat{e}_2' CA + \cdots + \hat{e}_{\nu}' CA^{\nu-1}.$$

6. Set $\tilde{A} \triangleq A + b\hat{e}' C$ and compute e', e_i': $1 \times p$ ($i \in \underline{\nu}$), such that

$$\ell' - e' C\tilde{A}^{\nu} = e_1' C + e_2' C\tilde{A} + \cdots + e_{\nu}' C\tilde{A}^{\nu-1}.$$

7. Set $T \triangleq W_0 + gm'$, $k_i' \triangleq h'T^{i-1}K$ ($i \in \underline{\nu}$) and compute k_i' from

$$k'_{\nu-i+1} = e_i' + \theta_i e' + \theta_{i+1}k_1' + \theta_{i+2}k_2' + \cdots + \theta_\nu k'_{\nu-i},$$

($i = \nu, \nu-1, \ldots, 1$). [These equations result by eliminating R from the appropriately dualized version of (31)].

8. Set $r_i' \triangleq h'T^{i-1}R$ ($i \in \underline{\nu}$) and compute r_i' from

$$r_i' = \hat{e}'C, \qquad r'_{i+1} = r_i'\tilde{A} + k_i'C, \qquad i \in \underline{\nu - 1}.$$

9. Compute

$$[K, R] = \begin{bmatrix} h' \\ h'T \\ \cdot \\ \cdot \\ \cdot \\ h'T^{\nu-1} \end{bmatrix}^{-1} \begin{bmatrix} k_1' & r_1' \\ \cdot & \cdot \\ \cdot & \cdot \\ \cdot & \cdot \\ k_\nu' & r_\nu' \end{bmatrix},$$

$W = T - Rbh'$, $G = uh'$, $H = u\hat{e}'$.

10. As a numerical example, let

$$A = \begin{bmatrix} 0 & 0 & 0 & 0 & 0 \\ 1 & 0 & 0 & 0 & 0 \\ 0 & 1 & 0 & 0 & 0 \\ 0 & 0 & 0 & 0 & 0 \\ 0 & 0 & 0 & 1 & 0 \end{bmatrix}, \quad B = \begin{bmatrix} 1 & 0 \\ 0 & 0 \\ 0 & 0 \\ 0 & 1 \\ 0 & 0 \end{bmatrix}, \quad C = \begin{bmatrix} 0 & 1 & 0 & 0 & 0 \\ 0 & 0 & 1 & 0 & 0 \\ 0 & 0 & 0 & 0 & 1 \end{bmatrix}.$$

Then $\nu = 1$ and one can take

$$H_0 = \begin{bmatrix} 0 & 0 & 0 \\ 0 & 1 & 0 \end{bmatrix}, \quad b = \begin{bmatrix} 1 \\ 0 \\ 0 \\ 0 \\ 0 \end{bmatrix}, \quad W_0 = 0, \quad h' = 1, \quad g = 1.$$

Setting double poles at $s = -1, -1 \pm i$, results finally in

$$K = [74 \;\; -28 \;\; 92], \quad W = -6, \quad G = \begin{bmatrix} 1 \\ 0 \end{bmatrix}, \quad H = \begin{bmatrix} -17 & 0 & -16 \\ 0 & 1 & 0 \end{bmatrix}.$$

3.12 Notes and References

The definition and fundamental properties of an observable system are due to Kalman [1]; see also Kalman, Ho, and Narendra [1], where the decomposition given in Ex. 3.6 was introduced. Minimal order dynamic observers were discovered by Luenberger [1], [2]; the treatment here and Lemma 3.5 follow Wonham [5]. The synthesis procedure of Ex. 3.5 mimics the algebraic development; see also Newmann [1]. The definition of detectability and the results of Sections 3.6 and 3.10 are due to Wonham [2]. For Ex. 3.11 see e.g., Denham [1], and for Ex. 3.12 cf. Hautus [1]. The main results in Section 3.8 (Theorem 3.5 and Lemma 3.9) are due to Brasch and Pearson [1]. See Shaw [1] for a caveat on the sensitivity of pole-shifting compensators with respect to small parameter changes. A 'geometric' treatment of the problem of Section 3.9 is given by Wonham and Morse [2]; for an alternative, computational approach see e.g., Murdoch [1], and for further discussion of low-order observers, Fortmann and Williamson [1].

CHAPTER 4

DISTURBANCE DECOUPLING AND OUTPUT STABILIZATION

In this chapter we first discuss a simple feedback synthesis problem, concerned with decoupling from the system output the effect of disturbances acting at the input. Examination of this problem leads naturally to the fundamental geometric concept of (A, B)-invariant subspace, which underlies many of our constructions and results in later chapters. As an immediate application, we show how state feedback may be utilized to stabilize outputs or, more generally, to realize a given set of characteristic exponents in the time response of output.

4.1 Disturbance Decoupling Problem (DDP)

Consider the system

$$\dot{x}(t) = Ax(t) + Bu(t) + Eq(t) , \qquad t \geq 0 , \tag{1}$$

$$z(t) = Dx(t) , \qquad t \geq 0 . \tag{2}$$

The new term q(t) in (1) represents a disturbance which is assumed not to be directly measurable by the controller. Our problem is to find (if possible) state feedback F such that $q(\cdot)$ has no influence on the controlled output $z(\cdot)$. Let us assume that $q(\cdot)$ belongs to a fairly rich function class $\underset{\sim}{Q}$, the choice reflecting in some measure our ignorance of the specific features of the disturbances to be encountered. This choice is not crucial: we adopt the continuous $\mathbb{R}^{\nu}$-valued functions on $[0, \infty)$, set $\mathcal{Q} \triangleq \mathbb{R}^{\nu}$, and assume $E: \mathcal{Q} \to \mathcal{X}$ is a time-invariant map.

We say that the system (1), (2) is disturbance decoupled relative to the pair $q(\cdot), z(\cdot)$ if, for each initial state $x(0) \in \mathcal{X}$, the output $z(t)$, $t \geq 0$, is the same for every $q(\cdot) \in \underset{\sim}{Q}$. Thus disturbance decoupling simply means that the forced response

$$z(t) = D\int_0^t e^{(t-s)A}\, Eq(s)\, ds = 0 \tag{3}$$

for all $q(\cdot) \in \underset{\sim}{Q}$ and $t \geq 0$.

Write $\mathcal{K} \triangleq \operatorname{Ker} D$ and $\mathcal{E} \triangleq \operatorname{Im} E$. The following result is easy to see from (3).

LEMMA 4.1. The system (1), (2) is disturbance decoupled if and only if $\langle A|\mathcal{D}\rangle \subset \mathcal{K}$.

Thus in algebraic terms the realization of disturbance decoupling by state feedback amounts to the following.

Disturbance Decoupling Problem (DDP)

Given A: $\mathcal{X} \to \mathcal{X}$, B: $\mathcal{U} \to \mathcal{X}$, $\mathcal{D} \subset \mathcal{X}$, and $\mathcal{K} \subset \mathcal{X}$, find (if possible) F: $\mathcal{X} \to \mathcal{U}$ such that

$$\langle A+BF|\mathcal{D}\rangle \subset \mathcal{K}. \tag{4}$$

Observe that the subspace on the left in (4) is (A+BF)-invariant and, if (4) is true, belongs to $\mathcal{K}$. Intuitively, DDP will be solvable if and only if the 'largest' subspace having these properties contains $\mathcal{D}$. To make this remark precise we must introduce a new concept.

4.2 (A, B)-Invariant Subspaces

We say that a subspace $\mathcal{V} \subset \mathcal{X}$ is (A, B)-invariant if it is A-invariant (mod $\mathcal{B}$), i.e.,

$$A\mathcal{V} \subset \mathcal{V} + \mathcal{B}. \tag{5}$$

We denote the class of (A, B)-invariant subspaces of $\mathcal{X}$ by $\underline{\mathcal{J}}(A, B; \mathcal{X})$, or simply $\underline{\mathcal{J}}(\mathcal{X})$ when A and B are fixed in the discussion.

Observe that any A-invariant subspace is automatically (A, B)-invariant. The essential fact about an (A, B)-invariant subspace is that it can be made (A+BF)-invariant for a suitable choice of F.

LEMMA 4.2. Let $\mathcal{V} \subset \mathcal{X}$. There exists F: $\mathcal{X} \to \mathcal{U}$ such that

$$(A+BF)\mathcal{V} \subset \mathcal{V} \tag{6}$$

if and only if $\mathcal{V} \in \underline{\mathcal{J}}(A, B; \mathcal{X})$.

PROOF: If $v \in \mathcal{V}$, (6) implies $(A+BF)v = w$ for some $w \in \mathcal{V}$, or

$$Av = w - BFv \in \mathcal{V} + \mathcal{B}.$$

Conversely let $\{v_1, \ldots, v_\mu\}$ be a basis for $\mathcal{V}$. By (5) there exist $w_i \in \mathcal{V}$ and $u_i \in \mathcal{U}$ ($i \in \underline{\mu}$) such that

$$Av_i = w_i - Bu_i, \qquad i \in \underline{\mu}.$$

Define $F_0: \mathcal{V} \to \mathcal{U}$ by

$$F_0 v_i = u_i, \qquad i \in \underline{\mu},$$

and let F be any extension of F_0 to $\mathcal{X}$. ▮

If $\mathcal{V} \in \underline{\mathcal{I}}(A, B; \mathcal{X})$ we write $\underline{F}(A, B; \mathcal{V})$, or simply $\underline{F}(\mathcal{V})$, for the class of maps $F: \mathcal{X} \to \mathcal{U}$ such that $(A + BF)\mathcal{V} \subset \mathcal{V}$. From the proof of Lemma 4.2 we see that if $F \in \underline{F}(\mathcal{V})$ then $\tilde{F} \in \underline{F}(\mathcal{V})$ if and only if $(\tilde{F} - F)\mathcal{V} \subset B^{-1}\mathcal{V}$; in particular $(\tilde{F} - F) | \mathcal{V} = 0$ if B is monic and $\mathcal{B} \cap \mathcal{V} = 0$.

The following observation is not required for the solution of DDP, but will find application later.

PROPOSITION 4.1. *Let* (A, B) *be controllable and let* $\mathcal{V} \in \underline{\mathcal{I}}(A, B; \mathcal{X})$, *with* $d(\mathcal{V}) = \nu$. *If* $F_0 \in \underline{F}(A, B; \mathcal{V})$ *and* $\overline{\Lambda}$ *is a symmetric set of* $n - \nu$ *complex numbers, there exists* $F: \mathcal{X} \to \mathcal{U}$ *such that*

$$F | \mathcal{V} = F_0 | \mathcal{V} \tag{7}$$

and

$$\sigma(A + BF) = \sigma[(A + BF) | \mathcal{V}] \,\dot{\cup}\, \overline{\Lambda}.$$

PROOF: Let $P: \mathcal{X} \to \mathcal{X}/\mathcal{V}$ be the canonical projection, write

$$\overline{A}_0 = \overline{A + BF_0}$$

for the map induced by $A + BF_0$ in $\mathcal{X}/\mathcal{V}$, and let $\overline{B} \triangleq PB$. By Proposition 1.2 the pair $(\overline{A}_0, \overline{B})$ is controllable, hence by Theorem 2.1 there exists $\overline{F}_1: \mathcal{X}/\mathcal{V} \to \mathcal{U}$ such that

$$\sigma(\overline{A}_0 + \overline{B}\overline{F}_1) = \overline{\Lambda}.$$

Define

$$F \triangleq F_0 + \overline{F}_1 P.$$

Clearly (7) holds, so that $F \in \underline{F}(\mathcal{V})$. If $\overline{A}_F$ is the map induced in $\mathcal{X}/\mathcal{V}$ by $A + BF$ we have that $\overline{A}_F$ is defined uniquely by the relation $\overline{A}_F P = P(A + BF)$. But

$$(\overline{A}_0 + \overline{B}\overline{F}_1) P = P(A + BF_0) + PB\overline{F}_1 P = P(A + BF)$$

and therefore $\overline{A}_F = \overline{A}_0 + \overline{B}\overline{F}_1$. There follows

$$\sigma(A + BF) = \sigma[(A + BF) | \mathcal{V}] \,\dot{\cup}\, \sigma(\overline{A}_F) = \sigma[(A + BF) | \mathcal{V}] \,\dot{\cup}\, \overline{\Lambda} \quad \text{as claimed.}$$ ▮

The following closure property will be crucial.

LEMMA 4.3. <u>The class of subspaces $\underline{\mathcal{I}}(A, B; \mathcal{X})$ is closed under the operation of subspace addition.</u>

PROOF: From (5) it is clear that if $\mathcal{V}_1, \mathcal{V}_2 \in \underline{\mathcal{I}}(\mathcal{X})$ then

$$A(\mathcal{V}_1 + \mathcal{V}_2) = A\mathcal{V}_1 + A\mathcal{V}_2 \subset \mathcal{V}_1 + \mathcal{V}_2 + \mathcal{B},$$

hence $\mathcal{V}_1 + \mathcal{V}_2 \in \underline{\mathcal{I}}(\mathcal{X})$. ▌

Lemma 4.3 can be phrased more technically by saying that $\underline{\mathcal{I}}(A, B; \mathcal{X})$ is an upper semi-lattice relative to subspace inclusion and addition. But it is not true in general that the property of (A, B)-invariance is preserved by subspace intersection, and therefore $\underline{\mathcal{I}}(A, B; \mathcal{X})$ is not a sublattice of the lattice of all subspaces of $\mathcal{X}$.

If $\underline{\mathcal{V}}$ is a family of subspaces of $\mathcal{X}$, we define the <u>largest</u> or <u>supremal</u> element $\mathcal{V}^*$ of $\underline{\mathcal{V}}$ to be that member of $\underline{\mathcal{V}}$ (when it exists) which contains every member of $\underline{\mathcal{V}}$. Thus $\mathcal{V}^* \in \underline{\mathcal{V}}$, and if $\mathcal{V} \in \underline{\mathcal{V}}$ then $\mathcal{V} \subset \mathcal{V}^*$. It is clear that $\mathcal{V}^*$ is unique. We write

$$\mathcal{V}^* = \sup\{\mathcal{V}: \mathcal{V} \in \underline{\mathcal{V}}\},$$

or simply

$$\mathcal{V}^* = \sup \underline{\mathcal{V}}.$$

LEMMA 4.4. <u>Let $\underline{\mathcal{V}}$ be a nonempty class of subspaces of $\mathcal{X}$, closed under addition. Then $\underline{\mathcal{V}}$ contains a supremal element $\mathcal{V}^*$.</u>

PROOF: Appealing to the axiom of choice, construct a chain in $\underline{\mathcal{V}}$, of the form

$$\mathcal{V}_1 \subset \mathcal{V}_1 + \mathcal{V}_2 \subset \mathcal{V}_1 + \mathcal{V}_2 + \mathcal{V}_3 \subset \cdots,$$

where $\mathcal{V}_i \in \underline{\mathcal{V}}$ and each inclusion is strict. As $d(\mathcal{X}) < \infty$, and the sums increase in dimension by at least one at each stage, the chain cannot be continued beyond, say, k terms. Set $\mathcal{V}^* = \mathcal{V}_1 + \cdots + \mathcal{V}_k$. Clearly $\mathcal{V}^* \in \underline{\mathcal{V}}$, and $\mathcal{V}^*$ contains every $\mathcal{V} \in \underline{\mathcal{V}}$. ▌

Now let $\mathcal{K} \subset \mathcal{X}$ be arbitrary, and let $\underline{\mathcal{I}}(A, B; \mathcal{K})$ denote the subclass of (A, B)-invariant subspaces contained in $\mathcal{K}$:

$$\underline{\mathcal{I}}(A, B; \mathcal{K}) \triangleq \{\mathcal{V}: \mathcal{V} \in \underline{\mathcal{I}}(A, B; \mathcal{X}) \ \& \ \mathcal{V} \subset \mathcal{K}\}.$$

With A and B fixed, we write simply $\underline{\mathcal{I}}(\mathcal{K}) \triangleq \underline{\mathcal{I}}(A, B; \mathcal{K})$. Now trivially, $0 \in \underline{\mathcal{I}}(\mathcal{K})$, so $\underline{\mathcal{I}}(\mathcal{K}) \neq \emptyset$. Since $\mathcal{K}$ is a subspace, Lemma 4.3 implies that $\underline{\mathcal{I}}(\mathcal{K})$ is closed under addition. Then

Lemma 4.4 guarantees the existence of the supremal element

$$\mathcal{V}^* \triangleq \sup \underline{\mathcal{I}}(\mathcal{K}) .$$

This simple but fundamental result is important enough to state formally.

THEOREM 4.1. Let A: $\mathcal{X} \to \mathcal{X}$ and B: $\mathcal{U} \to \mathcal{X}$. Every subspace $\mathcal{K} \subset \mathcal{X}$ contains a unique supremal (A, B)-invariant subspace [written $\sup \underline{\mathcal{I}}(A, B; \mathcal{K})$, or simply $\sup \underline{\mathcal{I}}(\mathcal{K})$ when A, B are understood from context].

In order to give Theorem 4.1 a systemic interpretation we now return to the problem of disturbance decoupling introduced in Section 4.1.

4.3 Solution of DDP

From the preceding considerations there follows immediately

THEOREM 4.2. DDP is solvable if and only if

$$\mathcal{V}^* \supset \mathcal{S} , \tag{8}$$

where

$$\mathcal{V}^* \triangleq \sup \underline{\mathcal{I}}(A, B; \mathcal{K}) .$$

PROOF: (If) Choose, by Lemma 4.2, $F \in \underline{F}(\mathcal{V}^*)$, i.e., $(A + BF)\mathcal{V}^* \subset \mathcal{V}^*$. Using (8), we have

$$\langle A + BF | \mathcal{S} \rangle \subset \langle A + BF | \mathcal{V}^* \rangle = \mathcal{V}^* \subset \mathcal{K} .$$

(Only if) If F solves DDP, the subspace

$$\mathcal{V} \triangleq \langle A + BF | \mathcal{S} \rangle$$

clearly belongs to $\underline{\mathcal{I}}(\mathcal{K})$, and therefore

$$\mathcal{V}^* \supset \mathcal{V} \supset \mathcal{S} . \blacksquare$$

So far our approach to DDP has been somewhat abstract. To conclude this section we give an algorithm by which $\mathcal{V}^*$ can be computed efficiently in a finite number of steps. With $\mathcal{V}^*$ so determined, checking the condition (8) of Theorem 4.2 becomes trivial. If it is satisfied, any $F \in \underline{F}(\mathcal{V}^*)$ provides a solution to DDP, and such F is easy to construct, as in the proof of Lemma 4.2.

For the computation of $\mathcal{V}^*$ we have the following.

THEOREM 4.3. Let A: $\mathcal{X} \to \mathcal{X}$, B: $\mathcal{U} \to \mathcal{X}$, and $\mathcal{K} \subset \mathcal{X}$. Define the sequence $\mathcal{V}^\mu$ according to

$$\mathcal{V}^0 = \mathcal{K}$$
$$\mathcal{V}^\mu = \mathcal{K} \cap A^{-1}(\mathcal{B} + \mathcal{V}^{\mu-1}), \qquad \mu \in \underline{n} .$$

Then $\mathcal{V}^\mu \subset \mathcal{V}^{\mu-1}$, and for some $k \le d(\mathcal{K})$,

$$\mathcal{V}^k = \sup \underline{\mathcal{I}}(A, B; \mathcal{K}) .$$

PROOF: Recall the properties of the function A^{-1} (Section 0.4). We first observe that $\mathcal{V}^\mu \downarrow$, i.e., the sequence $\mathcal{V}^\mu$ is nonincreasing: clearly $\mathcal{V}^1 \subset \mathcal{V}^0$, and if $\mathcal{V}^\mu \subset \mathcal{V}^{\mu-1}$, then

$$\mathcal{V}^{\mu+1} = \mathcal{K} \cap A^{-1}(\mathcal{B} + \mathcal{V}^\mu) \subset \mathcal{K} \cap A^{-1}(\mathcal{B} + \mathcal{V}^{\mu-1}) = \mathcal{V}^\mu .$$

Thus for some $k \le d(\mathcal{K})$, $\mathcal{V}^\mu = \mathcal{V}^k$ $(\mu \ge k)$. Now $\mathcal{V} \in \underline{\mathcal{I}}(\mathcal{K})$ if and only if

$$\mathcal{V} \subset \mathcal{K}, \qquad \mathcal{V} \subset A^{-1}(\mathcal{V} + \mathcal{B}) . \tag{9}$$

From (9), $\mathcal{V} \subset \mathcal{V}^0$, and if $\mathcal{V} \subset \mathcal{V}^{\mu-1}$,

$$\mathcal{V} \subset \mathcal{K} \cap A^{-1}(\mathcal{V} + \mathcal{B}) \subset \mathcal{K} \cap A^{-1}(\mathcal{V}^{\mu-1} + \mathcal{B}) = \mathcal{V}^\mu .$$

Therefore $\mathcal{V} \subset \mathcal{V}^k \in \underline{\mathcal{I}}(\mathcal{K})$, and as $\mathcal{V}$ was arbitrary the result follows. ▮

Theorems 4.2 and 4.3 furnish a constructive solution to the disturbance decoupling problem. But it should be pointed out that condition (8) is quite special, and cannot be satisfied generically in the space of data points (A, B, D, E) (Ex. 4.8). For this reason complete disturbance decoupling is typically not possible in practice. Even if DDP is solvable, we have no guarantee that state feedback F can be chosen to satisfy additional reasonable requirements, for example, that A + BF be stable. Nonetheless, the results of Theorems 4.2 and 4.3 will be of considerable value in various applications later, where generic solvability can be demonstrated. Also, a more realistic version of DDP will be solved by use of controllability subspaces in Chapter 5.

We turn now to an application of greater practical interest in its own right.

4.4 Output Stabilization Problem (OSP)

Consider the system

$$\dot{x} = Ax + Bu , \qquad t \ge 0 ,$$
$$z = Dx , \qquad t \ge 0 . \tag{10}$$

We pose the problem of stabilizing the output $z(\cdot)$ by means of state feedback: precisely, in terms of the triple (D, A, B) find conditions for the existence of state feedback F such that

$$De^{t(A+BF)} \to 0, \qquad t \to \infty. \tag{11}$$

More generally, we may seek F such that the characteristic exponents of the time function of (11) belong to a 'good' subset $\mathbb{C}_g \subset \mathbb{C}$. Our problem is thus to generalize the condition of Theorem 2.2.

We begin by translating the systems problem into purely algebraic terms. For arbitrary $F: \mathcal{X} \to \mathcal{U}$, write

$$\mathcal{N}_F \triangleq \bigcap_{i=1}^{n} \operatorname{Ker}[D(A+BF)^{i-1}].$$

Since $\mathcal{N}_F$ is the unobservable subspace of the pair $(D, A+BF)$, it is almost obvious that the exponents which appear in $De^{t(A+BF)}$ are simply the eigenvalues of the map $\overline{A+BF}$ induced by $A+BF$ in $\overline{\mathcal{X}} \triangleq \mathcal{X}/\mathcal{N}_F$. To justify this remark, recall from Lemma 3.2 that $(\overline{D}, \overline{A+BF})$ is observable. Introduce the complexifications $\mathcal{X}_{\mathbb{C}}$ and $\mathcal{Z}_{\mathbb{C}}$ of $\mathcal{X}$ and $\mathcal{Z}$, and suppose $\lambda \in \sigma(\overline{A+BF})$. Then $\overline{A+BF}\,\overline{x}_0 = \lambda \overline{x}_0$ for some $\overline{x}_0 \in \overline{\mathcal{X}}_{\mathbb{C}}$, $\overline{x}_0 \neq \overline{0}$. With $u = Fx$ in (10), we have

$$\dot{\overline{x}}(t) = \overline{A+BF}\,\overline{x}(t), \qquad t \geq 0,$$

so if $\overline{x}(0) = \overline{x}_0$ there results

$$z(t) = \overline{D}e^{\lambda t}\overline{x}_0, \qquad t \geq 0.$$

It is clear that $z(\cdot)$ is identically zero only if there is a nontrivial $\overline{A+BF}$-invariant subspace in $\operatorname{Ker} \overline{D}$, namely $\operatorname{Span}\{\overline{x}_0\}$; and observability rules this out. So, the exponents which appear in $De^{t(A+BF)}$ all belong to $\mathbb{C}_g$ if and only if

$$\sigma(\overline{A+BF}) \subset \mathbb{C}_g, \tag{12}$$

as claimed.

Now revert to the usual setting with field $\mathbb{R}$. To express (12) in a more geometric form we shall need

LEMMA 4.5. Let $\mathcal{S} \subset \mathcal{X}$, $A\mathcal{S} \subset \mathcal{S}$, and $\overline{\mathcal{X}} = \mathcal{X}/\mathcal{S}$. Let $P: \mathcal{X} \to \overline{\mathcal{X}}$ be the canonical projection, and $\overline{A}$ the map induced by A in $\overline{\mathcal{X}}$. Then $\sigma(\overline{A}) \subset \mathbb{C}_g$ if and only if $\mathcal{X}_b(A) \subset \mathcal{S}$.

PROOF: (If) Let $\overline{x} \in \overline{\mathcal{X}}$. Then

$$\alpha_g(\bar{A})\bar{x} = \alpha_g(\bar{A})Px = P\alpha_g(A)x \in P \operatorname{Ker} \alpha_b(A) \subset P\mathscr{S} = \bar{0}\ .$$

Thus the m.p. of $\bar{A}$ divides α_g; that is, $\sigma(\bar{A}) \subset \mathbb{C}_g$.

(Only if) Let $x \in \mathscr{X}_b(A) \triangleq \operatorname{Ker} \alpha_b(A)$. For suitable polynomials μ, ν we have

$$x = \mu(A)\alpha_g(A)x + \nu(A)\alpha_b(A)x = \mu(A)\alpha_g(A)x$$

and so $\bar{x} = Px = \mu(\bar{A})\alpha_g(\bar{A})\bar{x}$. But $\sigma(\bar{A}) \subset \mathbb{C}_g$ implies that the m.p. $\bar{\alpha}$ of $\bar{A}$ is a divisor of α_g. Thus $\alpha_g(\bar{A})\bar{x} = \bar{0}$, so that $Px = \bar{0}$, i.e., $x \in \mathscr{S}$. ▮

Applying Lemma 4.5 to A + BF and with $\mathscr{N}_F$ in place of $\mathscr{S}$, we see that (12) is true if and only if

$$\mathscr{X}_b(A + BF) \subset \mathscr{N}_F\ . \tag{13}$$

Observe finally that $\mathscr{X}_b(A + BF)$ is an (A + BF)-invariant subspace of Ker D, whereas $\mathscr{N}_F$ is the <u>largest</u> (A + BF)-invariant subspace of Ker D. Therefore, (13) can hold if and only if $\mathscr{X}_b(A + BF) \subset \operatorname{Ker} D$. On this basis we can state our original, generalized problem as follows:

<u>Given the maps</u> A: $\mathscr{X} \to \mathscr{X}$, B: $\mathscr{U} \to \mathscr{X}$, <u>and</u> D: $\mathscr{X} \to \mathscr{Z}$, <u>together with a symmetric partition</u> $\mathbb{C} = \mathbb{C}_g \dot{\cup} \mathbb{C}_b$, <u>find</u> F: $\mathscr{X} \to \mathscr{U}$ <u>such that</u>

$$\mathscr{X}_b(A + BF) \subset \operatorname{Ker} D\ . \tag{14}$$

We shall refer to the foregoing as the <u>Output Stabilization Problem</u> (<u>OSP</u>). Here 'stabilization' is to be understood in the general sense indicated.

THEOREM 4.4. <u>OSP is solvable if and only if</u>

$$\mathscr{X}_b(A) \subset \langle A|\mathscr{B}\rangle + \mathscr{V}^*\ , \tag{15}$$

<u>where</u>

$$\mathscr{V}^* \triangleq \sup \underline{\mathscr{I}}(A, B;\ \operatorname{Ker} D)\ .$$

Intuitively, (15) states that 'the bad modes of A are either controllable, or unobservable at the output'. In view of Theorem 4.2 the condition is entirely constructive.

For the proof we shall need

LEMMA 4.6. <u>Let</u> $\mathscr{V}$ <u>be any subspace such that</u> $A\mathscr{V} \subset \mathscr{V}$; <u>write</u> $\bar{\mathscr{X}} = \mathscr{X}/\mathscr{V}$; <u>let</u> P: $\mathscr{X} \to \mathscr{X}/\mathscr{V}$ <u>be the canonical projection; write</u> $\bar{A}$ <u>for the map induced in</u> $\bar{\mathscr{X}}$; <u>and relative to</u> $\bar{A}$ <u>define</u> $\bar{\alpha}_b, \bar{\mathscr{X}}_b(\bar{A})$ <u>etc. as in Section 2.3. Then</u>

$$\bar{\mathscr{X}}_b(\bar{A}) = P\mathscr{X}_b(A) .$$

PROOF: Let $Px \in \bar{\mathscr{X}}_b(\bar{A})$. Since $\bar{\mathscr{X}}_b(\bar{A}) = \operatorname{Ker} \bar{\alpha}_b(\bar{A})$, we have

$$P\bar{\alpha}_b(A)x = \bar{\alpha}_b(\bar{A})Px = \bar{0} ;$$

so $\bar{\alpha}_b(A)x \in \mathscr{V}$. As $\bar{\alpha}_b(\lambda) | \alpha_b(\lambda)$ there follows $\alpha_b(A)x \in \mathscr{V}$. Now

$$x = \rho(A)\alpha_g(A)x + \sigma(A)\alpha_b(A)x$$

for suitable $\rho, \sigma \in \mathbb{R}[\lambda]$. Since

$$\rho(A)\alpha_g(A)x \in \operatorname{Ker}\alpha_b(A) , \qquad \sigma(A)\alpha_b(A)x \in \mathscr{V} ,$$

we have

$$Px \in P \operatorname{Ker}\alpha_b(A)$$

and therefore $\bar{\mathscr{X}}_b(\bar{A}) \subset P\mathscr{X}_b(A)$.

For the reverse inclusion let $x \in \mathscr{X}_b(A)$, so that $\alpha_b(A)x = 0$, and if $\bar{x} = Px$,

$$\alpha_b(\bar{A})\bar{x} = P\alpha_b(A)x = \bar{0} . \tag{16}$$

If the m.p. of $\bar{x}$ relative to $\bar{A}$ is $\bar{\xi} = \bar{\xi}_b\bar{\xi}_g$ then (16) implies $\bar{\xi}_b\bar{\xi}_g | \alpha_b$, hence $\bar{\xi}_g = 1$, that is, $\bar{\xi} | \bar{\alpha}_b$. Therefore, $\bar{\alpha}_b(\bar{A})\bar{x} = \bar{0}$, or

$$\bar{x} = Px \in \bar{\mathscr{X}}_b(\bar{A}) . \ \blacksquare$$

PROOF of Theorem 4.4: Clearly $\mathscr{N}_F \in \underline{\mathscr{I}}(\operatorname{Ker} D)$ and therefore $\mathscr{N}_F \subset \mathscr{V}^*$ for all F. Write

$$\mathscr{S} \triangleq \langle A | \mathscr{B} \rangle + \mathscr{V}^* .$$

Since $\langle A | \mathscr{B} \rangle = \langle A + BF | \mathscr{B} \rangle$ for all F, and $A\mathscr{V}^* \subset \mathscr{V}^* + \mathscr{B}$, we have

$$(A + BF)\mathscr{S} \subset \mathscr{S}$$

for all F. Thus for every F the diagram (17) commutes. In (17) the vertical arrows represent canonical projections and bars denote the induced maps (cf. Ex. 0.10).

$$
\begin{array}{ccc}
\mathscr{X} & \xrightarrow{A+BF} & \mathscr{X} \\
\downarrow & & \downarrow \\
\mathscr{X}/\mathscr{N}_F & \xrightarrow{\overline{A+BF}} & \mathscr{X}/\mathscr{N}_F \\
\downarrow & & \downarrow \\
\mathscr{X}/\mathscr{S} & \xrightarrow{\overline{\overline{A+BF}}} & \mathscr{X}/\mathscr{S}
\end{array}
\tag{17}
$$

Let Q: $\mathscr{X} \to \mathscr{X}/\mathscr{S}$ be the canonical projection. The map $\overline{\overline{A+BF}}$ is uniquely determined by the relation

$$\overline{\overline{A+BF}}\, Q = Q(A+BF) = QA \ .$$

As $\bar{\bar{A}}Q = QA$, we therefore have

$$\overline{\overline{A+BF}} = \bar{\bar{A}}$$

for all F.

Now suppose OSP is solvable, so that (14), and hence (13), hold for some F. This with Lemma 4.6 yields

$$Q\mathscr{X}_b(A) = \bar{\bar{\mathscr{X}}}_b(\bar{\bar{A}}) = \bar{\bar{\mathscr{X}}}_b(\overline{\overline{A+BF}}) = Q\mathscr{X}_b(A+BF) \subset Q\mathscr{N}_F = \bar{\bar{0}} \ ,$$

so that $\mathscr{X}_b(A) \subset \operatorname{Ker} Q = \mathscr{S}$, as claimed.

Conversely, suppose (15) holds, that is, $\mathscr{X}_b(A) \subset \mathscr{S}$. Choose F_0 arbitrarily such that $(A+BF_0)\mathscr{V}^* \subset \mathscr{V}^*$, and consider the diagram (17) with F_0 in place of F. Application of Lemma 4.6 as before yields

$$Q\mathscr{X}_b(A+BF_0) = \bar{\bar{\mathscr{X}}}_b(\overline{\overline{A+BF_0}}) = \bar{\bar{\mathscr{X}}}_b(\bar{\bar{A}}) = Q\mathscr{X}_b(A) \subset Q\mathscr{S} = \bar{\bar{0}} \ ,$$

hence $\mathscr{X}_b(A+BF_0) \subset \operatorname{Ker} Q = \mathscr{S}$. Let P: $\mathscr{X} \to \mathscr{X}/\mathscr{V}^*$ be the canonical projection and note that

$$\mathscr{V}^* = \bigcap_{i=1}^{n} (A+BF_0)^{-i+1} \operatorname{Ker} D = \mathscr{N}_{F_0} \ .$$

Thus, we have

$$
\begin{aligned}
\bar{\mathscr{X}}_b(\overline{A+BF_0}) &= P\mathscr{X}_b(A+BF_0) \subset P(\langle A \,|\, \mathscr{B}\rangle + \mathscr{V}^*) \\
&= P\langle A \,|\, \mathscr{B}\rangle = P\langle A+BF_0 \,|\, \mathscr{B}\rangle = \langle \overline{A+BF_0} \,|\, \bar{\mathscr{B}}\rangle \ ,
\end{aligned}
\tag{18}
$$

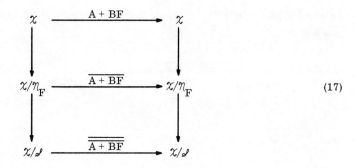

where $\overline{\mathcal{B}} \triangleq \operatorname{Im}\overline{B} = \operatorname{Im}(PB)$. Theorem 2.2 with (18) now implies the existence of $\overline{F}_1: \mathcal{X}/\mathcal{V}^* \to \mathcal{U}$ such that

$$\sigma(\overline{A+BF_0} + \overline{B}\,\overline{F}_1) \subset \mathbb{C}_g$$

or

$$\overline{\mathcal{X}}_b(\overline{A+BF_0} + \overline{B}\,\overline{F}_1) = \overline{0} \ . \tag{19}$$

Let $F_1 = \overline{F}_1 P$ and $F = F_0 + F_1$. Then

$$(\overline{A+BF_0} + \overline{B}\,\overline{F}_1)\,P = P(A+BF) \ ,$$

and by uniqueness of the induced map there follows

$$\overline{A+BF_0} + \overline{B}\,\overline{F}_1 = \overline{A+BF} \ . \tag{20}$$

By (19), (20), and Lemma 4.6 there results

$$P\mathcal{X}_b(A+BF) = \overline{\mathcal{X}}_b(\overline{A+BF}) = \overline{0} \ ,$$

and so

$$\mathcal{X}_b(A+BF) \subset \operatorname{Ker} P = \mathcal{V}^* \subset \operatorname{Ker} D$$

as required. ▮

Remark 1.

In Theorem 2.2 we had, in effect, $D = 1$ and $\operatorname{Ker} D = 0$; thus Theorem 4.4 is the generalization promised at the beginning of this section.

Remark 2.

Whereas (15) is a weaker condition than that of Theorem 2.2 it guarantees only that the output $z(\cdot)$ is well-behaved: nothing is said about $(A+BF)\,|\,\mathcal{N}_F$, the system map on the unobservable subspace, and this map could, for instance, be unstable. In Chapter 5, we shall see how further stability requirements can be accommodated.

4.5 Exercises

4.1 Give an example to show that if $\mathcal{V}_1, \mathcal{V}_2$ are (A, B)-invariant, $\mathcal{V}_1 \cap \mathcal{V}_2$ need not be. HINT: Take $d(\mathcal{X}) = 3$, $d(\mathcal{B}) = 1$, $d(\mathcal{V}_i) = 2$ $(i \in \underline{2})$. Thus A, B have matrices of size 3×3, 3×1; and $\mathcal{V}_i = \operatorname{Im} V_i$, with V_i of size 3×2. A random assignment of values to the 24 entries of these matrices will almost surely satisfy the problem conditions. Why?

4.2 Develop a procedure for the numerical computation of $\mathcal{V}^* = \sup \underline{\mathfrak{I}}(A, B; \operatorname{Ker} D)$. HINT: Write in matrix format the algorithm of Theorem 4.3; the ingredients are obtained from Ex. 0.11. The following terminology will be useful: if M, X, Y are matrices, with M given, a <u>maximal solution</u> of the equation $MX = 0$ (resp. $YM = 0$) is a solution X (resp. Y) of maximal rank, having linearly independent columns (resp. rows) when it is not the zero column (resp. row). With reference to Theorem 4.3, setting $\mathcal{K} = \operatorname{Ker} D$, let $\mathcal{V}^{\mu} = \operatorname{Im} V_{\mu}$, with V_0 a max. sol. of $DV_0 = 0$. Let W_{μ} be a max. sol. of

$$W_{\mu}[B, V_{\mu-1}] = 0\,, \qquad \mu = 1, 2, \ldots\,;$$

and obtain V_{μ} as a max. sol. of

$$\begin{bmatrix} D \\ W_{\mu}A \end{bmatrix} V_{\mu} = 0\,, \qquad \mu = 1, 2, \ldots\,.$$

At each stage one has $\mathcal{V}^{\mu} \subset \mathcal{V}^{\mu-1}$, i.e. (as a check),

$$\operatorname{Rank}[V_{\mu-1}, V_{\mu}] = \operatorname{Rank} V_{\mu-1}\,;$$

and the stopping rule is $\mathcal{V}_{\mu} = \mathcal{V}_{\mu-1}$, i.e.,

$$\operatorname{Rank} V_{\mu} = \operatorname{Rank} V_{\mu-1}\,.$$

As an illustration, let

$$A = \begin{bmatrix} 0 & 1 & 0 & 0 & 0 \\ 0 & 0 & 1 & 0 & 0 \\ 0 & 0 & 0 & 0 & 0 \\ 0 & 0 & 0 & 0 & 1 \\ 0 & 0 & 0 & 0 & 0 \end{bmatrix}, \qquad B = \begin{bmatrix} 0 & 0 \\ 0 & 0 \\ 1 & 0 \\ 0 & 1 \\ 0 & 0 \end{bmatrix}, \qquad D = \begin{bmatrix} 1 & 0 & 0 & 0 & 0 \\ 0 & 0 & 0 & 1 & 0 \end{bmatrix}.$$

This gives

$$V_0 = \begin{bmatrix} 0 & 0 & 0 \\ 1 & 0 & 0 \\ 0 & 1 & 0 \\ 0 & 0 & 0 \\ 0 & 0 & 1 \end{bmatrix}, \qquad W_1 = \begin{bmatrix} 1 & 0 & 0 & 0 & 0 \end{bmatrix},$$

$$V_1 = \begin{bmatrix} 0 & 0 \\ 0 & 0 \\ 1 & 0 \\ 0 & 0 \\ 0 & 1 \end{bmatrix}, \qquad W_2 = \begin{bmatrix} 1 & 0 & 0 & 0 & 0 \\ 0 & 1 & 0 & 0 & 0 \end{bmatrix},$$

$$V_2 = \begin{bmatrix} 0 \\ 0 \\ 0 \\ 0 \\ 1 \end{bmatrix}, \qquad W_3 = \begin{bmatrix} 1 & 0 & 0 & 0 & 0 \\ 0 & 1 & 0 & 0 & 0 \end{bmatrix},$$

and $\operatorname{Im} V_3 = \operatorname{Im} V_2$; i.e., $\mathcal{V}^* = \mathcal{V}^2 = \operatorname{Im} V_2$.

4.3 Construct a numerical example (say with $n = 5$, $m = 2$, $p = 3$) to illustrate the application of Theorems 4.2 and 4.3. Draw the signal flow graph and indicate the feedback branches. HINT: Let

$$A = \begin{bmatrix} 0 & 1 & 0 & 0 & 0 \\ 0 & 0 & 1 & 0 & 0 \\ 0 & 0 & 0 & 0 & 0 \\ 0 & 0 & 0 & 1 & 0 \\ 0 & 0 & 0 & 0 & 0 \end{bmatrix}, \qquad B = \begin{bmatrix} 0 & 0 \\ 0 & 0 \\ 1 & 0 \\ 0 & 0 \\ 0 & 1 \end{bmatrix}$$

$$D = \begin{bmatrix} 1 & 0 & 0 & -1 & 0 \\ 1 & -1 & 0 & 0 & 0 \\ 0 & 0 & 0 & 1 & -1 \end{bmatrix}, \qquad E = \begin{bmatrix} 1 \\ 1 \\ 1 \\ 1 \\ 1 \end{bmatrix}.$$

Verify that $\mathcal{V}^* = \operatorname{Im} E$, and that

$$F = \begin{bmatrix} 0 & 0 & 1 & 0 & 0 \\ 0 & 0 & 0 & 0 & 1 \end{bmatrix} \in \underline{F}(\mathcal{V}^*)$$

is a solution. Note that since $\mathcal{B} \cap \mathcal{V}^* = 0$ and B is monic, all solutions F coincide on $\mathcal{V}^*$; furthermore, $\sigma[(A+BF)|\mathcal{V}^*] = \{1\}$, i.e., disturbance decoupling is only obtained at the price of instability.

4.4 Construct an example to illustrate the application of Theorem 4.4 and also that $\sigma[(A+BF)|\mathcal{N}_F]$ may necessarily be bad. HINT: The example in Ex. 4.2 will serve.

4.5 Show that $(D, A+BF)$ is observable for all F if and only if $\sup \underline{\mathcal{J}}(A, B; \operatorname{Ker} D) = 0$.

4.6 Problem of perfect tracking. Prove that

$$\mathcal{T}^* \triangleq \mathcal{B} \cap A^{-1}\mathcal{B}$$

is the largest subspace of $\mathcal{X}$ such that

$$A\mathcal{T} + \mathcal{T} \subset \mathcal{B} .$$

From this show that if $r(\cdot)$ is continuously differentiable, $r(t) \in \mathcal{T}^*$ for all $t \geq 0$, and $x(0) = r(0)$, there exists a continuous control $u(t)$, $t \geq 0$, such that $x(t) = r(t)$, $t \geq 0$, where

$$\dot{x}(t) = Ax(t) + Bu(t) .$$

Furthermore, $\mathcal{T}^*$ is the largest subspace of $\mathcal{X}$ with this property.

4.7 Let $A\mathcal{N} \subset \mathcal{N}$. Show that there exists $F: \mathcal{X} \to \mathcal{U}$ such that $\mathcal{X}^+(A+BF) \subset \mathcal{N} \cap \operatorname{Ker} F$, if and only if

$$\mathcal{X}^+(A) \subset \langle A | \mathcal{B} \rangle + \mathcal{N} .$$

With the help of this result solve the following: Given $D: \mathcal{X} \to \mathcal{Z}$ and the system $\dot{x} = Ax + Bu$, $z = Dx$, find a necessary and sufficient condition for the existence of $F: \mathcal{X} \to \mathcal{U}$ such that, if $u = Fx$, then $z(t) \to 0$ and $u(t) \to 0$ $(t \to \infty)$ for every initial state $x(0)$.

4.8 Verify that DDP is not generically solvable (in fact is generically unsolvable!) in the space of data points (A, B, D, E). HINT: Note that DDP is solvable only if $DE = 0$. What can be said if D and E are fixed, $DE = 0$, and the data point is (A, B)?

4.9 System invertibility. Let $H(\lambda)$ be the transfer matrix (Section 0.17) of the complete triple (C, A, B), where C: $p \times n$ and B: $n \times m$, with $p \geq m$. Show that, as a matrix over the field $\mathbb{R}(\lambda)$, $H(\lambda)$ has a left inverse, if and only if B is monic and the subspace

$$\operatorname{Im} B \cap \sup \underline{\mathcal{J}}(A, B; \operatorname{Ker} C) = 0 .$$

What are the dual statement and conditions, in case $m \geq p$? HINT: Consider

$$y(t) = \int_0^t Ce^{(t-\tau)A} Bu(\tau)\, d\tau$$

with u(·) analytic. Under what conditions does the vanishing of $y'(0), y''(0), \ldots$, imply that of $u(0), u'(0), \ldots$?

4.10 Consider the system

$$\dot{x} = Ax + Bu \,, \qquad z = Dx + Eu$$

and the family of subspaces

$$\underline{\mathcal{V}} \triangleq \{\mathcal{V}: \mathcal{V} \subset \mathcal{X} \;\;\&\;\; \exists F: \mathcal{X} \to \mathcal{U}, (A+BF)\mathcal{V} \subset \mathcal{V} \subset \operatorname{Ker}(D+EF)\} \,.$$

Show that $\underline{\mathcal{V}}$ is closed under addition, and compute its supremal element. HINT: Take the external direct sum $\mathcal{X} \oplus \mathcal{Z}$ and define the maps

$$A_e \triangleq \begin{bmatrix} A & 0 \\ D & 0 \end{bmatrix}: \mathcal{X} \oplus \mathcal{Z} \to \mathcal{X} \oplus \mathcal{Z}, \qquad B_e \triangleq \begin{bmatrix} B \\ E \end{bmatrix}: \mathcal{U} \to \mathcal{X} \oplus \mathcal{Z} \,.$$

Now consider $\underline{\mathcal{I}}(A_e, B_e; \mathcal{X})$.
How could you exploit the alternative approach indicated in Section 0.16?

4.11 Show that in the algorithm of Theorem 4.3, A can be replaced by A + BF, for any F, without changing the result. HINT: For all F,

$$\underline{\mathcal{I}}(A+BF, B; \mathcal{K}) = \underline{\mathcal{I}}(A, B; \mathcal{K}).$$

4.6 Notes and References

The idea of (A, B)-invariant subspace and results equivalent to Theorems 4.2 and 4.3 were discovered independently by Basile and Marro [2], [3], and by Wonham and Morse [1]. The treatment of output stabilization is adapted from Bhattacharyya, Pearson, and Wonham [1]. The tracking problem of Ex. 4.6 is taken from Basile and Marro [1], and the results of Ex. 4.7 are due to Bhattacharyya [1]. The geometric significance of system invertibility (Ex. 4.9) has been pointed out by Silverman and Payne [1]. For further information related to Ex. 4.10 see Morse [1].

CHAPTER 5

CONTROLLABILITY SUBSPACES

Given a system pair (A, B) we consider all pairs (A + BF, BG) which can be formed by means of state feedback F and the connection of a 'gain' matrix G at the system input (Fig. 5.1). The controllable subspace of (A + BF, BG) is called a controllability subspace (c.s.) of the original pair (A, B). The family of c.s. of a fixed pair (A, B) is a subfamily, in general proper, of the (A, B)-invariant subspaces: the importance of c.s. derives from the fact that the restriction of A + BF to an (A + BF)-invariant c.s. can be assigned an arbitrary spectrum by suitable choice of F.

For the single-input system corresponding to a pair (A, b) the family of c.s. obviously comprises simply 0 and $\langle A \mid b \rangle$. However, in the multi-input situation, where $d(\mathcal{B}) \geq 2$, the family of c.s. is in general nontrivial. This fact, together with the spectral assignability already mentioned, indicates that c.s. is a central geometric concept in the state space theory of linear multivariable control.

This chapter is devoted to the basic properties of c.s.; the main applications, to tracking, regulation and noninteraction, are treated in the chapters to follow.

5.1 Controllability Subspaces

Let A: $\mathcal{X} \to \mathcal{X}$ and B: $\mathcal{U} \to \mathcal{X}$. A subspace $\mathcal{R} \subset \mathcal{X}$ is a controllability subspace (c.s.) of the pair (A, B) if there exist maps F: $\mathcal{X} \to \mathcal{U}$ and G: $\mathcal{U} \to \mathcal{U}$ such that

$$\mathcal{R} = \langle A + BF \mid \mathrm{Im}(BG) \rangle . \tag{1}$$

Thus $\mathcal{R}$ is precisely the controllable subspace of the pair (A + BF, BG). We adopt the notation $\underline{\mathcal{C}}(A, B; \mathcal{X})$, or simply $\underline{\mathcal{C}}(\mathcal{X})$, for the class of c.s. of (A, B).

The appearance of G in (1) is eliminated by use of the following observation.

PROPOSITION 5.1. If $\hat{\mathcal{B}} \subset \mathcal{B}$ and $\langle A \mid \hat{\mathcal{B}} \rangle = \mathcal{R}$ then $\langle A \mid \mathcal{B} \cap \mathcal{R} \rangle = \mathcal{R}$. Conversely if $\langle A \mid \mathcal{B} \cap \mathcal{R} \rangle = \mathcal{R}$, there exists G: $\mathcal{U} \to \mathcal{U}$ such that

$$\langle A \mid \mathrm{Im}(BG) \rangle = \mathcal{R} .$$

PROOF: If $\langle A \mid \hat{\mathcal{B}} \rangle = \mathcal{R}$ then $\hat{\mathcal{B}} \subset \mathcal{R}$, i.e., $\hat{\mathcal{B}} \subset \mathcal{B} \cap \mathcal{R}$, so

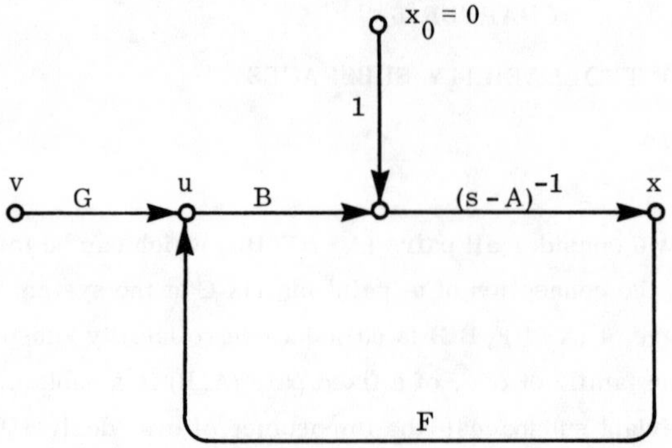

Fig. 5.1.

Controllability Subspace:
$\mathcal{R} = \langle A + BF \mid \operatorname{Im}(BG) \rangle$ is the subspace of states $x(1)$ generated by allowing $v(\cdot)$ to vary over (say) all continuous inputs defined for $0 \le t \le 1$, with $x(0) = 0$.

$$\mathcal{R} = \langle A | \hat{\mathcal{B}} \rangle \subset \langle A | \mathcal{B} \cap \mathcal{R} \rangle .$$

Clearly $A\mathcal{R} \subset \mathcal{R}$, hence $\langle A | \mathcal{B} \cap \mathcal{R} \rangle \subset \mathcal{R}$, and so

$$\langle A | \mathcal{B} \cap \mathcal{R} \rangle = \mathcal{R} .$$

For the converse let $\{b_1, \dots, b_r\}$ be a basis for $\mathcal{B} \cap \mathcal{R}$. Then $b_i = Bu_i$ ($u_i \in \mathcal{U}$), where the u_i ($i \in \underline{r}$) are independent. Let $\{u_1, \dots, u_m\}$ be a basis for $\mathcal{U}$, and define

$$Gu_i = u_i , \qquad i \in \underline{r} ,$$

$$Gu_i = 0 , \qquad i = r+1, \dots, m .$$

Then $\mathrm{Im}(BG) = \mathcal{B} \cap \mathcal{R}$. ▌

As an immediate consequence, we have

PROPOSITION 5.2. <u>A subspace</u> $\mathcal{R}$ <u>belongs to</u> $\underline{\mathcal{C}}(A, B; \mathcal{X})$ <u>if and only if there exists a map</u> F: $\mathcal{X} \to \mathcal{U}$ <u>such that</u>

$$\mathcal{R} = \langle A + BF | \mathcal{B} \cap \mathcal{R} \rangle .$$

Recall the notation $\underline{F}(A, B; \mathcal{J})$, or $\underline{F}(\mathcal{J})$, for the class of maps F: $\mathcal{X} \to \mathcal{U}$ such that $(A + BF)\mathcal{J} \subset \mathcal{J}$. Thus $\underline{F}(\mathcal{J}) \neq \emptyset$ if and only if $\mathcal{J}$ is (A, B)-invariant. If $\mathcal{R} \in \underline{\mathcal{C}}(A, B; \mathcal{X})$ clearly $\underline{F}(\mathcal{R}) \neq \emptyset$, and we have

PROPOSITION 5.3. <u>If</u> $\mathcal{R} \in \underline{\mathcal{C}}(A, B; \mathcal{X})$ <u>then</u>

$$\mathcal{R} = \langle A + BF | \mathcal{B} \cap \mathcal{R} \rangle$$

<u>for every map</u> $F \in \underline{F}(\mathcal{R})$.

PROOF: By Proposition 5.2 there is a map F_0: $\mathcal{X} \to \mathcal{U}$ such that

$$\mathcal{R} = \langle A + BF_0 | \mathcal{B} \cap \mathcal{R} \rangle .$$

Clearly $F_0 \in \underline{F}(\mathcal{R})$. Let $F_1 \in \underline{F}(\mathcal{R})$ and write

$$\mathcal{R}_1 \triangleq \langle A + BF_1 | \mathcal{B} \cap \mathcal{R} \rangle . \qquad (2)$$

Then $\mathcal{R}_1 \subset \mathcal{R}$. For the reverse inclusion suppose

$$(A+BF_0)^{i-1}(\mathcal{B}\cap\mathcal{R})\subset\mathcal{R}_1, \qquad i\in\underline{k}, \tag{3}$$

for some $k\in\underline{n}$. With (3) as induction hypothesis, we have

$$\begin{aligned}\sum_{i=1}^{k+1}(A+BF_0)^{i-1}(\mathcal{B}\cap\mathcal{R}) &= \mathcal{B}\cap\mathcal{R}+(A+BF_0)\sum_{i=1}^{k}(A+BF_0)^{i-1}(\mathcal{B}\cap\mathcal{R})\\ &\subset \mathcal{B}\cap\mathcal{R}+(A+BF_0)\mathcal{R}_1\\ &= \mathcal{B}\cap\mathcal{R}+[A+BF_1+B(F_0-F_1)]\mathcal{R}_1\\ &\subset \mathcal{B}\cap\mathcal{R}+(A+BF_1)\mathcal{R}_1+B(F_0-F_1)\mathcal{R}_1 .\end{aligned} \tag{4}$$

Let $x\in\mathcal{R}_1$. Then $B(F_0-F_1)x\in\mathcal{B}$ and, since $\mathcal{R}_1\subset\mathcal{R}$,

$$B(F_0-F_1)x=(A+BF_0)x-(A+BF_1)x\in\mathcal{R}.$$

Hence the subspace on the right in (4) is contained in

$$\mathcal{B}\cap\mathcal{R}+(A+BF_1)\mathcal{R}_1\subset\mathcal{R}_1 . \tag{5}$$

By (4) and (5)

$$(A+BF_0)^k(\mathcal{B}\cap\mathcal{R})\subset\mathcal{R}_1 .$$

Since (2) implies that (3) is true for $k=1$, we have that (3) is true for $k\in\underline{n}$, hence $\mathcal{R}\subset\mathcal{R}_1$. ▌

The foregoing result provides a way of checking whether a given subspace $\mathcal{R}\subset\mathcal{X}$ is a c.s.: Verify first that $\mathcal{R}\in\underline{\mathcal{I}}(A,B;\mathcal{X})$, i.e., $A\mathcal{R}\subset\mathcal{R}+\mathcal{B}$. If this is so, construct any F such that $(A+BF)\mathcal{R}\subset\mathcal{R}$, and then check that

$$\langle A+BF\,|\,\mathcal{B}\cap\mathcal{R}\rangle=\mathcal{R}.$$

5.2 Spectral Assignability

It will be shown that the family of controllability subspaces can be characterized in terms of the spectral assignability property of controllable pairs. A simple consequence of Theorem 2.1 these results, especially the first, are basic to the applications.

THEOREM 5.1. Let $\mathcal{R}\in\underline{\mathcal{C}}(A,B;\mathcal{X})$ with $d(\mathcal{R})=\rho\geq 1$. Let $0\neq b\in\mathcal{B}\cap\mathcal{R}$. For every symmetric set Λ of ρ complex numbers there exists a map $F:\ \mathcal{X}\to\mathcal{U}$ such that

$$\mathcal{R} = \langle A + BF | b \rangle$$

and

$$\sigma[(A + BF) | \mathcal{R}] = \Lambda .$$

PROOF: Suppose

$$\mathcal{R} = \langle A + BF_0 | \mathcal{B} \cap \mathcal{R} \rangle \tag{6}$$

and choose G: $\mathcal{U} \to \mathcal{U}$, such that

$$\operatorname{Im}(BG) = \mathcal{B} \cap \mathcal{R} . \tag{7}$$

Define A_0: $\mathcal{R} \to \mathcal{R}$ and B_0: $\mathcal{U} \to \mathcal{R}$ according to

$$A_0 \triangleq (A + BF_0) | \mathcal{R} , \qquad B_0 \triangleq BG .$$

By (6) and (7), we have

$$\langle A_0 | \mathcal{B}_0 \rangle = \mathcal{R} .$$

Then application of Theorem 2.1 to the pair (A_0, B_0) yields the existence of F_1: $\mathcal{R} \to \mathcal{U}$, such that

$$\mathcal{R} = \langle A_0 + B_0 F_1 | b \rangle$$

and

$$\sigma(A_0 + B_0 F_1) = \Lambda .$$

Let F_2: $\mathcal{X} \to \mathcal{U}$ be any extension of F_1 from $\mathcal{R}$ to $\mathcal{X}$. Then

$$F \triangleq F_0 + GF_2$$

is a map with the properties required. ▌

As a converse to Theorem 5.1 we prove the following criterion for a given subspace to be a c.s.

THEOREM 5.2. Let $\mathcal{R} \subset \mathcal{X}$ be a subspace with $d(\mathcal{R}) = \rho \geq 1$. Suppose that for every symmetric set Λ of ρ complex numbers there exists a map F: $\mathcal{X} \to \mathcal{U}$ such that

$$(A + BF)\mathcal{R} \subset \mathcal{R} , \qquad \sigma[(A + BF) | \mathcal{R}] = \Lambda . \tag{8}$$

Then

$$\mathcal{R} \in \underline{\mathcal{C}}(A, B; \mathcal{X}) .$$

PROOF: Fix $F_0 \in \underline{F}(\mathcal{R})$ and write $A_0 \triangleq (A+BF_0)|\mathcal{R}$. We have $F \in \underline{F}(\mathcal{R})$ if and only if $B(F-F_0)\mathcal{R} \subset \mathcal{B} \cap \mathcal{R}$. Let $B_0: \mathcal{U} \to \mathcal{R}$ be an arbitrary map with $\operatorname{Im} B_0 = \mathcal{B} \cap \mathcal{R}$. Then if $F \in \underline{F}(\mathcal{R})$, there exists $F_1: \mathcal{R} \to \mathcal{U}$ such that

$$B_0F_1 = B(F-F_0)|\mathcal{R} .$$

Thus (8) implies that for every Λ there exists F_1 such that

$$\sigma(A_0 + B_0F_1) = \Lambda .$$

By Theorem 2.1, the pair (A_0, B_0) is controllable. Hence

$$\mathcal{R} = \langle A_0 | \mathcal{B}_0 \rangle = \langle A + BF_0 | \mathcal{B} \cap \mathcal{R} \rangle$$

and therefore $\mathcal{R}$ is a c.s. ▮

5.3 Controllability Subspace Algorithm

In this section we characterize controllability subspaces by means of an algorithm which computes $\mathcal{R}$ without explicitly constructing $F \in \underline{F}(\mathcal{R})$. This result will be useful in obtaining general properties of the family $\underline{C}(A, B; \mathcal{X})$.

For an arbitrary, fixed subspace $\mathcal{R} \subset \mathcal{X}$ define a family $\underline{\mathcal{S}}$ of subspaces $\mathcal{S} \subset \mathcal{X}$ according to

$$\underline{\mathcal{S}} \triangleq \{\mathcal{S}: \mathcal{S} = \mathcal{R} \cap (A\mathcal{S} + \mathcal{B})\} . \tag{9}$$

It will be shown that $\underline{\mathcal{S}}$ has a unique least member.

LEMMA 5.1. <u>There is a unique element $\mathcal{S}_* \in \underline{\mathcal{S}}$ such that $\mathcal{S}_* \subset \mathcal{S}$ for every $\mathcal{S} \in \underline{\mathcal{S}}$.</u>

PROOF: Define a sequence $\mathcal{S}^\mu \subset \mathcal{X}$ according to

$$\mathcal{S}^0 = 0 ; \quad \mathcal{S}^\mu = \mathcal{R} \cap (A\mathcal{S}^{\mu-1} + \mathcal{B}) , \qquad \mu \in \underline{n} . \tag{10}$$

The $\mathcal{S}^\mu$ sequence is nondecreasing: clearly $\mathcal{S}^1 \supset \mathcal{S}^0$, and if $\mathcal{S}^\mu \supset \mathcal{S}^{\mu-1}$ then

$$\mathcal{S}^{\mu+1} = \mathcal{R} \cap (A\mathcal{S}^\mu + \mathcal{B}) \supset \mathcal{R} \cap (A\mathcal{S}^{\mu-1} + \mathcal{B}) = \mathcal{S}^\mu .$$

Thus there exists $k \in \underline{n}$ such that

$$\mathcal{S}^\mu = \mathcal{S}^k , \qquad \mu \ge k ,$$

and we set $\mathscr{R}_* \triangleq \mathscr{R}^k$. Clearly $\mathscr{R}_* \in \underline{\mathscr{R}}$. To show that $\mathscr{R}_*$ is infimal, let $\mathscr{R} \in \underline{\mathscr{R}}$. Then $\mathscr{R} \supset \mathscr{R}^0$, and if $\mathscr{R} \supset \mathscr{R}^\mu$, we have

$$\mathscr{R} = \mathcal{R} \cap (A\mathscr{R} + \mathcal{B}) \supset \mathcal{R} \cap (A\mathscr{R}^\mu + \mathcal{B}) = \mathscr{R}^{\mu+1} .$$

So $\mathscr{R} \supset \mathscr{R}^\mu$ for all μ, hence $\mathscr{R} \supset \mathscr{R}_*$. ▮

The algorithm (10) in the proof of Lemma 5.1 will be used often in the sequel: we call it the <u>controllability subspace algorithm</u> (CSA). Thus, we have

LEMMA 5.2. <u>The least element $\mathscr{R}_*$ of $\underline{\mathscr{R}}$ is given by</u>

$$\mathscr{R}_* = \lim \mathscr{R}^\mu = \mathscr{R}^n , \tag{11}$$

<u>where $\mathscr{R}^\mu$ is computed by CSA:</u>

$$\mathscr{R}^0 = 0 \; ; \quad \mathscr{R}^\mu = \mathcal{R} \cap (A\mathscr{R}^{\mu-1} + \mathcal{B}) , \quad \mu \in \underline{n} . \tag{10 bis}$$

The next two lemmas will link the $\mathscr{R}^\mu$ to the definition of c.s.

LEMMA 5.3. <u>Let $\mathcal{R} \in \underline{\mathscr{C}}(A, B; \mathcal{X})$. If $F \in \underline{F}(\mathcal{R})$ and $\hat{\mathcal{R}} \subset \mathcal{R}$ then</u>

$$\mathcal{B} \cap \mathcal{R} + (A + BF)\hat{\mathcal{R}} = \mathcal{R} \cap (A\hat{\mathcal{R}} + \mathcal{B}) .$$

PROOF: $F \in \underline{F}(\mathcal{R})$ implies $(A + BF)\hat{\mathcal{R}} \subset \mathcal{R}$; also

$$A\hat{\mathcal{R}} + \mathcal{B} = (A + BF)\hat{\mathcal{R}} + \mathcal{B} .$$

By the modular distributive rule (0.2),

$$\mathcal{R} \cap (A\hat{\mathcal{R}} + \mathcal{B}) = \mathcal{R} \cap [(A + BF)\hat{\mathcal{R}} + \mathcal{B}] = (A + BF)\hat{\mathcal{R}} + \mathcal{B} \cap \mathcal{R} . \; ▮$$

LEMMA 5.4. <u>Let $\mathcal{R} \in \underline{\mathscr{C}}(A, B; \mathcal{X})$, let $F \in \underline{F}(\mathcal{R})$, and define $\mathscr{R}^\mu$ by CSA. Then</u>

$$\mathscr{R}^\mu = \sum_{j=1}^{\mu} (A + BF)^{j-1}(\mathcal{B} \cap \mathcal{R}) , \quad \mu \in \underline{n} . \tag{12}$$

PROOF: Clearly (12) is true for $\mu = 1$. If it is true for $\mu = \nu$, then

$$\sum_{j=1}^{\nu+1} (A+BF)^{j-1}(\mathcal{B}\cap\mathcal{R}) = \mathcal{B}\cap\mathcal{R} + (A+BF)\mathcal{S}^{\nu}$$
$$= \mathcal{R}\cap(A\mathcal{S}^{\nu}+\mathcal{B}) \quad \text{(by Lemma 5.3)}$$
$$= \mathcal{S}^{\nu+1} . \blacksquare$$

We can now give the promised characterization of c.s.

THEOREM 5.3. Let $\mathcal{R}\subset\mathcal{X}$ and define the family $\mathcal{S}$ by (9). Then $\mathcal{R}\in\underline{\mathcal{C}}(A, B; \mathcal{X})$ if and only if

$$\mathcal{R}\in\underline{\mathcal{I}}(A, B; \mathcal{X}) \qquad [\text{i.e., } A\mathcal{R}\subset\mathcal{R}+\mathcal{B}] , \tag{13}$$

and

$$\mathcal{R} = \mathcal{S}_* . \tag{14}$$

Here $\mathcal{S}_*$ is the least member of $\mathcal{S}$ and is computable by CSA, as in (11).

PROOF: If (13) is true then $\underline{F}(\mathcal{R}) \neq \emptyset$. Taking $F\in\underline{F}(\mathcal{R})$, we have from (14), (11) and (12)

$$\mathcal{R} = \mathcal{S}_* = \mathcal{S}^n = \langle A+BF\,|\,\mathcal{B}\cap\mathcal{R}\rangle ,$$

so that $\mathcal{R}$ is a c.s. Conversely, if $\mathcal{R}$ is a c.s. then $\underline{F}(\mathcal{R}) \neq \emptyset$, so that (13) is true; and if $F\in\underline{F}(\mathcal{R})$

$$\mathcal{R} = \langle A+BF\,|\,\mathcal{B}\cap\mathcal{R}\rangle = \mathcal{S}^n = \mathcal{S}_*$$

by (12) and (11). $\blacksquare$

5.4 Supremal Controllability Subspace

In this section we show that the family of c.s. of a fixed pair (A, B) is a semilattice with respect to inclusion and vector addition, and hence that the family of c.s. which belong to a given subspace contains a supremal element. This property of c.s. is crucial in the applications.

LEMMA 5.5. The class of subspaces $\underline{\mathcal{C}}(A, B; \mathcal{X})$ is closed under the operation of subspace addition.

PROOF: The proof is based on the characterization of c.s. in Theorem 5.3. Clearly,

$$A(\mathcal{R}_1+\mathcal{R}_2)\subset\mathcal{R}_1+\mathcal{R}_2+\mathcal{B} .$$

Also, $\mathcal{R}_i = \mathcal{S}_i^n$ ($i \in \underline{2}$), where

$$\mathcal{S}_i^0 = 0 ; \qquad \mathcal{S}_i^\mu = \mathcal{R}_i \cap \left(A\mathcal{S}_i^{\mu-1} + \mathcal{B}\right), \qquad \mu \in \underline{n} .$$

Define $\mathcal{S}^\mu$ according to

$$\mathcal{S}^0 = 0 ; \qquad \mathcal{S}^\mu = (\mathcal{R}_1 + \mathcal{R}_2) \cap (A\mathcal{S}^{\mu-1} + \mathcal{B}) , \qquad \mu \in \underline{n} .$$

We have $\mathcal{S}^0 = 0 = \mathcal{S}_i^0$ ($i \in \underline{2}$), and if $\mathcal{S}^\mu \supset \mathcal{S}_i^\mu$ then

$$\mathcal{S}^{\mu+1} \supset \mathcal{R}_i \cap \left(A\mathcal{S}_i^\mu + \mathcal{B}\right) = \mathcal{S}_i^{\mu+1} , \qquad i \in \underline{2} ,$$

and so $\mathcal{S}^{\mu+1} \supset \mathcal{S}_1^\mu + \mathcal{S}_2^\mu$. Therefore,

$$\mathcal{R}_1 + \mathcal{R}_2 = \mathcal{S}_1^n + \mathcal{S}_2^n \subset \mathcal{S}^n \subset \mathcal{R}_1 + \mathcal{R}_2 ,$$

hence $\mathcal{R}_1 + \mathcal{R}_2 = \mathcal{S}^n$, and the result follows by Theorem 5.3. ▮

Now let $\mathcal{K} \subset \mathcal{X}$ be an arbitrary subspace, and write $\underline{\mathcal{C}}(A, B; \mathcal{K})$, or simply $\underline{\mathcal{C}}(\mathcal{K})$, for the family of c.s. in $\mathcal{K}$, i.e.,

$$\underline{\mathcal{C}}(A, B; \mathcal{K}) \triangleq \{\mathcal{R} : \mathcal{R} \in \underline{\mathcal{C}}(A, B; \mathcal{X}) \ \& \ \mathcal{R} \subset \mathcal{K}\} .$$

THEOREM 5.4. Let $A: \mathcal{X} \to \mathcal{X}$ and $B: \mathcal{U} \to \mathcal{X}$. Every subspace $\mathcal{K} \subset \mathcal{X}$ contains a unique supremal controllability subspace [written $\sup \underline{\mathcal{C}}(A, B; \mathcal{K})$, or simply $\sup \underline{\mathcal{C}}(\mathcal{K})$].

PROOF: The family $\underline{\mathcal{C}}(A, B; \mathcal{K})$ possesses at least one member, namely 0; and by Lemma 5.5, it is closed under addition. The result now follows by Lemma 4.4. ▮

The supremal element $\sup \underline{\mathcal{C}}(\mathcal{K})$ will often be denoted by $\mathcal{R}^*$. We now describe two ways of computing $\mathcal{R}^*$. Both of these require a prior computation of $\mathcal{V}^* = \sup \underline{\mathcal{J}}(A, B; \mathcal{K})$. An algorithm which computes $\mathcal{V}^*$ was presented in Theorem 4.3.

THEOREM 5.5. Let $\mathcal{V}^* \triangleq \sup \underline{\mathcal{J}}(A, B; \mathcal{K})$, $\mathcal{R}^* \triangleq \sup \underline{\mathcal{C}}(A, B; \mathcal{K})$. If $F \in \underline{F}(A, B; \mathcal{V}^*)$ then

$$\mathcal{R}^* = \langle A + BF \,|\, \mathcal{B} \cap \mathcal{V}^* \rangle . \tag{15}$$

For the proof we need two preliminary results. The first of these is a generalization of Lemma 2.1.

LEMMA 5.6. Let $\mathcal{V} \in \underline{\mathcal{J}}(A, B; \mathcal{X})$, $\mathcal{B}_0 \subset \mathcal{B} \cap \mathcal{V}$, $F_0 \in \underline{F}(\mathcal{V})$, and define

$$\mathcal{R} \triangleq \langle A + BF_0 | \mathcal{B}_0 \rangle .$$

<u>If</u> $F \in \underline{F}(\mathcal{V})$ <u>and</u> $B(F - F_0)\mathcal{V} \subset \mathcal{B}_0$ <u>then</u>

$$\mathcal{R} = \langle A + BF | \mathcal{B}_0 \rangle .$$

PROOF: Write

$$\mathcal{R}_1 = \langle A + BF | \mathcal{B}_0 \rangle$$

and

$$\mathcal{V}^i = \sum_{j=1}^{i} (A + BF_0)^{j-1} \mathcal{B}_0 , \qquad i \in \underline{n} .$$

Then $\mathcal{V}^1 = \mathcal{B}_0 \subset \mathcal{R}_1$. Suppose $\mathcal{V}^i \subset \mathcal{R}_1$. We have

$$\mathcal{V}^{i+1} = \mathcal{B}_0 + (A + BF_0)\mathcal{V}^i \subset \mathcal{B}_0 + (A + BF)\mathcal{V}^i + B(F - F_0)\mathcal{V}^i .$$

Since $F \in \underline{F}(\mathcal{R}_1)$,

$$(A + BF)\mathcal{V}^i \subset \mathcal{R}_1 ;$$

and because $F \in \underline{F}(\mathcal{V})$ and $\mathcal{B}_0 \subset \mathcal{V}$, we have that $\mathcal{R}_1 \subset \mathcal{V}$, hence

$$B(F - F_0)\mathcal{V}^i \subset B(F - F_0)\mathcal{R}_1 \subset \mathcal{B}_0 \subset \mathcal{R}_1 .$$

Therefore, $\mathcal{V}^{i+1} \subset \mathcal{R}_1$, so that $\mathcal{V}^i \subset \mathcal{R}_1$ ($i \in \underline{n}$) and

$$\mathcal{R} = \mathcal{V}^n \subset \mathcal{R}_1 .$$

By interchanging the roles of F and F_0, we infer that $\mathcal{R}_1 \subset \mathcal{R}$, and the result follows. ▌

LEMMA 5.7. <u>Let both</u> $\mathcal{R}$ <u>and</u> $\mathcal{V} \in \underline{\mathcal{J}}(A, B; \mathcal{X})$, <u>and suppose</u> $\mathcal{R} \subset \mathcal{V}$. <u>If</u> $F_0 \in \underline{F}(\mathcal{R})$ <u>there exists</u> $F \in \underline{F}(\mathcal{V}) \cap \underline{F}(\mathcal{R})$ <u>such that</u>

$$F | \mathcal{R} = F_0 | \mathcal{R} .$$

PROOF: Let $\mathcal{R} \oplus \mathcal{S} = \mathcal{V}$ and let $\{s_1, \ldots, s_q\}$ be a basis for $\mathcal{S}$. Then

$$As_i = v_i + Bu_i , \qquad i \in \underline{q} ,$$

for some $v_i \in \mathcal{V}$ and $u_i \in \mathcal{U}$. Let $F: \mathcal{X} \to \mathcal{U}$ be any map such that $Fx = F_0 x$ ($x \in \mathcal{R}$) and $Fs_i = -u_i$ ($i \in \underline{q}$). Then F has the required properties. ▌

PROOF of Theorem 5.5. With $F \in \underline{F}(\mathcal{V}^*)$, write

$$\mathcal{R} = \langle A + BF | \mathcal{B} \cap \mathcal{V}^* \rangle .$$

Since $\mathcal{B} \cap \mathcal{V}^* = \mathrm{Im}(BG)$ for some $G: \mathcal{U} \to \mathcal{U}$, and since

$$(A + BF)^{j-1} (\mathcal{B} \cap \mathcal{V}^*) \subset \mathcal{V}^* \subset \mathcal{X} , \qquad j \in \underline{n} ,$$

it is clear that $\mathcal{R} \in \underline{\mathcal{C}}(\mathcal{X})$. Let $\mathcal{R}_0 \in \underline{\mathcal{C}}(\mathcal{X})$ be arbitrary. Then

$$\mathcal{R}_0 = \langle A + BF_0 | \mathcal{B} \cap \mathcal{R}_0 \rangle$$

for some F_0. Since $(A + BF_0)\mathcal{R}_0 \subset \mathcal{R}_0$, clearly

$$\mathcal{R}_0 \subset \sup \underline{\mathcal{J}}(\mathcal{X}) = \mathcal{V}^* . \tag{16}$$

Choose, by Lemma 5.7, $F_1 \in \underline{F}(\mathcal{R}_0) \cap \underline{F}(\mathcal{V}^*)$, such that $F_1 | \mathcal{R}_0 = F_0 | \mathcal{R}_0$. If $x \in \mathcal{V}^*$,

$$B(F - F_1)x = (A + BF)x - (A + BF_1)x \in \mathcal{V}^* ,$$

so that $B(F - F_1)\mathcal{V}^* \subset \mathcal{B} \cap \mathcal{V}^*$. Then

$$\begin{aligned} \mathcal{R}_0 &= \langle A + BF_1 | \mathcal{B} \cap \mathcal{R}_0 \rangle \subset \langle A + BF_1 | \mathcal{B} \cap \mathcal{V}^* \rangle \quad \text{by (16)} \\ &= \langle A + BF | \mathcal{B} \cap \mathcal{V}^* \rangle \qquad \text{by Lemma 5.6} \\ &= \mathcal{R} . \end{aligned}$$

Therefore $\mathcal{R} \in \underline{\mathcal{C}}(\mathcal{X})$ is supremal and so $\mathcal{R} = \mathcal{R}^*$. ▌

COROLLARY 5.1. If $\mathcal{V}^* = \sup \underline{\mathcal{J}}(\mathcal{X})$ and $\mathcal{R}^* = \sup \underline{\mathcal{C}}(\mathcal{X})$, then

$$\underline{F}(\mathcal{V}^*) \subset \underline{F}(\mathcal{R}^*) . \tag{17}$$

PROOF: The assertion is immediate from (15). ▌

We turn now to a second method of computing $\mathcal{R}^*$, which does not require the prior computation of an $F \in \underline{F}(\mathcal{V}^*)$. This is a generalization of CSA.

THEOREM 5.6. Define the sequence $\mathcal{S}^\mu$ according to

$$\mathcal{S}^0 = 0 ; \qquad \mathcal{S}^\mu = \mathcal{V}^* \cap (A\mathcal{S}^{\mu-1} + \mathcal{B}) , \qquad \mu \in \underline{n} . \tag{18}$$

Then $\mathcal{S}^\mu = \mathcal{R}^*$ for $\mu \geq d(\mathcal{V}^*)$.

PROOF: Induction shows that $\mathscr{S}^{\mu} \uparrow$ and so $\mathscr{S}^{\mu} = \mathscr{S}^{k}$ for $\mu \geq k \triangleq d(\mathscr{V}^*)$. Write $\mathscr{S}_* \triangleq \mathscr{S}^k$. Since $\mathscr{S}^{\mu} \subset \mathscr{V}^*$ and $A\mathscr{V}^* \subset \mathscr{V}^* + \mathscr{B}$, we have

$$A\mathscr{S}^{\mu} \subset (\mathscr{V}^* + \mathscr{B}) \cap (A\mathscr{S}^{\mu} + \mathscr{B}) = \mathscr{V}^* \cap (A\mathscr{S}^{\mu} + \mathscr{B}) + \mathscr{B} = \mathscr{S}^{\mu+1} + \mathscr{B},$$

so that $A\mathscr{S}_* \subset \mathscr{S}_* + \mathscr{B}$. Since

$$\mathscr{S}^{\mu} \subset \mathscr{S}_* \subset \mathscr{V}^*, \qquad \mu \in \underline{n},$$

(18) implies

$$\mathscr{S}^{\mu} = \mathscr{S}_* \cap (A\mathscr{S}^{\mu-1} + \mathscr{B}), \qquad \mu \in \underline{n}.$$

We conclude from Theorem 5.3 that $\mathscr{S}_* \in \underline{\mathscr{C}}(\mathscr{K})$, and so $\mathscr{S}_* \subset \mathscr{R}^*$. On the other hand $\mathscr{R}^* = \mathscr{R}^n$, where

$$\mathscr{R}^0 = 0; \qquad \mathscr{R}^{\mu} = \mathscr{R}^* \cap (A\mathscr{R}^{\mu-1} + \mathscr{B}), \qquad \mu \in \underline{n}.$$

Since $\mathscr{R}^* \subset \mathscr{V}^*$ it follows easily by induction on μ that $\mathscr{R}^{\mu} \subset \mathscr{S}^{\mu}$ ($\mu \in \underline{n}$) and therefore $\mathscr{R}^* \subset \mathscr{S}_*$. ∎

To conclude this section we give a result on feedback maps and spectral assignability which generalizes the discussion in Section 2.3.

THEOREM 5.7. <u>Let</u> $\mathscr{V} \in \underline{\mathscr{I}}(A, B; \mathscr{X})$ <u>and let</u> $\mathscr{R}^* \triangleq \sup \underline{\mathscr{C}}(A, B; \mathscr{V})$. <u>For</u> $F \in \underline{F}(\mathscr{V})$ <u>write</u> $A_F \triangleq A + BF$ <u>and</u> $\overline{A}_F$ <u>for the map induced in</u> $\mathscr{V}/\mathscr{R}^*$ <u>by</u> A_F. <u>Then</u> $\overline{A}_F$ <u>is independent of</u> $F \in \underline{F}(\mathscr{V})$.

PROOF: By Corollary 5.1 with $\mathscr{K} = \mathscr{V}$, we have $A_F\mathscr{R}^* \subset \mathscr{R}^*$, so $\overline{A}_F$ is well defined. Let $P: \mathscr{V} \to \mathscr{V}/\mathscr{R}^*$ be the canonical projection. If $F_i \in \underline{F}(\mathscr{V})$ ($i \in \underline{2}$) and $\overline{x} = Px \in \mathscr{V}/\mathscr{R}^*$ then

$$\begin{aligned} \overline{A}_{F_1}\overline{x} - \overline{A}_{F_2}\overline{x} &= PA_{F_1}x - PA_{F_2}x = P\left(A_{F_1} - A_{F_2}\right)x = PB(F_1 - F_2)x \\ &\in P(\mathscr{B} \cap \mathscr{V}) \qquad [\text{since } x \in \mathscr{V} \text{ and } F_1, F_2 \in \underline{F}(\mathscr{V})] \\ &\subset P\mathscr{R}^* = \overline{0}. \end{aligned}$$ ∎

COROLLARY 5.2. <u>Under the conditions of Theorem 5.7, if</u> $F \in \underline{F}(\mathscr{V})$ <u>then</u>

$$\sigma[(A + BF)\,|\,\mathscr{V}] = \sigma_F \,\dot{\cup}\, \sigma_0,$$

<u>where</u>

$$\sigma_F \triangleq \sigma[(A + BF)\,|\,\mathscr{R}^*]$$

<u>is freely assignable by suitable choice of</u> $F \in \underline{F}(\mathcal{V})$, <u>and</u>

$$\sigma_0 \triangleq \sigma(\overline{A+BF})$$

<u>is fixed for all</u> $F \in \underline{F}(\mathcal{V})$.

5.5 Disturbance Decoupling with Stability

Most of the preceding ideas are illustrated by the problem of disturbance decoupling introduced in Section 4.1. But this time we impose the additional, realistic constraint that the closed loop system map $A+BF$ be stable or, more generally, have its spectrum in the 'good' part of the complex plane. Thus let $A: \mathcal{X} \to \mathcal{X}$, $B: \mathcal{U} \to \mathcal{X}$, $\mathcal{S} \subset \mathcal{X}$ and $\mathcal{K} \subset \mathcal{X}$, and let $\mathbb{C} = \mathbb{C}_g \dot{\cup} \mathbb{C}_b$ be a symmetric partition of the complex plane. We pose the problem of <u>Disturbance Decoupling with Stability</u> (DDPS):

<u>Find (if possible)</u> $F: \mathcal{X} \to \mathcal{U}$ <u>such that</u>

$$\langle A+BF \,|\, \mathcal{S} \rangle \subset \mathcal{K}, \qquad \sigma(A+BF) \subset \mathbb{C}_g . \tag{19}$$

To solve DDPS we start with the same heuristic approach as in Chapter 4. Noting that the subspace $\langle A+BF \,|\, \mathcal{S} \rangle$ is (A, B)-invariant and ought to be contained in $\mathcal{K}$, we introduce the family of subspaces

$$\underline{\mathcal{V}} \triangleq \{\mathcal{V}: \mathcal{V} \in \underline{\mathcal{I}}(\mathcal{K}), \ \& \ \exists F \in \underline{F}(\mathcal{V}), \ \sigma[(A+BF)\,|\,\mathcal{V}] \subset \mathbb{C}_g\} . \tag{20}$$

It is natural to conjecture that $\underline{\mathcal{V}}$ has a largest member $\mathcal{V}_g^*$. If $\mathcal{V}_g^*$ can be found, it is clearly enough to check that $\mathcal{V}_g^* \supset \mathcal{S}$, and then that the spectrum of the induced map in $\mathcal{X}/\mathcal{V}_g^*$ can also be assigned to $\mathbb{C}_g$.

We carry out this program as follows. Let

$$\mathcal{V}^* \triangleq \sup \underline{\mathcal{I}}(A, B; \mathcal{K}), \qquad \mathcal{R}^* \triangleq \sup \underline{\mathcal{C}}(A, B; \mathcal{K}) .$$

Choose $F_0 \in \underline{F}(\mathcal{V}^*)$, write $A_0 = A + BF_0$, let $P: \mathcal{X} \to \mathcal{X}/\mathcal{R}^*$ be the canonical projection, and let $\overline{A}_0$ be the map induced in $\mathcal{X}/\mathcal{R}^*$ by A_0: since by (17), $F_0 \in \underline{F}(\mathcal{R}^*)$, $\overline{A}_0$ is well-defined. We have that $\mathcal{V}^*/\mathcal{R}^*$ is $\overline{A}_0$-invariant, for

$$\overline{A}_0\left(\frac{\mathcal{V}^*}{\mathcal{R}^*}\right) = \overline{A}_0 P\mathcal{V}^* = P A_0 \mathcal{V}^* \subset P\mathcal{V}^* = \frac{\mathcal{V}^*}{\mathcal{R}^*} .$$

Also, by Theorem 5.7 the restriction of $\overline{A}_0$ to $\mathcal{V}^*/\mathcal{R}^*$ is independent of the choice of $F_0 \in \underline{F}(\mathcal{V}^*)$. Let $\beta(\lambda)$ be the m.p. of $\overline{A}_0\,|\,(\mathcal{V}^*/\mathcal{R}^*)$. Factor $\beta(\lambda) = \beta_g(\lambda)\,\beta_b(\lambda)$, where the zeros of β_g (resp. β_b) in $\mathbb{C}$ belong to $\mathbb{C}_g$ (resp. $\mathbb{C}_b$); and write

$$\overline{\mathcal{X}}_g^* \triangleq \left(\frac{\mathcal{V}^*}{\mathcal{R}^*}\right) \cap \operatorname{Ker} \beta_g(\overline{A}_0), \qquad \overline{\mathcal{X}}_b^* \triangleq \left(\frac{\mathcal{V}^*}{\mathcal{R}^*}\right) \cap \operatorname{Ker} \beta_b(\overline{A}_0).$$

Let us now take stock. In $\mathcal{R}^*$ we have that $\sigma(A_0|\mathcal{R}^*)$ can be assigned arbitrarily, hence to $\mathbb{C}_g$, by suitable choice of $F_0 \in \underline{F}(\mathcal{V}^*)$; whereas nothing can be done with such F_0 to change $\sigma[\overline{A}_0|\mathcal{V}^*/\mathcal{R}^*]$. Now, β_g and β_b coprime implies

$$\frac{\mathcal{V}^*}{\mathcal{R}^*} = \overline{\mathcal{X}}_g^* \oplus \overline{\mathcal{X}}_b^*. \tag{21}$$

Thus the subspace of 'good' modes of $A_0|\mathcal{V}^*$ can be made to be just that subspace $\mathcal{V} \subset \mathcal{V}^*$ for which

$$\sigma(A_0|\mathcal{V}) = \sigma(A_0|\mathcal{R}^*) \,\dot{\cup}\, \sigma(\overline{A}_0|\overline{\mathcal{X}}_g^*). \tag{22}$$

With (22) as objective, define

$$\mathcal{V}_g^* \triangleq P^{-1}\overline{\mathcal{X}}_g^*. \tag{23}$$

Now we can prove

LEMMA 5.8. <u>The subspace $\mathcal{V}_g^*$ defined by (23) is the largest member of the family $\underline{\mathcal{V}}$ defined by (20).</u>

PROOF: We first check that $\mathcal{V}_g^* \in \underline{\mathcal{V}}$. Now

$$P\mathcal{V}_g^* = P\left(P^{-1}\overline{\mathcal{X}}_g^*\right) = \overline{\mathcal{X}}_g^* \subset P\mathcal{V}^* \tag{24}$$

and therefore $\mathcal{V}_g^* \subset \mathcal{V}^* + \mathcal{R}^* = \mathcal{V}^* \subset \operatorname{Ker} D$. Also

$$PA_0\mathcal{V}_g^* = PA_0P^{-1}\overline{\mathcal{X}}_g^* = \overline{A}_0P\left(P^{-1}\overline{\mathcal{X}}_g^*\right) = \overline{A}_0\overline{\mathcal{X}}_g^* \subset \overline{\mathcal{X}}_g^*,$$

hence $A_0\mathcal{V}_g^* \subset P^{-1}\overline{\mathcal{X}}_g^* = \mathcal{V}_g^*$, and so $A\mathcal{V}_g^* \subset \mathcal{V}_g^* + \mathcal{B}$. Since $F_0 \in \underline{F}(\mathcal{V}^*)$ was arbitrary, we have also shown that $\underline{F}(\mathcal{V}^*) \subset \underline{F}(\mathcal{V}_g^*)$. Next, as $\mathcal{V}_g^* \supset \operatorname{Ker} P = \mathcal{R}^*$, we can indeed choose

$$F_0 \in \underline{F}(\mathcal{V}^*) \subset \underline{F}(\mathcal{R}^*) \cap \underline{F}(\mathcal{V}_g^*)$$

such that $\sigma(A_0|\mathcal{R}^*) \subset \mathbb{C}_g$. Then (21), (23) and (24) imply that (22) holds with $\mathcal{V} = \mathcal{V}_g^*$, and so finally $\mathcal{V}_g^* \in \underline{\mathcal{V}}$.

To show that $\mathcal{V}_g^*$ is supremal, choose an arbitrary $\mathcal{V} \in \underline{\mathcal{V}}$. By Lemma 5.7 we take $F \in \underline{F}(\mathcal{V}) \cap \underline{F}(\mathcal{V}^*)$, and write $A_F \triangleq A + BF$. Since $F \in \underline{F}(\mathcal{R}^*)$, the induced map $\overline{A}_F$ on $\mathcal{X}/\mathcal{R}^*$ exists, and by Theorem 5.7 coincides on $\mathcal{V}^*/\mathcal{R}^*$ with $\overline{A}_0$. Then, as $\overline{A}_FP\mathcal{V} = PA_F\mathcal{V} \subset P\mathcal{V}$, $P\mathcal{V}$ is also $\overline{A}_0$-invariant. From (21) and the fact that β_g and β_b are coprime we can therefore write

$$P\mathcal{V} = (P\mathcal{V}) \cap \bar{\mathcal{X}}_g^* \oplus (P\mathcal{V}) \cap \bar{\mathcal{X}}_b^* . \tag{25}$$

From (25) and the assumption $\mathcal{V} \in \underline{\mathcal{V}}$ there follows $(P\mathcal{V}) \cap \bar{\mathcal{X}}_b^* = \bar{0}$, hence $P\mathcal{V} \subset \bar{\mathcal{X}}_g^*$. Then

$$\mathcal{V} \subset P^{-1}\bar{\mathcal{X}}_g^* = \mathcal{V}_g^* ,$$

hence $\mathcal{V}_g^*$ is supremal, as claimed. ▌

The inclusion relations involved in the foregoing discussion are summarized in the lattice diagrams, Fig. 5.2.

It is now easy to prove the main result.

THEOREM 5.8. <u>Suppose</u> (A, B) <u>is controllable. Then DDPS is solvable if and only if</u>

$$\mathcal{V}_g^* \supset \mathcal{S} . \tag{26}$$

Since $\mathcal{V}^* \supset \mathcal{V}_g^*$, the condition (26) strengthens the condition $\mathcal{V}^* \supset \mathcal{S}$ given by Theorem 4.2 for solvability of DDP.

PROOF: Suppose (26) holds. We have already shown that there exists $F_0 \in \underline{F}(\mathcal{V}_g^*)$ such that

$$\sigma[(A + BF_0)\,|\,\mathcal{V}_g^*] \subset \mathbb{C}_g .$$

Since $(A + BF_0, B)$ is controllable, by Proposition 1.2 the corresponding pair $(\tilde{A}_0, \tilde{B})$ induced in $\mathcal{X}/\mathcal{V}_g^*$ is also controllable, hence there exists $\tilde{F}$: $\mathcal{X}/\mathcal{V}_g^* \to \mathcal{U}$ such that

$$\sigma(\tilde{A}_0 + \tilde{B}\tilde{F}) \subset \mathbb{C}_g . \tag{27}$$

Let Q: $\mathcal{X} \to \mathcal{X}/\mathcal{V}_g^*$ be the canonical projection and set $F = F_0 + \tilde{F}Q$. Then it follows immediately that F has the required properties (19).

Conversely if (19) is true then, as already noted, $\mathcal{S} \subset \mathcal{V}$ for some $\mathcal{V} \in \underline{\mathcal{V}}$, hence by Lemma 5.8, $\mathcal{S} \subset \mathcal{V}_g^*$. ▌

Using the condition for spectral assignment in Theorem 2.2, the hypothesis of controllability in Theorem 5.8 can be weakened. Define $\mathcal{X}_b(A)$ as in Section 2.3. Then it can be shown that DDPS is solvable if and only if

$$\mathcal{V}_g^* \supset \mathcal{S} \quad \text{and} \quad \mathcal{X}_b(A) \subset \langle A\,|\,\mathcal{B}\rangle . \tag{28}$$

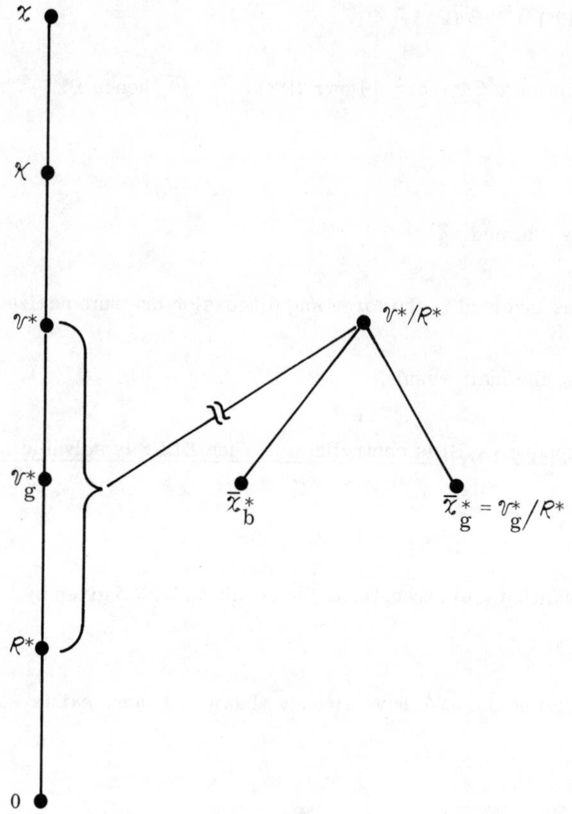

Fig. 5.2.

Lattice Diagrams: Construction of $\mathcal{V}^*_g$

5.6 Controllability Indices

In this chapter we have studied several constructions involving the transformation of a given controllable pair (A, B) into a new pair (A + BF, BG). It is of some interest to ask what properties, if any, of (A, B) remain invariant under all such transformations. We shall investigate this question under the restriction that the admissible maps G: $\mathcal{U} \to \mathcal{U}$ are precisely the automorphisms of $\mathcal{U}$; it is then clear that, as far as BG is concerned, the sole invariant is the 'geometric' invariant $\mathcal{B} = \operatorname{Im} B \subset \mathcal{X}$. As for A + BF, we already know that $\sigma(A + BF)$ can be assigned arbitrarily by suitable choice of F. This suggests that most of the linear algebraic structure of A is deleted if we let F vary through the set of all possible maps from $\mathcal{X}$ to $\mathcal{U}$. What is left will depend on how $\mathcal{B}$ is intertwined with the geometric structure of A.

To make the problem precise we fix n and m ($1 \le m \le n$), and consider the subset of all matrix pairs

$$(A, B) \in \mathbb{R}^{n \times n} \times \mathbb{R}^{n \times m}$$

for which B is monic and (A, B) is controllable, namely

$$\operatorname{Rank} B = m \tag{29a}$$

and

$$\operatorname{Rank}[B, AB, \ldots, A^{n-1}B] = n \,. \tag{29b}$$

Listing the elements of A and B in some arbitrary order, we regard (A, B) as a point $\underline{p} \in \mathbb{R}^N$, $N = n^2 + nm$. Denote by $\underline{S}$ the subset of $\mathbb{R}^N$ determined by (29): clearly $\underline{S}$ is the complement of a proper algebraic variety in $\mathbb{R}^N$. Next, introduce the class $\mathfrak{G}$ of transformations $\mathfrak{g}$ on $\mathbb{R}^N$ defined by

$$\mathfrak{g}\underline{p} \triangleq \mathfrak{g}(A, B) \triangleq (T^{-1}(A + BF)\,T, T^{-1}BG) \,. \tag{30}$$

That is, each $\mathfrak{g} \in \mathfrak{G}$ is represented by a distinct triple of matrices

$$(T, F, G) \in \mathbb{R}^{n \times n} \times \mathbb{R}^{m \times n} \times \mathbb{R}^{m \times m} \,,$$

where T, and also G, are required to be nonsingular. It is easy to see that the action (30) assigns to $\mathfrak{G}$ the structure of a transformation group, with identity

$$1 = (I_n, 0, I_m) \,,$$

inverse

$$\mathfrak{g}^{-1} = (T^{-1}, -G^{-1}FT, G^{-1}) \,,$$

and composition rule

$$\mathfrak{g}_2 \circ \mathfrak{g}_1 = \left(T_1 T_2, F_1 + G_1 F_2 T_1^{-1}, G_1 G_2 \right) .$$

If (A, B) is controllable and B is monic, clearly the pair $\mathfrak{g}$(A, B) given by (30) also has these properties for each $\mathfrak{g} \in \mathfrak{G}$; namely $\underline{S}$ is invariant under the action of $\mathfrak{G}$:

$$\mathfrak{G}\underline{S} \triangleq \bigcup_{\mathfrak{g} \in \mathfrak{G}} \mathfrak{g}\underline{S} = \underline{S} .$$

Fix $\underline{p} \in \underline{S}$. The subset

$$\mathfrak{G}\underline{p} \triangleq \{\mathfrak{g}\underline{p}: \mathfrak{g} \in \mathfrak{G}\} \subset \underline{S}$$

is the _orbit_ of $\underline{p}$ under $\mathfrak{G}$. It is easy to see that the orbits partition $\underline{S}$ into disjoint subsets. In other words $\mathfrak{G}$ induces on $\underline{S}$ an equivalence relation by the definition: $\underline{p}_1, \underline{p}_2 \in \underline{S}$ are _equivalent_ if and only if $\underline{p}_1, \underline{p}_2$ belong to the same orbit, namely $\underline{p}_2 = \mathfrak{g}\underline{p}_1$ for some $\mathfrak{g} \in \mathfrak{G}$. Denote the set of orbits by $\underline{\Omega} \triangleq \underline{S}/\mathfrak{G}$. Translated into the present setting, our original problem is simply to parametrize $\underline{\Omega}$ in some effective way, and to identify with each $\underline{\omega} \in \underline{\Omega}$ a unique element $\underline{p}^* = \underline{p}^*(\underline{\omega}) \in \underline{\omega}$ which exhibits the invariant structure of all $\underline{p} = (A, B)$ on the orbit $\underline{\omega}$. Without posing this problem formally and abstractly, we shall pass immediately to the main results, which are self-explanatory.

THEOREM 5.9. _There is a bijection from $\underline{\Omega}$ to the set of all lists of integers_

$$\varkappa = (\varkappa_1, \varkappa_2, \ldots, \varkappa_m)$$

with the properties

$$\varkappa_1 \geq \varkappa_2 \geq \cdots \geq \varkappa_m \geq 1$$

and

$$\varkappa_1 + \varkappa_2 + \cdots + \varkappa_m = n .$$

Thus if n = 8 and m = 3, there are exactly five distinct orbits, corresponding to the lists

$$(3,3,2),\ (4,2,2),\ (4,3,1),\ (5,2,1),\ (6,1,1) .$$

From now on we write $\varkappa^*(\underline{\omega})$ for the list $\varkappa$ which labels $\underline{\omega} \in \underline{\Omega}$. Our second result assigns to $\varkappa^*(\underline{\omega})$ its geometric meaning relative to A and B.

THEOREM 5.10. _Let $\underline{p} = (A, B)$ in $\underline{\omega}$ and let $\varkappa^*(\underline{\omega}) = (\varkappa_1, \ldots, \varkappa_m)$. There are_ (A, B)-_controllability subspaces $\mathcal{R}_1, \ldots, \mathcal{R}_m$ with $d(\mathcal{R}_i) = \varkappa_i$, such that_

$$\bigoplus_{i=1}^{m} \mathcal{R}_i = \mathcal{X} . \tag{31}$$

COROLLARY 5.3. Under the conditions of Theorem 5.10, there are bases for $\mathcal{X}$ and $\mathcal{U}$, and a map F: $\mathcal{X} \to \mathcal{U}$, such that

$$\mathrm{Mat}(A + BF) = \mathrm{Mat}\, A^* \triangleq \mathrm{diag}[A_1, \dots, A_m]$$

and

$$\mathrm{Mat}\, B = \mathrm{Mat}\, B^* \triangleq \mathrm{diag}[b_1, \dots, b_m] .$$

Here A_i and b_i are given by

$$A_i = \begin{bmatrix} 0 & 1 & 0 & \cdot & \cdot & \cdot & 0 \\ 0 & 0 & 1 & \cdot & \cdot & \cdot & 0 \\ \cdot & \cdot & \cdot & \cdot & \cdot & \cdot & \cdot \\ 0 & \cdot & \cdot & \cdot & \cdot & 0 & 1 \\ 0 & \cdot & \cdot & \cdot & \cdot & \cdot & 0 \end{bmatrix}_{\varkappa_i \times \varkappa_i}, \qquad b_i = \begin{bmatrix} 0 \\ \cdot \\ \cdot \\ \cdot \\ 0 \\ 1 \end{bmatrix}_{\varkappa_i \times 1} .$$

Thus any matrix pair (A, B) in $\underline{S}$ can be transformed into exactly one pair (A^*, B^*) by suitable choice of (T, F, G). Conversely, to any list $\varkappa$ there corresponds exactly one orbit in $\underline{S}$, namely the set of all transforms under $\mathfrak{G}$ of the corresponding matrix pair (A^*, B^*). If $\underline{p} = (A, B) \in \underline{\omega}$ we define $\underline{p}^*(\underline{\omega}) = (A^*, B^*)$, and call this pair the canonical form of (A, B) under $\mathfrak{G}$. The canonical form exhibits the original 'system' $\dot{x} = Ax + Bu$, after transformation, as a parallel array of m decoupled 'subsystems' of dynamic order $\varkappa_1, \dots, \varkappa_m$.[(1)]

If $\underline{p} = (A, B) \in \underline{\omega}$ and $\varkappa^*(\underline{\omega}) = (\varkappa_1, \dots, \varkappa_m)$, the integers $\varkappa_i$ $(i \in \underline{m})$ are the controllability indices of (A, B). With some abuse of terminology $\varkappa_1$, the largest controllability index, is called 'the' controllability index of (A, B); as will be clear from (36), below,

$$\varkappa_1 = \min\{j:\ 1 \le j \le n,\ \mathcal{B} + A\mathcal{B} + \cdots + A^{j-1}\mathcal{B} = \mathcal{X}\} .$$

For the proof of Theorems 5.9 and 5.10 we need

LEMMA 5.9. If $b \in \mathcal{B}$ has the properties

$$A^k b \in \mathcal{B} + A\mathcal{B} + \cdots + A^{k-1}\mathcal{B},$$

and

$$A^{k-1} b \notin \mathcal{B} + A\mathcal{B} + \cdots + A^{k-2}\mathcal{B}$$

for some k $(2 \le k \le n)$, then there exists F: $\mathcal{X} \to \mathcal{U}$ such that

---

(1) In applications, however, these subsystems need have no particular physical identity. Moreover, the $\mathcal{R}_i$ themselves, unlike $\varkappa$, are in general not unique.

$$(A + BF)^k b = 0 .$$

<u>Further, the vectors</u>

$$b,\ (A + BF)b,\ \ldots,\ (A + BF)^{k-1} b$$

<u>are linearly independent.</u>

PROOF: By assumption, there exist vectors $b_1, \ldots, b_k \in \mathcal{B}$ such that

$$A\Big(\cdots A((Ab - b_1) - b_2) \cdots - b_{k-1}\Big) - b_k = 0 ;$$

and the vectors $x_1, \ldots, x_k$, given by

$$b,\ Ab - b_1,\ \ldots,\ A^{k-1}b - A^{k-2}b_1 - \cdots - b_{k-1} ,$$

are linearly independent. Define $F: \mathcal{X} \to \mathcal{U}$ such that $BFx_i = -b_i$ ($i \in \underline{k}$); then F has the required properties. ∎

We define the controllability indices $\varkappa_i$ of (A, B) as follows. Write

$$\mathcal{S}_j \triangleq \mathcal{B} + A\mathcal{B} + \cdots + A^j \mathcal{B} \tag{32}$$

for $j = 0, 1, \ldots, n-1$; and let

$$\rho_0 \triangleq m ; \qquad \rho_j \triangleq d\left(\frac{\mathcal{S}_j}{\mathcal{S}_{j-1}}\right), \qquad j \in \underline{n-1} . \tag{33}$$

It is easy to check (Ex. 5.11) that

$$\rho_0 \geq \rho_1 \geq \cdots \geq \rho_{n-1} \geq 0 \tag{34}$$

and

$$\rho_0 + \rho_1 + \cdots + \rho_{n-1} = n . \tag{35}$$

Now define, for $i \in \underline{m}$,

$$\varkappa_i \triangleq \text{number of integers in the set } \{\rho_0, \rho_1, \ldots, \rho_{n-1}\} \text{ which are } \geq i . \tag{36}$$

Thus

$$\varkappa_1 \geq \varkappa_2 \geq \cdots \geq \varkappa_m$$

and by (35),

$$\varkappa_1 + \varkappa_2 + \cdots + \varkappa_m = n .$$

Since for any F: $\mathcal{X} \to \mathcal{U}$,

$$\mathcal{S}_j = \mathcal{B} + (A+BF)\mathcal{B} + \cdots + (A+BF)^j \mathcal{B} \quad , \tag{37}$$

it is clear that the ρ_j and $\varkappa_j$ are invariant under a transformation $A \mapsto A+BF$.

PROOF of Theorems 5.9 and 5.10. Let $b_1, \ldots, b_m$ be a basis for $\mathcal{B}$; write down the list

$$b_1, \ldots, b_m \;;\; Ab_1, \ldots, Ab_m \;;\; \cdots \;;\; A^{n-1}b_1, \ldots, A^{n-1}b_m \;;$$

and working from left to right, delete each vector which is linearly dependent on its predecessors. After a relabelling of the b_i, if necessary, the list will then look like

$$b_m, \ldots, b_1; \cdots ; A^{\varkappa_m - 1} b_m, \ldots, A^{\varkappa_m - 1} b_1;$$

$$A^{\varkappa_m} b_{m-1}, \ldots, A^{\varkappa_m} b_1; \cdots ; A^{\varkappa_{m-1}-1} b_{m-1}, \ldots, A^{\varkappa_{m-1}-1} b_1;$$

$$\cdots\cdots\cdots\cdots\cdots\cdots\cdots\cdots\cdots$$

$$A^{\varkappa_3} b_2, A^{\varkappa_3} b_1; \cdots ; A^{\varkappa_2 - 1} b_2, A^{\varkappa_2 - 1} b_1 ;$$

$$A^{\varkappa_2} b_1; \cdots ; A^{\varkappa_1 - 1} b_1 .$$

Here the $\varkappa_i$ ($i \in \underline{m}$) are the controllability indices of (A, B): that the list takes the form shown is an immediate consequence of their definition. Thus for $j \in \underline{m}$,

$$A^{\varkappa_j} b_j \in \mathcal{B} + A\mathcal{B} + \cdots + A^{\varkappa_j - 1} \mathcal{B} \tag{38}$$

but

$$A^{\varkappa_j - 1} b_j \notin \mathcal{B} + A\mathcal{B} + \cdots + A^{\varkappa_j - 2} \mathcal{B} . \tag{39}$$

Furthermore, by the list ordering,

$$\varkappa_{j+1} \geq i \geq \varkappa_j - 1 \quad \text{and} \quad j-1 \geq k \geq 1$$

implies

$$A^i b_k \cap \left(\mathcal{B} + A\mathcal{B} + \cdots + A^{i-1}\mathcal{B} + A^i b_j + \cdots + A^i b_{k+1} \right) = 0 . \tag{40}$$

Now apply Lemma 5.9 to $b_1, \ldots, b_m$ in that order. By (38)–(40) there exists F: $\mathcal{X} \to \mathcal{U}$ such that the subspaces

$$\mathcal{R}_i \triangleq \langle A+BF \,|\, b_i \rangle , \qquad i \in \underline{m} ,$$

are independent and have dimension $\varkappa_i$; furthermore, F can be defined so that

$$(A+BF)^{\varkappa_i} \mathcal{R}_i = 0 . \tag{41}$$

By the remark following (37) it is obvious that $\varkappa = (\varkappa_1, \ldots, \varkappa_m)$ is invariant on the $\mathfrak{G}$-orbit of the matrix pair (A, B). Furthermore, distinct orbits $\underline{\omega}_1, \underline{\omega}_2$ yield distinct evaluations of $\varkappa^*(\omega_1), \varkappa^*(\omega_2)$: for if $\underline{p}_i \in \underline{\omega}_i$ and $\varkappa^*(\underline{\omega}_i) = \varkappa$ ($i \in \underline{2}$), there exist $\mathfrak{g}_i \in \mathfrak{G}$ such that $\mathfrak{g}_i \underline{p}_i = \underline{p}^*$, where $\underline{p}^*$ is the canonical pair (A^*, B^*) with indices $\varkappa$; therefore $\underline{p}_2 = \mathfrak{g}_2^{-1} \mathfrak{g}_1 \underline{p}_1$ and so $\underline{\omega}_2 = \underline{\omega}_1$. Theorems 5.9 and 5.10 are now proved, and Corollary 5.3 follows by choosing F according to (41). ▮

From symmetry considerations one would expect that generically, the dimensions $\varkappa_i$ of the $\mathcal{R}_i$ in (31) would all be about equal. This is the content of

COROLLARY 5.4. Let $1 \le m \le n$ and suppose $n = km + \nu$ for some ν, $0 \le \nu < m$. Then in $\mathbb{R}^N$ ($N = n^2 + nm$), generically,

$$\varkappa_i = \begin{cases} k+1 , & 1 \le i \le \nu \\ k & \nu+1 \le i \le m . \end{cases}$$

PROOF: The result is immediate by (32)–(36), if we note that, generically,

$$d(\mathcal{B} + A\mathcal{B} + \cdots + A^{j-1}\mathcal{B}) = \min(n, jm) . \;▮$$

To conclude this section we cite the following amusing application.

THEOREM 5.11. Let (A, B) be controllable, with controllability indices $(\varkappa_1, \ldots, \varkappa_m)$. Then the possible dimensions of the nonzero c.s. of (A, B) are given by the list:

$$\begin{aligned} &\varkappa_m ; \\ &\varkappa_{m-1}, \varkappa_{m-1}+1, \ldots, \varkappa_{m-1}+\varkappa_m ; \\ &\varkappa_{m-2}, \varkappa_{m-2}+1, \ldots, \varkappa_{m-2}+\varkappa_{m-1}+\varkappa_m ; \\ &\cdots\cdots\cdots\cdots\cdots\cdots\cdots\cdots \\ &\varkappa_1, \varkappa_1+1, \ldots, \varkappa_1+\varkappa_2+\cdots+\varkappa_m . \end{aligned} \tag{42}$$

There is exactly one c.s. of dimension $r \ne 0$ if (i) $r = n$, or (ii) for some $j \in \underline{m-1}$,

$$\varkappa_j > r = \varkappa_{j+1} + \varkappa_{j+2} + \cdots + \varkappa_m . \tag{43}$$

If $r \ne n$ and (43) fails, but r is in the list (42), there are nondenumerably many distinct c.s. of dimension r.

For example, if $\varkappa = (5, 2, 1)$, there are nonzero c.s. of dimension r if and only if $1 \le r \le 8$ and $r \neq 4$. These c.s. are unique if r = 1, 3 or 8 but are nondenumerably many if r = 2, 5, 6, or 7.

The proof is left as Ex. 5.12.

5.7 Exercises

5.1 Develop a procedure for the numerical computation of $\mathcal{R}^* \triangleq \sup \underline{\mathcal{C}}(A, B; \operatorname{Ker} D)$. HINT: First compute $\mathcal{V}^* \triangleq \sup \underline{\mathcal{I}}(A, B; \operatorname{Ker} D)$ by the procedure of Ex. 4.2. Then implement the algorithm of Theorem 5.6, as follows. Let $\mathcal{V}^* = \operatorname{Im} V^*$ and let W^* be a maximal solution of $W^*V^* = 0$. Define $\mathcal{S}_\mu = \operatorname{Im} S_\mu$ and let T_μ be a max. sol. of $T_\mu[AS_{\mu-1}, B] = 0$, with $S_0 = 0$. Then S_μ is obtained as a max. sol. of

$$\begin{bmatrix} W^* \\ T_\mu \end{bmatrix} S_\mu = 0, \qquad \mu \in \underline{n}.$$

Since $\mathcal{S}_{\mu+1} \supset \mathcal{S}_\mu$ one has as a check, $\operatorname{Rank}[S_{\mu+1}, S_\mu] = \operatorname{Rank} S_{\mu+1}$; and the stopping test is $\operatorname{Rank} S_{k+1} = \operatorname{Rank} S_k$, i.e., $\mathcal{R}^* = \operatorname{Im} S_k$.

As an illustration suppose

$$A = \begin{bmatrix} 1 & 0 & 0 & 0 & 1 & 0 \\ 0 & 0 & 1 & 0 & 0 & 0 \\ 0 & -1 & 0 & 0 & 0 & 0 \\ 0 & 0 & 0 & 0 & 1 & 0 \\ 0 & 0 & 0 & 1 & 0 & 0 \\ 0 & 0 & 0 & 0 & 0 & 1 \end{bmatrix}, \qquad B = \begin{bmatrix} 0 & 1 & 0 \\ 0 & 0 & 0 \\ 1 & 0 & 0 \\ 0 & 0 & 1 \\ 0 & 0 & 0 \\ 0 & 0 & 0 \end{bmatrix},$$

$$V^* = \begin{bmatrix} 1 & 0 & 0 & 1 & 2 \\ 0 & 1 & 0 & 0 & 0 \\ 0 & 0 & 1 & 0 & 0 \\ 0 & 0 & 0 & 0 & 0 \\ 1 & 0 & 0 & 0 & 0 \\ 0 & 0 & 0 & 0 & 1 \end{bmatrix}.$$

Then $W^* = [0\ 0\ 0\ 1\ 0\ 0]$ and

$$T_1 = \begin{bmatrix} 0 & 1 & 0 & 0 & 0 & 0 \\ 0 & 0 & 0 & 0 & 1 & 0 \\ 0 & 0 & 0 & 0 & 0 & 1 \end{bmatrix}, \qquad S_1 = \begin{bmatrix} 1 & 0 \\ 0 & 0 \\ 0 & 1 \\ 0 & 0 \\ 0 & 0 \\ 0 & 0 \end{bmatrix},$$

$$T_2 = \begin{bmatrix} 0 & 0 & 0 & 0 & 1 & 0 \\ 0 & 0 & 0 & 0 & 0 & 1 \end{bmatrix}, \qquad S_2 = \begin{bmatrix} 1 & 0 & 0 \\ 0 & 1 & 0 \\ 0 & 0 & 1 \\ 0 & 0 & 0 \\ 0 & 0 & 0 \\ 0 & 0 & 0 \end{bmatrix}.$$

This leads to Rank S_3 = Rank S_2, i.e., $\mathcal{R}^* = \operatorname{Im} S_2$.

5.2 Construct an example to illustrate Theorem 5.7. HINT: Continuing from Ex. 5.1, first compute $\underline{F}(\mathcal{V}^*)$, namely those $F: \mathcal{X} \to \mathcal{U}$ such that $(A + BF)\mathcal{V}^* \subset \mathcal{V}^*$. In matrices, these F are the solutions of

$$W^*(A + BF)V^* = 0 ,$$

or $W^*BFV^* = -W^*AV^*$. In this case, we get

$$[0 \;\; 0 \;\; 1]\, F^{3 \times 6} \begin{bmatrix} 1 & 0 & 0 & 1 & 2 \\ 0 & 1 & 0 & 0 & 0 \\ 0 & 0 & 1 & 0 & 0 \\ 0 & 0 & 0 & 0 & 0 \\ 1 & 0 & 0 & 0 & 0 \\ 0 & 0 & 0 & 0 & 1 \end{bmatrix} = -[1 \;\; 0 \;\; 0 \;\; 0 \;\; 0] .$$

Writing $F = [f_{ij}]$ ($i \in \underline{3}$, $j \in \underline{6}$) and solving,

$$F = \begin{bmatrix} f_{11} & f_{12} & f_{13} & f_{14} & f_{15} & f_{16} \\ f_{21} & f_{22} & f_{23} & f_{24} & f_{25} & f_{26} \\ 0 & 0 & 0 & f_{34} & -1 & 0 \end{bmatrix},$$

where the elements written f_{ij} are unrestricted. The general structure of A + BF, $F \in \underline{F}(\mathcal{V}^*)$ is now, by inspection,

$$A + BF = \begin{bmatrix} 1+f_{21} & f_{22} & f_{23} & f_{24} & 1+f_{25} & f_{26} \\ 0 & 0 & 1 & 0 & 0 & 0 \\ f_{11} & -1+f_{12} & f_{13} & f_{14} & f_{15} & f_{16} \\ 0 & 0 & 0 & f_{34} & 0 & 0 \\ 0 & 0 & 0 & 1 & 0 & 0 \\ 0 & 0 & 0 & 0 & 0 & 1 \end{bmatrix}.$$

Next compute the matrix of $(A + BF) \,|\, \mathcal{V}^*$ and exhibit the action on $\mathcal{R}^*$: write $\mathcal{V}^* = \mathcal{R}^* \oplus \mathcal{S}$, where $\mathcal{S}$ is an arbitrary complement of $\mathcal{R}^*$ in $\mathcal{V}^*$; select a basis of $\mathcal{V}^*$ adapted to this decomposition; and transform the matrix to this basis. For example, with $\mathcal{R}^* = \operatorname{Im} S_2$ above,

$$\mathcal{V}^* = \operatorname{Im}\begin{bmatrix} 1 & 0 & 0 \\ 0 & 1 & 0 \\ 0 & 0 & 1 \\ 0 & 0 & 0 \\ 0 & 0 & 0 \\ 0 & 0 & 0 \end{bmatrix} \oplus \operatorname{Im}\begin{bmatrix} 1 & 2 \\ 0 & 0 \\ 0 & 0 \\ 0 & 0 \\ 1 & 0 \\ 0 & 1 \end{bmatrix}.$$

Computing the action of $A+BF$ on these basis vectors yields the matrix

$$(A+BF)\,|\mathcal{V}^* \sim \left[\begin{array}{ccc|cc} 1+f_{21} & f_{22} & f_{23} & 2+f_{21}+f_{25} & 2f_{21}+f_{26} \\ 0 & 0 & 1 & 0 & 0 \\ f_{11} & -1+f_{12} & f_{13} & f_{11}+f_{15} & 2f_{11}+f_{16} \\ \hline 0 & 0 & 0 & 0 & 0 \\ 0 & 0 & 0 & 0 & 1 \end{array}\right].$$

From this the matrix of the fixed induced map $\overline{A+BF}$ on $\mathcal{V}^*/\mathcal{R}^*$ is read off as $\begin{bmatrix} 0 & 0 \\ 0 & 1 \end{bmatrix}$. Finally it can be verified that the spectrum of $(A+BF)\,|\mathcal{R}^*$, i.e., of the upper left block, is arbitrarily assignable by setting $f_{13} = f_{23} = 0$, $f_{22} = 1$, and suitably choosing f_{11}, f_{12} and f_{21}.

5.3 Construct an example to illustrate DDPS and Theorem 5.8. HINT: Arrange, for instance, that $\mathcal{V}^* = \mathcal{R}^* \oplus \mathcal{S}_g \oplus \mathcal{S}_b$, $\mathcal{X} = \mathcal{V}^* \oplus \mathcal{W}$, with $d(\mathcal{R}^*) = d(\mathcal{S}_g) = d(\mathcal{S}_b) = 1$, $d(\mathcal{W}) = 2$. By inspection, the following data satisfy these conditions.

$$A = \left[\begin{array}{c|c|c|cc} 0 & 0 & 0 & 0 & 0 \\ \hline 0 & -1 & 0 & 0 & 0 \\ \hline 0 & 0 & 0 & 1 & 0 \\ \hline 0 & 0 & 0 & 0 & 1 \\ 0 & 0 & 0 & 0 & 0 \end{array}\right], \quad B = \left[\begin{array}{cc} 1 & 0 \\ 0 & 0 \\ 0 & 0 \\ \hline 0 & 0 \\ 0 & 1 \end{array}\right], \quad D = [0\ 0\ 0\ 1\ 0].$$

Here 'good' means 'stable'. A solution is

$$F = \begin{bmatrix} -1 & 0 & 0 & 0 & 0 \\ 0 & 0 & -1 & -3 & -3 \end{bmatrix};$$

all eigenvalues are then assigned to $s = -1$. The decoupled disturbances are those for which

$$\mathcal{S} \subset \mathcal{V}_g^* = \mathcal{R}^* \oplus \mathcal{S}_g = \operatorname{Im} \begin{bmatrix} 1 & 0 \\ 0 & 1 \\ 0 & 0 \\ 0 & 0 \\ 0 & 0 \end{bmatrix} .$$

Note that while (A, B) is not controllable, the condition (28) is satisfied. Note also that the example could be made to look more impressive by disguising the structure: replace A by $A + B\hat{F}$ for a random $\hat{F}$, and apply a random similarity transformation

$$(D, A + B\hat{F}, B) \mapsto (DT^{-1}, T(A + B\hat{F})T^{-1}, TB) .$$

Now solve the disguised version by computing, in this order: $\mathcal{V}^*$, $\mathcal{R}^*$, $F_0 \in \underline{F}(\mathcal{V}^*)$, $\mathcal{V}_g^*$, $Q: \mathcal{X} \to \mathcal{X}/\mathcal{V}_g^*$, $\tilde{F}: \mathcal{X}/\mathcal{V}_g^* \to \mathcal{U}$, and finally $F = F_0 + \tilde{F}Q$, just as in the proof of Theorem 5.8. Here F_0 is chosen to make $(A + BF_0)|\mathcal{R}^*$ stable.

5.4 Construct a numerical illustration of Theorems 5.9 and 5.10 by working through the proof with, say, n = 8, m = 3 and randomly chosen A, B.

5.5 Verify the assertion at the end of Section 5.5.

5.6 A necessary condition that $\mathcal{R}$ be a c.s. is that $\mathcal{R} + \mathcal{B} = A\mathcal{R} + \mathcal{B}$. Is this condition sufficient?

5.7 Show by an example that the intersection of two c.s. need not be a c.s., or even be (A, B)-invariant. Show, however, that the family of c.s. of (A, B) is a lattice relative to the operations + and $\wedge$, where

$$\mathcal{R}_1 \wedge \mathcal{R}_2 \triangleq \sup \underline{\mathcal{C}}(A, B; \mathcal{R}_1 \cap \mathcal{R}_2) .$$

Is this lattice modular?

5.8 Let $\mathcal{S} \subset \mathcal{X}$ be a fixed subspace and consider the family $\underline{\mathcal{F}}$ of c.s. $\mathcal{R}$ such that $\mathcal{R} \supset \mathcal{S}$. Show by example that in general $\underline{\mathcal{F}}$ does not possess a (unique) smallest element. Show, however, that if $\underline{\mathcal{F}}$ is nonempty it possesses at least one <u>minimal</u> element $\mathcal{R}_0$, such that $\mathcal{R}_0 \supset \mathcal{R} \in \underline{\mathcal{F}}$ implies $\mathcal{R} = \mathcal{R}_0$.

5.9 Given $\dot{x} = Ax + Bu$ and $\mathcal{T} \subset \mathcal{X}$, show that the largest c.s. $\mathcal{R}^* \subset \mathcal{T}$ is characterized by the following property: $\mathcal{R}^*$ is the largest subspace $\mathcal{S} \subset \mathcal{T}$ such that, if $x(0) = 0$ and $x \in \mathcal{S}$, there exists a continuous control $u(t)$, $0 \le t \le 1$, for which $x(t) \in \mathcal{T}$, $0 \le t \le 1$, and

$x(1) = x$. Thus $\mathcal{R}^*$ is the largest subspace of $\mathcal{T}$ all of whose states can be reached from $x(0) = 0$ by a continuous path lying entirely in $\mathcal{T}$.

5.10 Let $A\mathcal{N} \subset \mathcal{N} \subset \mathcal{T} \subset \mathcal{X}$ and $P: \mathcal{X} \to \overline{\mathcal{X}} \triangleq \mathcal{X}/\mathcal{N}$ the canonical projection. If $\mathcal{V}^*, \mathcal{R}^*$ (resp. $(\overline{\mathcal{V}})^*$, $(\overline{\mathcal{R}})^*$) have their usual meaning relative to $\mathcal{T}$ (resp. $\overline{\mathcal{T}}$), show that

$$\overline{\mathcal{V}^*} = (\overline{\mathcal{V}})^*$$

and

$$\overline{\mathcal{R}^*} = (\overline{\mathcal{R}})^* .$$

5.11 Show that, for arbitrary subspaces $\mathcal{R} \subset \mathcal{S} \subset \mathcal{X}$ and a map $P: \mathcal{X} \to \mathcal{X}$,

$$d\left(\frac{\mathcal{S}}{\mathcal{R}}\right) = d\left(\frac{P\mathcal{S}}{P\mathcal{R}}\right) + d\left(\frac{\mathcal{S} \cap \operatorname{Ker} P}{\mathcal{R} \cap \operatorname{Ker} P}\right);$$

and if $\mathcal{T} \subset \mathcal{X}$,

$$d\left(\frac{\mathcal{S}}{\mathcal{R}}\right) = d\left(\frac{\mathcal{S} + \mathcal{T}}{\mathcal{R} + \mathcal{T}}\right) + d\left(\frac{\mathcal{S} \cap \mathcal{T}}{\mathcal{R} \cap \mathcal{T}}\right).$$

Applying these results to the $\mathcal{S}_j$ defined by (32) show that (for $j = 0, 1, \ldots, n-1$)

$$d\left(\frac{\mathcal{S}_j}{\mathcal{S}_{j-1}}\right) = d\left(\frac{\mathcal{S}_{j+1}}{\mathcal{S}_j}\right) + d\left(\frac{\mathcal{B} \cap A\mathcal{S}_j}{\mathcal{B} \cap A\mathcal{S}_{j-1}}\right) + d\left(\frac{\mathcal{S}_j \cap \operatorname{Ker} A}{\mathcal{S}_{j-1} \cap \operatorname{Ker} A}\right),$$

where $\mathcal{S}_{-1} \triangleq 0$.

5.12 Prove Theorem 5.11. HINT: First prove the result for $m = 2$. In this case, to construct a c.s. $\mathcal{R}$ with $d(\mathcal{R}) = \kappa_1 + k$ $(1 \le k \le \kappa_2 - 1)$ take (A, B) in canonical form, and as a basis for $\mathcal{R}$ the vectors $x_1, \ldots, x_{\kappa_1 + k}$ given by

$$b_1,\ Ab_1,\ \ldots,\ A^{\mu-1} b_1,$$

$$A^{\mu} b_1 + b_2,\ A^{\mu+1} b_1 + Ab_2,\ \ldots,\ A^{\kappa_1 - 1} b_1 + A^{\kappa_1 - \mu - 1} b_2,$$

$$A^{\kappa_1 - \mu} b_2,\ \ldots,\ A^{\kappa_2 - 1} b_2,$$

where $\mu \triangleq \kappa_1 + k - \kappa_2$; then define $F: \mathcal{X} \to \mathcal{U}$ according to

$$BFx_i = 0, \quad i \ne \mu; \qquad BFx_{\mu} = b_2 .$$

Show next that there is no c.s. with dimension k': $k' < \kappa_2$ or $\kappa_2 < k' < \kappa_1$; and finally, check uniqueness. The generalization to arbitrary m is now easy.

5.13 Suppose (A, B) is controllable and $A\mathcal{R} \subset \mathcal{R}$. Write $\mathcal{X} = \mathcal{R} \oplus \mathcal{S}$, and in a compatible basis let

$$A = \begin{bmatrix} A_1 & A_3 \\ 0 & A_2 \end{bmatrix}, \qquad B = \begin{bmatrix} B_1 \\ B_2 \end{bmatrix}.$$

Show that (A_1, B_1) is controllable if and only if $\mathcal{R}$ is a c.s., but (A_2, B_2) is always controllable. If $\mathcal{R}$ is a c.s. show that there exists G such that $\hat{B} \triangleq BG$ has the matrix

$$\hat{B} = \begin{bmatrix} \hat{B}_{11} & \hat{B}_{12} \\ 0 & \hat{B}_{22} \end{bmatrix},$$

where $(A_1, \hat{B}_{11})$ is controllable.

5.8 Notes and References

The concept of controllability subspace was introduced by Wonham and Morse [1]. Most of the results of this chapter were presented in the reference cited, and by Morse and Wonham [1]. The results of Section 5.5 were reported informally by Wonham [6]. Section 5.6 is adapted from Brunovsky [1] and Wonham and Morse [2], except for Theorem 5.11, which is due to Warren and Eckberg [1]. For alternative approaches to the subject of controllability indices, via Kronecker or 'minimal' indices, see Rosenbrock [1] and Kalman [4].

CHAPTER 6

TRACKING AND REGULATION I: OUTPUT STABILIZATION

A typical multivariable control problem requires the design of dynamic compensation to guarantee the following desirable behavior of the closed loop system.

1. Each of an assigned set of output variables converges to, or tracks, a corresponding observed reference input from a specified function class. This is the servo problem.

2. Each of an assigned set of output variables converges to zero from arbitrary initial values, when the system is perturbed by possibly nonmeasurable disturbances in a specified function class. This is the regulator problem; the convergent variables are said to be regulated; and zero represents the desired or set-point value.

Very often both features are present in the same problem: the system is required to track in the presence of disturbances. Indeed, the formal distinction between the servo and regulator problems disappears if we regard each tracking error (the difference between a reference input and the corresponding output) as a variable to be regulated. For this reason we may safely restrict attention to the regulator problem alone.

We shall also assume that the disturbance variables (including reference inputs) satisfy known, time-invariant, linear differential equations of finite order. After writing these in state-variable format, we include them together with the equations of the plant (for an example, see Section 7.7). The combined system equations then take the standard form

$$\dot{x}(t) = Ax(t) + Bu(t), \qquad t \geq 0, \tag{1}$$

$$y(t) = Cx(t), \qquad t \geq 0, \tag{2}$$

and

$$z(t) = Dx(t), \qquad t \geq 0. \tag{3}$$

Here $y(\cdot)$ is the vector of directly measured outputs and $z(\cdot)$ is the variable to be regulated. Thus it is required that for every initial state $x(0+)$, we have

$$z(t) \to 0, \qquad t \to \infty. \tag{4}$$

Typically the triple (C, A, B) is not controllable and observable, or even stabilizable and detectable: if it were, the problem would be solved by an immediate application of the results of Sections 3.5–3.7. Stabilizability may fail because the 'exogenous' variables – disturbances and reference signals – cannot be controlled; and detectability may fail if, for instance, certain disturbance variables happen to be decoupled from the measured outputs.

We turn now to a detailed discussion of how these constraints affect solvability of the problem.

6.1 Restricted Regulator Problem (RRP)

Let $\mathcal{N}$ denote the unobservable subspace of (C, A):

$$\mathcal{N} \triangleq \bigcap_{i=1}^{n} \operatorname{Ker}(CA^{i-1}) .$$

Write $\bar{\mathcal{X}} \triangleq \mathcal{X}/\mathcal{N}$ and let $P: \mathcal{X} \to \bar{\mathcal{X}}$ be the canonical projection. As noted in Section 3.2, the 'observable subsystem' may be identified with the triple $(\bar{C}, \bar{A}, \bar{B})$ in the commutative diagram below:

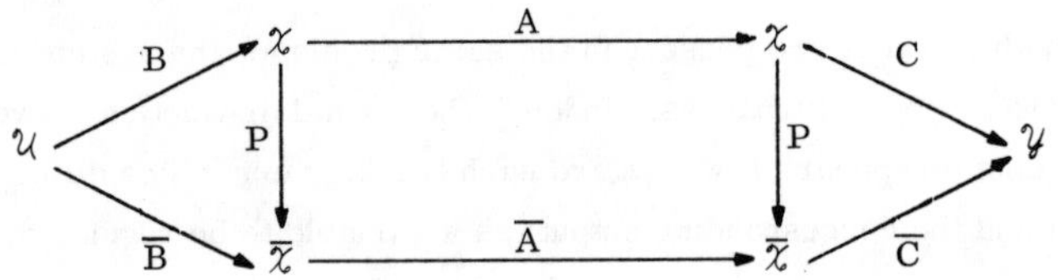

Since $A\mathcal{N} \subset \mathcal{N}$, the induced map $\bar{A}: \bar{\mathcal{X}} \to \bar{\mathcal{X}}$ is defined, and as $\operatorname{Ker} C \supset \mathcal{N}$, there exists $\bar{C}: \bar{\mathcal{X}} \to \mathcal{Y}$ with $\bar{C}P = C$; finally, we set $PB = \bar{B}$.

Since the pair $(\bar{C}, \bar{A})$ is observable we know from Section 3.3 that maps $\bar{J}: \bar{\mathcal{X}} \to \bar{\mathcal{X}}$ and $\bar{K}: \mathcal{Y} \to \bar{\mathcal{X}}$ exist such that the auxiliary system

$$\dot{\bar{w}}(t) = \bar{J}\bar{w}(t) + \bar{K}y(t) + \bar{B}u(t) , \qquad t \geq 0 ,$$

is a dynamic observer for the system (1), (2) reduced mod $\mathcal{N}$. Namely we select $\bar{K}$ such that

$$\sigma(\bar{A} - \bar{K}\bar{C}) \subset \mathbb{C}^-$$

and set $\bar{J} \triangleq \bar{A} - \bar{K}\bar{C}$, $\bar{e}(t) \triangleq \bar{x}(t) - \bar{w}(t)$. Since

$$\dot{\bar{x}}(t) = \bar{A}\bar{x}(t) + \bar{B}u(t) , \qquad t \geq 0 ,$$

there follows $\dot{\bar{e}}(t) = \bar{J}\bar{e}(t)$ $(t \geq 0)$, so that $\bar{e}(t) \to 0$ $(t \to \infty)$. Since $\sigma(\bar{J})$ can be assigned arbitrarily by suitable choice of $\bar{K}$, convergence can in principle be made arbitrarily exponentially fast. Now suppose $u(t) = \overline{F}\,\overline{w}(t)$ for some $\overline{F}: \overline{\mathcal{X}} \to \mathcal{U}$. Setting $F = \overline{F}P$ and noting that

$$u = \overline{F}(\overline{x} - \overline{e}) = \overline{F}(Px - \overline{e}) = Fx - \overline{F}\overline{e}$$

we obtain from (1),

$$\dot{x} = (A + BF)x - B\overline{F}\overline{e}\,, \qquad t \geq 0\,. \tag{5}$$

From (3), (4) and (5) we conclude that regulation is achieved with the control law $u = \overline{F}\overline{w}$ if and only if

$$De^{t(A+BF)}\left[x(0+) - \int_0^t e^{-\tau(A+BF)}B\overline{F}\overline{e}(\tau)\,d\tau\right] \to 0$$

as $t \to \infty$, for all $x(0+)$, $\overline{e}(0+)$. Equivalently

$$De^{t(A+BF)} \to 0\,, \qquad t \to \infty\,, \tag{6}$$

and

$$\int_0^t De^{(t-\tau)(A+BF)}B\overline{F}e^{\tau\overline{J}}\,d\tau \to 0\,, \qquad t \to \infty\,. \tag{7}$$

Suppose (6) is true. Since $\overline{J}$ is stable, the integral in (7) is the convolution of functions having Laplace transforms which are analytic in $\mathbb{C}^+$, and (7) follows. On this basis we can (and shall) ignore the term containing $\overline{e}$ in (5), assume that the state $\overline{x}$ of the observable reduced system is directly observable at the start, and admit a priori all controls of the form $u = \overline{F}\overline{x}$. A control $u = Fx$ can be written in this form if and only if $F = \overline{F}P$ for some $\overline{F}$, that is, $\operatorname{Ker} F \supset \mathcal{N}$, and this version of the observability constraint will be used in the sequel. We remark that exactly the same reasoning applies if the observer is chosen to be of minimal dynamic order given by

$$d(\operatorname{Ker}\overline{C}) = d(\operatorname{Ker} C) - d(\mathcal{N}),$$

along the lines of Section 3.4.

Finally, as shown in Section 4.4, a condition equivalent to (6) is $\mathcal{X}^+(A + BF) \subset \operatorname{Ker} D$.

In this way we are led to formulate the <u>Restricted Regulator Problem (RRP).</u> <u>Given the maps</u> $A: \mathcal{X} \to \mathcal{X}$, $B: \mathcal{U} \to \mathcal{X}$, $D: \mathcal{X} \to \mathcal{Z}$, <u>and a subspace</u> $\mathcal{N} \subset \mathcal{X}$ <u>with</u> $A\mathcal{N} \subset \mathcal{N}$, <u>find</u> $F: \mathcal{X} \to \mathcal{U}$ <u>such that</u>

$$\operatorname{Ker} F \supset \mathcal{N}$$

<u>and</u>

$$\mathcal{X}^+(A + BF) \subset \operatorname{Ker} D\,. \tag{8}$$

RRP is 'restricted' in the sense that no provision is made for dynamic compensation other than that tacitly introduced by the observer. Actually, we shall exploit dynamic compensation later, using a technique of state space extension which will bring our results to a satisfactory completion.

6.2 Solvability of RRP

In this section we obtain necessary and sufficient conditions for the solvability of RRP. As they stand, these conditions are not constructive in the sense of providing an algorithmic solution of the problem when a solution exists; nevertheless they can made so in combination with state space extension, as will be shown in Section 6.3.

THEOREM 6.1. RRP is solvable if and only if there exists a subspace $\mathcal{V} \subset \mathcal{X}$ such that

$$\mathcal{V} \subset \operatorname{Ker} D \cap A^{-1}(\mathcal{V} + \mathcal{B}) \tag{9}$$

$$\mathcal{X}^+(A) \cap \mathcal{N} + A(\mathcal{V} \cap \mathcal{N}) \subset \mathcal{V} \tag{10}$$

and

$$\mathcal{X}^+(A) \subset \langle A \mid \mathcal{B} \rangle + \mathcal{V} . \tag{11}$$

We remark that condition (9) is equivalent to $\mathcal{V} \in \underline{\mathcal{I}}(A, B; \operatorname{Ker} D)$; we employ the more explicit version for greater directness.

Before proving Theorem 6.1 we note various structural features of conditions (9)–(11). Introduce the family of subspaces

$$\underline{\mathcal{V}} = \{\mathcal{V}: \ \mathcal{V} \in \underline{\mathcal{I}}(A, B; \operatorname{Ker} D) \ \& \ A(\mathcal{V} \cap \mathcal{N}) \subset \mathcal{V}\} .$$

In general $\underline{\mathcal{V}}$ is not closed under addition and it is not true that $\underline{\mathcal{V}}$ contains a supremal element (in the sense of Section 4.2). However, as $\underline{\mathcal{V}}$ is nonempty ($0 \in \underline{\mathcal{V}}$) it always has, possibly many, maximal elements: by definition, $\mathcal{V}^M \in \underline{\mathcal{V}}$ is maximal if $\mathcal{V} \in \underline{\mathcal{V}}$ and $\mathcal{V} \supset \mathcal{V}^M$ imply $\mathcal{V} = \mathcal{V}^M$. We have

COROLLARY 6.1. RRP is solvable if and only if

$$\mathcal{X}^+(A) \cap \mathcal{N} \subset \operatorname{Ker} D , \tag{12}$$

and for some maximal element $\mathcal{V}^M \in \underline{\mathcal{V}}$,

$$\mathcal{X}^+(A) \subset \langle A \mid \mathcal{B} \rangle + \mathcal{V}^M . \tag{13}$$

The difficulty in verifying (13) is that of effectively parametrizing the subfamily of all $\mathcal{V}^M$. Actually, in many cases which arise in practice it happens that $\underline{\mathcal{V}}$ does contain a (unique) supremal element, namely the familiar

$$\mathcal{V}^* \triangleq \sup \underline{\mathcal{I}}(A, B; \operatorname{Ker} D) .$$

That is, $\mathcal{V}^*$ satisfies the second defining condition in (10):

$$A(\mathcal{V}^* \cap \mathcal{N}) \subset \mathcal{V}^* . \tag{14}$$

Then, of course, the $\mathcal{V}^M$ all coincide with $\mathcal{V}^*$ and solvability of RRP is constructively verifiable by the algorithm of Theorem 4.3:

$$\mathcal{V}^0 = \operatorname{Ker} D$$

$$\mathcal{V}^j = \operatorname{Ker} D \cap A^{-1}(\mathcal{V}^{j-1} + \mathcal{B}) , \qquad j \in \underline{n} \tag{15}$$

$$\mathcal{V}^* = \mathcal{V}^n .$$

A sufficient condition for (14) to be true is included in the following.

COROLLARY 6.2. Suppose

$$A(\mathcal{N} \cap \operatorname{Ker} D) \subset \operatorname{Ker} D . \tag{16}$$

Then RRP is solvable if and only if

$$\mathcal{X}^+(A) \cap \mathcal{N} \subset \operatorname{Ker} D$$

and

$$\mathcal{X}^+(A) \subset \langle A | \mathcal{B} \rangle + \mathcal{V}^* .$$

The proof of these results depends on four lemmas, of which the first has already been proved as Theorem 4.4.

LEMMA 6.1. Let $\mathcal{K} \subset \mathcal{X}$. There exists a map F: $\mathcal{X} \to \mathcal{U}$ such that

$$\mathcal{X}^+(A + BF) \subset \mathcal{K}$$

if and only if

$$\mathcal{X}^+(A) \subset \langle A | \mathcal{B} \rangle + \mathcal{T}^* ,$$

where

$$\mathcal{T}^* \triangleq \sup \underline{\mathcal{I}}(A, B; \mathcal{K}) .$$

LEMMA 6.2. Let A: $\mathcal{X} \to \mathcal{X}$, A_1: $\mathcal{X} \to \mathcal{X}$ and $\mathcal{N} \subset \mathcal{X}$, with $A\mathcal{N} \subset \mathcal{N}$ and $A_1 | \mathcal{N} = A | \mathcal{N}$. Then

$$\mathcal{X}^+(A_1) \cap \mathcal{N} = \mathcal{X}^+(A) \cap \mathcal{N}.$$

PROOF: Denote by α_1^+ (resp. α^+) the unstable factor of the m.p. of A_1 (resp. A). Let $x \in \mathcal{X}^+(A_1) \cap \mathcal{N}$. Then $x \in \operatorname{Ker} \alpha_1^+(A_1)$. Since A coincides with A_1 on $\mathcal{N}$, $A^j x = A_1^j x$ $(j = 1, 2, \ldots)$ and therefore

$$\alpha_1^+(A)x = \alpha_1^+(A_1)x = 0 .$$

Let $\alpha_x(\lambda)$ be the A-m.p. of x. Then $\alpha_x | \alpha_1^+$, that is, the complex zeros of α_x belong to $\mathbb{C}^+$. Let $\alpha = \alpha^+\alpha^-$ be the m.p. of A. Then also $\alpha_x | \alpha$, and therefore $\alpha_x | \alpha^+$. Thus $x \in \operatorname{Ker} \alpha^+(A)$; that is, $x \in \mathcal{X}^+(A) \cap \mathcal{N}$. We have shown that

$$\mathcal{X}^+(A_1) \cap \mathcal{N} \subset \mathcal{X}^+(A) \cap \mathcal{N} ,$$

and the reverse inclusion follows by symmetry. ▮

LEMMA 6.3. <u>Let</u> $A\mathcal{V} \subset \mathcal{V} + \mathcal{B}$ <u>and</u> $A_1 = A + BF_1$. <u>Then the relation</u>

$$\mathcal{X}^+(A) \subset \langle A | \mathcal{B} \rangle + \mathcal{V} \tag{17}$$

<u>implies</u>

$$\mathcal{X}^+(A_1) \subset \langle A_1 | \mathcal{B} \rangle + \mathcal{V} .$$

PROOF: By (17) and Lemma 6.1 (with $\mathcal{K} = \mathcal{J}^* = \mathcal{V}$) there exists F: $\mathcal{X} \to \mathcal{U}$ such that $\mathcal{X}^+(A + BF) \subset \mathcal{V}$. Setting $F_0 = F - F_1$ we have $\mathcal{X}^+(A_1 + BF_0) \subset \mathcal{V}$ and so, again by Lemma 6.1,

$$\mathcal{X}^+(A_1) \subset \langle A_1 | \mathcal{B} \rangle + \mathcal{V} . \ ▮$$

LEMMA 6.4. <u>For arbitrary</u> F: $\mathcal{X} \to \mathcal{U}$,

$$\mathcal{X}^+(A + BF) + \langle A | \mathcal{B} \rangle = \mathcal{X}^+(A) + \langle A | \mathcal{B} \rangle . \tag{18}$$

PROOF: If P: $\mathcal{X} \to \mathcal{X}/\langle A | \mathcal{B} \rangle$ is the canonical projection and a bar denotes the induced map in $\mathcal{X}/\langle A | \mathcal{B} \rangle$, then $\overline{A + BF} = \overline{A}$ and

$$\begin{aligned} P\mathcal{X}^+(A + BF) &= \overline{\mathcal{X}}^+(\overline{A + BF}) \quad \text{(by Lemma 4.6)} \\ &= \overline{\mathcal{X}}^+(\overline{A}) = P\mathcal{X}^+(A) . \end{aligned} \tag{19}$$

From (19), (18) follows at once. ▮

PROOF of Theorem 6.1. (If) Let $\mathcal{V}$ have the properties (9)–(11). Then

$$A\mathcal{V} \subset \mathcal{V} + \mathcal{B} , \qquad A(\mathcal{V} \cap \mathcal{N}) \subset \mathcal{V} . \tag{20}$$

By (20) there exists $F_0\colon \mathcal{X} \to \mathcal{U}$ such that

$$(A + BF_0)\mathcal{V} \subset \mathcal{V}, \qquad F_0(\mathcal{V} \cap \mathcal{N}) = 0 .$$

Let

$$\mathcal{V} + \mathcal{N} = \hat{\mathcal{V}} \oplus \mathcal{V} \cap \mathcal{N} \oplus \hat{\mathcal{N}} ,$$

where $\hat{\mathcal{V}} \subset \mathcal{V}$ and $\hat{\mathcal{N}} \subset \mathcal{N}$. Define $F_1\colon \mathcal{X} \to \mathcal{U}$ such that $F_1|\mathcal{V} = F_0|\mathcal{V}$ and $F_1|\hat{\mathcal{N}} = 0$. Then $F_1\mathcal{N} = 0$ and $(A + BF_1)\mathcal{V} \subset \mathcal{V}$. Write $A_1 \triangleq A + BF_1$, let $P\colon \mathcal{X} \to \mathcal{X}/\mathcal{V}$ be the canonical projection, and consider the commutative diagram below.

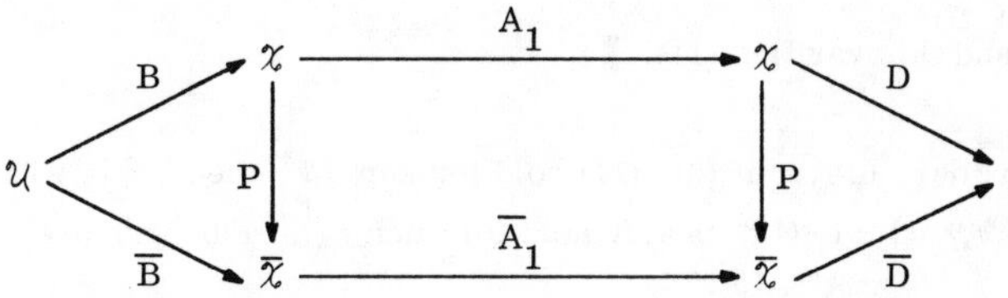

Here $\bar{A}_1$ is the induced map on $\bar{\mathcal{X}} \triangleq \mathcal{X}/\mathcal{V}$, and $\bar{D}$ exists since $\operatorname{Ker} D \supset \mathcal{V}$. Now $A_1|\mathcal{N} = A|\mathcal{N}$, so by Lemma 6.2 and (10),

$$\mathcal{X}^+(A_1) \cap \mathcal{N} = \mathcal{X}^+(A) \cap \mathcal{N} \subset \mathcal{V} .$$

Thus

$$\mathcal{N} = \mathcal{N} \cap \mathcal{X}^+(A_1) \oplus \mathcal{N} \cap \mathcal{X}^-(A_1) \subset \mathcal{X}^-(A_1) + \mathcal{V}$$

so that

$$\bar{\mathcal{N}} \triangleq P\mathcal{N} \subset \bar{\mathcal{X}}^-(\bar{A}_1) . \tag{21}$$

Also, Lemma 6.3 and (11) yield

$$\mathcal{X}^+(A_1) \subset \langle A_1|\mathcal{B}\rangle + \mathcal{V}$$

so

$$\bar{\mathcal{X}}^+(\bar{A}_1) \subset \langle \bar{A}_1|\bar{\mathcal{B}}\rangle . \tag{22}$$

By (21) and (22) there exists $\bar{F}_2\colon \bar{\mathcal{X}} \to \mathcal{U}$ such that $\operatorname{Ker} \bar{F}_2 \supset \bar{\mathcal{N}}$ and $\bar{A}_1 + \bar{B}\bar{F}_2$ is stable. Define $F_2 = \bar{F}_2 P$. Then $F_2\mathcal{N} = \bar{F}_2\bar{\mathcal{N}} = 0$. Let $F = F_1 + F_2$. Then $F\mathcal{N} = 0$. Also, $F_2\mathcal{V} = 0$ implies

$$(A + BF)|\mathcal{V} = A_1|\mathcal{V} ,$$

so $(A + BF)\mathcal{V} \subset \mathcal{V}$. For the induced map $\overline{A + BF}$ on $\bar{\mathcal{X}}$ we have

$$\bar{\mathcal{X}}^+(\overline{A + BF}) = \bar{\mathcal{X}}^+(\bar{A}_1 + \bar{B}\bar{F}_2) = \bar{0} ,$$

so that

$$\mathcal{X}^+(A + BF) \subset \mathcal{V} \subset \operatorname{Ker} D \qquad \text{as required.}$$

(Only if) Let $\mathcal{V} = \mathcal{X}^+(A+BF)$. Then (9) is clear from (8). Since Ker F $\supset \mathcal{N}$, we have

$$(A+BF)|\mathcal{N} = A|\mathcal{N}$$

and by Lemma 6.2

$$\mathcal{V} \cap \mathcal{N} = \mathcal{X}^+(A+BF) \cap \mathcal{N} = \mathcal{X}^+(A) \cap \mathcal{N} ,$$

so that $A(\mathcal{V} \cap \mathcal{N}) \subset \mathcal{V} \cap \mathcal{N}$, proving (10). Finally

$$\mathcal{V} + \langle A|\mathcal{B}\rangle = \mathcal{X}^+(A+BF) + \langle A|\mathcal{B}\rangle = \mathcal{X}^+(A) + \langle A|\mathcal{B}\rangle ,$$

by Lemma 6.4, and this verifies (11). ▮

PROOF of Corollary 6.1. If (9) – (11) hold for some $\mathcal{V}$, then $\mathcal{V} \in \underline{\mathcal{V}}$. There is some $\mathcal{V}^M \in \underline{\mathcal{V}}$ with $\mathcal{V}^M \supset \mathcal{V}$, and (9) – (11) clearly hold for such $\mathcal{V}^M$. Furthermore,

$$\mathcal{X}^+(A) \cap \mathcal{N} \subset \mathcal{V} \subset \text{Ker } D .$$

For the converse, set $\mathcal{V} = \mathcal{V}^M$. By (12), $\mathcal{X}^+(A) \cap \mathcal{N}$ is an A-invariant subspace of $\mathcal{N} \cap \text{Ker } D$, hence certainly belongs to each $\mathcal{V}^M$: indeed if $\mathcal{V} \in \underline{\mathcal{V}}$ then

$$\left[\mathcal{V} + \mathcal{X}^+(A) \cap \mathcal{N}\right] \cap \mathcal{N} = \mathcal{V} \cap \mathcal{N} + \mathcal{X}^+(A) \cap \mathcal{N}$$

and therefore $\mathcal{V} + \mathcal{X}^+(A) \cap \mathcal{N} \in \underline{\mathcal{V}}$. ▮

PROOF of Corollary 6.2. By (16), $A(\mathcal{N} \cap \text{Ker } D) \subset \mathcal{N} \cap \text{Ker } D$, so $\mathcal{N} \cap \text{Ker } D \subset \mathcal{V}^*$. Therefore

$$\mathcal{V}^* \cap \mathcal{N} \subset \text{Ker } D \cap \mathcal{N} \subset \mathcal{V}^* \cap \mathcal{N} .$$

Thus $\mathcal{V}^* \cap \mathcal{N} = \text{Ker } D \cap \mathcal{N}$ is A-invariant, so $\mathcal{V}^* \in \underline{\mathcal{V}}$. Therefore $\mathcal{V}^M = \mathcal{V}^*$ for all $\mathcal{V}^M$, and the result follows by Corollary 6.1. ▮

To conclude this section we give a description of the subspaces $\mathcal{V}^M$ which will be useful later.

PROPOSITION 6.1. Let

$$\mathcal{V}_0 \triangleq \bigcap_{i=1}^{n} A^{-i+1}(\text{Ker } D \cap \mathcal{N}) .$$

Each subspace $\mathcal{V}^M$ is of the form

$$\mathcal{V}^M = \mathcal{V}_0 \oplus \mathcal{V}_1 ,$$

<u>where</u>

$$\mathcal{V}_1 = \sup\left\{\mathcal{V}:\ \mathcal{V} \subset \mathcal{W} \cap A^{-1}(\mathcal{B} + \mathcal{V}_0 + \mathcal{V})\right\}$$

<u>and</u> $\mathcal{W}$ <u>is a suitable complement of</u> $\mathcal{N} \cap \operatorname{Ker} D$ <u>in</u> $\operatorname{Ker} D$.

The idea is illustrated by the lattice diagram, Fig. 6.1.

PROOF: Suppose $\mathcal{V}^M$ is maximal, and write

$$\mathcal{V}^M = \mathcal{V}^M \cap \mathcal{N} \oplus \mathcal{V}_1^M ,$$

$$\operatorname{Ker} D = \operatorname{Ker} D \cap \mathcal{N} \oplus \mathcal{V}_1^M \oplus \mathcal{W}_1$$

and

$$\mathcal{V}_1^M \oplus \mathcal{W}_1 = \mathcal{W} .$$

It will be shown that

$$\mathcal{V}^M \cap \mathcal{N} = \mathcal{V}_0 \tag{23}$$

and

$$\mathcal{V}_1^M = \mathcal{V}_1 . \tag{24}$$

As to (23), observe that

$$\mathcal{V}_0 = \sup\{\mathcal{V}:\ \mathcal{V} \subset \mathcal{N} \cap \operatorname{Ker} D,\ A\mathcal{V} \subset \mathcal{V}\} , \tag{25}$$

hence the subspace

$$\left(\mathcal{V}^M + \mathcal{V}_0\right) \cap \mathcal{N} = \mathcal{V}^M \cap \mathcal{N} + \mathcal{V}_0$$

is A-invariant, so $\mathcal{V}^M + \mathcal{V}_0 \in \underline{\mathcal{V}}$. By maximality of $\mathcal{V}^M$, $\mathcal{V}^M \supset \mathcal{V}_0$, i.e., $\mathcal{V}^M \cap \mathcal{N} \supset \mathcal{V}_0$. But as $\mathcal{V}^M \cap \mathcal{N}$ is A-invariant and belongs to $\mathcal{N} \cap \operatorname{Ker} D$, it follows by (25) that $\mathcal{V}^M \cap \mathcal{N} \subset \mathcal{V}_0$, and (23) is proved. For (24), we have first

$$A\mathcal{V}_1^M \subset A\mathcal{V}^M \subset \mathcal{V}^M + \mathcal{B} = \mathcal{V}^M \cap \mathcal{N} + \mathcal{V}_1^M + \mathcal{B} = \mathcal{V}_0 + \mathcal{B} + \mathcal{V}_1^M ,$$

and therefore $\mathcal{V}_1^M \subset \mathcal{V}_1$. Now $\mathcal{V}_1 \cap \mathcal{N} = 0$, as $\mathcal{V}_1 \subset \mathcal{W}$ and $\mathcal{W} \cap \mathcal{N} = 0$. Hence the subspace

$$(\mathcal{V}_0 \oplus \mathcal{V}_1) \cap \mathcal{N} = \mathcal{V}_0$$

is A-invariant. Since also $\mathcal{V}_0 \oplus \mathcal{V}_1 \subset \operatorname{Ker} D$, and

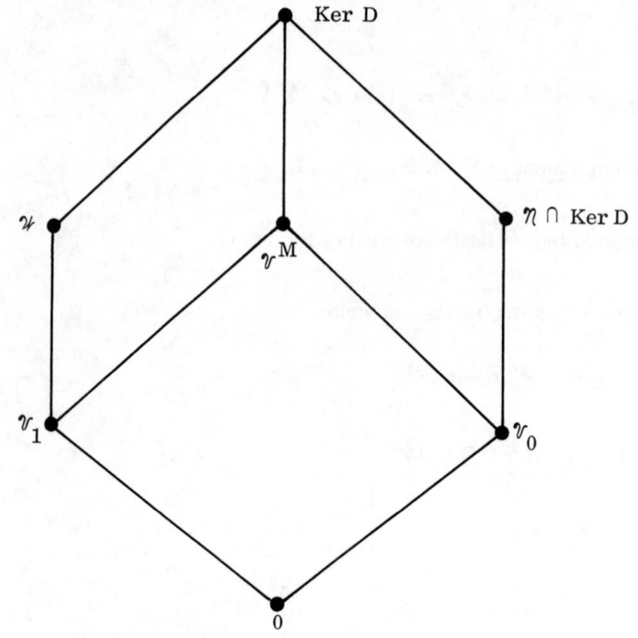

Fig. 6.1.

Lattice Diagram: Structure of $\mathcal{V}^M$

$$A(\mathcal{V}_0 \oplus \mathcal{V}_1) \subset \mathcal{V}_0 + \mathcal{V}_1 + \mathcal{B},$$

there results $\mathcal{V}_0 \oplus \mathcal{V}_1 \in \underline{\mathcal{V}}$. But since

$$\mathcal{V}_0 \oplus \mathcal{V}_1 \supset \mathcal{V}_0 \oplus \mathcal{V}_1^M = \mathcal{V}^M, \tag{26}$$

the maximality of $\mathcal{V}^M$ implies that equality holds in (26), and because $\mathcal{V}_1 \supset \mathcal{V}_1^M$, (24) results. ▮

6.3 Extended Regulator Problem (ERP)

To exploit the advantages of dynamic compensation we bring in auxiliary dynamic elements (integrators), according to the equations

$$\dot{x}_a = B_a u_a, \qquad y_a = C_a x_a,$$

where $u_a \in \mathcal{U}_a$, $x_a \in \mathcal{X}_a$, $y_a \in \mathcal{Y}_a$. Here $B_a: \mathcal{U}_a \approx \mathcal{X}_a$ and $C_a: \mathcal{X}_a \approx \mathcal{Y}_a$ are arbitrary isomorphisms. Introduce the external direct sums

$$\mathcal{U}_e = \mathcal{U} \oplus \mathcal{U}_a, \qquad \mathcal{X}_e = \mathcal{X} \oplus \mathcal{X}_a, \qquad \mathcal{Y}_e = \mathcal{Y} \oplus \mathcal{Y}_a$$

for the extended control, state and (observed) output spaces, and accordingly define the extended maps

$$\begin{aligned}
&A_e: \mathcal{X}_e \to \mathcal{X}_e; \quad && A_e|\mathcal{X} = A, \quad && A_e|\mathcal{X}_a = 0;\\
&B_e: \mathcal{U}_e \to \mathcal{X}_e; && B_e|\mathcal{U} = B, && B_e|\mathcal{U}_a = B_a;\\
&C_e: \mathcal{X}_e \to \mathcal{Y}_e; && C_e|\mathcal{X} = C, && C_e|\mathcal{X}_a = C_a;\\
&D_e: \mathcal{X}_e \to \mathcal{Z}; && D_e|\mathcal{X} = D, && D_e|\mathcal{X}_a = 0.
\end{aligned}$$

Writing $d(\mathcal{X}_e) = n_e$, we have

$$\mathcal{N}_e = \bigcap_{i=1}^{n_e} \operatorname{Ker}\left(C_e A_e^{i-1}\right) = \mathcal{N};$$

also

$$\operatorname{Ker} D_e = \operatorname{Ker} D \oplus \mathcal{X}_a.$$

We define the Extended Regulator Problem (ERP) as that of finding suitable $\mathcal{X}_a$ (that is, $d(\mathcal{X}_a)$) and then $F_e: \mathcal{X}_e \to \mathcal{U}_e$, such that

$$\operatorname{Ker} F_e \supset \mathcal{N}$$

and

$$\mathcal{X}_e^+(A_e + B_e F_e) \subset \operatorname{Ker} D \oplus \mathcal{X}_a .$$

The main result of this chapter is the following.

THEOREM 6.2. Let RRP be defined as in Section 6.1. Then ERP is solvable if and only if, for RRP,

$$\mathcal{X}^+(A) \cap \mathcal{N} \subset \operatorname{Ker} D \tag{27}$$

and

$$\mathcal{X}^+(A) \subset \langle A \mid \mathcal{B} \rangle + \mathcal{V}^* , \tag{28}$$

where

$$\mathcal{V}^* \triangleq \sup \underline{\mathcal{J}}(A, B; \operatorname{Ker} D) .$$

Furthermore, if ERP is solvable, it is possible to take

$$d(\mathcal{X}_a) \le d\left[\frac{\mathcal{N} \cap \mathcal{V}^*}{\left(\mathcal{N} \cap \bigcap_{i=1}^{n} A^{-i+1}\mathcal{V}^*\right)}\right]. \tag{29}$$

For the proof we shall need

LEMMA 6.5. Suppose $\mathcal{V} \subset \mathcal{X}$ and $\mathcal{N} \subset \mathcal{X}$ with $A\mathcal{N} \subset \mathcal{N}$. Define extended spaces and maps as above, with

$$\mathcal{X}_a \approx \frac{\mathcal{N} \cap \mathcal{V}}{\left(\mathcal{N} \cap \bigcap_{i=1}^{n} A^{-i+1}\mathcal{V}\right)} . \tag{30}$$

There exists a map $E: \mathcal{X}_e \to \mathcal{X}_e$ with $\operatorname{Im} E = \mathcal{X}_a$, such that the subspace $\mathcal{V}_e = (1 + E)\mathcal{V}$ has the property

$$\mathcal{N} \cap \bigcap_{i=1}^{n} A^{-i+1}\mathcal{V} + A_e(\mathcal{V}_e \cap \mathcal{N}) \subset \mathcal{V}_e .$$

PROOF: Write

$$\mathcal{V}_0 = \mathcal{N} \cap \bigcap_{i=1}^{n} A^{-i+1}\mathcal{V}$$

and let

$$\mathcal{V} \cap \mathcal{N} = \mathcal{V}_0 \oplus \mathcal{V}_1 ,$$

$$\mathcal{V} = \mathcal{V} \cap \mathcal{N} \oplus \mathcal{V}_2 .$$

Let $E: \mathcal{X}_e \to \mathcal{X}_e$ be any map such that

$$\mathrm{Ker}\, E \supset \mathcal{V}_0 \oplus \mathcal{V}_2 ,$$
$$\mathrm{Ker}\, E \cap \mathcal{V}_1 = 0 ,$$
$$E\mathcal{V}_1 = \mathcal{X}_a .$$

Such a map exists by (30). Now

$$\mathcal{V}_e \cap \mathcal{N} = [\mathcal{V}_0 \oplus (1+E)\mathcal{V}_1 \oplus \mathcal{V}_2] \cap \mathcal{N} = \mathcal{V}_0 ,$$

so that

$$A_e(\mathcal{V}_e \cap \mathcal{N}) = A\mathcal{V}_0 \subset \mathcal{V}_0 = \mathcal{V}_e \cap \mathcal{N}$$

as required. ▌

PROOF of Theorem 6.2. (If) Choose $\mathcal{X}_a$ according to (30) (with $\mathcal{V}^*$ in place of $\mathcal{V}$). Construct $\mathcal{V}_e^* = (1+E)\mathcal{V}^*$ as in Lemma 6.5. Thus

$$\mathcal{N} \cap \bigcap_{i=1}^{n} A^{-i+1}\mathcal{V}^* + A_e\left(\mathcal{V}_e^* \cap \mathcal{N}\right) \subset \mathcal{V}_e^* . \tag{31}$$

We shall verify that the conditions of Theorem 6.1 hold for the extended problem. Now

$$\mathcal{V}_e^* \subset \mathcal{V}^* \oplus \mathcal{X}_a \subset \mathrm{Ker}\, D \oplus \mathcal{X}_a = \mathrm{Ker}\, D_e$$

and

$$A_e \mathcal{V}_e^* = A\mathcal{V}^* \subset \mathcal{V}^* + \mathcal{B} \subset (1+E)\mathcal{V}^* + \mathcal{B} + \mathcal{X}_a = \mathcal{V}_e^* + \mathcal{B}_e .$$

Next

$$\mathcal{X}_e^+(A_e) \cap \mathcal{N} = \left[\mathcal{X}^+(A) \oplus \mathcal{X}_a\right] \cap \mathcal{N} = \mathcal{X}^+(A) \cap \mathcal{N} .$$

As $\mathcal{X}^+(A) \cap \mathcal{N}$ is A-invariant and by (27) belongs to Ker D, we get

$$\mathcal{X}_e^+(A_e) \cap \mathcal{N} \subset \mathcal{N} \cap \bigcap_{i=1}^{n} A^{-i+1}\mathcal{V}^* \subset \mathcal{V}_e^* \quad \text{(by (31))}$$

and this verifies the extended version of (10). Finally

$$\begin{aligned} \mathcal{X}_e^+(A_e) &= \mathcal{X}^+(A) \oplus \mathcal{X}_a \subset \langle A|\mathcal{B}\rangle + \mathcal{V}^* + \mathcal{X}_a \\ &= \langle A|\mathcal{B}\rangle + (1+E)\mathcal{V}^* + \mathcal{X}_a = \langle A_e|\mathcal{B}_e\rangle + \mathcal{V}_e^* , \end{aligned}$$

which verifies the extended version of (11).

(Only if) Let Q be the projection on $\mathcal{X}$ along $\mathcal{X}_a$. Applied to ERP, Theorem 6.1 provides a subspace $\mathcal{V}_e \subset \mathcal{X}_e$ which satisfies the extended version of (9) – (11). In particular (10) implies

$$\operatorname{Ker} D_e \supset \mathcal{X}_e^+(A_e) \cap \mathcal{N} = \left[\mathcal{X}^+(A) \oplus \mathcal{X}_a\right] \cap \mathcal{N} = \mathcal{X}^+(A) \cap \mathcal{N}$$

so that

$$\mathcal{X}^+(A) \cap \mathcal{N} \subset Q \operatorname{Ker} D_e = \operatorname{Ker} D ,$$

proving (27). Next, (11) applied to ERP yields

$$\mathcal{X}_e^+(A_e) \subset \langle A_e | \mathcal{B}_e \rangle + \mathcal{V}_e$$

and so, with $\mathcal{V} = Q\mathcal{V}_e$,

$$\mathcal{X}^+(A) = Q\mathcal{X}_e^+(A_e) \subset \langle A | \mathcal{B} \rangle + \mathcal{V} . \tag{32}$$

Finally we note that $\mathcal{V}_e \subset \operatorname{Ker} D_e$ implies $\mathcal{V} \subset \operatorname{Ker} D$, and $A_e\mathcal{V}_e \subset \mathcal{V}_e + \mathcal{B}_e$ implies

$$A\mathcal{V} = AQ\mathcal{V}_e = QA_e\mathcal{V}_e \subset Q(\mathcal{V}_e + \mathcal{B}_e) = \mathcal{V} + \mathcal{B} .$$

Hence $\mathcal{V} \subset \mathcal{V}^*$, and (28) follows from (32). ∎

If $\mathcal{V}_e$ is a solution of ERP then by (10)

$$A_e(\mathcal{V}_e \cap \mathcal{N}) \subset \mathcal{V}_e ; \tag{33}$$

but it is not true in general that $A(\mathcal{V} \cap \mathcal{N}) \subset \mathcal{V}$ with $\mathcal{V} = Q\mathcal{V}_e$. Deduction of the last-written inclusion from (33) would be immediate if

$$Q(\mathcal{V}_e \cap \mathcal{N}) = Q\mathcal{V}_e \cap Q\mathcal{N} ;$$

and, as $\operatorname{Ker} Q = \mathcal{X}_a$ and $\mathcal{N} \cap \mathcal{X}_a = 0$, this would be true if and only if

$$(\mathcal{V}_e + \mathcal{N}) \cap \mathcal{X}_a = \mathcal{V}_e \cap \mathcal{X}_a . \tag{34}$$

But in general (34) fails; indeed the construction of Lemma 6.5 has

$$(\mathcal{V}_e + \mathcal{N}) \cap \mathcal{X}_a = \mathcal{X}_a , \qquad \mathcal{V}_e \cap \mathcal{X}_a = 0 .$$

This heuristic reasoning suggests that in some cases ERP is solvable when RRP is not, a conjecture borne out by the following example.

6.4 Example

Let

$$A = \begin{bmatrix} 0 & 1 & 0 \\ -1 & -2 & 0 \\ 0 & 0 & 1 \end{bmatrix}, \qquad B = \begin{bmatrix} 0 \\ 1 \\ 0 \end{bmatrix},$$

$$C = [0 \quad 0 \quad 1], \qquad D = [\alpha \quad -\alpha \quad -1] .$$

Assume $\alpha \neq 0$. We have

$$\mathcal{N} = \text{Im} \begin{bmatrix} 1 & 0 \\ 0 & 1 \\ 0 & 0 \end{bmatrix}, \qquad \text{Ker } D = \text{Im} \begin{bmatrix} 1 & 1 \\ 1 & 0 \\ 0 & \alpha \end{bmatrix},$$

$$\langle A | \mathcal{B} \rangle = \text{Im} \begin{bmatrix} 1 & 0 \\ 0 & 1 \\ 0 & 0 \end{bmatrix}, \qquad \mathcal{X}^+(A) = \text{Im} \begin{bmatrix} 0 \\ 0 \\ 1 \end{bmatrix}.$$

The algorithm (15) yields $\mathcal{V}^* = \text{Ker } D$, so that

$$\mathcal{X}^+(A) \subset \mathcal{X} = \langle A | \mathcal{B} \rangle + \mathcal{V}^* .$$

Since in addition $\mathcal{X}^+(A) \cap \mathcal{N} = 0$, Theorem 6.2 asserts that ERP is solvable. We find

$$\mathcal{N} \cap \bigcap_{i=1}^{3} A^{-i+1} \mathcal{V}^* = 0$$

so we can take

$$d(\mathcal{X}_a) = d(\mathcal{N} \cap \mathcal{V}^*) = d\left(\text{Im} \begin{bmatrix} 1 \\ 1 \\ 0 \end{bmatrix} \right) = 1 .$$

Write explicitly

$$E \, \text{col}[1 \ 1 \ 0 \ 0] = \text{col}[1 \ 1 \ 0 \ 1] \ ;$$

then

$$\mathcal{V}_e^* = (1 + E) \mathcal{V}^* = \text{Im} \begin{bmatrix} 1 & 1 \\ 1 & 0 \\ 0 & \alpha \\ 1 & 0 \end{bmatrix}.$$

ERP is now essentially solved: it only remains to compute a feedback map F_e such that $\text{Ker } F_e \supset \mathcal{N}$, $(A_e + B_e F_e) \mathcal{V}_e^* \subset \mathcal{V}_e^*$, and the induced map $\overline{A_e + B_e F_e}$ on $\mathcal{X}_e / \mathcal{V}_e^*$ is stable. In this example these requirements lead to the unique result

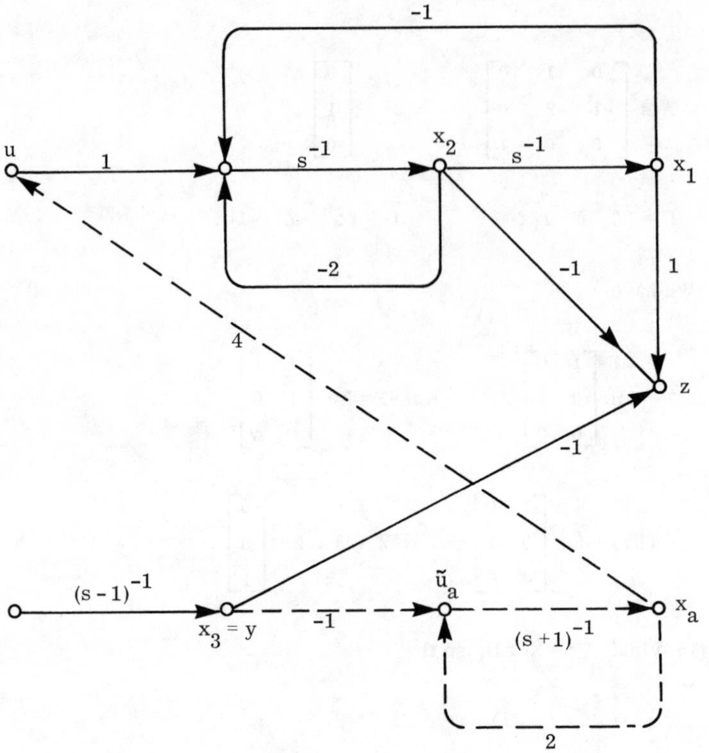

Fig. 6.2.

Signal Flow Graph:
Example, Section 6.4.
Controller connections shown dotted; $\alpha = 1$.

$$F_e = \begin{bmatrix} 0 & 0 & 0 & 4 \\ 0 & 0 & -\alpha^{-1} & 1 \end{bmatrix}.$$

Controller structure is evident from the signal flow graph, Fig. 6.2. The given system has two stable, unobservable 'modes' (with state variables x_1, x_2) and one unstable, observable mode (x_3). Only x_1 and x_2 are controllable. The regulated variable is $z = \alpha x_1 - \alpha x_2 - x_3$. To interpret the role of dynamic compensation suppose first that all states had been observable and consider the corresponding RRP, with $\mathcal{N} = 0$. A simple computation shows that output regulation is achieved, with state feedback $u = f_1 x_1 + f_2 x_2 + f_3 x_3$, only if $f_1 + f_2 = 4$. But then $(A + BF) | \langle A | \mathcal{B} \rangle$ has the spectrum $\{1, 1 - f_1\}$, i.e., the controllable subsystem is destabilized. Returning to the example, we have that $\langle A | \mathcal{B} \rangle$ is unobservable. The compensator can be thought of as simulating the 'stable' unobservable variable $x_1 + x_2$ according to the equation $\dot{x}_a = -x_a + \tilde{u}_a$. Then the feedback law

$$u = 4x_a, \qquad \tilde{u}_a = -\alpha^{-1} x_3 + 2x_a$$

produces the required internal instability. The resulting transfer function from the exponential 'disturbance' $x_3(\cdot)$ to the regulated output is

$$\frac{\hat{z}(s)}{\hat{x}_3(s)} = -\frac{(s+3)(s-1)}{(s+1)^2}.$$

Of course the example is artificial, and from a sensitivity viewpoint ill-posed, but it exhibits disturbance decoupling as a distinct, fundamental role of linear state feedback and compensation. A second role, observer action, is inoperative by virtue of our initial assumption $\operatorname{Ker} C = \mathcal{N}$; a third, pole-shifting, is not possible here because the controllable observable state subspace is zero.

To verify that RRP is not solvable we apply Proposition 6.1. Clearly

$$\mathcal{N} \cap \operatorname{Ker} D = \operatorname{Im} \operatorname{col}[1 \ 1 \ 0]$$

is not A-invariant, so $\mathcal{V}_0 = 0$. Every subspace $\mathcal{W}$, such that $\mathcal{W} \oplus \mathcal{N} \cap \operatorname{Ker} D = \operatorname{Ker} D$, can be written

$$\mathcal{W}_\mu = \operatorname{Im}\left(\mu \begin{bmatrix} 1 \\ 1 \\ 0 \end{bmatrix} + \begin{bmatrix} 1 \\ 0 \\ \alpha \end{bmatrix}\right) = \operatorname{Im} \begin{bmatrix} \mu + 1 \\ \mu \\ \alpha \end{bmatrix}, \qquad \mu \in \mathbb{R}.$$

Application of (15), with $\mathcal{W}_\mu$ in place of Ker D, yields

$$\mathcal{V}_{\mu}^{M} = 0 . \tag{35}$$

To satisfy the condition (13) of Corollary 6.1 would require

$$\operatorname{Im}\begin{bmatrix}0\\0\\1\end{bmatrix} \subset \operatorname{Im}\begin{bmatrix}1 & 0\\0 & 1\\0 & 0\end{bmatrix} + \mathcal{V}_{\mu}^{M}$$

and this is clearly incompatible with (35).

6.5 Concluding Remark

To continue the general discussion, we note that if $A(\mathcal{V}^* \cap \mathcal{N}) \subset \mathcal{V}^*$, the right side of (29) reduces to 0, so that RRP is solvable whenever ERP is solvable, and no dynamic compensation is required. Examination of the proof of Lemma 6.5 together with condition (12) of Corollary 6.1 reveals that dynamic compensation is necessary only if the stable, unobservable state subspace $\mathcal{X}^-(A) \cap \mathcal{N}$ is nonzero. This fact and the foregoing example indicate that the decoupling action of the adjoined dynamics is realized via the simulation only of stable unobservable modes. The significance of this assertion will appear more clearly in Chapter 7.

Next, there was nothing special about the partition $\mathbb{C} = \mathbb{C}^+ \dot{\cup} \mathbb{C}^-$. In practice one might well require that convergence in (3) take place with exponents in some 'good' subset $\mathbb{C}_g \subset \mathbb{C}^-$, where $\mathbb{C}_g$ is symmetric with respect to the real axis and $\mathbb{C}_g \cap \mathbb{R} \neq \emptyset$. Writing $\mathbb{C}_b$ for the 'bad' complement $\mathbb{C} - \mathbb{C}_g$, and replacing $\mathcal{X}^+$ (resp. $\mathcal{X}^-$) by the corresponding subspaces $\mathcal{X}_b$ (resp. $\mathcal{X}_g$), one obtains the corresponding results by exactly the same procedure.

The main result of this chapter (Theorem 6.2) can be paraphrased by saying that output regulation is achievable, at least with dynamic compensation, if and only if (i) the unstable, unobservable modes of the system are nulled at the regulated output, and (ii) output stabilization is possible without regard to observability constraints. The result is constructive and offers significant structural insight. It has, however, the shortcoming that no condition has been imposed to ensure internal stability, that is, stability of controllable and observable modes. Indeed the example of Section 6.4 serves to show that output regulation and internal stability are not always compatible. In Chapter 7 we solve the more realistic problem of achieving both those desirable system properties.

6.6 Exercises

6.1 For the example in Section 6.4, with $\alpha = 1$, work out the Laplace transform $\hat{z}(s)$ as an explicit function of the initial values $x_1(0+), x_2(0+), x_3(0+)$, and $x_a(0+)$, and verify directly that $z(t) \to 0$ as $t \to \infty$.

6.2 Say that the system structure specified by (1) – (3) <u>admits indirect feedback control</u> if the observations y(·) permit reconstruction of z(·), i.e., $\mathcal{N} \subset \operatorname{Ker} D$. What can be said about the solvability of RRP? of ERP? In particular show that dynamic compensation is necessary only if $\mathcal{N} \not\subset \operatorname{Ker} D$, and so the system must in this sense operate partially 'open-loop'.

6.3 Verify in detail that ERP is solvable when RRP is not, only if $\mathcal{X}^{-}(A) \cap \mathcal{N} \neq 0$.

6.7 Notes and References

The discussion in this chapter closely follows Wonham [7].

CHAPTER 7

TRACKING AND REGULATION II: INTERNAL STABILIZATION

In this chapter we continue the discussion in Chapter 6 on output regulation for the system

$$\dot{x}(t) = Ax(t) + Bu(t) \, , \tag{1}$$

$$y(t) = Cx(t) \, , \tag{2}$$

$$z(t) = Dx(t) \, .$$

As before, we regard $y(\cdot)$ as the measured variable and $z(\cdot)$ as the variable to be regulated. We postulate also that a dynamic observer is utilized; equivalently, as shown in Section 6.1 we can replace C by any map $\hat{C}$ such that

$$\operatorname{Ker} \hat{C} = \mathcal{N} \triangleq \bigcap_{i \geq 1} \operatorname{Ker}(CA^{i-1}) \, .$$

For regulation of $z(\cdot)$ it is required to find a feedback map $F: \mathcal{X} \to \mathcal{U}$ such that

$$\mathcal{X}^+(A + BF) \subset \operatorname{Ker} D \, . \tag{3}$$

To respect the observability constraint, F must satisfy the condition

$$\operatorname{Ker} F \supset \mathcal{N} \, . \tag{4}$$

Necessary and sufficient conditions for the existence of F subject to (3) and (4) were given in Chapter 6.

In this chapter we impose the additional requirement that F stabilize all the unstable modes of A which are both controllable and observable. Precisely, regard $\mathcal{X}/\mathcal{N}$ as the state space of the system (1), (2) made observable by projection mod $\mathcal{N}$. The controllable, observable subspace is then $(\langle A|\mathcal{B}\rangle + \mathcal{N})/\mathcal{N}$. We require that the map induced on $(\langle A|\mathcal{B}\rangle + \mathcal{N})/\mathcal{N}$, by the closed-loop system map, be stable. Equivalently, any observable, unstable modes of $A + BF$ must be uncontrollable; that is,

$$\frac{\mathcal{X}^+(A + BF) + \mathcal{N}}{\mathcal{N}} \cap \frac{\langle A|\mathcal{B}\rangle + \mathcal{N}}{\mathcal{N}} = 0 \, . \tag{5}$$

It is natural to call a system in which F has been chosen to satisfy (5), <u>internally stable</u>. In this way, we are led to formulate the

Regulator Problem with Internal Stability (RPIS):

Given the maps A: $\mathcal{X} \to \mathcal{X}$, B: $\mathcal{U} \to \mathcal{X}$, D: $\mathcal{X} \to \mathcal{Z}$, and a subspace $\mathcal{N} \subset \mathcal{X}$ with $A\mathcal{N} \subset \mathcal{N}$, find F: $\mathcal{X} \to \mathcal{U}$ such that

$$\operatorname{Ker} F \supset \mathcal{N} \tag{6}$$

$$\mathcal{X}^+(A+BF) \cap (\langle A|\mathcal{B}\rangle + \mathcal{N}) \subset \mathcal{N} \tag{7}$$

and

$$\mathcal{X}^+(A+BF) \subset \operatorname{Ker} D\,. \tag{8}$$

Here it is easily checked that (7) is equivalent to (5).

The 'restricted regulator problem' (RRP) defined in Chapter 6 is identical to RPIS except that the internal stability requirement (7) is absent. We recall that RRP may be solvable when RPIS is not: that is, internal stability need not be compatible with output regulation, as was shown by the example in Section 6.4.

In Section 7.1 we obtain a preliminary set of necessary and sufficient conditions that RPIS be solvable. While not constructive, they are exploited to show that in this problem dynamic compensation in the sense of Section 6.3 is redundant. In Section 7.2 we give constructive necessary and sufficient conditions in the case $\mathcal{N} = 0$, and in Section 7.3 extend them to the general case. In Section 7.4 the theory is applied to step disturbance rejection, and in Section 7.5 to steady-state decoupling with step inputs. Numerical examples are presented in Sections 7.6 and 7.7.

7.1 Solvability of RPIS: General Considerations

THEOREM 7.1. RPIS is solvable if and only if there exists a subspace $\mathcal{V} \subset \mathcal{X}$ such that

$$\mathcal{V} \subset \operatorname{Ker} D \cap A^{-1}(\mathcal{V} + \mathcal{B}) \tag{9}$$

$$\mathcal{X}^+(A) \cap \mathcal{N} + A(\mathcal{V} \cap \mathcal{N}) \subset \mathcal{V} \tag{10}$$

$$\mathcal{V} \cap (\langle A|\mathcal{B}\rangle + \mathcal{N}) \subset \mathcal{N} \tag{11}$$

and

$$\mathcal{X}^+(A) \subset \langle A|\mathcal{B}\rangle + \mathcal{V}\,. \tag{12}$$

We observe that conditions (9), (10) and (12) are equivalent to solvability of RRP, as shown by Theorem 6.1; only condition (11) is new. The proof follows exactly the same lines as for the theorem cited, and so need only be sketched.

PROOF: Suppose RPIS is solvable and put $\mathcal{V} = \mathcal{X}^+(A+BF)$. Since $A\mathcal{N} \subset \mathcal{N}$ and $\operatorname{Ker} F \supset \mathcal{N}$, we have by Lemma 6.2,

$$\mathcal{X}^+(A+BF) \cap \mathcal{N} = \mathcal{X}^+(A) \cap \mathcal{N}\,.$$

Then (9)−(11) follow immediately from (6)−(8), and (12) follows from the general identity (Lemma 6.4)

$$\langle A|\mathcal{B}\rangle + \mathcal{X}^+(A) = \langle A|\mathcal{B}\rangle + \mathcal{X}^+(A+BF) \; . \tag{13}$$

Conversely, if (9) and (10) are true there exists $F_0: \mathcal{X}\to\mathcal{U}$ such that $\operatorname{Ker} F_0 \supset \mathcal{N}$ and $(A+BF_0)\mathcal{V}\subset\mathcal{V}$. Write $A_0 = A+BF_0$. By (12) and (13)

$$\mathcal{X}^+(A_0) \subset \langle A_0|\mathcal{B}\rangle + \mathcal{V} \, . \tag{14}$$

Furthermore, by (10),

$$\mathcal{X}^+(A_0) \cap \mathcal{N} = \mathcal{X}^+(A) \cap \mathcal{N} \subset \mathcal{V} \, . \tag{15}$$

Just as in the proof of Theorem 6.1, (14) and (15) imply the existence of $F_1: \mathcal{X}\to\mathcal{U}$ such that $\operatorname{Ker} F_1 \supset \mathcal{N}$ and $\mathcal{X}^+(A_0+BF_1)\subset\mathcal{V}$. Then $F = F_0 + F_1$ has all the properties required. ∎

While Theorem 7.1 does not indicate how to find a suitable $\mathcal{V}$ if one exists, it is well suited to showing that if RPIS is not solvable, then no solution can be obtained by broadening the assumptions to include the possibility of state space extension, that is, dynamic compensation. We may interpret this result as a 'deterministic separation theorem' which asserts that, after insertion of a dynamic observer, no further dynamic signal processing is required to achieve the stated design objectives, if these objectives can be achieved at all.*

To be precise, introduce extended spaces and maps exactly as in Section 6.3. In the notation used there, we now define the Extended Regulator Problem with Internal Stability (ERPIS) as that of finding suitable $\mathcal{X}_a$ (that is, $d(\mathcal{X}_a)$) and then $F_e: \mathcal{X}_e \to \mathcal{U}_e$, such that

$$\operatorname{Ker} F_e \supset \mathcal{N}$$

$$\mathcal{X}_e^+(A_e + B_e F_e) \cap (\langle A_e|\mathcal{B}_e\rangle + \mathcal{N}) \subset \mathcal{N}$$

and
$$\mathcal{X}_e^+(A_e + B_e F_e) \subset \operatorname{Ker} D \oplus \mathcal{X}_a \, .$$

THEOREM 7.2. <u>ERPIS is solvable only if RPIS is solvable.</u>

PROOF: If ERPIS is solvable Theorem 7.1 implies the existence of $\mathcal{V}_e \subset \mathcal{X}_e$ such that

---

* It should be borne in mind that as yet our problem formulation takes no account of the sensitivity of the synthesis to parameter variations. If this is done, additional dynamic elements may be used to advantage, as will be shown in Chapter 8.

$$\mathscr{V}_e \subset (\operatorname{Ker} D \oplus \mathscr{X}_a) \cap A_e^{-1}(\mathscr{V}_e + \mathscr{B} + \mathscr{B}_a) , \tag{16}$$

$$\mathscr{X}_e^+(A_e) \cap \mathscr{N} + A_e(\mathscr{V}_e \cap \mathscr{N}) \subset \mathscr{V}_e , \tag{17}$$

$$\mathscr{V}_e \cap (\langle A | \mathscr{B} \rangle + \mathscr{X}_a + \mathscr{N}) \subset \mathscr{N} , \tag{18}$$

and

$$\mathscr{X}_e^+(A_e) \subset \langle A | \mathscr{B} \rangle + \mathscr{X}_a + \mathscr{V}_e . \tag{19}$$

Here we have used the facts (cf. Section 6.3) that $\mathscr{N}_e = \mathscr{N}$, $\operatorname{Ker} D_e = \operatorname{Ker} D \oplus \mathscr{X}_a$, and

$$\langle A_e | \mathscr{B}_e \rangle = \langle A | \mathscr{B} \rangle \oplus \mathscr{X}_a .$$

Let P: $\mathscr{X}_e \to \mathscr{X}_e$ be the projection on $\mathscr{X}$ along $\mathscr{X}_a$ and define $\mathscr{V} = P\mathscr{V}_e$. It is enough to show that $\mathscr{V}$ has the properties (9)–(12), and this requires only the application of P to both sides of the relations (16)–(19). By definition of P and A_e, $PA_e = A_eP$ and $A_e | \mathscr{X} = A$. Using these facts and rewriting (16) as

$$\mathscr{V}_e \subset \operatorname{Ker} D \oplus \mathscr{X}_a , \qquad A_e\mathscr{V}_e \subset \mathscr{V}_e + \mathscr{B} + \mathscr{B}_a$$

there follows

$$\mathscr{V} \subset \operatorname{Ker} D , \qquad A\mathscr{V} \subset \mathscr{V} + \mathscr{B}$$

which is equivalent to (9). Next, the obvious relation

$$\mathscr{X}_e^+(A_e) = \mathscr{X}^+(A) \oplus \mathscr{X}_a \tag{20}$$

together with (19), establishes (12). To verify (11) from (18) we use the following general result for a map P and subspaces $\mathscr{R}, \mathscr{S}$ (0.7, 0.8):

$$P(\mathscr{R} \cap \mathscr{S}) = (P\mathscr{R}) \cap (P\mathscr{S}) \tag{21}$$

if and only if

$$(\mathscr{R} + \mathscr{S}) \cap \operatorname{Ker} P = \mathscr{R} \cap \operatorname{Ker} P + \mathscr{S} \cap \operatorname{Ker} P . \tag{22}$$

With $\operatorname{Ker} P = \mathscr{X}_a$, $\mathscr{R} = \mathscr{V}_e$ and $\mathscr{S} = \langle A | \mathscr{B} \rangle + \mathscr{X}_a + \mathscr{N}$, (22) follows at once, and then (21) applied to (18) yields (11). It remains to check (10) from (17). By (20)

$$\mathscr{X}^+(A_e) \cap \mathscr{N} = \mathscr{X}^+(A) \cap \mathscr{N}$$

and so

$$\mathscr{X}^+(A) \cap \mathscr{N} \subset P\mathscr{V}_e = \mathscr{V} . \tag{23}$$

Also, by (21), (22) we shall have

$$P(\mathscr{V}_e \cap \mathscr{N}) = \mathscr{V} \cap \mathscr{N} \tag{24}$$

provided

$$(\mathcal{V}_e + \mathcal{N}) \cap \mathcal{X}_a = \mathcal{V}_e \cap \mathcal{X}_a + \mathcal{N} \cap \mathcal{X}_a . \tag{25}$$

As for (25) let

$$x_a = v_e + n \in (\mathcal{V}_e + \mathcal{N}) \cap \mathcal{X}_a$$

with $v_e \in \mathcal{V}_e$ and $n \in \mathcal{N}$. Then

$$v_e = x_a - n \in \mathcal{X}_a + \mathcal{N}$$

and by (18), $v_e \in \mathcal{N}$. Therefore $x_a \in \mathcal{N} \cap \mathcal{X}_a = 0$, that is,

$$\mathcal{X}_a \cap (\mathcal{V}_e + \mathcal{N}) = 0$$

proving (25). Then (24) is true, and (17) yields

$$\mathcal{V} \supset PA_e(\mathcal{V}_e \cap \mathcal{N}) = A(\mathcal{V} \cap \mathcal{N}) . \tag{26}$$

Finally, (10) results from (23) and (26). ▌

7.2 Constructive Solution of RPIS: $\mathcal{N} = 0$

Let

$$\mathcal{V}^* \triangleq \sup \underline{\mathcal{I}}(A, B; \operatorname{Ker} D)$$

and

$$\mathcal{R}^* \triangleq \sup \underline{\mathcal{C}}(A, B; \operatorname{Ker} D) .$$

Recall from Theorem 5.5 that $\mathcal{R}^* \subset \mathcal{V}^*$, and from Corollary 5.1 that $\underline{F}(A, B; \mathcal{V}^*) \subset \underline{F}(A, B; \mathcal{R}^*)$. If $F \in \underline{F}(\mathcal{V}^*)$ ($\triangleq \underline{F}(A, B; \mathcal{V}^*)$) and $A_F \triangleq A + BF$, let $\bar{A}_F$ denote the map induced in $\mathcal{X}/\mathcal{R}^*$ by A_F. Then (Theorem 5.7) the restriction $\bar{A}_F | (\mathcal{V}^*/\mathcal{R}^*)$ is independent of the choice of $F \in \underline{F}(\mathcal{V}^*)$.

Let $A\mathcal{T} \subset \mathcal{T}$ and $A\mathcal{R} \subset \mathcal{R} \subset \mathcal{T}$. The subspace $\mathcal{R}$ <u>decomposes</u> $\mathcal{T}$ <u>relative to</u> A if there exists a subspace $\mathcal{S}$ such that $A\mathcal{S} \subset \mathcal{S}$ and $\mathcal{R} \oplus \mathcal{S} = \mathcal{T}$. An elementary and constructive criterion that $\mathcal{R}$ decompose $\mathcal{T}$ was given in Section 0.11; it amounts to the fact that decomposability is equivalent to the existence of a solution to Sylvester's linear matrix equation.

THEOREM 7.3. <u>Let $\mathcal{N} = 0$. Then RPIS is solvable if and only if</u>

$$\mathcal{X}^+(A) \subset \langle A | \mathcal{B} \rangle + \mathcal{V}^* , \tag{27}$$

<u>and in $\mathcal{X}/\mathcal{R}^*$, with $F \in \underline{F}(\mathcal{V}^*)$, the subspace</u>

$$\frac{\mathcal{V}^* \cap \mathcal{X}^+(A_F) \cap \langle A | \mathcal{B} \rangle + \mathcal{R}^*}{\mathcal{R}^*}$$

<u>decomposes the subspace</u>

$$\frac{\mathcal{V}^* \cap \mathcal{X}^+(A_F) + \mathcal{R}^*}{\mathcal{R}^*}$$

<u>relative to the map induced by</u> A_F <u>in</u> $\mathcal{V}^*/\mathcal{R}^*$.

It is clear that this solvability criterion is constructive, as $\mathcal{V}^*, \mathcal{R}^*$ are computable by simple algorithms (Theorems 4.3 and 5.6), an (arbitrary) $F \in \underline{F}(\mathcal{V}^*)$ is readily constructed (Lemma 4.2) and decomposability is verifiable in the way already described.

PROOF: (If) We shall construct a subspace $\mathcal{V}$ which satisfies the conditions of Theorem 7.1. While the details are somewhat intricate, the construction is readily visualized with the aid of the lattice diagrams of Fig. 7.1. For simplicity, the reader might first consider what happens when $\mathcal{R}^*$ is zero.

Let $F \in \underline{F}(\mathcal{V}^*)$. By (27) and Lemma 6.4,

$$\mathcal{X}^+(A_F) \subset \langle A|\mathcal{B}\rangle + \mathcal{V}^* .$$

As the subspaces on the right are A_F-invariant, we have

$$\mathcal{X}^+(A_F) = \langle A|\mathcal{B}\rangle \cap \mathcal{X}^+(A_F) + \mathcal{V}^* \cap \mathcal{X}^+(A_F) . \tag{28}$$

Also, by the assumption of decomposability, there exists a subspace $\mathcal{W} \subset \mathcal{X}$ such that

$$A_F \mathcal{W} \subset \mathcal{W} \tag{29}$$

$$\mathcal{R}^* \subset \mathcal{W} \subset \mathcal{V}^* \cap \mathcal{X}^+(A_F) + \mathcal{R}^* \tag{30}$$

and

$$\frac{\mathcal{V}^* \cap \mathcal{X}^+(A_F) + \mathcal{R}^*}{\mathcal{R}^*} = \frac{\mathcal{V}^* \cap \langle A|\mathcal{B}\rangle \cap \mathcal{X}^+(A_F) + \mathcal{R}^*}{\mathcal{R}^*} \oplus \frac{\mathcal{W}}{\mathcal{R}^*} . \tag{31}$$

We remark that with $\mathcal{W}$ fixed, (29)–(31) hold for all $F \in \underline{F}(\mathcal{V}^*)$. By (31),

$$\mathcal{V}^* \cap \mathcal{X}^+(A_F) \subset \mathcal{V}^* \cap \langle A|\mathcal{B}\rangle \cap \mathcal{X}^+(A_F) + \mathcal{W} \tag{32}$$

and by (28) and (32),

$$\mathcal{X}^+(A_F) \subset \langle A|\mathcal{B}\rangle + \mathcal{V}^* \cap \mathcal{X}^+(A_F) \subset \langle A|\mathcal{B}\rangle + \mathcal{W} . \tag{33}$$

Clearly

$$\mathcal{W} \subset \mathcal{V}^* . \tag{34}$$

Also, by(31)

$$\frac{\mathcal{W}}{\mathcal{R}^*} \cap \frac{\langle A|\mathcal{B}\rangle}{\mathcal{R}^*} = 0$$

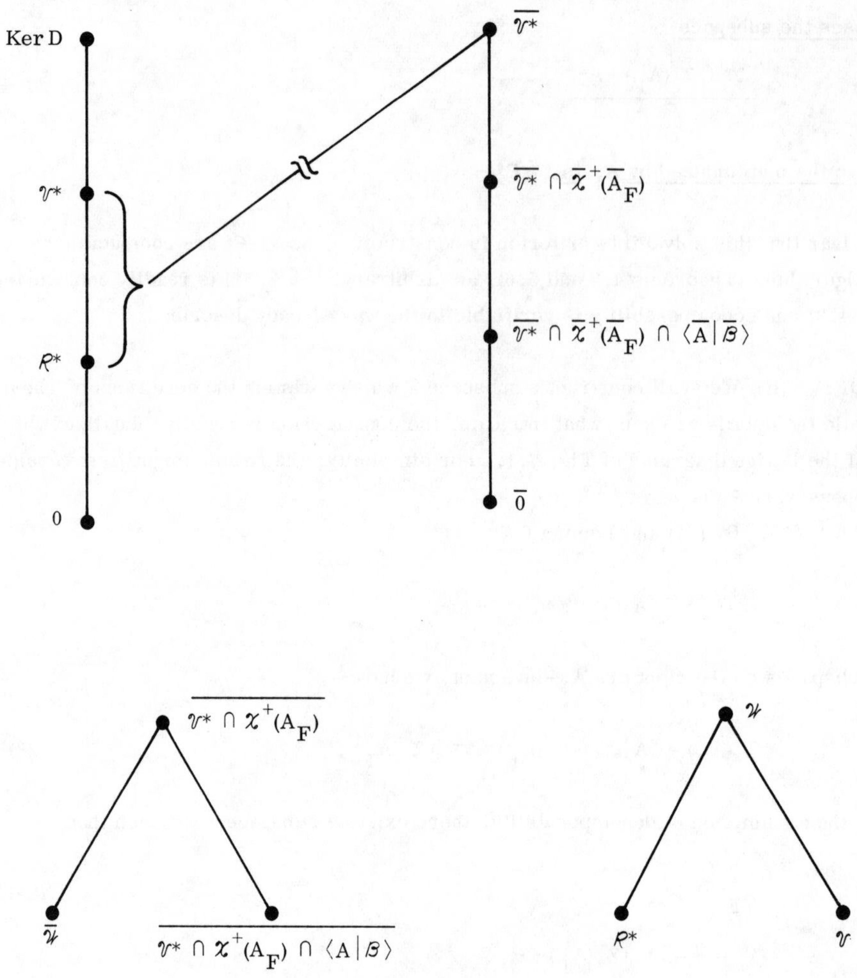

Fig. 7.1.

Lattice Diagrams:
Construction of Subspace $\mathcal{V}$.
(Bars denote projections mod $\mathcal{R}^*$)

so that

$$\mathcal{W} \cap \langle A|\mathcal{B}\rangle = \mathcal{R}^* . \tag{35}$$

Finally, let $\overline{A}_F$ denote the map induced by A_F in $\mathcal{X}/\mathcal{R}^*$, and choose $F \in \underline{F}(\mathcal{V}^*)$ such that

$$\sigma(A_F|\mathcal{R}^*) \cap \sigma\left(\overline{A}_F \left| \left(\frac{\mathcal{W}}{\mathcal{R}^*}\right)\right.\right) = \emptyset .$$

Since the two spectra are now disjoint, $\mathcal{R}^*$ certainly decomposes $\mathcal{W}$ relative to A_F; that is, there exists $\mathcal{V} \subset \mathcal{W}$ (depending on F) such that

$$A_F \mathcal{V} \subset \mathcal{V} \tag{36}$$

and

$$\mathcal{R}^* \oplus \mathcal{V} = \mathcal{W} . \tag{37}$$

From (33)–(37) we conclude that

$$\mathcal{V} \subset \operatorname{Ker} D \cap A^{-1}(\mathcal{V} + \mathcal{B}) ,$$

$$\mathcal{V} \cap \langle A|\mathcal{B}\rangle = 0 ,$$

and

$$\mathcal{X}^+(A) \subset \langle A|\mathcal{B}\rangle + \mathcal{V} .$$

It follows by Theorem 7.1 that RPIS is solvable.

(Only if) If RPIS is solvable, Theorem 7.1 supplies a subspace $\mathcal{V}$ such that

$$\mathcal{V} \subset \operatorname{Ker} D \cap A^{-1}(\mathcal{V} + \mathcal{B})$$

and

$$\mathcal{X}^+(A) \subset \langle A|\mathcal{B}\rangle \oplus \mathcal{V} . \tag{38}$$

Since $\mathcal{V} \cap \langle A|\mathcal{B}\rangle = 0$ we have $\mathcal{V} \cap \mathcal{R}^* = 0$, so that $\mathcal{V}^* \supset \mathcal{R}^* \oplus \mathcal{V}$. From this it is clear that $F \in \underline{F}(\mathcal{V}) \cap \underline{F}(\mathcal{V}^*)$ can be chosen such that $A_F|\mathcal{R}^*$ is stable. By (38) and Lemma 6.4 we have

$$\mathcal{X}^+(A_F) \subset \langle A|\mathcal{B}\rangle \oplus \mathcal{V} \subset \langle A|\mathcal{B}\rangle + \mathcal{V}^* .$$

Since all the subspaces here are A_F-invariant there follows

$$\begin{aligned}\mathcal{X}^+(A_F) &\subset \langle A|\mathcal{B}\rangle \cap \mathcal{X}^+(A_F) \oplus \mathcal{V} \cap \mathcal{X}^+(A_F) \\ &\subset \langle A|\mathcal{B}\rangle \cap \mathcal{X}^+(A_F) + \mathcal{V}^* \cap \mathcal{X}^+(A_F) \subset \mathcal{X}^+(A_F)\end{aligned}$$

and therefore

$$\mathcal{V}^* \cap \mathcal{X}^+(A_F) \subset \langle A|\mathcal{B}\rangle \cap \mathcal{X}^+(A_F) \oplus \mathcal{V} \cap \mathcal{X}^+(A_F) .$$

Intersecting both sides with $\mathcal{V}^*$ and using $\mathcal{V}^* \supset \mathcal{V}$, we obtain

$$\mathcal{V}^* \cap \mathcal{X}^+(A_F) = \langle A|\mathcal{B}\rangle \cap \mathcal{X}^+(A_F) \cap \mathcal{V}^* \oplus \mathcal{V} \cap \mathcal{X}^+(A_F) = \mathcal{S} \oplus \mathcal{T}, \text{ say.} \tag{39}$$

Let $P: \mathcal{X} \to \mathcal{X}/\mathcal{R}^*$ be the canonical projection. By the stability of $A_F|\mathcal{R}^*$ we have

$$(\mathcal{S} \oplus \mathcal{T}) \cap \operatorname{Ker} P = (\mathcal{S} \oplus \mathcal{T}) \cap \mathcal{R}^* \subset \mathcal{X}^+(A_F) \cap \mathcal{R}^* = 0$$

$$= \mathcal{S} \cap \operatorname{Ker} P \oplus \mathcal{T} \cap \operatorname{Ker} P$$

and therefore

$$(P\mathcal{S}) \cap (P\mathcal{T}) = P(\mathcal{S} \cap \mathcal{T}) = 0 . \tag{40}$$

By (39), (40) we have finally

$$P\left[\mathcal{V}^* \cap \mathcal{X}^+(A_F)\right] = P\left[\langle A|\mathcal{B}\rangle \cap \mathcal{X}^+(A_F) \cap \mathcal{V}^*\right] \oplus P\left[\mathcal{V} \cap \mathcal{X}^+(A_F)\right],$$

a decomposition of the type required. ▮

Remark 1

The foregoing proof of sufficiency made no essential use of the fact that $\mathcal{V}^*$ is actually the supremal element of the family of subspaces

$$\underline{\mathcal{V}} = \{\tilde{\mathcal{V}}: \tilde{\mathcal{V}} \subset \operatorname{Ker} D \cap A^{-1}(\tilde{\mathcal{V}} + \mathcal{B})\} .$$

The sole reason for stating Theorem 7.3 in terms of $\mathcal{V}^*$ is that this element of $\underline{\mathcal{V}}$ is readily computable algorithmically and so the obtained conditions are constructive. It is clear from the proof that the conclusion of Theorem 7.3 is valid provided the stated conditions hold for some element $\tilde{\mathcal{V}} \in \underline{\mathcal{V}}$, with $\mathcal{R}^*$ replaced by the largest c.s. $\tilde{\mathcal{R}} \subset \tilde{\mathcal{V}}$.

Remark 2

In applications it is often true that the map $\tilde{A}$ (say), induced by A in $\tilde{\mathcal{X}} \triangleq \mathcal{X}/\langle A|\mathcal{B}\rangle$, is completely unstable, i.e., $\sigma(\tilde{A}) \subset \mathbb{C}^+$. This merely reflects the fact that $\tilde{A}$ models the dynamic structure of the disturbance and reference signals external to the plant. Under this condition Theorem 7.3 can be stated more simply as follows.

COROLLARY 7.1. Let $\mathcal{N} = 0$ and assume that the map induced by A in $\mathcal{X}/\langle A|\mathcal{B}\rangle$ has its spectrum in $\mathbb{C}^+$. Then RPIS is solvable if and only if

$$\langle A|\mathcal{B}\rangle + \mathcal{V}^* = \mathcal{X},$$

and in $\mathcal{X}/\mathcal{R}^*$, with $F \in \underline{F}(\mathcal{V}^*)$, the subspace $(\mathcal{V}^* \cap \langle A|\mathcal{B}\rangle)/\mathcal{R}^*$ decomposes the subspace $\mathcal{V}^*/\mathcal{R}^*$ relative to the map induced by A_F in $\mathcal{V}^*/\mathcal{R}^*$.

We emphasize again that the decomposability condition need be checked only for a single, arbitrarily selected map $F \in \underline{F}(\mathcal{V}^*)$.

The proof is left as Ex. 7.9.

7.3 Constructive Solution of RPIS: $\mathcal{N}$ Arbitrary

It is not difficult to extend Theorem 7.3 to the general case. Suppose first that RPIS is solvable with the map F. Since $\operatorname{Ker} F \supset \mathcal{N}$ we have by Lemma 6.2 that

$$\mathcal{X}^+(A) \cap \mathcal{N} = \mathcal{X}^+(A+BF) \cap \mathcal{N} \tag{41}$$

is (A + BF)-invariant. Let

$$P: \mathcal{X} \to \overline{\mathcal{X}} = \frac{\mathcal{X}}{\mathcal{X}^+(A) \cap \mathcal{N}}$$

be the canonical projection, and let bars designate the maps induced in $\overline{\mathcal{X}}$. As $\operatorname{Ker} F \supset \operatorname{Ker} P$, $\overline{F}: \overline{\mathcal{X}} \to \mathcal{U}$ exists uniquely such that $\overline{F}P = F$, and it is easily seen that $P \operatorname{Ker} F = \operatorname{Ker} \overline{F}$. Similarly, by (8) and (41), $\overline{D}: \overline{\mathcal{X}} \to \mathcal{Z}$ exists uniquely such that $\overline{D}P = D$, and $P \operatorname{Ker} D = \operatorname{Ker} \overline{D}$. Finally, define $\overline{B}: \mathcal{U} \to \overline{\mathcal{X}}$ by $\overline{B} = PB$.

Now $\overline{A+BF} = \overline{A} + \overline{B}\overline{F}$ so (by Lemma 4.6 applied to A + BF)

$$P\mathcal{X}^+(A+BF) = \overline{\mathcal{X}}^+(\overline{A} + \overline{B}\overline{F}) .$$

Also

$$[\mathcal{X}^+(A+BF) + \langle A | \mathcal{B} \rangle + \mathcal{N}] \cap \operatorname{Ker} P = \mathcal{X}^+(A) \cap \mathcal{N}$$

$$= \mathcal{X}^+(A+BF) \cap \operatorname{Ker} P + (\langle A | \mathcal{B} \rangle + \mathcal{N}) \cap \operatorname{Ker} P.$$

With these observations we may project both sides of (6) – (8) to obtain

$$\operatorname{Ker} \overline{F} \supset \overline{\mathcal{N}} \tag{42}$$

$$\overline{\mathcal{X}}^+(\overline{A} + \overline{B}\overline{F}) \cap (\langle \overline{A} | \overline{\mathcal{B}} \rangle + \overline{\mathcal{N}}) \subset \overline{\mathcal{N}} \tag{43}$$

$$\overline{\mathcal{X}}^+(\overline{A} + \overline{B}\overline{F}) \subset \operatorname{Ker} \overline{D} . \tag{44}$$

Automatically

$$\overline{\mathcal{X}}^+(\overline{A}) \cap \overline{\mathcal{N}} = \overline{0}$$

or equivalently

$$\overline{\mathcal{N}} \subset \overline{\mathcal{X}}^-(\overline{A}) . \tag{45}$$

We have shown that if RPIS is solvable, so is the reduced problem (42) – (44) in $\overline{\mathcal{X}}$, and (45) is true as well. Conversely, suppose

$$\mathcal{X}^+(A) \cap \mathcal{N} \subset \operatorname{Ker} D \tag{46}$$

and that $\overline{F}$: $\overline{\mathcal{X}} \to \mathcal{U}$ exists such that (42)–(44) are true. Define $F = \overline{F}P$. By reversing the steps which led to (42)–(44) it is routine to verify that (6)–(8) are true, that is, RPIS is solvable. We therefore have

LEMMA 7.1. RPIS is solvable if and only if the reduced problem (42)–(44) is solvable under the assumption (46).

Next we show that in (43) we may set $\overline{\mathcal{N}} = \overline{0}$.

LEMMA 7.2. If (42)–(46) are true then

$$\overline{\mathcal{X}}^+(\overline{A} + \overline{B}\overline{F}) \cap \langle \overline{A} | \overline{\mathcal{B}} \rangle = \overline{0} \, . \tag{47}$$

Conversely if (47) holds, so does (43).

PROOF: By (43)

$$\begin{aligned}\overline{\mathcal{X}}^+(\overline{A} + \overline{B}\overline{F}) \cap (\langle \overline{A} | \overline{\mathcal{B}} \rangle + \overline{\mathcal{N}}) &\subset \overline{\mathcal{N}} \cap \overline{\mathcal{X}}^+(\overline{A} + \overline{B}\overline{F}) \\ &= \overline{\mathcal{N}} \cap \overline{\mathcal{X}}^+(\overline{A}) \quad \text{(by (42))} = \overline{0} \, .\end{aligned}$$

Conversely, the left side of (43) can be written

$$\begin{aligned}&\overline{\mathcal{X}}^+(\overline{A} + \overline{B}\overline{F}) \cap \left[\langle \overline{A} | \overline{\mathcal{B}} \rangle \cap \overline{\mathcal{X}}^+(\overline{A} + \overline{B}\overline{F}) + \langle \overline{A} | \overline{\mathcal{B}} \rangle \cap \overline{\mathcal{X}}^-(\overline{A} + \overline{B}\overline{F}) + \overline{\mathcal{N}} \cap \overline{\mathcal{X}}^-(\overline{A})\right] \\ &= \overline{\mathcal{X}}^+(\overline{A} + \overline{B}\overline{F}) \cap \langle \overline{A} | \overline{\mathcal{B}} \rangle = \overline{0} \, . \ \blacksquare\end{aligned}$$

By Lemmas 7.1 and 7.2 the solvability of RPIS is equivalent to solvability of the reduced problem (42), (44), (47) under the assumption (46). Our next result implies that the condition (42) is redundant. For simplicity of notation we temporarily drop bars.

LEMMA 7.3. Let F_0: $\mathcal{X} \to \mathcal{U}$ be such that

$$\mathcal{X}^+(A + BF_0) \cap \langle A | \mathcal{B} \rangle = 0 \, .$$

There exists F_1: $\mathcal{X} \to \mathcal{U}$ such that

$$\operatorname{Ker} F_1 \supset \mathcal{X}^-(A) \tag{48}$$

and

$$\mathcal{X}^+(A + BF_1) = \mathcal{X}^+(A + BF_0) \, . \tag{49}$$

PROOF: In this proof, primes are used as indices. The lemma will be proved in three steps. First, let $P^+: \langle A|\mathcal{B}\rangle \to \langle A|\mathcal{B}\rangle \cap \mathcal{X}^+(A)$ be the natural projection on $\langle A|\mathcal{B}\rangle \cap \mathcal{X}^+(A)$ along $\langle A|\mathcal{B}\rangle \cap \mathcal{X}^-(A)$, and write

$$A^+ \triangleq A|[\langle A|\mathcal{B}\rangle \cap \mathcal{X}^+(A)], \qquad B^+ \triangleq P^+B .$$

Since

$$\langle A|\mathcal{B}\rangle \cap \mathcal{X}^+(A) = P^+\langle A|\mathcal{B}\rangle = \langle A^+|\mathcal{B}^+\rangle$$

we have that (A^+, B^+) is controllable, so there exists $F^+: \langle A|\mathcal{B}\rangle \cap \mathcal{X}^+(A) \to \mathcal{U}$ such that $A^+ + B^+F^+$ is stable. Choose $\mathcal{S}^-$ such that

$$\langle A|\mathcal{B}\rangle \cap \mathcal{X}^-(A) \oplus \mathcal{S}^- = \mathcal{X}^-(A)$$

and then $\mathcal{S}$ such that $\mathcal{S} \supset \mathcal{S}^-$ and $\langle A|\mathcal{B}\rangle \oplus \mathcal{S} = \mathcal{X}$. Now define $F_0': \mathcal{X} \to \mathcal{U}$ according to

$$F_0'|[\langle A|\mathcal{B}\rangle \cap \mathcal{X}^+(A)] = F^+$$
$$F_0'|[\langle A|\mathcal{B}\rangle \cap \mathcal{X}^-(A) \oplus \mathcal{S}] = 0 .$$

Write $A_0' = A + BF_0'$ and $F_0'' = F_0 - F_0'$. It is then clear that

$$\operatorname{Ker} F_0' \supset \mathcal{X}^-(A) \tag{50}$$

$$\mathcal{X}^+(A_0') \cap \langle A|\mathcal{B}\rangle = 0$$

and

$$\mathcal{X}^+(A_0' + BF_0'') \cap \langle A|\mathcal{B}\rangle = 0 . \tag{51}$$

As the second step we claim there exists $F_1': \mathcal{X} \to \mathcal{U}$ such that

$$\operatorname{Ker} F_1' \supset \langle A|\mathcal{B}\rangle \tag{52}$$

and

$$\mathcal{X}^+(A_0' + BF_1') = \mathcal{X}^+(A_0' + BF_0'') \qquad (= \mathcal{X}^+(A + BF_0)) . \tag{53}$$

For this, let

$$F_1'|\langle A|\mathcal{B}\rangle = 0$$
$$F_1'|\mathcal{X}^+(A_0' + BF_0'') = F_0''|\mathcal{X}^+(A_0' + BF_0'')$$

and let $F_1'|\mathcal{T}$ be defined arbitrarily on some complement $\mathcal{T}$ of $\mathcal{X}^+(A_0' + BF_0'') + \langle A|\mathcal{B}\rangle$ ($= \mathcal{X}^+(A) + \langle A|\mathcal{B}\rangle$) in $\mathcal{X}$. Write

$$A_0'' = A_0' + BF_0'' , \qquad A_1' = A_0' + BF_1' .$$

Since $\mathcal{X}^+(A_0'')$ is A_0''-invariant, and

$$A_1' | \mathcal{X}^+(A_0'') = A_0'' | \mathcal{X}^+(A_0'')$$

there follows by Lemma 6.2,

$$\mathcal{X}^+(A_1') \cap \mathcal{X}^+(A_0'') = \mathcal{X}^+(A_0'')$$

so that

$$\mathcal{X}^+(A_0'') \subset \mathcal{X}^+(A_1') . \tag{54}$$

Similarly we have

$$\mathcal{X}^+(A_1') \cap \langle A | \mathcal{B} \rangle = \mathcal{X}^+(A_0') \cap \langle A | \mathcal{B} \rangle = 0 .$$

By Lemma 6.4 there results

$$\langle A | \mathcal{B} \rangle \oplus \mathcal{X}^+(A_0'') = \langle A | \mathcal{B} \rangle \oplus \mathcal{X}^+(A_1') \tag{55}$$

and (53) follows at once from (54) and (55).

As the last step we prove the existence of $F_1'': \mathcal{X} \to \mathcal{U}$ such that

$$\operatorname{Ker} F_1'' \supset \mathcal{X}^-(A) + \langle A | \mathcal{B} \rangle \tag{56}$$

$$\mathcal{X}^+(A_0' + BF_1'') = \mathcal{X}^+(A_0' + BF_1') . \tag{57}$$

A bar will denote a subspace or induced map in $\overline{\mathcal{X}} = \mathcal{X}/\langle A | \mathcal{B} \rangle$. Let $P: \mathcal{X} \to \overline{\mathcal{X}}$ be the canonical projection. We have $\overline{\mathcal{X}} = \overline{\mathcal{X}}^+(\overline{A}) \oplus \overline{\mathcal{X}}^-(\overline{A})$, and by (51), $F_1' = \overline{F}_1' P$ for some $\overline{F}_1': \overline{\mathcal{X}} \to \mathcal{U}$. Define $F_1'' = \overline{F}_1'' P$, where

$$\overline{F}_1'' | \overline{\mathcal{X}}^+(\overline{A}) = \overline{F}_1' | \overline{\mathcal{X}}^+(\overline{A})$$

$$\overline{F}_1'' | \overline{\mathcal{X}}^-(\overline{A}) = 0 .$$

Then

$$P \operatorname{Ker} F_1'' = \operatorname{Ker} \overline{F}_1'' \supset \overline{\mathcal{X}}^-(\overline{A})$$

so that

$$\mathcal{X}^-(A) \subset \operatorname{Ker} F_1'' + \langle A | \mathcal{B} \rangle = \operatorname{Ker} F_1''$$

and (56) is true. Also if $x \in \mathcal{X}^+(A_0' + BF_1')$ then $Px \in \overline{\mathcal{X}}^+(\overline{A})$, so

$$F_1'' x = \overline{F}_1'' Px = \overline{F}_1' Px = F_1' x ;$$

therefore

$$(A_0' + BF_1'') | \mathcal{X}^+(A_0' + BF_1') = (A_0' + BF_1') | \mathcal{X}^+(A_0' + BF_1')$$

and there follows

$$\mathcal{X}^+(A_0' + BF_1'') \supset \mathcal{X}^+(A_0' + BF_1') . \qquad (58)$$

Similarly, as $\langle A|\mathcal{B}\rangle \subset \operatorname{Ker} F_1' \cap \operatorname{Ker} F_1''$,

$$(A_0' + BF_1'')|\langle A|\mathcal{B}\rangle = (A_0' + BF_1')|\langle A|\mathcal{B}\rangle ,$$

and so

$$\mathcal{X}^+(A_0' + BF_1'') \cap \langle A|\mathcal{B}\rangle = \mathcal{X}^+(A_0' + BF_1') \cap \langle A|\mathcal{B}\rangle = 0 \text{ (by (51) and (53)).}$$

This means

$$\mathcal{X}^+(A_0' + BF_1'') \approx \overline{\mathcal{X}}^+(\overline{A_0' + BF_1''}) = \overline{\mathcal{X}}^+(\overline{A_0' + BF_1'}) \approx \mathcal{X}^+(A_0' + BF_1') \qquad (59)$$

and (57) follows by (58) and (59).

It remains only to define

$$F_1 = F_0' + F_1'' .$$

Then (48) follows by (50), (56); and (49) by (53), (57). ∎

It is now easy to prove our main result. For this we revert to the notation introduced at the beginning of this section.

THEOREM 7.4. <u>In the general case $\mathcal{N} \neq 0$, RPIS is solvable if and only if</u>

(i) $$\mathcal{X}^+(A) \cap \mathcal{N} \subset \operatorname{Ker} D \qquad (60)$$

<u>and</u>

(ii) <u>In the factor space $\overline{\mathcal{X}} = \mathcal{X}/[\mathcal{X}^+(A) \cap \mathcal{N}]$ the reduced problem is solvable: that is, there exists $\overline{F}_0 : \overline{\mathcal{X}} \to \mathcal{U}$ such that</u>

$$\overline{\mathcal{X}}^+(\overline{A} + \overline{B}\overline{F}_0) \subset \operatorname{Ker} \overline{D} \qquad (61)$$

<u>and</u>

$$\overline{\mathcal{X}}^+(\overline{A} + \overline{B}\overline{F}_0) \cap \langle \overline{A}|\overline{\mathcal{B}}\rangle = \overline{0} . \qquad (62)$$

Of course the reduced problem (ii) is identical in form to the one solved by Theorem 7.3.

PROOF: (If) Suppose the reduced problem (RP) defined by (61), (62) is solvable. Lemma 7.3 applied to RP yields a map $\overline{F} : \overline{\mathcal{X}} \to \mathcal{U}$ such that

$$\operatorname{Ker} \overline{F} \supset \overline{\mathcal{X}}^-(\overline{A})$$

and $\overline{F}$ satisfies (44) and (47). Since $\overline{\mathcal{X}}^-(\overline{A}) \supset \overline{\mathcal{N}}$ we have that (42) is true as well. As already noted, Lemmas 7.1 and 7.2 now imply that RPIS is solvable.

(Only if) The necessity of (60) is immediate from (9), (10); and that of (61), (62) follows by Lemmas 7.1 and 7.2. ▌

7.4 Application: Regulation Against Step Disturbances

As a simple application of Theorem 7.3, consider the system

$$\dot{x}_1 = A_1 x_1 + A_3 x_2 + B_1 u$$
$$\dot{x}_2 = 0$$
$$z = D_1 x_1 + D_2 x_2 \,.$$

We assume that $y = x$ and (A_1, B_1) is controllable. The equations represent a controllable plant subjected to step disturbances which enter both dynamically and directly at the regulated output, a situation common in industrial process control.

In basis-free terms our assumptions amount to the following:

$$\mathcal{N} = 0 \,, \tag{63}$$
$$\operatorname{Im} A \subset \langle A \,|\, \mathcal{B} \rangle \,. \tag{64}$$

We now have

THEOREM 7.5. <u>Subject to the assumptions (63) and (64) RPIS is solvable if and only if</u>

$$\langle A \,|\, \mathcal{B} \rangle + \operatorname{Ker} D \cap A^{-1} \mathcal{B} = \mathcal{X} \,. \tag{65}$$

PROOF: (If) Exploiting the remark after the proof of Theorem 7.3, let

$$\tilde{\mathcal{V}} = \operatorname{Ker} D \cap A^{-1} \mathcal{B} \,. \tag{66}$$

From (65), (66) it is clear, first, that

$$\mathcal{X}^{+}(A) \subset \langle A \,|\, \mathcal{B} \rangle + \tilde{\mathcal{V}} \,.$$

Also, as $A\tilde{\mathcal{V}} \subset \mathcal{B}$ there exists $F \in \underline{F}(\tilde{\mathcal{V}})$ such that $A_F \tilde{\mathcal{V}} = 0$, where $A_F = A + BF$. Then

$$\tilde{\mathcal{V}} \subset \operatorname{Ker} A_F \subset \mathcal{X}^{+}(A_F)$$

so

$$\tilde{\mathcal{V}} \cap \mathcal{X}^{+}(A_F) \cap \langle A \,|\, \mathcal{B} \rangle = \tilde{\mathcal{V}} \cap \langle A \,|\, \mathcal{B} \rangle \,.$$

According to Theorem 5.5 the supremal c.s. $\tilde{\mathcal{R}}$ in $\tilde{\mathcal{V}}$ is given by

$$\tilde{\mathcal{R}} = \langle A_F | \mathcal{B} \cap \tilde{\mathcal{V}} \rangle = \mathcal{B} \cap \tilde{\mathcal{V}} .$$

The second condition of Theorem 7.3 (with $\tilde{\mathcal{V}}$ in place of $\mathcal{V}^*$) will thus be satisfied if

$$\frac{\tilde{\mathcal{V}} \cap \langle A | \mathcal{B} \rangle}{\mathcal{B} \cap \tilde{\mathcal{V}}}$$

decomposes $\tilde{\mathcal{V}}/(\mathcal{B} \cap \tilde{\mathcal{V}})$ relative to the map induced by A_F in $\tilde{\mathcal{V}}/(\mathcal{B} \cap \tilde{\mathcal{V}})$. Since $A_F | \tilde{\mathcal{V}} = 0$ this is trivial, and the result follows.

(Only if) Let $\bar{\mathcal{X}} \triangleq \mathcal{X}/\langle A | \mathcal{B} \rangle$ and now use bars for subspaces and induced maps in $\bar{\mathcal{X}}$. By (64), $\bar{A} = 0$ and, since $\bar{\mathcal{X}}^-(\bar{A}) = \bar{0}$, we have $\mathcal{X}^-(A) \subset \langle A | \mathcal{B} \rangle$. Let F solve RPIS. Since $\bar{A}_F = \bar{A} = 0$ for all F, and since $\mathcal{X}^+(A_F) \cap \langle A | \mathcal{B} \rangle = 0$, we have $\mathcal{X}^+(A_F) = \operatorname{Ker} A_F$. Now $\operatorname{Ker} A_F \subset A^{-1}\mathcal{B}$ for any F, so

$$\mathcal{X}^+(A_F) \subset \operatorname{Ker} D \cap A^{-1}\mathcal{B} . \tag{67}$$

By application of Lemma 6.3 to (67) there results

$$\mathcal{X}^+(A) \subset \langle A | \mathcal{B} \rangle + \operatorname{Ker} D \cap A^{-1}\mathcal{B}$$

and therefore

$$\mathcal{X} = \mathcal{X}^-(A) \oplus \mathcal{X}^+(A) \subset \langle A | \mathcal{B} \rangle + \mathcal{X}^+(A) \subset \langle A | \mathcal{B} \rangle + \operatorname{Ker} D \cap A^{-1}\mathcal{B} \subset \mathcal{X} . \quad \blacksquare$$

7.5 Application: Static Decoupling

Many control processes call for the occasional resetting of scalar output variables to new values, which are then held constant for time intervals long compared to the time constants of the process. It is convenient to associate a reset control v_i with each such output w_i so that if, for some fixed i, v_i alone is given a step change at $t = 0$, then

$$w_i(t) \to v_i(0+) , \qquad t \to \infty .$$

In addition it is required that the remaining variables return to their initial values, possibly after an intervening transient, i.e.,

$$w_j(t) \to w_j(0-) , \qquad j \neq i, \quad t \to \infty .$$

It is straightforward to treat this situation with the methods already developed. We have the plant equation

$$\dot{x}_1 = A_1 x_1 + B_1 u$$

and assume (A_1, B_1) controllable. The output equation is

$$w = D_1 x_1 .$$

Denote the reset control vector by x_2, so that

$$\dot{x}_2(t) = 0 , \qquad t > 0 .$$

For simplicity we assume that both the plant state x_1 and (reasonably enough) the reset control x_2 are observable. We require state feedback F_1 and reset gain F_2 such that, if

$$u = F_1 x_1 + F_2 x_2 ,$$

then $w(t) - x_2(t) \to 0$ $(t \to \infty)$. In addition, we ask for internal (plant) stabilization. Thus, defining

$$z = D_1 x_1 - x_2$$

we obtain a problem of the typed solved in Section 7.4.

7.6 Example 1: RPIS Unsolvable

It is instructive to return to the example in Section 6.4 and verify that the conditions of Theorem 7.4 fail. We had

$$A = \begin{bmatrix} 0 & 1 & 0 \\ -1 & -2 & 0 \\ 0 & 0 & 1 \end{bmatrix}, \qquad B = \begin{bmatrix} 0 \\ 1 \\ 0 \end{bmatrix},$$

$$C = [0 \quad 0 \quad 1], \qquad D = [\alpha \quad -\alpha \quad -1],$$

where $\alpha \neq 0$ is arbitrary. This yields

$$\mathcal{N} = \operatorname{Im} \begin{bmatrix} 1 & 0 \\ 0 & 1 \\ 0 & 0 \end{bmatrix}, \qquad \operatorname{Ker} D = \operatorname{Im} \begin{bmatrix} 1 & 1 \\ 1 & 0 \\ 0 & \alpha \end{bmatrix},$$

$$\langle A|\mathcal{B}\rangle = \text{Im}\begin{bmatrix}1 & 0\\0 & 1\\0 & 0\end{bmatrix}, \qquad \mathcal{X}^+(A) = \text{Im}\begin{bmatrix}0\\0\\1\end{bmatrix}.$$

Since $\mathcal{X}^+(A) \cap \mathcal{N} = 0$, the 'reduced problem' of Theorem 7.4 is simply the problem given, with $\mathcal{N}$ replaced by zero. Now

$$A \operatorname{Ker} D \subset \operatorname{Ker} D + \mathcal{B},$$

hence $\mathcal{V}^* = \operatorname{Ker} D$; and $\mathcal{B} \cap \mathcal{V}^* = 0$ implies $\mathcal{R}^* = 0$. The map

$$F = [0 \quad 4 \quad 0]$$

is in $\underline{F}(\mathcal{V}^*)$;

$$A_F = \begin{bmatrix}0 & 1 & 0\\-1 & 2 & 0\\0 & 0 & 1\end{bmatrix};$$

and $\mathcal{X}^+(A_F) = \mathcal{X}$.

Since now $\mathcal{N} = 0$, we use Theorem 7.3. Clearly

$$\langle A|\mathcal{B}\rangle + \mathcal{V}^* = \mathcal{X}$$

and so condition (27) holds. Since $\mathcal{R}^* = 0$, we must check (for the decomposability condition) whether

$$\mathcal{V}^* \cap \langle A|\mathcal{B}\rangle \cap \mathcal{X}^+(A_F) = \text{Im}\begin{bmatrix}1\\1\\0\end{bmatrix}$$

decomposes

$$\mathcal{V}^* \cap \mathcal{X}^+(A_F) = \text{Im}\begin{bmatrix}1 & 1\\1 & 0\\0 & \alpha\end{bmatrix}$$

relative to the map $A_F|\mathcal{V}^*$. For this, let

$$e_1 = \begin{bmatrix}1\\1\\0\end{bmatrix}, \qquad e_2 = \begin{bmatrix}1\\0\\\alpha\end{bmatrix}$$

and write $\mathcal{E}_1$ for the span of e_1. In the basis $\{e_1, e_2\}$

$$\text{Mat}(A_F|\mathcal{V}^*) = \begin{bmatrix}1 & -1\\0 & 1\end{bmatrix} = A_F^*, \text{ say.} \tag{68}$$

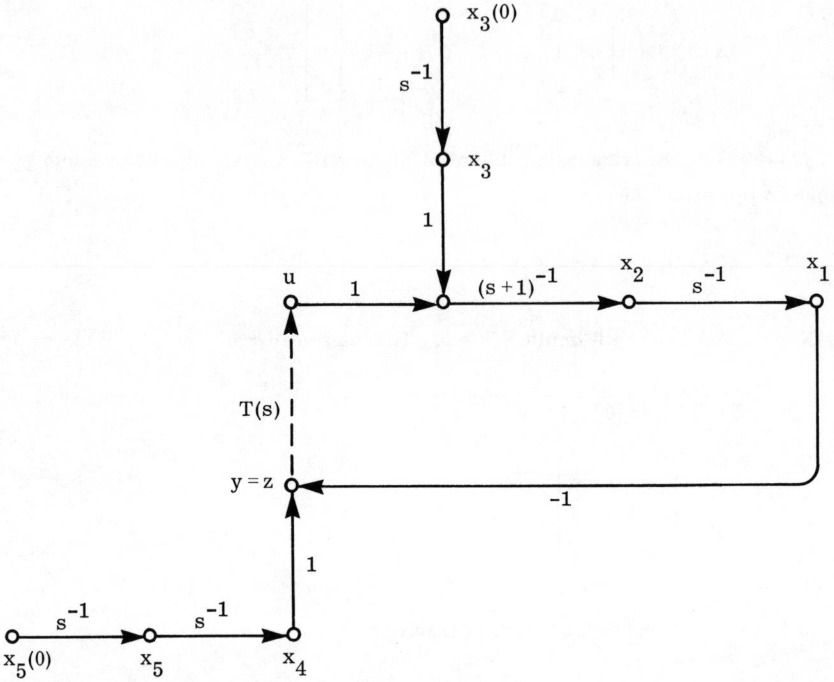

Fig. 7.2.

Signal Flow Graph:
Servo-Regulator, Section 7.7.
T(s) combines observer-compensator.

Since

$$\sigma(A_F^*) = \{1,1\} ,$$

it is clear that e_1 decomposes $\mathcal{V}^*$ relative to A_F^* if and only if there is a vector of form $\begin{bmatrix}\beta\\1\end{bmatrix}$ such that

$$A_F^* \begin{bmatrix}\beta\\1\end{bmatrix} = \begin{bmatrix}\beta\\1\end{bmatrix} .$$

A trivial computation shows that no such vector exists, hence decomposability fails, and RPIS is not solvable.

Referring to Proposition 0.5 we could alternatively check the condition on elementary divisors (e.d.). By inspection of (68) we see that $A_F^*|e_1$ has e.d. $\lambda-1$, as does the induced map $\overline{A}_F^*$ on $\mathcal{V}^*/e_1$; but A_F^* has the single e.d. $(\lambda-1)^2$, which shows again that decomposability fails.

7.7 Example 2: Servo-Regulator

We shall design a controller for the single-input, single-output system with the signal-flow graph of Fig. 7.2. The state and output equations are:

$$\begin{aligned}
\dot{x}_1 &= x_2 \\
\dot{x}_2 &= -x_2 + x_3 + u \\
\dot{x}_3 &= 0 \\
\dot{x}_4 &= x_5 \\
\dot{x}_5 &= 0 \\
y = z &= -x_1 + x_4 .
\end{aligned}$$

The system represents a second-order plant (state variables x_1, x_2) subject to a step load disturbance x_3, to be designed to track a ramp input x_4. The tracking error $x_4 - x_1$ is assumed to be the only variable accessible to direct measurement. What is required is a suitable compensator T(s).

We have

$$A = \begin{bmatrix} 0 & 1 & 0 & 0 & 0 \\ 0 & -1 & 1 & 0 & 0 \\ 0 & 0 & 0 & 0 & 0 \\ 0 & 0 & 0 & 0 & 1 \\ 0 & 0 & 0 & 0 & 0 \end{bmatrix}, \qquad B = \begin{bmatrix} 0 \\ 1 \\ 0 \\ 0 \\ 0 \end{bmatrix},$$

$$C = D = [-1\ \ 0\ \ 0\ \ 1\ \ 0]\ .$$

There follows

$$\mathcal{N} = \operatorname{Im}\begin{bmatrix} 1 & 0 \\ 0 & 1 \\ 0 & 1 \\ 1 & 0 \\ 0 & 1 \end{bmatrix}, \qquad \mathcal{X}^{+}(A) = \operatorname{Im}\begin{bmatrix} 1 & 0 & 0 & 0 \\ 0 & 1 & 0 & 0 \\ 0 & 1 & 0 & 0 \\ 0 & 0 & 1 & 0 \\ 0 & 0 & 0 & 1 \end{bmatrix}.$$

Thus $\mathcal{N} \cap \mathcal{X}^{+}(A) = \mathcal{N} \subset \operatorname{Ker} D$, as required by the first condition (60) of Theorem 7.4. To examine the 'reduced' problem in $\mathcal{X}/\mathcal{N}$, write $\mathcal{X} = \mathcal{M} \oplus \mathcal{N}$, with

$$\mathcal{M} = \operatorname{Im}\begin{bmatrix} 1 & 0 & 0 \\ 0 & 1 & 0 \\ 0 & 0 & 1 \\ 0 & 0 & 0 \\ 0 & 0 & 0 \end{bmatrix}.$$

The projection $P: \mathcal{X} \to \mathcal{X}/\mathcal{N}$ is represented by the natural projection $P: \mathcal{M} \oplus \mathcal{N} \to \mathcal{M}$ defined by $P|\mathcal{M} = 1_{\mathcal{M}}$, $P|\mathcal{N} = 0$. This gives

$$P = \begin{bmatrix} 1 & 0 & 0 & -1 & 0 \\ 0 & 1 & 0 & 0 & -1 \\ 0 & 0 & 1 & 0 & -1 \end{bmatrix}.$$

The induced maps

$$\overline{A}: \mathcal{M} \to \mathcal{M}, \qquad \overline{B}: \mathcal{U} \to \mathcal{M}, \qquad \overline{D}: \mathcal{M} \to \mathcal{Z},$$

determined by

$$\overline{A}P = PA\ , \qquad \overline{B} = PB\ , \qquad \overline{D}P = D\ ,$$

are then

$$\overline{A} = \begin{bmatrix} 0 & 1 & 0 \\ 0 & -1 & 1 \\ 0 & 0 & 0 \end{bmatrix}, \qquad \overline{B} = \begin{bmatrix} 0 \\ 1 \\ 0 \end{bmatrix}, \qquad \overline{D} = [-1\ \ 0\ \ 0]\ . \tag{69}$$

The reduced problem is solvable if the conditions of Theorem 7.3 are satisfied by the triple (69). We have by simple computations

$$\overline{\mathcal{X}}^{+}(\overline{A}) = \operatorname{Im}\begin{bmatrix} 1 & 0 \\ 0 & 1 \\ 0 & 1 \end{bmatrix}, \qquad \langle \overline{A}|\overline{\mathcal{B}} \rangle = \operatorname{Im}\begin{bmatrix} 1 & 0 \\ 0 & 1 \\ 0 & 0 \end{bmatrix}, \qquad \overline{\mathcal{V}}^{*} = \operatorname{Im}\begin{bmatrix} 0 \\ 0 \\ 1 \end{bmatrix}, \tag{70}$$

so (27) holds. The condition of decomposability is trivially satisfied, as $\bar{\mathcal{V}}^* \cap \langle \bar{A} | \bar{\mathcal{B}} \rangle = \bar{0}$.

Having verified that RPIS is solvable, we construct a solution in three stages: first a controller for the reduced problem with data (69), second an observer to generate $\bar{x} = Px \in \mathcal{M}$, and third the compensator T(s) in which controller and observer are combined.

1. For the controller we could follow the constructive procedure in the proof (sufficiency half) of Theorem 7.3, or alternatively look directly for a subspace $\bar{\mathcal{V}}$ with properties (9) – (12) of Theorem 7.1. Since our problem is of low dimension, the latter method is quicker. Referring to (70) we see that $\mathcal{X}^+(\bar{A}) \not\subset \langle \bar{A} | \bar{\mathcal{B}} \rangle$, hence to satisfy (11) and (12) (with $\mathcal{N} = 0$) $\bar{\mathcal{V}}$ must be of the form

$$\bar{\mathcal{V}} = \operatorname{Im} \begin{bmatrix} \alpha \\ \beta \\ 1 \end{bmatrix} \tag{71}$$

for some α, β. Applying (9), we require

$$\bar{A}\bar{\mathcal{V}} \subset \bar{\mathcal{V}} + \bar{\mathcal{B}}, \qquad \bar{\mathcal{V}} \subset \operatorname{Ker} \bar{D}\,. \tag{72}$$

From (69), (71), (72) there results

$$\bar{\mathcal{V}} = \operatorname{Im} \begin{bmatrix} 0 \\ 0 \\ 1 \end{bmatrix};$$

thus $\bar{\mathcal{V}} = \bar{\mathcal{V}}^*$, as was also clear from (70) and (71). Next choose $\bar{F}_0 \in \underline{F}(\bar{\mathcal{V}})$ arbitrarily, e.g., $\bar{F}_0 = [\,0 \;\; 0 \;\; -1\,]$; then

$$\bar{A}_0 = \bar{A} + \bar{B}\bar{F} = \begin{bmatrix} 0 & 1 & 0 \\ 0 & -1 & 0 \\ 0 & 0 & 0 \end{bmatrix}.$$

It remains to choose $\bar{F}_1$ such that $\mathcal{X}^+(\bar{A}_0 + \bar{B}\bar{F}_1) \subset \bar{\mathcal{V}}$ and $(\bar{A}_0 + \bar{B}\bar{F}_1) | \langle \bar{A} | \bar{\mathcal{B}} \rangle$ is stable. Write $\bar{F}_1 = [\gamma \;\; \delta \;\; \epsilon]$, so

$$\bar{A}_0 + \bar{B}\bar{F}_1 = \begin{bmatrix} 0 & 1 & 0 \\ \gamma & -1+\delta & \epsilon \\ 0 & 0 & 0 \end{bmatrix}$$

and

$$(\bar{A}_0 + \bar{B}\bar{F}_1) | \langle \bar{A} | \bar{\mathcal{B}} \rangle \sim \begin{bmatrix} 0 & 1 \\ \gamma & -1+\delta \end{bmatrix}.$$

Assigning the spectrum on $\langle \overline{A} | \overline{\mathscr{B}} \rangle$ as $\{-2, -2\}$ we get $\gamma = -4$, $\delta = -3$; then

$$\overline{\mathscr{X}}^{+}(\overline{A}_0 + \overline{B}\overline{F}_1) = \operatorname{Im}\begin{bmatrix} \epsilon \\ 0 \\ 4 \end{bmatrix},$$

which belongs to $\overline{\mathscr{V}}$ if $\epsilon = 0$. Finally

$$\overline{F} = \overline{F}_0 + \overline{F}_1 = [-4 \quad -3 \quad -1]\,. \tag{73}$$

2. For the observer design we utilize again the decomposition $\mathscr{X} = \mathscr{M} \oplus \mathscr{N}$, the pair $(\overline{A}, \overline{B})$ of (69), and measured output matrix

$$\overline{C} = [-1 \quad 0 \quad 0]$$

determined by $\overline{C}P = C$. We adopt an observer of minimal order 2 with spectrum $\{-4, -4\}$. Applied to $(\overline{C}, \overline{A}, \overline{B})$ the procedure of Ex. 3.4 yields the observer equation

$$\dot{\overline{w}} = \begin{bmatrix} -8 & 1 \\ -16 & 0 \end{bmatrix} \overline{w} + \begin{bmatrix} 40 \\ 112 \end{bmatrix} y + \begin{bmatrix} 1 \\ 0 \end{bmatrix} u \tag{74}$$

and asymptotic evaluation

$$\overline{x} = \begin{bmatrix} -1 & 0 & 0 \\ -7 & 1 & 0 \\ -16 & 0 & 1 \end{bmatrix} \begin{bmatrix} y \\ \overline{w}_1 \\ \overline{w}_2 \end{bmatrix}. \tag{75}$$

From (73) and (75) the control is given by

$$u = \overline{F}\overline{x} = 41y - 3\overline{w}_1 - \overline{w}_2\,. \tag{76}$$

3. The compensator T(s) is now obtained as the transfer function from y to u determined by (74) and (76). The result is

$$T(s) = \frac{41s^2 + 96s + 64}{s(s+11)}\,.$$

A straightforward computation from the signal flow graph yields, as a check,

$$\hat{z}(s) = \frac{s(s+11)\left[-\hat{x}_3(s) + s(s+1)\hat{x}_4(s)\right]}{(s+2)^2 (s+4)^2}\,. \tag{77}$$

It is clear from (77) that the system is internally stable and that the tracking error $z(t) \to 0$ $(t \to \infty)$ in the presence of step disturbances

$$\hat{x}_3(s) = x_3(0+)\, s^{-1}$$

and ramp command signals

$$\hat{x}_4(s) = x_4(0+)\, s^{-1} + x_5(0+)\, s^{-2}\ .$$

7.8 Exercises

The first four exercises are directed to programming a solution F of RPIS when a solution exists. It is assumed that the results of Exs. 0.11, 2.2, 4.2 and 5.1 are available as subprocedures.

7.1 Regulator synthesis. Given $A, B, \mathcal{V}, \mathcal{N}$ with the properties

$$A\mathcal{V} \subset \mathcal{V} + \mathcal{B}\ , \qquad \langle A|\mathcal{B}\rangle \oplus \mathcal{V} = \mathcal{X}\ ,$$
$$A\mathcal{N} \subset \mathcal{N} \subset \langle A|\mathcal{B}\rangle \cap \mathcal{X}^-(A)\ ,$$

compute $F \in \underline{F}(\mathcal{V})$ such that $\operatorname{Ker} F \supset \mathcal{N}$ and $(A+BF)|\langle A|\mathcal{B}\rangle$ is stable. HINT: 1. Choose a basis adapted to the decomposition

$$\mathcal{X} = \langle A|\mathcal{B}\rangle \cap \mathcal{X}^-(A) \oplus \langle A|\mathcal{B}\rangle \cap \mathcal{X}^+(A) \oplus \mathcal{V}\ .$$

2. In this basis, compute

$$A = \left[\begin{array}{cc|c} A_1^- & 0 & A_3^- \\ 0 & A_1^+ & A_3^+ \\ \hline 0 & 0 & A_2 \end{array}\right], \qquad B = \left[\begin{array}{c} B_1^- \\ B_1^+ \\ \hline 0 \end{array}\right].$$

3. Compute $F_0 = [\,0\ \ 0\ \ F_2\,]$ such that $(A+BF_0)\mathcal{V} \subset \mathcal{V}$. 4. Compute $F_1 = \left[\,0\ \ F_1^+\ \ 0\,\right]$ such that $A_1^+ + B_1^+ F_1^+$ is stable. 5. Set $F \triangleq F_0 + F_1$.

7.2 Decomposition. Given $A, \mathcal{R}, \mathcal{T}$ with $A\mathcal{T} \subset \mathcal{T}$ and $A\mathcal{R} \subset \mathcal{R} \subset \mathcal{T}$, compute $\mathcal{S}$ such that $A\mathcal{S} \subset \mathcal{S}$ and $\mathcal{R} \oplus \mathcal{S} = \mathcal{T}$. HINT: 1. Compute any $\hat{\mathcal{S}}$ such that $\mathcal{T} = \mathcal{R} \oplus \hat{\mathcal{S}}$. 2. Compute $A|\mathcal{T}$ in a basis adapted to the decomposition in 1, so that

$$A|\mathcal{T} = \begin{bmatrix} A_1 & A_3 \\ 0 & A_2 \end{bmatrix}.$$

3. Compute any solution Q of

$$A_1 Q - Q A_2 - A_3 = 0\ .$$

If no solution exists, $\mathcal{R}$ does not decompose $\mathcal{T}$ relative to A. 4. Represent $\mathcal{S}$ as

$$\mathcal{S} = \mathrm{Ker}\,[I, Q] = \mathrm{Im}\begin{bmatrix} -Q \\ I \end{bmatrix}.$$

7.3 Solution of reduced RPIS. Given A, B, C, D such that

$$\mathcal{N} \subset \mathcal{X}^-(A) \subset \langle A|\mathcal{B}\rangle, \tag{78}$$

compute (if one exists) a solution F of RPIS. HINT: 1. Compute $\langle A|\mathcal{B}\rangle, \mathcal{V}^*, \mathcal{V}^* \cap \langle A|\mathcal{B}\rangle, \mathcal{R}^*$ and any $\mathcal{T}$ such that $\mathcal{R}^* \oplus \mathcal{T} = \mathcal{V}^*$ [$\mathcal{T}$ coordinatizes $\mathcal{V}^*/\mathcal{R}^*$]. 2. Check $\langle A|\mathcal{B}\rangle + \mathcal{V}^* = \mathcal{X}$. If this condition fails, RPIS is not solvable. 3. Compute arbitrary $F_0 \in \underline{F}(\mathcal{V}^*)$ [without regard to the constraint $\mathrm{Ker}\,F \supset \mathcal{N}$], and set $A_0 \triangleq A + BF_0$. 4. Compute $A_0|\mathcal{V}^*, \mathcal{B} \cap \mathcal{V}^*$ in a basis adapted to the decomposition $\mathcal{V}^* = \mathcal{R}^* \oplus \mathcal{T}$:

$$\hat{A}_0 \triangleq A_0|\mathcal{V}^* = \begin{bmatrix} A_{01} & A_{03} \\ 0 & A_{02} \end{bmatrix}, \qquad \mathcal{B} \cap \mathcal{V}^* = \mathrm{Im}\begin{bmatrix} B_1 \\ 0 \end{bmatrix}. \tag{79}$$

5. Check the condition $\sigma(A_{01}) \cap \sigma(A_{02}) = \emptyset$. If it fails, achieve it by replacing A_{01} with $A_{01} + B_1 F_{01}$ for suitable (random!) F_{01}: i.e., exploit controllability of (A_{01}, B_1). 6. Redefine $\mathcal{T}$ as the $\hat{A}_0$-invariant complement of $\mathcal{R}^*$ in $\mathcal{V}^*$: namely, if π_2 is the ch.p. of A_{02}, then $\mathcal{T} \triangleq \mathrm{Ker}\,\pi_2(\hat{A}_0)$. The result of steps 5 and 6 is to ensure $A_{03} = 0$ in (79). 7. Compute $\mathcal{T}_1 \triangleq \mathcal{V}^* \cap \langle A|\mathcal{B}\rangle \cap \mathcal{T}$: its representation in $\mathcal{V}^*$ is of form $\mathrm{Im}\begin{bmatrix} 0 \\ T_1 \end{bmatrix}$, and in $\mathcal{T}$ is $\mathrm{Im}\,T_1$. 8. Using Ex. 7.2 compute $\mathcal{T}_2 = \mathrm{Im}\,T_2 \subset \mathcal{T}$ such that $A_{02}\mathcal{T}_2 \subset \mathcal{T}_2$ and $\mathcal{T}_1 \oplus \mathcal{T}_2 = \mathcal{T}$. If this step fails, RPIS is not solvable. 9. Compute any $\mathcal{S}$ such that $\mathcal{X} = \mathcal{R}^* \oplus \mathcal{T} \oplus \mathcal{S}$ and set

$$\mathcal{V} \triangleq \mathrm{Im}\begin{bmatrix} 0 \\ T_2 \\ 0 \end{bmatrix}.$$

10. Compute a solution F by Ex. 7.1 applied to $A, B, \mathcal{V}, \mathcal{N}$.

7.4 Reduction of general RPIS. Given A, B, C, D compute reduced versions $(\bar{A}, \bar{B}, \bar{C}, \bar{D})$ for which (78) holds. Check solvability of RPIS for the original data. HINT: 1. The first condition of (78) is equivalent to $\bar{\mathcal{N}} \cap \bar{\mathcal{X}}^+(\bar{A}) = \bar{0}$. To achieve it, first check that $\mathcal{N} \cap \mathcal{X}^+(A) \subset \mathrm{Ker}\,D$. If this condition fails, RPIS is not solvable. 2. Compute arbitrary $\hat{\mathcal{X}}$ such that $\mathcal{N} \cap \mathcal{X}^+(A) \oplus \hat{\mathcal{X}} = \mathcal{X}$, then $P: \mathcal{X} \to \hat{\mathcal{X}}$ to satisfy $P(\mathcal{N} \cap \mathcal{X}^+(A)) = 0$, $P|\hat{\mathcal{X}} = 1_{\hat{\mathcal{X}}}$. With $\hat{\mathcal{X}}$ as a representation of $\bar{\mathcal{X}}$, compute the induced maps $\bar{A}$ etc. according to $\bar{A}P = PA$, $\bar{B} = PB$, $\bar{C}P = C$ and $\bar{D}P = D$. 3. The second condition of (78) states that the map induced by A on $\mathcal{X}/\langle A|\mathcal{B}\rangle$ is completely unstable. To achieve this, set $\bar{\mathcal{X}}_1 \triangleq \langle \bar{A}|\bar{\mathcal{B}}\rangle$, compute arbitrary $\bar{\mathcal{X}}_2$ such that $\bar{\mathcal{X}}_1 \oplus \bar{\mathcal{X}}_2 = \bar{\mathcal{X}}$, and compute $\bar{A}$ in a compatible basis as

$$\overline{A} = \begin{bmatrix} \overline{A}_1 & \overline{A}_3 \\ 0 & \overline{A}_2 \end{bmatrix} .$$

4. Split $\overline{\mathcal{X}}_2$ according to

$$\overline{\mathcal{X}}_2 = \overline{\mathcal{X}}_2^+(\overline{A}_2) \oplus \overline{\mathcal{X}}_2^-(\overline{A}_2) .$$

5. With a compatible sub-basis for $\overline{\mathcal{X}}_2$ the maps are now

$$\overline{A} = \begin{bmatrix} \overline{A}_1 & \overline{A}_3^+ & \overline{A}_3^- \\ 0 & \overline{A}_2^+ & 0 \\ 0 & 0 & \overline{A}_2^- \end{bmatrix}, \qquad \overline{B} = \begin{bmatrix} \overline{B}_1 \\ 0 \\ 0 \end{bmatrix},$$

$$\overline{C} = \begin{bmatrix} \overline{C}_1 & \overline{C}_2^+ & \overline{C}_2^- \end{bmatrix}, \qquad \overline{D} = \begin{bmatrix} \overline{D}_1 & \overline{D}_2^+ & \overline{D}_2^- \end{bmatrix}.$$

To obtain the final versions of $\overline{A}$ etc. delete the third (block) row and column of $\overline{A}$, the third row of $\overline{B}$, and third column of $\overline{C}$ and $\overline{D}$.

7.5 Apply the procedures of Exs. 7.1–7.4 to solve a realistic multivariable example with at least two inputs to be tracked and at least one disturbance to be rejected. The physical origin of the example should be plausible, and the parameter values representative of the application. Check the final design by an analog simulation. HINT: The example to follow illustrates the main steps, in a contrived situation of minimal complexity (Fig. 7.3). To make the problem more impressive, disguise it by a random change of basis in $\mathcal{U}, \mathcal{X}, \mathcal{Y}, \mathcal{Z}$. For the signal flow graph illustrated we have

$$A = \begin{bmatrix} 1 & 1 & 0 & 0 & 0 & 0 & 0 & 0 \\ 0 & 0 & 0 & 0 & 0 & 0 & 0 & 0 \\ 0 & 0 & 2 & 0 & 0 & 0 & 0 & 0 \\ 0 & 0 & 0 & 1 & 1 & 0 & 0 & 0 \\ 0 & 0 & 0 & 0 & -2 & 1 & 0 & 0 \\ 0 & 0 & 0 & 0 & 0 & 0 & 0 & 0 \\ 0 & 0 & 0 & 0 & 0 & 0 & 0 & 0 \\ 0 & 0 & 0 & 0 & 0 & 0 & 0 & -3 \end{bmatrix}, \qquad B = \begin{bmatrix} 0 & 0 & 0 \\ 1 & 0 & 0 \\ 0 & 1 & 0 \\ 0 & 0 & 0 \\ 0 & 0 & 1 \\ 0 & 0 & 0 \\ 0 & 0 & 0 \\ 0 & 0 & 0 \end{bmatrix},$$

$$C = \begin{bmatrix} 1 & 0 & 0 & 0 & 0 & 0 & 0 & 0 \\ 0 & 0 & 1 & 0 & 0 & 0 & 0 & 0 \\ 0 & 0 & 0 & -1 & 0 & 0 & 1 & 0 \end{bmatrix}, \qquad D = \begin{bmatrix} 0 & 1 & 0 & 0 & 0 & 0 & 0 & 0 \\ 0 & 0 & 0 & -1 & 0 & 0 & 1 & 0 \\ 0 & 0 & 0 & 0 & 0 & 0 & 0 & 1 \end{bmatrix}.$$

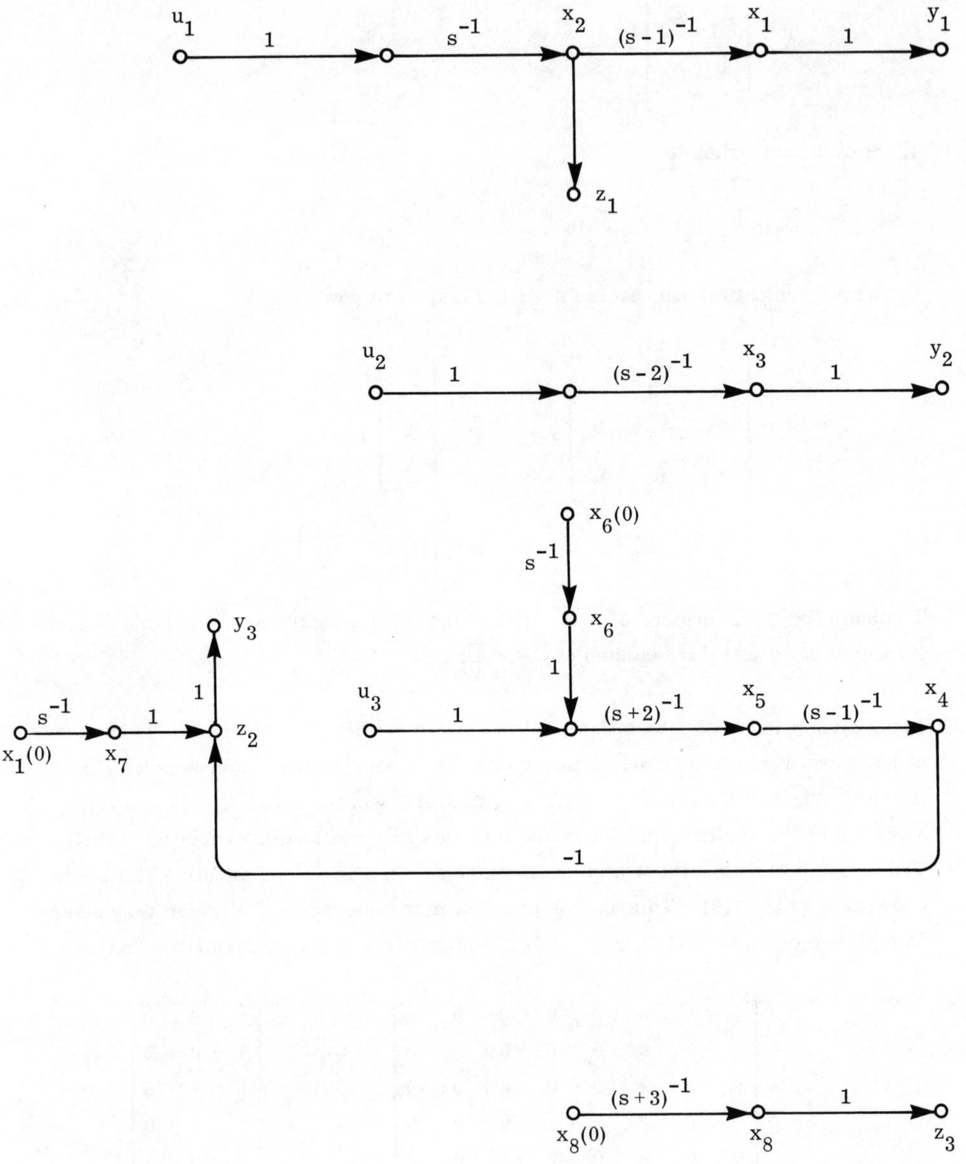

Fig. 7.3.

Signal Flow Graph: Ex. 7.5.

Exercise 7.4 yields

$$\mathcal{N} = \operatorname{Im}\begin{bmatrix} 0 & 0 \\ 0 & 0 \\ 0 & 0 \\ 1 & 0 \\ -1 & 0 \\ -2 & 0 \\ 1 & 0 \\ 0 & 1 \end{bmatrix} = \operatorname{Im}[n_1, n_2], \text{ say,}$$

where $An_1 = 0$, $An_2 = -3n_2$. Thus

$$\mathcal{N} \cap \mathcal{X}^-(A) = \operatorname{Span}\{n_2\} ,$$
$$\mathcal{N} \cap \mathcal{X}^+(A) = \operatorname{Span}\{n_1\} \subset \operatorname{Ker} D .$$

Writing e_i ($i \in \underline{8}$) for the unit vectors in $\mathbb{R}^8$, and taking

$$\hat{\mathcal{X}} = \operatorname{Im}[e_1\ e_2\ e_3\ e_4\ e_5\ e_6\ e_8] ,$$

one finds for $P: \mathcal{N} \cap \mathcal{X}^+(A) \oplus \hat{\mathcal{X}} \to \hat{\mathcal{X}}$ the matrix

$$P = \left[0^{7\times 1}, I^{7\times 7}\right]\left[n_1\, e_1\, e_2\, e_3\, e_4\, e_5\, e_6\, e_8\right]^{-1}$$

$$= \begin{bmatrix} 1 & 0 & 0 & 0 & 0 & 0 & 0 & 0 \\ 0 & 1 & 0 & 0 & 0 & 0 & 0 & 0 \\ 0 & 0 & 1 & 0 & 0 & 0 & 0 & 0 \\ 0 & 0 & 0 & 1 & 0 & 0 & -1 & 0 \\ 0 & 0 & 0 & 0 & 1 & 0 & 1 & 0 \\ 0 & 0 & 0 & 0 & 0 & 1 & 2 & 0 \\ 0 & 0 & 0 & 0 & 0 & 0 & 0 & 1 \end{bmatrix} .$$

From this (Ex. 7.4, step 2)

$$\overline{A} = \begin{bmatrix} 1 & 1 & 0 & 0 & 0 & 0 & 0 \\ 0 & 0 & 0 & 0 & 0 & 0 & 0 \\ 0 & 0 & 2 & 0 & 0 & 0 & 0 \\ 0 & 0 & 0 & 1 & 1 & 0 & 0 \\ 0 & 0 & 0 & 0 & -2 & 1 & 0 \\ 0 & 0 & 0 & 0 & 0 & 0 & 0 \\ 0 & 0 & 0 & 0 & 0 & 0 & -3 \end{bmatrix}, \qquad \overline{B} = \begin{bmatrix} 0 & 0 & 0 \\ 1 & 0 & 0 \\ 0 & 1 & 0 \\ 0 & 0 & 0 \\ 0 & 0 & 1 \\ 0 & 0 & 0 \\ 0 & 0 & 0 \end{bmatrix}, \qquad (80a)$$

$$\overline{C} = \begin{bmatrix} 1 & 0 & 0 & 0 & 0 & 0 & 0 \\ 0 & 0 & 1 & 0 & 0 & 0 & 0 \\ 0 & 0 & 0 & -1 & 0 & 0 & 0 \end{bmatrix}, \quad \overline{D} = \begin{bmatrix} 0 & 1 & 0 & 0 & 0 & 0 & 0 \\ 0 & 0 & 0 & -1 & 0 & 0 & 0 \\ 0 & 0 & 0 & 0 & 0 & 0 & 1 \end{bmatrix}. \qquad (80b)$$

To carry out steps 3–5, note that

$$\langle \overline{A} | \overline{\mathscr{B}} \rangle = \operatorname{Im}\left[\overline{e}_1 \ldots \overline{e}_6\right],$$

where $\overline{e}_i$ $(i \in \underline{7})$ are the unit vectors in $\mathbb{R}^7$. By inspection,

$$\overline{\mathscr{X}}_2 = \operatorname{Im}\left[\overline{e}_7, \overline{e}_8\right] = \overline{\mathscr{X}}_2^+(\overline{A}_2) \oplus \overline{\mathscr{X}}_2^-(\overline{A}_2) = \operatorname{Span}\{\overline{e}_7\} \oplus \operatorname{Span}\{\overline{e}_8\}.$$

The final versions, say $\tilde{A}$ etc., of $\overline{A}$ etc. are obtained by deleting the $8^{\underline{th}}$ row and column of $\overline{A}$, the $8^{\underline{th}}$ row of $\overline{B}$ and $8^{\underline{th}}$ column of $\overline{C}$ and $\overline{D}$. This yields

$$\tilde{A} = \begin{bmatrix} 1 & 1 & 0 & 0 & 0 & 0 \\ 0 & 0 & 0 & 0 & 0 & 0 \\ 0 & 0 & 2 & 0 & 0 & 0 \\ 0 & 0 & 0 & 1 & 1 & 0 \\ 0 & 0 & 0 & 0 & -2 & 1 \\ 0 & 0 & 0 & 0 & 0 & 0 \end{bmatrix}, \quad \tilde{B} = \begin{bmatrix} 0 & 0 & 0 \\ 1 & 0 & 0 \\ 0 & 1 & 0 \\ 0 & 0 & 0 \\ 0 & 0 & 1 \\ 0 & 0 & 0 \end{bmatrix}, \qquad (81a)$$

$$\tilde{C} = \begin{bmatrix} 1 & 0 & 0 & 0 & 0 & 0 \\ 0 & 0 & 1 & 0 & 0 & 0 \\ 0 & 0 & 0 & -1 & 0 & 0 \end{bmatrix}, \quad \tilde{D} = \begin{bmatrix} 0 & 1 & 0 & 0 & 0 & 0 \\ 0 & 0 & 0 & -1 & 0 & 0 \end{bmatrix}. \qquad (81b)$$

The meaning of these steps should be transparent from Fig. 7.3.

Next we carry out Ex. 7.3 with the data (81). Writing $\tilde{e}_i$ $(i \in \underline{6})$ for the unit vectors in $\mathbb{R}^6$ we have

$$\langle \tilde{A} | \tilde{\mathscr{B}} \rangle = \operatorname{Im}\left[\tilde{e}_1 \tilde{e}_2 \tilde{e}_3 \tilde{e}_4 \tilde{e}_5\right],$$

and after a short computation,

$$\tilde{\mathscr{V}}^* = \operatorname{Im}\left[\tilde{e}_1 \tilde{e}_3 \tilde{e}_6\right].$$

For $\tilde{F}_0 \in \underline{\tilde{F}}(\mathscr{V}^*)$ we may take

$$\tilde{F}_0 = \begin{bmatrix} & & 0 \\ 0^{3\times 5} & & 0 \\ & & -1 \end{bmatrix}, \qquad (82)$$

and then

$$\tilde{A}_0 = \tilde{A} + \tilde{B}\tilde{F}_0 = \begin{bmatrix} 1 & 1 & 0 & 0 & 0 & 0 \\ 0 & 0 & 0 & 0 & 0 & 0 \\ 0 & 0 & 2 & 0 & 0 & 0 \\ 0 & 0 & 0 & 1 & 1 & 0 \\ 0 & 0 & 0 & 0 & -2 & 0 \\ 0 & 0 & 0 & 0 & 0 & 0 \end{bmatrix}.$$

Next

$$\tilde{\mathcal{V}} = \tilde{\mathcal{R}}^* \oplus \tilde{\mathcal{T}} = \mathrm{Span}\{\tilde{e}_3\} \oplus \mathrm{Span}\{\tilde{e}_1, \tilde{e}_6\},$$

say. Since

$$\tilde{\mathcal{T}}_1 = \tilde{\mathcal{T}} \cap \langle \tilde{A} | \tilde{\mathcal{B}} \rangle = \mathrm{Span}\{\tilde{e}_1\},$$

and since

$$\tilde{A}_0 \tilde{e}_1 = \tilde{e}_1, \qquad \tilde{A}_0 \tilde{e}_6 = 0,$$

the decomposition of $\tilde{\mathcal{T}}$ yields

$$\tilde{\mathcal{V}} = \tilde{\mathcal{T}}_2 = \mathrm{Span}\{\tilde{e}_6\}. \tag{83}$$

To complete the solution we go to Ex. 7.1 with data (81)–(83); here $\tilde{\mathcal{N}} = 0$. The details are quite straightforward. Choosing $\tilde{F}_1$ such that $\tilde{F}_1 \tilde{\mathcal{V}} = 0$ and $(\tilde{A}_0 + \tilde{B}\tilde{F}_1) | \langle \tilde{A} | \tilde{\mathcal{B}} \rangle$ has spectrum at -1 we get, for instance,

$$\tilde{F}_1 = \begin{bmatrix} -4 & -3 & 0 & 0 & 0 & 0 \\ 0 & 0 & -3 & 0 & 0 & 0 \\ 0 & 0 & 0 & -4 & -1 & 0 \end{bmatrix},$$

and then

$$\tilde{F} = \tilde{F}_0 + \tilde{F}_1 = \begin{bmatrix} -4 & -3 & 0 & 0 & 0 & 0 \\ 0 & 0 & -3 & 0 & 0 & 0 \\ 0 & 0 & 0 & -4 & -1 & -1 \end{bmatrix}.$$

Writing $Q: \overline{\mathcal{X}} \to \tilde{\mathcal{X}}$ for the projection employed above, namely

$$Q = \begin{bmatrix} I^{6\times 6} & 0^{6\times 1} \end{bmatrix},$$

we have that $\overline{F} = \tilde{F}Q$, and finally

$$F = \overline{F}P = \begin{bmatrix} -4 & -3 & 0 & 0 & 0 & 0 & 0 & 0 \\ 0 & 0 & -3 & 0 & 0 & 0 & 0 & 0 \\ 0 & 0 & 0 & -4 & -1 & -1 & 1 & 0 \end{bmatrix}.$$

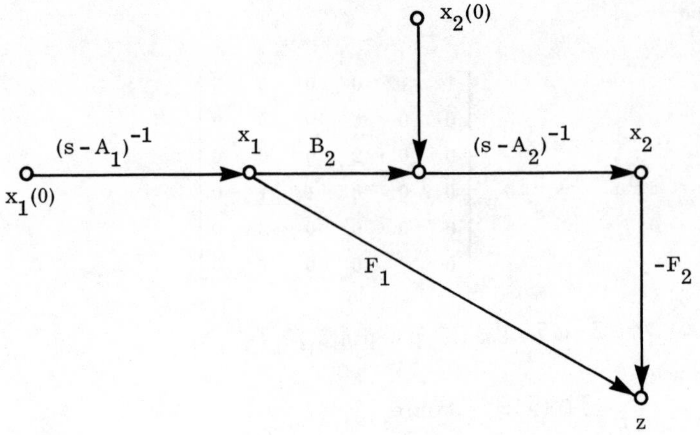

Fig. 7.4.

Signal Flow Graph: Ex. 7.6.

It is readily checked that F is indeed a solution of RPIS. Implementation of $u = Fx$ with an observer may be left to the reader; its order would be

$$d\left(\frac{\operatorname{Ker} C}{\mathcal{N}}\right) = 3 .$$

7.6 In the system shown in Fig. 7.4,

$$\sigma(A_1) \subset \mathbb{C}^+ \triangleq \{\lambda: \mathcal{R}e\,\lambda \geq 0\}$$

$$\sigma(A_2) \subset \mathbb{C}^- \triangleq \{\lambda: \mathcal{R}e\,\lambda < 0\}$$

and B_2, F_2 are arbitrary. Show that there exists F_1 such that, for all $x_1(0)$ and $x_2(0)$,

$$z(t) \triangleq F_1 x_1(t) - F_2 x_2(t) \to 0 , \qquad t \to \infty .$$

HINT: Let

$$Q(t) \triangleq \int_0^t e^{sA_2} B_2 e^{-sA_1}\, ds .$$

Show that

$$Q_\infty \triangleq \lim Q(t) , \qquad t \to \infty ,$$

exists, and is determined uniquely by

$$A_2 Q_\infty - Q_\infty A_1 + B_2 = 0 .$$

Then let $F_1 \triangleq F_2 Q_\infty$. Can you interpret Lemma 7.3 in the light of this result?

7.7 Carry out the routine verification indicated just before Lemma 7.1.

7.8 Extend Theorem 7.5 to the case $\mathcal{N} \neq 0$.

7.9 Prove Corollary 7.1. HINT: With $A\mathcal{R} \subset \mathcal{R} \subset \mathcal{X}$, note that $\mathcal{R}$ decomposes $\mathcal{X}$ relative to A if and only if $\mathcal{R} \cap \mathcal{X}^{\pm}(A)$ decomposes $\mathcal{X}^{\pm}(A)$ relative to A.

7.9 Notes and References

The material in this chapter is based on Wonham and Pearson [1].

CHAPTER 8

TRACKING AND REGULATION III: STRUCTURALLY STABLE SYNTHESIS

In this chapter we investigate the regulator problem with internal stability (RPIS) discussed in Chapter 7, from the viewpoint of well-posedness and genericity in the sense of Section 0.15, and of structurally stable implementation. Subject to mild restrictions it is shown that, if and only if RPIS is well-posed, a controller can be synthesized which preserves output regulation and loop stability in the presence of small parameter variations, of a specified type, in controller and plant. Synthesis is achieved by means of a feedback configuration which in general incorporates an invariant, and suitably redundant, copy of the dynamic model adopted for the exogenous reference and disturbance signals which the system is required to process.

8.1 Preliminaries

As in Chapter 7 we consider the system

$$\dot{x} = Ax + Bu , \qquad y = Cx , \qquad z = Dx \tag{1}$$

where y is the measured vector and z the vector to be regulated. The system pair (A, B) describes the plant (controllable subsystem) together with the exogenous reference and disturbance signals (e.g., steps, ramps, ...) with respect to which control is needed. As before, our spaces $\mathcal{X}, \mathcal{U}, \ldots$ and maps A, B, ... are regarded as defined initially over the field $\mathbb{R}$ but we sometimes adopt, without comment, the natural complexifications of $\mathcal{X}$ etc. However, if $\{x_1, x_2, \ldots\}$ is a set of vectors in $\mathcal{X}$, $\mathrm{Span}_{\mathbb{R}}\{\cdots\}$ or $\mathrm{Span}_{\mathbb{C}}\{\cdots\}$ will denote explicitly their span over $\mathbb{R}$ or $\mathbb{C}$, respectively.

In this chapter primes($'$) are used as indices; they will never denote dual elements. And to obviate fussy distinctions between maps or vectors and their matrices, it will help to employ the notation $x_1 \oplus x_2$ for elements of a direct sum $\mathcal{X}_1 \oplus \mathcal{X}_2$. In matrix notation $x_1 \oplus x_2$ could look like $\begin{bmatrix} x_1 \\ x_2 \end{bmatrix}$.

In the following we shall assume without essential loss of generality that the exogenous signals are completely unstable, namely the map $\bar{A}$ induced by A in $\bar{\mathcal{X}} \triangleq \mathcal{X}/\langle A|\mathcal{B}\rangle$ satisfies

$$\sigma(\bar{A}) \subset \mathbb{C}^+ \triangleq \{\lambda : \mathcal{R}e\,\lambda \geq 0\} . \tag{2}$$

It is also natural to assume that the pair (C, A) is detectable, namely

$$\mathcal{X}^+(A) \cap \mathcal{N}_C = 0, \tag{3}$$

since otherwise, by Theorem 7.4, RPIS can be reformulated in the factor space $\mathcal{X}/\mathcal{X}^+(A) \cap \mathcal{N}_C$. We then have the following result, as an immediate formal simplification of Theorem 7.1. This result will be our point of departure for the synthesis described later.

THEOREM 8.1. Subject to assumptions (2) and (3), RPIS is solvable if and only if there exists a subspace $\mathcal{V} \subset \mathcal{X}$ such that

$$\mathcal{V} \subset \operatorname{Ker} D \cap A^{-1}(\mathcal{V} + \mathcal{B}), \tag{4}$$

$$\mathcal{V} \cap \langle A|\mathcal{B}\rangle = 0, \tag{5}$$

and

$$\langle A|\mathcal{B}\rangle + \mathcal{V} = \mathcal{X}. \tag{6}$$

We may clearly assume that D: $\mathcal{X} \to \mathcal{Z}$ is epic (otherwise replace $\mathcal{Z}$ by Im D); then (4) and (6) imply

$$D\langle A|\mathcal{B}\rangle = \mathcal{Z}. \tag{7}$$

From now on we adopt (7) as a standing assumption.

8.2 Example 1: Structural Stability

To motivate further developments we point out here that naive application of the results of Chapter 7 may lead to systems which are highly unsatisfactory from a practical viewpoint. Consider the trivial RPIS defined by the following:

$$\dot{x}_1 = -ax_1 + u, \qquad a > 0$$

$$\dot{x}_2 = 0,$$

$$y = (x_1, x_2), \qquad z = x_2 - x_1,$$

where x_1, x_2 are scalars. Certainly a solution is furnished by

$$u = f_1 x_1 + f_2 x_2; \qquad f_1 = 0, \; f_2 = a;$$

with signal flow shown in Fig. 8.1. However, if the parameter a is not precisely known to the designer, who takes instead (say) $f_2 = a + \epsilon$, then

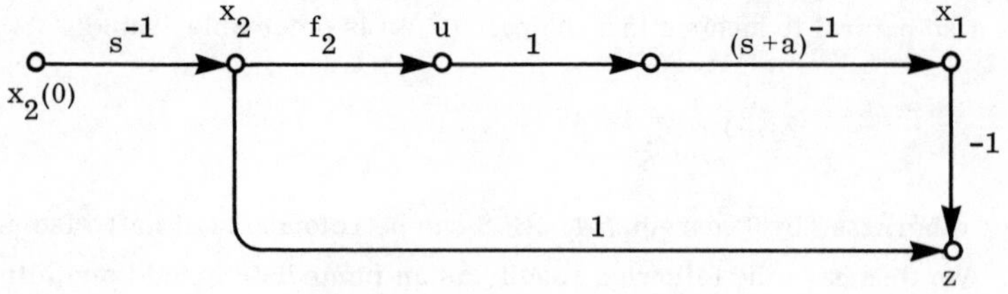

Fig. 8.1.

'Naive' Solution of RPIS.

Open-loop control: $f_2 = a$.

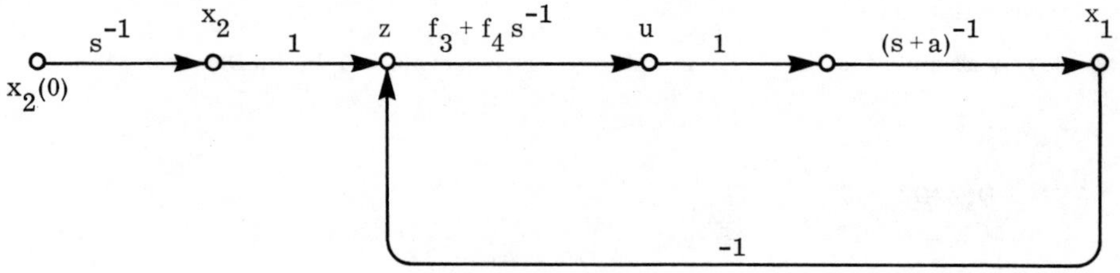

Fig. 8.2.

Structurally Stable Solution of RPIS.

Closed-loop control: integral compensation,

$f_3, f_4 > 0$ arbitrary.

$$\dot{z} = ax_1 - f_2x_2 = -az - \epsilon x_2 .$$

But now

$$z(t) \to \left(-\frac{\epsilon}{a}\right) x_2(0+) , \qquad t \to \infty ,$$

and output regulation fails.

Every engineer knows that the cure in this example is to adopt feedback control together with 'integral' compensation, according to Fig. 8.2. A short computation yields

$$\hat{z}(s) = \frac{s(s+a)}{s^2 + (a+f_3)s + f_4} \hat{x}_2(s) .$$

Then, with $\hat{x}_2(s) = x_2(0+)/s$, we shall have internal (loop) stability and output regulation, provided $a + f_3 > 0$ and $f_4 > 0$. The new design is structurally stable in the sense that internal stability and output regulation are both preserved in the presence of arbitrary variations in the parameters (a, f_3, f_4) of plant and controller, at least in a neighborhood of their nominal values. For the approach to succeed, of course, we must ensure that the loop integration s^{-1}, as well as the comparator which generates the error signal z, remain precisely fixed, but in practice this usually poses no serious problem.

The crucial features of the second design are the feedback loop topology of the signal flow, together with the presence in the loop of an 'internal model' (s^{-1}) of the dynamic system which generates the exogenous signal x_2 which the system is required to track. Now RPIS can always be formulated, as in the example of Section 7.8, to build in feedback from scratch: just assume $y = z$. The technique will work for the present example too, because the loop integration is supplied by the observer. But this simplistic approach is unduly restrictive and, it turns out, in the multivariable case may actually fail. To see why, and to develop a structurally stable synthesis in the general case, we place RPIS in a simple topological setting, along lines already sketched in Section 0.15.

8.3 Well-posedness and Genericity

Write $\mathcal{X}_1 \triangleq \langle A|\mathcal{B}\rangle$, $\mathcal{X} = \mathcal{X}_1 \oplus \mathcal{X}_2$, and fix a compatible basis to obtain matrix representations

$$A = \begin{bmatrix} A_1 & A_3 \\ 0 & A_2 \end{bmatrix}, \qquad B = \begin{bmatrix} B_1 \\ 0 \end{bmatrix},$$
$$C = \begin{bmatrix} C_1 & C_2 \end{bmatrix}, \qquad D = \begin{bmatrix} D_1 & D_2 \end{bmatrix}, \tag{8}$$

with dimensions A_1: $n_1 \times n_1$, A_2: $n_2 \times n_2$, B_1: $n_1 \times m$, C_i: $p \times n_i$ and D_i: $q \times n_i$. Here (A_1, B_1) is controllable and A_2 represents the map $\bar{A}$ defined above, so that

$$\sigma(A_2) \subset \mathbb{C}^+ . \tag{9}$$

Also, in view of (7) we shall assume at the outset

$$\text{Rank } D_1 = q . \tag{10}$$

Now fix (A_2, C, D) and, after listing the matrix elements in arbitrary order, regard (A_1, A_3, B_1) as a data point $\underline{p}$ in $\mathbb{R}^N$, $N = n_1^2 + n_1 n_2 + n_1 m$. In the spirit of Section 0.15 we shall say that RPIS is generically solvable if it is solvable at all $\underline{p}$ in the complement of a proper algebraic variety in $\mathbb{R}^N$, and that RPIS is well-posed at $\underline{p}$ if it is solvable at all points in some open neighborhood of $\underline{p}$.

Of course many other definitions of well-posedness are possible, the idea being to allow for uncertainty about the precise numerical values of various system parameters. We elect to fix C and D because 'typically' the variables which can be measured ($y = Cx$) or which must be regulated ($z = Dx$) are defined by the problem coordinatization in a way which is independent of small parameter variations, for instance when y is a position measurement and z a tracking error. Here we neglect any sensor or comparator imprecision. The matrix A_2 embodies the dynamic structure of disturbance and/or reference signals external to the plant: as such it is normally fixed by a priori specification of the class of exogenous signals which the regulator is to be designed to handle: steps, ramps and the like. Similarly the controllable subspace $\mathcal{X}_1$ (i.e., the plant state space) is or can be fixed by coordinatization: since (A_1, B_1) is controllable, so are all pairs (A_1', B_1') in some neighborhood of (A_1, B_1) in $\mathbb{R}^{n_1^2 + n_1 m}$. On the other hand, by allowing completely free small variations in (A_1, B_1) we tacitly ignore special features of plant structure often fixed by coordinatization, like definitional relations of the type $\xi_2 = \dot{\xi}_1$. More conservatively still, we allow free variations in the map A_3 which binds the exogenous signals into the plant. While somewhat unrealistic, such latitude is technically convenient, and it will turn out that our results are not unduly restrictive from a practical point of view.

The main results of this section are the following.

THEOREM 8.2. Subject to (2), (3) and (7) [equivalently (9), (3) and (10)], RPIS is well-posed at (A_1, A_3, B_1) if and only if

$$(A - \lambda)(\text{Ker } D \cap \langle A | \mathcal{B} \rangle) + \mathcal{B} = \langle A | \mathcal{B} \rangle \tag{11}$$

for all $\lambda \in \sigma(\bar{A})$ [or equivalently

$$\text{Rank} \begin{bmatrix} A_1 - \lambda I & B_1 \\ D_1 & 0 \end{bmatrix} = n_1 + q \tag{12}$$

for all $\lambda \in \sigma(A_2)$].

COROLLARY 8.1. Under the assumptions of Theorem 8.2, RPIS is generically solvable if and only if $m \geq q$. If $m < q$, no data point is well-posed.

PROOF of Theorem 8.2. (If) It will be shown that for each data point in a suitable neighborhood of $\underline{p} = (A_1, A_3, B_1)$ there exists a subspace $\mathcal{V}$ which satisfies the conditions of Theorem 8.1. We note first that (11) [or (12)] is equivalent to

$$(A_1 - \lambda)\,\mathrm{Ker}\, D_1 + \mathcal{B}_1 = \mathcal{X}_1, \qquad \lambda \in \sigma(A_2). \tag{13}$$

It is clear that if (13) holds at $\underline{p}$ then it holds throughout some neighborhood of $\underline{p}$, so it suffices to show that $\mathcal{V}$ can be constructed at $\underline{p}$ alone. For this take a complex Jordan decomposition of $\mathcal{X}_2$ relative to A_2. We treat the case where $\sigma(A_2)$ has a complex conjugate eigenvalue pair, leaving the real case to the reader. For this, select a cyclic prime subspace $\mathcal{X}_{2\lambda}$ of $\mathcal{X}_2$ with eigenvalue $\lambda = \alpha + i\beta$ ($\beta \neq 0$) and dimension k, choose a generator $g = g_1 + ig_2$, and define the basis

$$e_{2j} = \left(A_2 - \lambda\right)^{j-1} g, \qquad j \in \underline{k}.$$

Let

$$x_{2,2} = g_2, \qquad x_{2,1} = g_1$$

and

$$x_{2,2t} = \mathcal{I}m(A_2 - \alpha - i\beta)(x_{2,2t-3} + ix_{2,2t-2})$$

$$x_{2,2t-1} = \mathcal{R}e(A_2 - \alpha - i\beta)(x_{2,2t-3} + ix_{2,2t-2})$$

for $t = 2, \ldots, k$. Then

$$\mathcal{X}_{2\lambda} \oplus \mathcal{X}_{2\lambda^*} = \mathrm{Span}_{\mathbb{C}}\{x_{2,1}, x_{2,2}, \ldots, x_{2,2k-1}, x_{2,2k}\}$$

and we have the relations

$$x_{2,2t} = (A_2 - \alpha)x_{2,2t-2} - \beta x_{2,2t-3}$$

$$x_{2,2t-1} = \beta x_{2,2t-2} + (A_2 - \alpha)x_{2,2t-3}.$$

Since by (7) [or (10)] $D_1 : \mathcal{X}_1 \to \mathcal{Z}$ is epic, there exist $x'_{1,2t-2}, x'_{1,2t-3} \in \mathcal{X}_1$ such that

$$D_1 x'_{1,2t-2} + D_2 x_{2,2t-2} = 0,$$

$$D_1 x'_{1,2t-3} + D_2 x_{2,2t-3} = 0.$$

Suppose

$$x''_{1,2k}, \ldots, x''_{1,2t-1} \in \mathrm{Ker}\, D_1$$

and

$$b'_{1,2k}, \ldots, b'_{1,2t-1} \in \mathcal{B}_1$$

are already defined, and let

$$x_{1,\ell} = x'_{1,\ell} + x''_{1,\ell}, \qquad \ell = 2k, \ldots, 2t-1;$$

$$x_{1,2k+1} = 0,$$

$$x_{1,2k+2} = 0.$$

By (13) there exist $x''_{1,2t-2}, x''_{1,2t-3} \in \operatorname{Ker} D_1$ and $b_{1,2t-2}, b_{1,2t-3} \in \mathcal{B}_1$ such that

$$(A_1 - \alpha)x''_{1,2t-2} - \beta x''_{1,2t-3} + b_{1,2t-2}$$

$$= -(A_1 - \alpha)x'_{1,2t-2} + \beta x'_{1,2t-3} - A_3 x_{2,2t-2} + x_{1,2t}$$

and

$$\beta x''_{1,2t-2} + (A_1 - \alpha)x''_{1,2t-3} + b_{1,2t-3}$$

$$= -\beta x'_{1,2t-2} - (A_1 - \alpha)x'_{1,2t-3} - A_3 x_{2,2t-3} + x_{1,2t-1}.$$

Equivalently

$$(A_1 - \alpha)x_{1,2t-2} - \beta x_{1,2t-3} + b_{1,2t-2}$$

$$= -A_3 x_{2,2t-2} + x_{1,2t} \tag{14a}$$

and

$$\beta x_{1,2t-2} + (A_1 - \alpha)x_{1,2t-3} + b_{1,2t-3}$$

$$= -A_3 x_{2,2t-3} + x_{1,2t-1}, \tag{14b}$$

where

$$x_{1,2t-2} = x'_{1,2t-2} + x''_{1,2t-2},$$

and

$$x_{1,2t-3} = x'_{1,2t-3} + x'_{1,2t-3}.$$

Let

$$x_{2t-2} = x_{1,2t-2} \oplus x_{2,2t-2} \in \mathcal{X}_1 \oplus \mathcal{X}_2$$

and

$$x_{2t-3} = x_{1,2t-3} \oplus x_{2,2t-3} \in \mathcal{X}_1 \oplus \mathcal{X}_2.$$

By induction it follows that the vectors x_{2t-2}, x_{2t-3}, and $b_{1,2t-2}, b_{1,2t-3}$ can be determined so as to satisfy (14) for all $t = 2, \ldots, k$. Then the subspace

$$\mathscr{V}_\lambda \triangleq \mathrm{Span}_{\mathbb{R}}\{x_1, x_2, \ldots, x_{2k-1}, x_{2k}\}$$

has the properties (4) and (5).

For λ real the construction of a corresponding subspace $\mathscr{V}_\lambda$ is even simpler and runs parallel to the construction just given.

Finally, list the cyclic prime subspaces $\mathscr{P}$ of the Jordan decomposition of $\mathscr{X}_2$. Let $\mathscr{V}$ be the direct sum of the $\mathscr{V}_\lambda$ constructed, as above, for each real $\mathscr{P}$ and each conjugate pair $\mathscr{P}, \mathscr{P}^*$. It is then clear that $\mathscr{V}$ satisfies conditions (4)–(6), as required.

(Only if) We know that for each $\underline{p}'$ in a neighborhood of $\underline{p}$ there exists (dropping primes) a map $F: \mathscr{X} \to \mathscr{U}$ such that

$$\mathscr{X}^+(A+BF) \cap \langle A|\mathscr{B}\rangle = 0 \tag{15}$$

and

$$\mathscr{X}^+(A+BF) \subset \operatorname{Ker} D\,.$$

By (2) and (15) there is an operator isomorphism such that the diagram below commutes.

$$\begin{array}{ccc}
\mathscr{X}^+(A+BF) & \xrightarrow{\quad A+BF \quad} & \mathscr{X}^+(A+BF) \\
\downarrow \approx & & \downarrow \approx \\
\mathscr{X}/\langle A|\mathscr{B}\rangle & \xrightarrow{\quad \overline{A} \quad} & \mathscr{X}/\langle A|\mathscr{B}\rangle
\end{array}$$

Going to the basis used in the proof of sufficiency, writing $F = [F_1, F_2]$, and taking $\lambda \in \sigma(A_2)$ with eigenvector $x_1 \oplus x_2$, we see that the equations

$$(A_1 + B_1 F_1 - \lambda)x_1 + (A_3 + B_1 F_2)x_2 = 0$$

$$(A_2 - \lambda)x_2 = 0$$

$$D_1 x_1 + D_2 x_2 = 0$$

admit a solution with $x_2 \neq 0$. Fixing $A_1' = A_1$, $B_1' = B_1$ and the eigenvector x_2 of A_2, we conclude by well-posedness that for each A_3' near $A_3 \in \mathbb{R}^{n_3 n_2}$ there exist F_1', F_2' and x_1', x_1'' such that

$$(A_1 - \lambda)x_1'' + B_1 F_1' x_1' + B_1 F_2' x_2 = -(A_1 - \lambda)x_1' - A_3' x_2 - B_1 F_1' x_1'',$$

$$D_1 x_1' + D_2 x_2 = 0 , \tag{16}$$

and

$$D_1 x_1'' = 0 .$$

Define x_1' uniquely by fixing an arbitrary complement of $\mathrm{Ker}\, D_1$ in $\mathcal{X}_1$. Now

$$\mathrm{Span}_{\mathbb{R}}\{A_3' x_2 : A_3' \text{ near } A_3\} = \mathcal{X}_1 ,$$

where $\mathcal{X}_1$ is taken over $\mathbb{R}$ or $\mathbb{C}$ according as λ is real or has nonzero imaginary part: to see this, note that in the latter case $x_2 = x_2' + ix_2''$, say, where x_2', x_2'' are real and independent. It follows by (16) that for every $x_1 \in \mathcal{X}_1$ there exist $x_1'' \in \mathrm{Ker}\, D_1$ and $b_1 \in \mathcal{B}_1$ such that

$$(A_1 - \lambda) x_1'' + b_1 = x_1 .$$

That is,

$$(A_1 - \lambda)\, \mathrm{Ker}\, D_1 + \mathcal{B}_1 = \mathcal{X}_1$$

and (11) is proved. ▮

PROOF of Corollary 8.1. If RPIS is generically solvable there exists a well-posed data point $\underline{p}$. By Theorem 8.2, $\underline{p}$ satisfies (12), hence $n_1 + m \geq n_1 + q$, i.e., $m \geq q$. Conversely if $m \geq q$ and (10) is true, then (12) holds at all $\underline{p} = (A_1, A_3, B_1)$ except for those on the proper variety defined by the conditions

$$(\mathcal{R}e, \mathcal{I}m) \begin{vmatrix} A_1 - \lambda & B_1 \\ D_1 & 0 \end{vmatrix}_j^i = 0$$

for some $\lambda \in \sigma(A_2)$ and all i, j. Here $|\cdot|_j^i$ denotes the $(n_1 + q) \times (n_1 + q)$ minor determined by the row multi-index $i = (i_1, \ldots, i_{n_1+q})$ and column multi-index $j = (j_1, \ldots, j_{n_1+q})$. Finally, if $m < q$ then clearly (12) must fail at every data point $\underline{p}$. ▮

8.4 Synthesis, Case I: $C = D$, $\mathcal{N}_D = 0$

In the remainder of this chapter we show how to synthesize a controller which implements a solution of (well-posed) RPIS, and has the desirable property that internal stability and output regulation are preserved, when parameters of the plant and controller undergo small variations. In other words, the controller is 'flexible' enough to permit some uncertainty, at the design stage, about values of system parameters, and also to permit (slow) drift (with in limits) of these parameters while the system is in operation. It will be no surprise that a feedback configuration is used: less familiar is the result that the feedback compensator includes a (fixed) model of the external dynamics which in general must be reduplicated in a sense made precise below.

To present the main ideas most simply, we shall assume in this section that the measured variables y are precisely the regulated variables z and that the system (1) is completely observable from z; thus

$$C = D, \qquad \mathcal{N}_D \triangleq \bigcap_{i=1}^{n} \mathrm{Ker}(DA^{i-1}) = 0 . \tag{17}$$

As explained in Chapter 7 the control law $u = Fx$ provided by formal solution of RPIS can be implemented via a dynamic observer, which for simplicity we take to be of full dynamic order n. Set

$$u = Fw , \tag{18}$$

where $w \in \mathcal{W}$ is the state of the observer, determined by

$$\dot{w} = (A - KD + BF)w + Kz . \tag{19}$$

Comparing (1) and (18), (19) we get that the state estimation error $e \triangleq x - w \in \mathcal{X} \oplus \mathcal{W}$ is given by

$$\dot{e} = (A - KD)e ;$$

of course, $K: \mathcal{Z} \to \mathcal{W}$ is selected to make $A - KD$ stable.

Consider the observer map

$$T \triangleq A - KD + BF : \mathcal{W} \to \mathcal{W} . \tag{20}$$

With mild abuse of notation, the symbols A, D, B, F here denote copies of the corresponding maps defined before, but now with $\mathcal{X}$ replaced by $\mathcal{W}$; context will make the usage clear. Since F solves RPIS, we know that

$$\mathcal{W}^+(A + BF) \subset \mathrm{Ker}\, D ;$$

hence T restricts to $\mathcal{W}^+(A + BF)$, giving

$$T \,|\, \mathcal{W}^+(A + BF) = (A + BF) \,|\, \mathcal{W}^+(A + BF) \approx \bar{A} .$$

We can therefore write $\mathcal{W} = \mathcal{W}_1 \oplus \mathcal{W}_2$ with $\mathcal{W}_i \approx \mathcal{X}_i$, and choose a basis for $\mathcal{W}$ such that

$$T = \begin{bmatrix} T_1 & 0 \\ T_3 & A_2 \end{bmatrix}, \tag{21}$$

where A_2 is a copy of the matrix A_2 in (8).

The composite system comprising plant, observer and exogenous signal, with state vector

$$x_S \triangleq x_1 \oplus w \oplus x_2 \in \mathcal{X}_S \triangleq \mathcal{X}_1 \oplus \mathcal{W} \oplus \mathcal{X}_2$$

has differential equation $\dot{x}_S = A_S x_S$ where, by inspection of (8), (18), (19) and (20),

$$A_S \triangleq \begin{bmatrix} A_1 & B_1F & A_3 \\ KD_1 & T & KD_2 \\ 0 & 0 & A_2 \end{bmatrix}. \tag{22}$$

It is natural to introduce the 'loop' matrix

$$A_L \triangleq \begin{bmatrix} A_1 & B_1F \\ KD_1 & T \end{bmatrix}. \tag{23}$$

By (20) and the transformation $(x, w) \mapsto (x, e)$,

$$A_S \approx \begin{bmatrix} A+BF & -BF \\ 0 & A-KD \end{bmatrix}$$

and

$$A_L \approx \begin{bmatrix} A_1+B_1F_1 & -B_1F \\ 0 & A-KD \end{bmatrix}.$$

Thus

$$A_L \text{ is stable}, \tag{24}$$

as it should be; we have $\mathcal{X}_S^+(A_S) \approx \mathcal{X}_2$; and the regulation condition is equivalent to

$$\mathcal{X}_S^+(A_S) \subset \operatorname{Ker}\begin{bmatrix} D_1 & 0 & D_2 \end{bmatrix}. \tag{25}$$

We define a synthesis of RPIS (under condition (17)) to be a triple (F, T, K) such that, with A_S and A_L defined by (22) and (23), (24) and (25) are true. With A_2, D and T_3 fixed, A_S is parametrized by points

$$\underline{p}_S \triangleq (A_1, A_3, B_1, F, T_1, K) \in \mathbb{R}^{N_S}, \tag{26}$$

where

$$N_S = n_1^2 + n_1 n_2 + n_1 m + mn + n_1^2 + nq .$$

We shall say that $\underline{p}_S$ is a regular point if (24) and (25) are true throughout some (open) neighborhood of $\underline{p}_S$ in $\mathbb{R}^{N_S}$. Finally, writing $\underline{p} = (A_1, A_3, B_1)$ as before, we call a synthesis (F, T, K) strong at $\underline{p}$ if $\underline{p}_S$ is regular.*

Our objective is to show that, in a suitable sense, RPIS admits a strong synthesis. To construct one we shall need, in general, to modify our given RPIS by a process of 'outward extension'. For this, introduce an auxiliary state space $\mathcal{X}_a$ and extended state space $\mathcal{X}_e \triangleq \mathcal{X} \oplus \mathcal{X}_a$. Define extensions D_e, A_e, B_e of D, A, B according to

$$D_e: \mathcal{X}_e \to \mathcal{Z}: x \oplus x_a \mapsto Dx,$$

$$A_e: \mathcal{X}_e \to \mathcal{X}_e: x \oplus x_a \mapsto (Ax + A_{3a} x_a) \oplus A_{2a} x_a, \tag{27}$$

$$B_e: \mathcal{U} \to \mathcal{X}_e: u \mapsto Bu .$$

In terms of our previous choice of basis this amounts to writing

$$A_{3a} = \begin{bmatrix} A_{13} \\ A_{23} \end{bmatrix}, \quad A_e = \begin{bmatrix} A_1 & A_3 & A_{13} \\ 0 & A_2 & A_{23} \\ 0 & 0 & A_{2a} \end{bmatrix}, \quad B_e = \begin{bmatrix} B_1 \\ 0 \\ 0 \end{bmatrix}, \tag{28a}$$

and

$$D_e = \begin{bmatrix} D_1 & D_2 & 0 \end{bmatrix}. \tag{28b}$$

Here $d(\mathcal{X}_a)$ and A_{2a}, A_{3a} can be freely chosen.

Given that (D, A) is observable, we shall say that (D_e, A_e, B_e) is an outward extension of (D, A, B) if (27) [or (28)] holds and (D_e, A_e) is observable. It is obvious that if RPIS is solvable for (D_e, A_e, B_e) then it is solvable for (D, A, B) and that RPIS is imbedded in its extended version in a natural way. Thus, under assumption (17), we say that RPIS is strongly solvable at $\underline{p}$ if there is an outward extension of (D, A, B) for which the corresponding (extended) RPIS has a strong synthesis. Our main result is the following.

THEOREM 8.3. Let $C = D$, D be epic, and $\eta_D = 0$. Then RPIS is strongly solvable at $\underline{p}$ if and only if RPIS is well-posed at $\underline{p}$.

---

* The ad hoc term 'strong' is adopted in lieu of the more cumbersome 'structurally stable'.

For the proof we need four preliminary results.

LEMMA 8.1 (cf. Ex. 3.12). A pair (D, A) is observable if and only if

$$\operatorname{Ker} D \cap \operatorname{Ker}(A - \lambda) = 0\,, \qquad \lambda \in \mathbb{C}\,. \tag{29}$$

PROOF: We have

$$\mathcal{N}_D = \bigcap_{i \geq 1} \operatorname{Ker}(D A^{i-1})\,.$$

If (29) fails, there is $x \neq 0$ with $x \in \operatorname{Ker} D$ and $Ax = \lambda x$, hence $x \in \mathcal{N}_D$, so (D, A) is not observable. Conversely if $\mathcal{N}_D \neq 0$ then $A | \mathcal{N}_D$ has an eigenvalue $\lambda \in \sigma(A)$ and (29) fails for such λ. ∎

In matrix terms (29) reads

$$\begin{bmatrix} A - \lambda \\ D \end{bmatrix} \text{ is monic,} \qquad \lambda \in \mathbb{C}\,, \tag{30}$$

i.e., for each $\lambda \in \mathbb{C}$ the indicated matrix has maximal rank.

The extension described in the next lemma is crucial to the synthesis procedure.

LEMMA 8.2. With (D, A, B) as in (8), assume that (D, A) is observable, D_1 is epic, $\lambda \in \sigma(A_2)$ and

$$\nu \triangleq d\left(\operatorname{Ker}(A_2 - \lambda)\right) \leq q\,.$$

There exists an outward extension of (D, A, B) with the following properties. Write

$$A_{2e} \triangleq \begin{bmatrix} A_2 & A_{23} \\ 0 & A_{2a} \end{bmatrix}. \tag{31}$$

Then

(i) $$d\left(\operatorname{Ker}(A_{2e} - \lambda)\right) = q\,,$$

and (ii) if k is the dimension of the largest prime cyclic subspace of $\mathcal{X}_2$ corresponding to λ, we have

$$\operatorname{Ker}(A_{2e} - \lambda)^{k-1} = \operatorname{Im}(A_{2e} - \lambda)\,.$$

PROOF: We shall prove the assertion for complex λ, leaving the real case to the reader. Let $\lambda = \alpha + i\beta$, $\beta \neq 0$, and suppose

$$\mathcal{X}_0 \triangleq \operatorname{Ker}\left((A_2 - \alpha)^2 + \beta^2\right)^k$$

has Jordan decomposition

$$\mathcal{X}_0 = \mathcal{X}_2^{(1)} \oplus \cdots \oplus \mathcal{X}_2^{(\nu)},$$

so that

$$A_2^{(i)} \triangleq A_2 | \mathcal{X}_2^{(i)}$$

is cyclic, and

$$2d_i \triangleq d\left(\mathcal{X}_2^{(i)}\right) \le 2k, \qquad i \in \underline{\nu}.$$

Here

$$A_2^{(i)} = \begin{bmatrix} M & I_2 & & & O \\ & M & I_2 & & \\ & & \cdot & \cdot & \\ & O & & \cdot & I_2 \\ & & & & M \end{bmatrix}_{2d_i \times 2d_i}$$

and

$$M = \begin{bmatrix} \alpha & \beta \\ -\beta & \alpha \end{bmatrix}.$$

The proof amounts to imbedding each $\mathcal{X}_2^{(i)}$ in an extension of dimension 2k, then adjoining $q - \nu$ new cyclic components, also of dimension 2k. From this the dimensional assertions (i) and (ii) will follow immediately.

Step 1. Write

$$\mathcal{X}_{2,e}^{(i)} = \mathcal{X}_2^{(i)} \oplus \mathcal{X}_{2,a}^{(i)}, \qquad i \in \underline{\nu},$$

with

$$d\left(\mathcal{X}_{2,a}^{(i)}\right) = 2k - d\left(\mathcal{X}_2^{(i)}\right).$$

Now it is easy to construct a map $A_{2,e}^{(i)}$ on $\mathcal{X}_{2,e}^{(i)}$ which is cyclic with minimal polynomial $\left((s-\alpha)^2 + \beta^2\right)^k$ and extends $A_2^{(i)}$: formally, just enlarge the real Jordan matrix of $A_2^{(i)}$. We shall verify that, with this extension, observability is retained. For $\lambda = \alpha + i\beta$, condition (30) is equivalent to the condition

$$\begin{bmatrix} A - \alpha & -\beta \\ \beta & A - \alpha \\ D & 0 \\ 0 & D \end{bmatrix} \text{ is monic .}$$

Thus if

$$\left[\begin{array}{ccc|ccc} A_1-\alpha & A_3 & 0 & -\beta I_1 & 0 & 0 \\ 0 & A_2-\alpha & A_{23} & 0 & -\beta I_2 & 0 \\ 0 & 0 & A_{2a}-\alpha & 0 & 0 & -\beta I_{2a} \\ \hline \beta I_1 & 0 & 0 & A_1-\alpha & A_3 & 0 \\ 0 & \beta I_2 & 0 & 0 & A_2-\alpha & A_{23} \\ 0 & 0 & \beta I_{2a} & 0 & 0 & A_{2a}-\alpha \\ \hline D_1 & D_2 & 0 & 0 & 0 & 0 \\ \hline 0 & 0 & 0 & D_1 & D_2 & 0 \end{array}\right] \begin{bmatrix} x_1 \\ x_2 \\ x_{2a} \\ \xi_1 \\ \xi_2 \\ \xi_{2a} \end{bmatrix} = 0$$

then

$$\left[\begin{array}{cc|cc} A_2-\alpha & A_{23} & -\beta I_2 & 0 \\ 0 & A_{2a}-\alpha & 0 & -\beta I_{2a} \\ \hline \beta I_2 & 0 & A_2-\alpha & A_{23} \\ 0 & \beta I_{2a} & 0 & A_{2a}-\alpha \end{array}\right] \begin{bmatrix} x_2 \\ x_{2a} \\ \xi_2 \\ \xi_{2a} \end{bmatrix} = 0 .$$

This implies that $x_{2a} = \xi_{2a} = 0$, and hence

$$\left[\begin{array}{cc|cc} A_1-\alpha & A_3 & -\beta I_1 & 0 \\ 0 & A_2-\alpha & 0 & -\beta I_2 \\ \hline \beta I_1 & 0 & A_1-\alpha & A_3 \\ 0 & \beta I_2 & 0 & A_2-\alpha \\ \hline D_1 & D_2 & 0 & 0 \\ \hline 0 & 0 & D_1 & D_2 \end{array}\right] \begin{bmatrix} x_1 \\ x_2 \\ \xi_1 \\ \xi_2 \end{bmatrix} = 0 ;$$

therefore

$$\begin{bmatrix} x_1 \\ x_2 \\ \xi_1 \\ \xi_2 \end{bmatrix} = 0$$

by observability of the pair (D, A).

Step 2. To complete the extension, adjoin an auxiliary state subspace

$$\tilde{\mathcal{X}}_{2a} \triangleq \tilde{\mathcal{X}}_2^{(1)} \oplus \cdots \oplus \tilde{\mathcal{X}}_2^{(q-\nu)}$$

with

$$d\left(\tilde{\mathcal{X}}_2^{(i)}\right) = 2k , \qquad i \in \underline{q-\nu} .$$

We require that $\tilde{\mathcal{X}}_2^{(i)}$ be A_{2e}-invariant and define the restriction

$$\tilde{A}_{2e}^{(i)} = A_{2e} | \tilde{\mathcal{X}}_2^{(i)}$$

to be cyclic with minimal polynomial $\left((s-\alpha)^2+\beta^2\right)^k$.

With provision of a binding map S, the augmented pair looks like

$$A_e = \begin{bmatrix} A_1 & A_3 & S \\ 0 & A_2 & 0 \\ 0 & 0 & A_{2a} \end{bmatrix}, \qquad D_e = \begin{bmatrix} D_1 & D_2 & 0 \end{bmatrix},$$

where we assume for simplicity of notation that A_2 now denotes the extension constructed in Step 1. We shall show that S can be chosen in such a way that observability is preserved. Consider the matrix

$$\left[\begin{array}{ccc|ccc} A_1-\alpha & A_3 & S & -\beta I_1 & 0 & 0 \\ 0 & A_2-\alpha & 0 & 0 & -\beta I_2 & 0 \\ 0 & 0 & A_{2a}-\alpha & 0 & 0 & -\beta I_{2a} \\ \hline \beta I_1 & 0 & 0 & A_1-\alpha & A_3 & S \\ 0 & \beta I_2 & 0 & 0 & A_2-\alpha & 0 \\ 0 & 0 & \beta I_{2a} & 0 & 0 & A_{2a}-\alpha \\ \hline D_1 & D_2 & 0 & 0 & 0 & 0 \\ 0 & 0 & 0 & D_1 & D_2 & 0 \end{array}\right].$$

In view of the observability of (D, A), the matrix above is monic if and only if

$$\left\{\begin{bmatrix} S & 0 \\ 0 & S \end{bmatrix} \operatorname{Ker}\begin{bmatrix} A_{2a}-\alpha & -\beta I_{2a} \\ \beta I_{2a} & A_{2a}-\alpha \end{bmatrix}\right\} \cap \left\{ \begin{array}{l} \begin{bmatrix} A_1-\alpha & -\beta I_1 \\ \beta I_1 & A_1-\alpha \end{bmatrix} x^{(1)} + \begin{bmatrix} A_3 & 0 \\ 0 & A_3 \end{bmatrix} x^{(2)} : \\[2ex] \begin{bmatrix} A_2-\alpha & -\beta I_2 \\ \beta I_2 & A_2-\alpha \end{bmatrix} x^{(2)} = 0 \quad \& \\[2ex] \begin{bmatrix} D_1 & 0 \\ 0 & D_1 \end{bmatrix} x^{(1)} + \begin{bmatrix} D_2 & 0 \\ 0 & D_2 \end{bmatrix} x^{(2)} = 0 \end{array} \right\} = 0$$

and

$$\operatorname{Ker}\begin{bmatrix} S & 0 \\ 0 & S \end{bmatrix} \cap \operatorname{Ker}\begin{bmatrix} A_{2a}-\alpha & -\beta I_{2a} \\ \beta I_{2a} & A_{2a}-\alpha \end{bmatrix} = 0.$$

Now it is readily verified that

$$\begin{bmatrix} S & 0 \\ 0 & S \end{bmatrix} \operatorname{Ker} \begin{bmatrix} A_{2a}-\alpha & -\beta I_{2a} \\ \beta I_{2a} & A_{2a}-\alpha \end{bmatrix} = \operatorname{Im} \begin{bmatrix} S_1 & -S_2 \\ S_2 & S_1 \end{bmatrix}$$

for suitable $S_1, S_2 \in \mathbb{R}^{n_1 \times (q-\nu)}$. So we need only supply $S_1, S_2 \in \mathbb{R}^{n_1 \times (q-\nu)}$ such that $S_1 + iS_2 \in \mathbb{C}^{n_1 \times (q-\nu)}$ is monic, and

$$\operatorname{Im}(S_1 + iS_2) \cap \{(A_1 - \lambda)x_1 + A_3 x_2 :$$
$$(A_2 - \lambda)x_2 = 0 \ \ \& \ \ D_1 x_1 + D_2 x_2 = 0\} = 0 .$$

But

$$d\{(A_1 - \lambda)x_1 + A_3 x_2 : (A_2 - \lambda)x_2 = 0$$
$$\& \ \ D_1 x_1 + D_2 x_2 = 0\}$$
$$\leq d\left(\operatorname{Ker}(A_2 - \lambda)\right) + d(\operatorname{Ker} D_1) = \nu + (n_1 - q) = n_1 - (q - \nu) ,$$

so that S_1 and S_2 with the required properties clearly exist; indeed a 'random' choice will almost surely suffice. ▌

LEMMA 8.3. Under the conditions of Lemma 8.2, there exists an outward extension (D_e, A_e, B_e) of (D, A, B) such that, if $\bar{A}_e$ is the map induced by A_e in $\bar{\mathcal{X}}_e \triangleq \mathcal{X}_e / \langle A_e | \mathcal{B}_e \rangle$, then

$$d\left(\operatorname{Ker}(\bar{A}_e - \lambda)\right) = q$$

for each $\lambda \in \sigma(\bar{A})$. Furthermore, if $k(\lambda)$ is the dimension of the largest prime cyclic subspace of $\bar{\mathcal{X}}$ corresponding to $\lambda \in \sigma(\bar{A})$, then

$$\operatorname{Ker}(\bar{A}_e - \lambda)^{k(\lambda)-1} = \operatorname{Im}(\bar{A}_e - \lambda) . \tag{32}$$

To interpret Lemma 8.3 we make the following observation. If $A: \mathcal{X} \to \mathcal{X}$ and $\lambda \in \mathbb{C}$, call $\gamma_A(\lambda) \triangleq d\left(\operatorname{Ker}(A - \lambda)\right)$ the cyclic index of A at λ. Thus $\gamma_A(\lambda) = 0$ unless $\lambda \in \sigma(A)$, when $\gamma_A(\lambda)$ is the number of prime cyclic subspaces corresponding to λ in a Jordan decomposition of $\mathcal{X}$ relative to A. With $D: \mathcal{X} \to \mathcal{Z}$ epic and $d(\mathcal{Z}) = q$, the pair (D, A) is observable only if $\gamma_A(\lambda) \leq q$ for all λ. So Lemma 8.3 says that A can be extended in such a way that the output $z = D_e x_e$ now observes, for each λ of interest, the largest possible number (namely, q) of prime cyclic subspaces in $\bar{\mathcal{X}}_e$. The property (32) is equivalent to the statement that for each $\lambda \in \sigma(\bar{A})$ these prime cyclic subspaces have common dimension $k(\lambda)$.

PROOF of Lemma 8.3. List the distinct elements $\lambda', \lambda'', \ldots$ of $\sigma(A_2)$, take A_2 in corresponding diagonal block form $A_2 = \text{diag}[A_2', A_2'', \ldots]$, and carry out the construction of Lemma 8.2 for each $\lambda', \lambda'', \ldots$ to obtain $A_{2e}', A_{2e}'', \ldots$ and $A_{3e}', A_{3e}'', \ldots$. Then set

$$A_e = \begin{bmatrix} A_1 & A_{3e} \\ 0 & A_{2e} \end{bmatrix}, \qquad D_e = \begin{bmatrix} D_1, D_2', D_2'', \ldots \end{bmatrix},$$

where

$$A_{2e} = \text{diag}[A_{2e}', A_{2e}'', \ldots],$$

$$A_{3e} = [A_{3e}', A_{3e}'', \ldots],$$

and D_e is defined in the obvious way, to coincide with D on $\mathcal{X}_1 \oplus \mathcal{X}_2$ and to vanish on $\mathcal{X}_a$. The verification that this extension has the required properties is immediate. ▌

As our final preliminary result we have

LEMMA 8.4. Under the assumption (17), let RPIS be well-posed. If (D_e, A_e, B_e) is any outward extension of (D, A, B) such that the distinct elements of $\sigma(\overline{A}_e)$ coincide with those of $\sigma(\overline{A})$, then the extended RPIS for (D_e, A_e, B_e) is again well-posed.

PROOF: Immediate by definition of an outward extension and by Theorem 8.2. ▌

PROOF of Theorem 8.3. (Only if) Suppose RPIS is strongly solvable at p, hence, possibly after outward extension, possesses a strong synthesis. Because this synthesis is, in particular, an implementation by dynamic compensation which respects the observability constraints, we may apply Theorem 7.2 to conclude that RPIS is solvable at each data point in a neighborhood of p, hence that RPIS is well-posed at p.

(If) Suppose RPIS is well-posed at p. According to Lemmas 8.3 and 8.4 we can and do assume without loss of generality that, for $\lambda \in \sigma(\overline{A})$,

$$d\left(\text{Ker}(\overline{A} - \lambda)\right) = d(\mathcal{Y}) \quad (= q) \tag{33}$$

and

$$\text{Ker}(\overline{A} - \lambda)^{k(\lambda)-1} = \text{Im}(\overline{A} - \lambda), \tag{34}$$

where $k(\lambda)$ is the dimension of the largest prime cyclic subspace of $\overline{A}$ corresponding to λ. Now consider a synthesis with composite system map A_S as in (22). By (33) and (34),

$$d\left(\text{Ker}(A_2 - \lambda)\right) = q, \qquad \lambda \in \sigma(A_2), \tag{35}$$

and

$$\operatorname{Ker}(A_2 - \lambda)^{k(\lambda)-1} = \operatorname{Im}(A_2 - \lambda) . \tag{36}$$

It will be shown that this synthesis, maybe after slight modification, is strong. To this end consider first (21). If $T_3 \neq 0$, perturb T_1 a little to arrange

$$\sigma(T_1) \cap \sigma(A_2) = \emptyset , \tag{37}$$

and then redefine $\mathcal{W}_1$ to achieve

$$T = \operatorname{diag}[T_1, A_2] \tag{38}$$

on $\mathcal{W} = \mathcal{W}_1 \oplus \mathcal{W}_2$.

Next, with $F = [F_1, F_2]$, we claim that $F_2 : \mathcal{W}_2 \to \mathcal{U}$ can, if necessary, be perturbed a little to achieve

$$(A_1 - \lambda) \operatorname{Ker} D_1 + B_1 F_2 \operatorname{Ker}(A_2 - \lambda) = \mathcal{X}_1 , \qquad \lambda \in \sigma(A_2) . \tag{39}$$

To see this, recall from (11) (or (13)) that well-posedness implies

$$(A_1 - \lambda) \operatorname{Ker} D_1 + \mathcal{B}_1 = \mathcal{X}_1 , \qquad \lambda \in \sigma(A_2) . \tag{40}$$

Also, as (D, A) is observable so is (D_1, A_1), and therefore (Lemma 8.1)

$$(A_1 - \lambda) \operatorname{Ker} D_1 \approx \operatorname{Ker} D_1 , \qquad \lambda \in \mathbb{C} . \tag{41}$$

By (10), (40) and (41),

$$d\left[\frac{(A_1 - \lambda) \operatorname{Ker} D_1 + \mathcal{B}_1}{(A_1 - \lambda) \operatorname{Ker} D_1}\right] = n_1 - (n_1 - q) = q . \tag{42}$$

In view of (35) and (42) we shall have shown that (39) is true for all $F_2 \in \mathbb{R}^{m \times n_2}$ with the exception of those F_2 which, as points in $\mathbb{R}^{mn_2}$, belong to some proper algebraic variety in $\mathbb{R}^{mn_2}$, once we exhibit any $F_2 \in \mathbb{R}^{mn_2}$ which satisfies (39). For this suppose, for instance,

$$\lambda \in \sigma(A_2) , \qquad \lambda = \alpha + i\beta , \qquad \beta \neq 0 ,$$

and let

$$\mathcal{X}_0 \triangleq \operatorname{Ker}(A_2 - \lambda) = \operatorname{Span}_{\mathbb{C}}\{x_{2,1} + i\tilde{x}_{2,1}, \ldots, x_{2,q} + i\tilde{x}_{2,q}\} ,$$

where the $x_{2,j}$ and $\tilde{x}_{2,j}$ are real. Then the vectors

$$x_{2,1}, \tilde{x}_{2,1}, \ldots, x_{2,q}, \tilde{x}_{2,q}$$

are linearly independent over $\mathbb{R}$. Let $\{x_{1,j}, \ j \in \underline{n_1}\}$ be a basis for $\mathcal{X}_1$. From the well-posedness condition (40) there correspond vectors $d_\ell + i\tilde{d}_\ell$ ($\ell \in \underline{(n_1 - q)}$) with $d_\ell, \tilde{d}_\ell \in \operatorname{Ker} D_1$, and $u_r + i\tilde{u}_r$ ($r \in \underline{q}$) with $u_r, \tilde{u}_r$ real, such that

$$\mathcal{X}_1 = (A_1 - \lambda) \operatorname{Span}_{\mathbb{C}} \{d_\ell + i\tilde{d}_\ell, \ \ell \in \underline{n_1 - q}\}$$

$$\oplus B_1 \operatorname{Span}_{\mathbb{C}} \{u_r + i\tilde{u}_r, \ r \in \underline{q}\} .$$

Define a real matrix $F_2 : \mathcal{X}_2 \to \mathcal{U}$ such that

$$\left.\begin{aligned} F_2 x_{2j} &= u_j \\ F_2 \tilde{x}_{2j} &= \tilde{u}_j \end{aligned}\right\} \quad j \in \underline{q} .$$

F_2 is defined by the same process on the remaining eigenspaces of $\mathcal{X}_2$; and can be defined arbitrarily on a complement in $\mathcal{X}_2$ of

$$\bigoplus_{\lambda} \operatorname{Ker}(A_2 - \lambda) ,$$

where the sum is taken over the distinct elements of $\sigma(A_2)$. Such F_2 clearly satisfies (39).

From now on we assume that (37)–(39) hold; and it is clear that we still have that

$$A_L \text{ is stable .} \tag{43}$$

As in (26) let $\underline{p}_S$ denote the parameter of the synthesis as now defined. Since (37), (39) and (43) certainly hold throughout a neighborhood of $\underline{p}_S$, it is enough to show that these conditions guarantee the regulation property (25). A_L being stable, $\mathcal{X}_S^+(A_S)$ is uniquely operator-isomorphic to $\mathcal{X}_2$:

$$\begin{array}{ccc} \mathcal{X}_S^+(A_S) & \xrightarrow{\quad A_S \quad} & \mathcal{X}^+(A_S) \\ \downarrow \approx & & \downarrow \approx \\ \mathcal{X}_2 & \xrightarrow{\quad A_2 \quad} & \mathcal{X}_2 \end{array}$$

So, pick a cyclic prime subspace of $\mathcal{X}_2$ with eigenvalue λ, dimension k, generator g_2 and basis

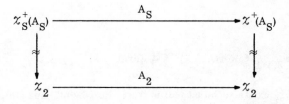

$$x_{2j} = (A_2 - \lambda)^{j-1} g_2 , \qquad j \in \underline{k} .$$

D_1 being epic, fix $x'_{1j} \in \mathcal{X}_1$ such that

$$D_1 x'_{1j} + D_2 x_{2j} = 0 , \qquad j \in \underline{k} . \tag{44}$$

Suppose $x''_{1k}, \ldots, x''_{1,j+1} \in \operatorname{Ker} D_1$ and $w_k, \ldots, w_{j+1} \in \mathcal{W}$ are already defined, with

$$\left.\begin{aligned} w_\ell &\triangleq w_{1\ell} \oplus w_{2\ell} \\ w_{1\ell} &= 0 \\ w_{2,k+1} &= 0 \\ (A_2 - \lambda) w_{2\ell} &= w_{2,\ell+1} \end{aligned}\right\} \tag{45}$$

for $\ell = k, \ldots, j+1$. Write also

$$x_{1\ell} = x'_{1\ell} + x''_{1\ell} , \qquad x_{1,k+1} = 0 , \tag{46}$$

and

$$w_{2\ell} = w'_{2\ell} + w''_{2\ell} \tag{47}$$

with $w''_{2\ell} \in \operatorname{Ker}(A_2 - \lambda)$. Now consider the equations

$$(A_1 - \lambda) x''_{1j} + B_1 F_2 w''_{2j}$$

$$= -(A_1 - \lambda) x'_{1j} - B_1 F_2 w'_{2j} - B_1 F_1 w_{1j} - A_3 x_{2j} + x_{1,j+1} , \tag{48a}$$

$$(T_1 - \lambda) w_{1j} = w_{1,j+1} , \tag{48b}$$

$$(A_2 - \lambda) w'_{2j} = w_{2,j+1} . \tag{48c}$$

Since by (45)

$$w_{2,j+1} \in \operatorname{Ker}(A_2 - \lambda)^{k-j} \subset \operatorname{Ker}(A_2 - \lambda)^{k-1} ,$$

(36) implies that w'_{2j} exists such that (48) is true. Next by (37) and (45), (48b) is satisfied if $w_{1j} = 0$. With the right side of (48a) thus determined, (39) now guarantees the existence of $x''_{1j} \in \operatorname{Ker} D_1$ and $w''_{2j} \in \operatorname{Ker}(A_2 - \lambda)$ such that (48a) is true. Thus it follows by backwards induction on j that x_{1j}, w_{1j} and w_{2j} exist which satisfy (44)–(48) for all $j \in \underline{k}$; in other words, for our fixed set of x_{2j} ($j \in \underline{k}$) there exist vectors $x_{1j} \in \mathcal{X}_1$ and $w_j = w_{1j} \oplus w_{2j} \in \mathcal{W}$ such that

$$x_{1j} \oplus w_j \oplus x_{2j} \in \mathcal{X}_S^+(A_S) \cap \mathrm{Ker}\left[D_1, 0, D_2\right].$$

Applying this argument to each prime cyclic component of a Jordan decomposition of $\mathcal{X}_2$, we conclude that

$$\mathcal{X}_S^+(A_S) \subset \mathrm{Ker}\left[D_1, 0, D_2\right] \tag{25 bis}$$

as required. ▮

Several features of the strong synthesis we have constructed are worth dwelling on, as they embody structural principles of fundamental importance. First, the compensator input is the regulated output z: in other words, a bona fide feedback structure is utilized. Secondly, the fixed part (A_2) of the compensator, where we do not and cannot permit parameter variations, will be in general a highly redundant, or 'reduplicated' model of the actual dynamics of the exogenous signals which the designer envisages a priori; the precise degree of redundancy is specified in the remark following Lemma 8.3. This redundancy is the price we pay for insisting on regulation in the presence of a very wide variety of parameter variations both internal to the feedback loop and also in the binding map which couples the loop to the exogenous signals. Finally we remark that the proof of Theorem 8.3 shows that our strong synthesis admits any and all perturbations in $\underline{p}_S$ (see (26)) which preserve the stability of A_L and the property (39). Under such perturbations the map $A_1 + B_1 F_1$ itself may cease to be stable and the compensator may give up its partial role as observer of the plant state.

8.5 Synthesis, Case II: Ker C ⊂ Ker D, $\mathcal{N}_D$ Minimal

In this section we relax the requirement C = D, but retain feedback structure by virtue of the assumption

$$\mathrm{Ker}\, C \subset \mathrm{Ker}\, D\,. \tag{49}$$

[Of course, (49) implies the existence of $E: \mathcal{Y} \to \mathcal{Z}$ such that $z = Ey$.] Fix (A_2, C, D) and consider the data point $\underline{p} = (A_1, A_3, B_1)$. It will be shown that the synthesis procedure of Section 8.4 is applicable generically, i.e., for all $\underline{p}$ in the complement of a proper algebraic variety. For this we require two preliminary results on generic observability. As usual we adopt the assumptions (7)–(10). We also write $\gamma(\lambda)$ for the cyclic index of $\bar{A}$ (or A_2) at λ, and remark that

$$\gamma \triangleq \max\{\gamma(\lambda): \lambda \in \mathbb{C}\}$$

is the cyclic index of $\bar{A}$ (or A_2), namely the number of cyclic components in a rational canonical decomposition of $\bar{\mathcal{X}}$ (or $\mathcal{X}_2$) relative to $\bar{A}$ (or A_2).

In the following the notation (g) means that the statement thus designated is true generically, i.e., except possibly on a proper variety in the space $\mathbb{R}^N$ of data points $\underline{p}$.

LEMMA 8.5. <u>If</u> $q \geq \gamma$ <u>then</u> (D, A) <u>is observable</u> (g).

PROOF: We have

$$\sigma(A_1) \cap \sigma(A_2) = \emptyset \quad (g) ,$$

so if $\lambda \in \sigma(A_2)$

$$d\left(\mathrm{Ker}(A_2 - \lambda)\right) = \gamma(\lambda) \leq \gamma \leq q ,$$

and therefore

$$d(\mathrm{Ker}\, D) + d\left(\mathrm{Ker}(A - \lambda)\right) \leq (n - q) + q = n .$$

Thus we shall have proved that

$$\mathrm{Ker}\, D \cap \mathrm{Ker}(A - \lambda) = 0 \quad (g) \tag{50}$$

as soon as we establish the intersection property at some $\underline{p}$. For this, fix A_1 with $\sigma(A_1) \cap \sigma(A_2) = \emptyset$ and (D_1, A_1) observable. From the discussion following Proposition 0.5, the operator

$$L(\cdot) \triangleq A_1(\cdot) - (\cdot)A_2 : \mathbb{R}^{n_1 \times n_2} \to \mathbb{R}^{n_1 \times n_2}$$

is then invertible. Furthermore, if

$$L(R) + A_3 = 0$$

then

$$\begin{bmatrix} I & -R \\ 0 & I \end{bmatrix} \begin{bmatrix} A_1 & A_3 \\ 0 & A_2 \end{bmatrix} \begin{bmatrix} I & R \\ 0 & I \end{bmatrix} = \begin{bmatrix} A_1 & 0 \\ 0 & A_2 \end{bmatrix}$$

and

$$\begin{bmatrix} D_1 & D_2 \end{bmatrix} \begin{bmatrix} I & R \\ 0 & I \end{bmatrix} = \begin{bmatrix} D_1, D_1 R + D_2 \end{bmatrix} ;$$

hence (D, A) is observable if and only if $(D_1 R + D_2, A_2)$ is observable. We show first that there exists $\tilde{R} \in \mathbb{R}^{n_1 \times n_2}$ such that $(D_1 \tilde{R}, A_2)$ is observable. For this let $g_1, \ldots, g_\gamma \in \mathbb{R}^{1 \times n_2}$ be a set of cyclic generators for A_2 (more properly, for the dual map, or transpose of A_2), and set

$$G \triangleq \begin{bmatrix} g_1 \\ \vdots \\ g_\gamma \\ 0 \end{bmatrix} \in \mathbb{R}^{q \times n_2} .$$

Let $\tilde{R} \triangleq \check{D}_1 G$, where $\check{D}_1 \in \mathbb{R}^{n_1 \times q}$ and $D_1 \check{D}_1 = I_q$ ($\check{D}_1$ exists since D_1 is epic). Clearly, $(D_1 \tilde{R}, A_2)$ is observable. It follows that $(D_1 \tilde{R} + \epsilon D_2, A_2)$ is observable for all ϵ sufficiently small. Fix such $\epsilon \neq 0$. Then $\left(D_1(\epsilon^{-1} \tilde{R}) + D_2, A_2\right)$ is observable. Choosing $A_3 = -L(\epsilon^{-1} \tilde{R})$ and $\underline{p} = (A_1, A_3, B_1)$ we have that (D, A) is observable, so by Lemma 8.1

$$\operatorname{Ker} D \cap \operatorname{Ker}(A - \lambda) = 0 ,$$

and (50) follows. ▮

COROLLARY 8.2. <u>Let</u> A_1 <u>be stable and</u> $q \geq \gamma$. <u>Then</u> A_3 <u>exists such that</u> (D, A) <u>is detectable.</u>

PROOF: We have (D_1, A_1) detectable and $\sigma(A_1) \cap \sigma(A_2) = \emptyset$. The preceding proof provides an A_3 such that $(D_1 R + D_2, A_2)$ is detectable, where $L(R) + A_3 = 0$. Thus (D, A) is detectable for such A_3. ▮

To adapt Lemma 8.5 to the case $q < \gamma$ we first prove

LEMMA 8.6. <u>Let</u> $A \in \mathbb{R}^{n \times n}$ <u>have rational canonical decomposition</u>

$$\mathcal{X} = \bigoplus_{j=1}^{\gamma} \mathcal{X}_j ,$$

<u>with</u> $d(\mathcal{X}_1) \geq \cdots \geq d(\mathcal{X}_\gamma)$, <u>and let</u> $B \in \mathbb{R}^{n' \times m}$ <u>be monic, with</u> $m < \gamma$. <u>Then for almost all</u> $R \in \mathbb{R}^{n \times n'}$ (<u>i.e., all</u> R <u>in the complement of a proper variety in</u> $\mathbb{R}^{nn'}$), <u>there is an A-operator isomorphism</u>

$$\langle A \,|\, \operatorname{Im}(RB) \rangle \approx \bigoplus_{j=1}^{m} \mathcal{X}_j .$$

PROOF: For $i \in \underline{m}$ let g_i be a cyclic generator for $\mathcal{X}_i$, set $G \triangleq [g_1, \ldots, g_m] \in \mathbb{R}^{n \times m}$, and $\tilde{R} \triangleq G\check{B}$ where $\check{B}B = I_m$, $\check{B} \in \mathbb{R}^{m \times n'}$. Then

$$\langle A \,|\, \operatorname{Im}(\tilde{R}B) \rangle = \bigoplus_{j=1}^{m} \mathcal{X}_j .$$

By uniqueness (within isomorphism) of the rational canonical decomposition,

$$d(\langle A|\operatorname{Im}(RB)\rangle) \le \sum_{j=1}^{m} d(\mathcal{X}_j), \qquad R \in \mathbb{R}^{n\times n'},$$

since the subspace on the left side is A-invariant and has at most m cyclic generators. Since equality holds at $\tilde{R}$, it clearly holds at almost all R. It follows by the dimensional maximality (Proposition 0.3) that for such R, $A|\langle A|\operatorname{Im}(RB)\rangle$ is similar to

$$A\Big|\bigoplus_{j=1}^{m} \mathcal{X}_j, \qquad \text{as claimed. } \blacksquare$$

COROLLARY 8.3. *Dualizing the result of Lemma 8.6 and applying it to the pair* (D_1, A_2), *we have that for almost all* $R \in \mathbb{R}^{n_1\times n_2}$,

$$\bigcap_{i=1}^{n_2} \operatorname{Ker}\left(D_1 R A_2^{i-1}\right) \approx \bigoplus_{j=q+1}^{\gamma} \mathcal{X}_{2j}, \tag{51}$$

where $\mathcal{X}_2$ *has rational canonical decomposition*

$$\bigoplus_{j=1}^{\gamma} \mathcal{X}_{2j}$$

relative to A_2.

LEMMA 8.7. *Let* $1 \le q < \gamma$ *and define the* $\mathcal{X}_{2j} \subset \mathcal{X}_2$ *as in (51). Then for almost all* p *there is an operator isomorphism according to the diagram:*

$$\begin{array}{ccc} \dfrac{\mathcal{N}_D + \mathcal{X}_1}{\mathcal{X}_1} & \xrightarrow{\quad \bar{A} \quad} & \dfrac{\mathcal{N}_D + \mathcal{X}_1}{\mathcal{X}_1} \\ \big\downarrow \approx & & \big\downarrow \approx \\ \bigoplus_{j=q+1}^{\gamma} \mathcal{X}_{2j} & \xrightarrow{\quad A_2 \quad} & \bigoplus_{j=q+1}^{\gamma} \mathcal{X}_{2j} \end{array} \tag{52}$$

The lemma states that generically one obtains maximal observability (i.e., minimal unobservability) from the pair (D, A), and the structure of the map induced by A on $\mathcal{X}/(\mathcal{N}_D + \mathcal{X}_1)$ is locally constant at almost all data points p.

PROOF: In (51) replace $D_1 R$ by $D_1 R + \epsilon D_2$ and proceed as in the proof of Lemma 8.5. $\blacksquare$

COROLLARY 8.4. Let A_1 be stable and $q < \gamma$. Then there exists A_3 for which the following is an A-operator isomorphism:

$$\frac{\mathcal{N}_D \cap \mathscr{X}^+(A) + \mathscr{X}_1}{\mathscr{X}_1} \approx \bigoplus_{j=q+1}^{\gamma} \mathscr{X}_{2j} .$$

We shall say that p is typical if $q \geq \gamma$ and (D, A) is observable, or if $q < \gamma$, (D_1, A_1) is observable and (52) holds. By Lemmas 8.6 and 8.7 almost all p are typical. Suppose $q \geq \gamma$, p is typical and RPIS is well-posed: we are then in the situation of Theorem 8.3 and can proceed as before. Now suppose $q < \gamma$ and p is typical. Since (D_1, A_1) is observable, we have $\mathcal{N}_D \cap \mathscr{X}_1 = 0$, hence by (52) obtain the diagram:

$$\begin{array}{ccc} \mathcal{N}_D & \xrightarrow{\quad A \quad} & \mathcal{N}_D \\ \big\downarrow \approx & & \big\downarrow \approx \\ \bigoplus_{j=q+1}^{\gamma} \mathscr{X}_{2j} & \xrightarrow{\quad A_2 \quad} & \bigoplus_{j=q+1}^{\gamma} \mathscr{X}_{2j} \end{array} \qquad (53)$$

Equivalently, we have the commutative diagram below.

$$\begin{array}{ccc} \dfrac{\mathscr{X}}{\mathcal{N}_D \oplus \mathscr{X}_1} & \xrightarrow{\quad \hat{A} \quad} & \dfrac{\mathscr{X}}{\mathcal{N}_D \oplus \mathscr{X}_1} \\ \big\downarrow \approx & & \big\downarrow \approx \\ \bigoplus_{j=1}^{q} \mathscr{X}_{2j} & \xrightarrow{\quad A_2 \quad} & \bigoplus_{j=1}^{q} \mathscr{X}_{2j} \end{array} \qquad (54)$$

Here $\hat{A}$ is the map induced by A in $\mathscr{X}/(\mathcal{N}_D \oplus \mathscr{X}_1)$. To exploit (54) we proceed exactly as in Section 8.4, except that (D, A, B) is replaced initially by the corresponding triple induced in $\mathscr{X}/\mathcal{N}_D$. It is entirely straightforward to verify that the resulting strong synthesis is actually strong for (D, A, B) in $\mathscr{X}$. Indeed, in the proof of Theorem 8.3 one need only adjoin additional 'blocks' to A_2 and A_3, corresponding to the D-unobservable cyclic subspaces diagrammed in (53). Splitting the latter into prime components (obviously of dimension no greater than those of $\mathscr{X}_{21}$), one applies exactly the same argument used before.

Before summarizing, we introduce the definition that $\mathcal{N}_D$ is minimal at p if $d(\mathcal{N}_D)$ is a minimum compatible with the fixed structure of D and A_2. It is clear that $\mathcal{N}_D$ is minimal if p is typical. Conversely if $\mathcal{N}_D$ is minimal, then (i) $q \geq \gamma$ implies $\mathcal{N}_D = 0$; and (ii) $q < \gamma$ implies that $d(\mathscr{X}/\mathcal{N}_D)$ is maximal, hence equal to

$$d(\mathscr{X}_1) + d\left(\bigoplus_{j=1}^{q} \mathscr{X}_{2j} \right) :$$

since minimality implies $\mathcal{N}_D \cap \mathscr{X}_1 = 0$, we conclude that (53) is true; hence p is typical.

We have now proved the following generalization of Theorem 8.3.

THEOREM 8.4. Assume that (2), (3), (7) and (49) hold, and let $\mathcal{N}_D$ be minimal at p. Then RPIS is strongly solvable at p if and only if RPIS is well-posed at p.

We remark that the (C, A)-detectability assumption (3) really plays no role, in view of the minimality of $\mathcal{N}_D$; it is imposed only for the sake of formal consistency with the conditions of Theorem 8.2.

8.6 Synthesis, Case III: $\operatorname{Ker} C \subset \operatorname{Ker} D$, Dual Observer

In the previous section we exploited the generic minimality of $\mathcal{N}_D$ to circumvent the use of an observer with input $y(\cdot)$, namely a 'y-observer'. In this section we describe a synthesis with two observers, a y-observer serving for prior plant stabilization and a z-observer for loop stabilization and output regulation. This procedure permits direct treatment of the non-generic case where $\mathcal{N}_D$ is not minimal. The latter situation may arise in practice when the spectra of A_1 and A_2 have points in common [i.e., the plant transfer matrix and $(sI - A_2)^{-1}$ have poles in common], as in the example of Section 7.7. Although one could separate the spectra by perturbing the plant model A_1 slightly, the penalty could be numerical ill-conditioning and we elect to proceed otherwise.

Step 1. Implementation of y-observer. By (2) we have $\mathcal{X}^-(A) \subset \langle A | \mathcal{B} \rangle$. From this and (3)

$$\begin{aligned} \mathcal{N}_C &= \mathcal{N}_C \cap \mathcal{X}^+(A) \oplus \mathcal{N}_C \cap \mathcal{X}^-(A) \\ &= \mathcal{N}_C \cap \mathcal{X}^-(A) \subset \langle A | \mathcal{B} \rangle . \end{aligned} \tag{55}$$

Write $\tilde{\mathcal{X}} \triangleq \mathcal{X}/\mathcal{N}_C$, let $P: \mathcal{X} \to \tilde{\mathcal{X}}$ be the canonical projection, and define maps $\tilde{C}, \tilde{A}, \tilde{B}$ according to the commutative diagram below.

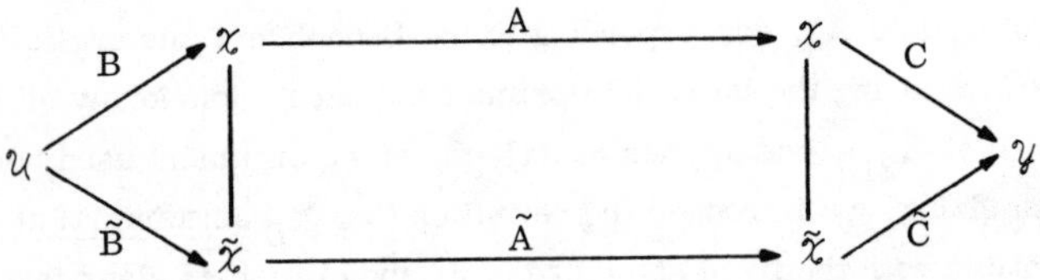

(56)

Next write $\mathcal{X}_{11} \triangleq \mathcal{N}_C$ and $\mathcal{X}_1 = \mathcal{X}_{11} \oplus \mathcal{X}_{12}$ for some complement $\mathcal{X}_{12}$, so that $\tilde{\mathcal{X}} \approx \mathcal{X}_{12} \oplus \mathcal{X}_2$. Then in a compatible basis the matrices appear as

$$A_1 = \begin{bmatrix} A_{11} & A_{13} \\ 0 & A_{12} \end{bmatrix}, \qquad A_3 = \begin{bmatrix} A_{31} \\ A_{32} \end{bmatrix},$$

$$B_1 = \begin{bmatrix} B_{11} \\ B_{12} \end{bmatrix}, \qquad C_1 = \begin{bmatrix} 0 & C_{12} \end{bmatrix}, \qquad D_1 = \begin{bmatrix} 0 & D_{12} \end{bmatrix}.$$

Thus we have the representations

$$\tilde{A} \sim \begin{bmatrix} A_{12} & A_{32} \\ 0 & A_2 \end{bmatrix}, \qquad \tilde{B} \sim \begin{bmatrix} B_{12} \\ 0 \end{bmatrix}, \qquad \tilde{C} \sim \begin{bmatrix} C_{12} & C_2 \end{bmatrix}.$$

As $(\tilde{C}, \tilde{A})$ is observable we introduce the y-observer

$$\dot{x}_a = (\tilde{A} - \tilde{J}\tilde{C})\,x_a + \tilde{J}\tilde{C}\tilde{x} + \tilde{B}u\,,$$

$$u = \tilde{H}x_a + v\,.$$

Here $x_a \in \mathcal{X}_a$ (the observer state space), $\tilde{x} = Px$, $\tilde{A} - \tilde{J}\tilde{C}$ is stable and v is an external control input. As $\mathcal{X}_a \approx \tilde{\mathcal{X}}$ we write, compatibly, $\tilde{H} = [H_{12} \;\; H_2]$; and as (A_{12}, B_{12}) is controllable we choose H_{12} such that $A_{12} + B_{12}H_{12}$ is stable.

Step 2. <u>Extended RPIS.</u> Now define the <u>extended system</u> according to $\mathcal{X}_{1e} \triangleq \mathcal{X}_1 \oplus \mathcal{X}_a$, $\mathcal{X}_e = \mathcal{X}_{1e} \oplus \mathcal{X}_2$ and

$$A_{1e} = \begin{bmatrix} A_1 & B_1\tilde{H} \\ \tilde{J}C_1 & \tilde{A} - \tilde{J}\tilde{C} + \tilde{B}\tilde{H} \end{bmatrix}, \qquad A_{3e} = \begin{bmatrix} A_3 \\ \tilde{J}C_2 \end{bmatrix},$$

$$B_{1e} = \begin{bmatrix} B_1 \\ \tilde{B} \end{bmatrix}, \qquad D_{1e} = \begin{bmatrix} D_1 & 0 \end{bmatrix},$$

$$A_e = \begin{bmatrix} A_{1e} & A_{3e} \\ 0 & A_2 \end{bmatrix}, \qquad B_e = \begin{bmatrix} B_{1e} \\ 0 \end{bmatrix}, \qquad D_e = \begin{bmatrix} D_{1e} & D_2 \end{bmatrix}.$$

Here A_{1e} is similar to

$$\begin{bmatrix} A_{11} & A_{13} + B_{11}H_{12} & B_{11}\tilde{H} \\ 0 & A_{12} + B_{12}H_{12} & B_{12}\tilde{H} \\ 0 & 0 & \tilde{A} - \tilde{J}\tilde{C} \end{bmatrix}$$

and so is stable.

Step 3. Strong synthesis. The extended system is

$$\dot{x}_e = A_e x_e + B_e v$$

$$z = D_e x_e .$$

In this context we define a strong synthesis of RPIS to be a strong synthesis, in the sense of Section 8.4, of RPIS for the extended system. Write $\underline{p} = (A_1, A_3, B_1)$ as before. We shall say that RPIS is strongly solvable at $\underline{p}$ if, for any system extension (with y-observer) of the type already described, the extended system admits a strong synthesis in the sense of Section 8.4. More precisely, the formal definition of 'strong solvability' given in Section 8.4 is now to be applied to the triple induced by (D_e, A_e, B_e) in $\mathcal{X}/\mathcal{N}_{D_e}$. On this basis we can prove

THEOREM 8.5. Assume that (2), (3), (7) and (49) hold. Then RPIS is strongly solvable at $\underline{p} = (A_1, A_3, B_1)$ if and only if RPIS is well-posed at $\underline{p}$.

PROOF: Necessity follows as in the proof of Theorem 8.3. For sufficiency, it will first be shown that RPIS is well-posed at $\underline{p}$ if and only if (extended) RPIS is well-posed at $\underline{p}_e \triangleq (A_{1e}, A_{3e}, B_{1e})$. Write

$$H_1 \triangleq \begin{bmatrix} 0 & H_2 \end{bmatrix} : \mathcal{X}_{11} \oplus \mathcal{X}_{12} \to \mathcal{U} .$$

We have well-posedness at $\underline{p}_e$ if and only if

$$(A_{1e} - \lambda)\,\mathrm{Ker}\, D_{1e} + \mathcal{B}_{1e} = \mathcal{X}_{1e}, \qquad \lambda \in \sigma(A_2) ,$$

or what is the same,

$$\begin{bmatrix} A_1 + B_1 H_1 - \lambda & B_1 \tilde{H} \\ 0 & \tilde{A} - \tilde{J}\tilde{C} - \lambda \end{bmatrix} \mathrm{Ker} \begin{bmatrix} D_1 & 0 \end{bmatrix}$$

$$+ \mathrm{Im} \begin{bmatrix} B_1 \\ 0 \end{bmatrix} = \mathcal{X}_{1e}, \qquad \lambda \in \sigma(A_2) .$$

Equivalently, as $\tilde{A} - \tilde{J}\tilde{C}$ is stable,

$$(A_1 + B_1 H_1 - \lambda)\,\mathrm{Ker}\, D_1 + \mathcal{B}_1 = \mathcal{X}_1, \qquad \lambda \in \sigma(A_2) ,$$

and this is equivalent in turn to well-posedness of RPIS at $\underline{p}$.

Now suppose that $q \geq \gamma$, the cyclic index of A_2. As A_{1e} is stable, Corollary 8.2 supplies a map $\hat{A}_{3e}: \mathcal{X}_2 \to \mathcal{X}_{1e}$ such that $(D_e, \hat{A}_e)$ is detectable, where

$$\hat{A}_e \triangleq \begin{bmatrix} A_{1e} & \hat{A}_{3e} \\ 0 & A_2 \end{bmatrix}.$$

Writing $\hat{\mathcal{N}}_{D_e}$ for the unobservable subspace of $(D_e, \hat{A}_e)$ we have [cf. (55)] that $\hat{\mathcal{N}}_{D_e} \subset \mathcal{X}_{1e}$.

Let $\bar{\bar{\mathcal{X}}}_e \triangleq \mathcal{X}_e/\hat{\mathcal{N}}_{D_e}$ and let $(\bar{\bar{D}}_e, \bar{\bar{A}}_e, \bar{\bar{B}}_e)$ be the maps induced by $(D_e, \hat{A}_e, B_e)$ relative to $\bar{\bar{\mathcal{X}}}_e$ [cf. (56)]. Also let $\mathcal{X}_{1e}^{(1)} \triangleq \mathcal{N}_{D_e}$ and write $\mathcal{X}_{1e} = \mathcal{X}_{1e}^{(1)} \oplus \mathcal{X}_{1e}^{(2)}$. Then $\bar{\bar{\mathcal{X}}}_e \approx \mathcal{X}_{1e}^{(2)} \oplus \mathcal{X}_2$ and in a compatible basis we have, say,

$$A_{1e} = \begin{bmatrix} A_{1e}^{(1)} & A_{1e}^{(3)} \\ 0 & A_{1e}^{(2)} \end{bmatrix}, \qquad A_{3e} = \begin{bmatrix} A_{3e}^{(1)} \\ A_{3e}^{(2)} \end{bmatrix},$$

$$B_{1e} = \begin{bmatrix} B_{1e}^{(1)} \\ B_{1e}^{(2)} \end{bmatrix}, \qquad D_{1e} = \begin{bmatrix} 0 & D_{1e}^{(2)} \end{bmatrix},$$

together with the representations

$$\bar{\bar{A}}_e \sim \begin{bmatrix} A_{1e}^{(2)} & A_{3e}^{(2)} \\ 0 & A_2 \end{bmatrix}, \qquad \bar{\bar{B}}_e \sim \begin{bmatrix} B_{1e}^{(2)} \\ 0 \end{bmatrix}, \qquad \bar{\bar{D}}_e \sim \begin{bmatrix} D_{1e}^{(2)} & D_2 \end{bmatrix}.$$

Next introduce the z-observer equations

$$\dot{w} = (\bar{\bar{A}}_e - \bar{\bar{K}}_e \bar{\bar{D}}_e) w + \bar{\bar{K}}_e \bar{\bar{D}}_e \bar{\bar{x}} + \bar{\bar{B}}_e v,$$

$$v = \bar{\bar{F}}_e w.$$

Here $w \in \mathcal{W} \approx \bar{\bar{\mathcal{X}}}_e$, $\bar{\bar{A}}_e - \bar{\bar{K}}_e \bar{\bar{D}}_e$ is stable and

$$\bar{\bar{F}}_e = \begin{bmatrix} 0, & F_2 \end{bmatrix}: \bar{\bar{\mathcal{X}}}_e \to \mathcal{U}.$$

In $\mathcal{X}_{1e} \oplus \mathcal{W} \oplus \mathcal{X}_2$ the composite system matrix is

$$A_S = \left[\begin{array}{cc|c} A_{1e} & B_{1e}\bar{\bar{F}}_e & A_{3e} \\ \bar{\bar{K}}_e D_{1e} & \bar{\bar{A}}_e - \bar{\bar{K}}_e \bar{\bar{D}}_e + \bar{\bar{B}}_e \bar{\bar{F}}_e & \bar{\bar{K}}_e D_2 \\ \hline 0 & 0 & A_2 \end{array}\right]; \qquad (57)$$

and the extended loop map (upper left block), being similar to

$$\begin{bmatrix} A_{1e} & B_{1e}\bar{\bar{F}}_e \\ 0 & \bar{\bar{A}}_e - \bar{\bar{K}}_e \bar{\bar{D}}_e \end{bmatrix},$$

is stable.

The proof of Theorem 8.3 now shows that the map A_S in (57) supplies, possibly after an outward extension, the strong synthesis required.

In the case $q < \gamma$ we apply Corollary 8.4 to obtain $\hat{A}_{3e}$ yielding maximal detectability of $(D_e, \hat{A}_e)$. The proof of existence of a strong synthesis in this case runs parallel to the proof of Theorem 8.4. ▮

8.7 Example 2: Ill-posed RPIS

The following is an example of an RPIS which is solvable but not well-posed. Let

$$A = \left[\begin{array}{ccc|c} -2 & 1 & 0 & 0 \\ 0 & -2 & 0 & 1 \\ 0 & 0 & -1 & 1 \\ \hline 0 & 0 & 0 & 0 \end{array}\right], \qquad B = \left[\begin{array}{cc} 0 & 0 \\ 1 & 0 \\ 0 & 1 \\ \hline 0 & 0 \end{array}\right]$$

$$D = \left[\begin{array}{ccc|c} -2 & 1 & 0 & 0 \\ 0 & 0 & 1 & 0 \end{array}\right].$$

The system consists of a controllable third-order plant with two regulated scalar outputs and subject to a scalar step disturbance. We assume $C = D$; it can be verified that (D, A) is observable. According to Theorem 7.5, RPIS is solvable if and only if

$$\langle A | \mathcal{B} \rangle + \operatorname{Ker} D \cap A^{-1}\mathcal{B} = \mathcal{X}. \qquad (58)$$

Now

$$\langle A|\mathcal{B}\rangle = \mathrm{Im}\begin{bmatrix}1 & 0 & 0\\ 0 & 1 & 0\\ 0 & 0 & 1\\ 0 & 0 & 0\end{bmatrix}$$

and

$$\mathrm{Ker}\,D \cap A^{-1}\mathcal{B} = \mathrm{Im}\begin{bmatrix}1 & 0\\ 2 & 0\\ 0 & 0\\ 0 & 1\end{bmatrix},$$

so that (58) is certainly true. Now let $\epsilon \neq 0$, $|\epsilon| < 1$ and consider

$$A_\epsilon \triangleq \left[\begin{array}{ccc|c}-2+2\epsilon & 1-\epsilon & 0 & \epsilon\\ 0 & -2 & 0 & 1\\ 0 & 0 & -1 & 1\\ \hline 0 & 0 & 0 & 0\end{array}\right] \tag{59}$$

with B and D as before. Then $\langle A|\mathcal{B}\rangle$ is unchanged but now

$$\mathrm{Ker}\,D \cap A^{-1}\mathcal{B} = \mathrm{Im}\begin{bmatrix}1\\ 2\\ 0\\ 0\end{bmatrix},$$

and the solvability condition (58) fails. In the notation of Corollary 7.3, we find that

$$\mathcal{V}_\epsilon^* = \mathrm{Ker}\,D, \qquad \mathcal{R}_\epsilon^* = 0$$

for all $|\epsilon| < 1$. Taking

$$F_\epsilon = \begin{bmatrix}0 & 2 & 0 & -1+2\epsilon\\ 0 & 0 & 0 & -1\end{bmatrix} \in \underline{F}(\mathcal{V}_\epsilon^*)$$

and

$$\mathcal{V}_\epsilon^* = \mathrm{Im}\begin{bmatrix}1 & 0\\ 2 & 0\\ 0 & 0\\ 0 & 1\end{bmatrix},$$

we find that in this basis for $\mathcal{V}_\epsilon^*$,

$$(A_\epsilon + BF_\epsilon)|\mathcal{V}_\epsilon^* \sim \begin{bmatrix}0 & \epsilon\\ 0 & 0\end{bmatrix} \tag{60}$$

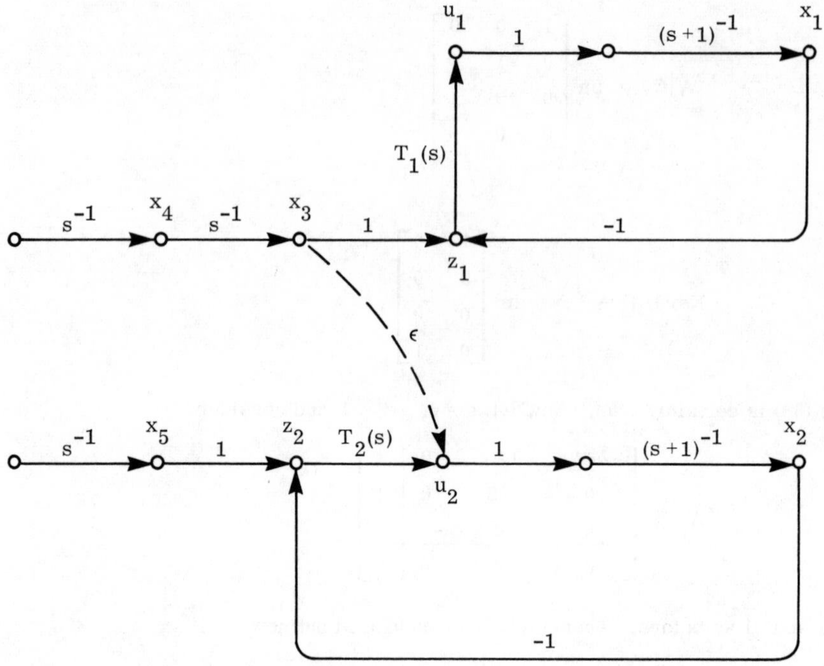

Fig. 8.3.

Structural Instability in a Multivariable System.

and

$$\langle A_\epsilon | \mathcal{B} \rangle \cap \mathcal{V}_\epsilon^* \sim \operatorname{Im} \begin{bmatrix} 1 \\ 0 \end{bmatrix}. \tag{61}$$

It is clear that the subspace (61) indeed fails to decompose $\mathcal{V}_\epsilon^*$ relative to the map (60), unless $\epsilon = 0$.

More directly, setting $\lambda = 0$ in the criterion of Theorem 8.2, one verifies quickly that

$$A(\operatorname{Ker} D \cap \langle A | \mathcal{B} \rangle) + \mathcal{B} = \mathcal{B} \neq \langle A | \mathcal{B} \rangle ,$$

and well-posedness fails. The conclusion is that our original (solvable) RPIS is surely rendered unsolvable by <u>some</u> appropriately chosen perturbation, arbitrarily small.

8.8 Example 3: Well-posed RPIS: Strong Synthesis

Let

$$A = \left[\begin{array}{cc|ccc} -1 & 0 & & A_3 & \\ 0 & -1 & & & \\ \hline & & 0 & 1 & 0 \\ & O & 0 & 0 & 0 \\ \hline 0 & 0 & 0 & 0 & 0 \end{array}\right], \qquad B = \left[\begin{array}{cc} 1 & 0 \\ 0 & 1 \\ \hline & \\ & O \\ & \end{array}\right], \tag{62}$$

$$D = \begin{bmatrix} -1 & 0 & 1 & 0 & 0 \\ 0 & -1 & 0 & 0 & 1 \end{bmatrix},$$

and suppose first that $A_3 = 0$. The system represents two identical, decoupled first-order lags (state variables x_1, x_2) which are required to track, respectively, a ramp (x_3, x_4) or step (x_5). The pair (D, A) is observable and we assume $C = D$.

If no account is taken of possible perturbations of A_3, 'naive' implementation of a feedback controller with a (minimal-order) observer could take the form shown in solid lines in Fig. 8.3. Here, the compensators

$$T_1(s) = \frac{6s+1}{16s^2}, \qquad T_2(s) = \frac{1}{s}$$

guarantee internal stability and output regulation for each decoupled subsystem.

It is clear, however, that if $A_3 = 0$ is perturbed to

$$A_{3\epsilon} = \begin{bmatrix} 0 & 0 & 0 \\ \epsilon & 0 & 0 \end{bmatrix}, \qquad \epsilon \neq 0,$$

as shown by the dotted branch in Fig. 8.3, then the second loop will fail to reject the ramp disturbance $x_3(\cdot)$, giving an offset (asymptotic) error

$$z_2(\infty) = -\epsilon x_4(0+) .$$

A simple cure, obvious by inspection, is to replace $T_2(s)$ by $\tilde{T}_2(s) = T_1(s)$. The system then maintains internal stability and output regulation in the face of arbitrary small perturbations in (A_1, A_3, B_1), provided the 'internal models' represented by the double integrators $(1/s^2)$ remain fixed in each loop. Observe that the same is true if the lower right block in A_2 (scalar 0) is extended to $\begin{bmatrix} 0 & 1 \\ 0 & 0 \end{bmatrix}$, as the result is only to modify the flow graph branch

$$\circ \xrightarrow{s^{-1}} \circ\; x_5 \qquad \text{to} \qquad \circ \xrightarrow{s^{-1}} \underset{x_6}{\circ} \xrightarrow{s^{-1}} \circ\; x_5$$

As an illustrative exercise we shall carry out the formal synthesis described in Section 8.4. The first step (after checking well-posedness) is to form an outward extension with the properties listed in Lemmas 8.2 and 8.3. For this we need merely set

$$A_{2e} = \left[\begin{array}{cc|cc} 0 & 1 & & \\ 0 & 0 & \multicolumn{2}{c}{O} \\ \hline & & 0 & 1 \\ \multicolumn{2}{c|}{O} & 0 & 0 \end{array}\right], \tag{63}$$

namely (comparing (62), (63) with (31)),

$$A_{2a} = 0 , \qquad A_{23} = \begin{bmatrix} 0 \\ 0 \\ 1 \end{bmatrix} .$$

With $\lambda = 0$ and $k = q = 2$, we have

$$d\left(\mathrm{Ker}(A_{2e} - \lambda)\right) = 2 = q$$

and

$$\mathrm{Ker}(A_{2e} - \lambda)^{k-1} = \mathrm{Im}\begin{bmatrix} 1 & 0 \\ 0 & 0 \\ 0 & 1 \\ 0 & 0 \end{bmatrix} = \mathrm{Im}(A_{2e} - \lambda) ,$$

as required. With $A_{13} = 0$, (D_e, A_e) is observable. It remains only to construct a solution of (extended) RPIS along the lines described in Chapter 7: indeed, the small perturbations of T_3 and F_2, introduced in the proof of Theorem 8.3 to create the 'generic' situation, will in practice almost never be required. In this simple example the extended RPIS decomposes into two identical, decoupled, single-input single-output servo problems of low order. On solving each one independently with identical second-order (minimal) observer and assignment of poles, we recover the second design described above.

8.9 On Practical Synthesis

Our results so far have established that a structurally stable synthesis of RPIS can be implemented under the rather mild condition (Theorem 8.2) of well-posedness on the problem data. In this section we summarize informally one possible synthesis procedure, starting from the representation (8), and our standing assumptions

$$\mathcal{X}^{+}(A) \cap \mathcal{N}_C = 0 \tag{3 bis}$$

$$\sigma(A_2) \subset \mathbb{C}^{+} \tag{9 bis}$$

$$\text{Rank } D_1 = q \tag{10 bis}$$

$$\text{Ker } C \subset \text{Ker } D \,. \tag{49 bis}$$

The final configuration will take the form displayed by the signal flow graph, Fig. 8.4.

Step 1. Exploiting (C, A)-detectability (3), design a compensator to stabilize the plant, thus completing the inner loop, with parameters (G', G'', R, H). The compensator may be designed around a standard full-order or minimal-order observer, or by means of the possibly more efficient scheme of Section 3.8. Its equations will be of the form

$$\dot{q} = Rq + Hy \tag{64a}$$

$$u = G'q + G''y + v \,. \tag{64b}$$

Combining (64) with (8) yields the composite system

$$\begin{bmatrix} \dot{x}_1 \\ \dot{q} \\ \hline \dot{x}_2 \end{bmatrix} = \left[\begin{array}{cc|c} A_1 + B_1G'' & B_1G' & B_1G''C_2 + A_3 \\ HC_1 & R & HC_2 \\ \hline 0 & 0 & A_2 \end{array}\right] \begin{bmatrix} x_1 \\ q \\ \hline x_2 \end{bmatrix} + \begin{bmatrix} B_1 \\ 0 \\ \hline 0 \end{bmatrix} v \,. \tag{65}$$

In (65) the (x_1, q)-subsystem, corresponding to the upper left block of the system matrix, is stable; it need not be (completely) controllable from v, but this fact is of no importance. To simplify notation, redefine

$$x_1 = (x_1)_{\text{new}} \triangleq \text{col}(x_1, q)_{\text{old}} \,,$$

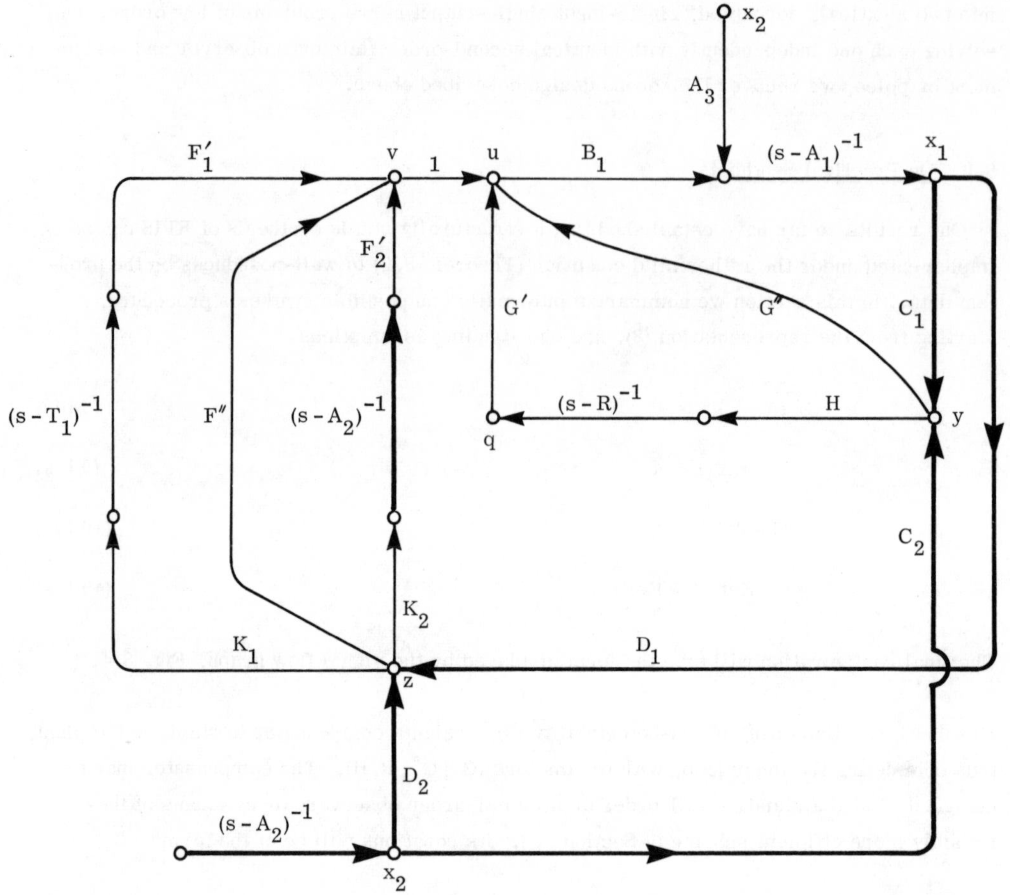

Fig. 8.4.

Signal Flow in Structurally Stable Multivariable Regulator. Heavy branches have fixed transmissions, light branches admit small parameter perturbations. A_2 is assumed augmented. In general $D = EC$, i.e., $z = Ey$ for some fixed E (not shown).

redefine A_1, A_3, B_1 as displayed in (65), and start afresh from (8) with the assurance that now

$$A_1 \text{ is stable.}$$

Step 2. If $\mathcal{N}_D \cap \mathcal{X}^+(A) \neq 0$, compute the induced maps $(\overline{D}, \overline{A}, \overline{B})$ relative to the factor space $\mathcal{X}/\mathcal{N}_D \cap \mathcal{X}^+(A)$, redefine

$$(D, A, B)_{new} = (\overline{D}, \overline{A}, \overline{B})_{old},$$

and start afresh from (8) with the assurance that now

$$\mathcal{N}_D \cap \mathcal{X}^+(A) = 0. \tag{66}$$

Step 3. Transform A_2 to real Jordan form, and accordingly transform A_3, D_2. In practice A_2 is typically modelled in Jordan form at the start. By inspection, extend A_2, A_3 and D_2 as in the proofs of Lemmas 8.2 and 8.3. Namely: 1. For each real λ read off the dimension $k(\lambda)$ of the largest associated Jordan block. 2. Enlarge any smaller block to size $k(\lambda)$. 3. Adjoin new blocks, if necessary, to bring the total number for each λ to q. 4. Repeat this process for the real blocks, of size $2k(\lambda)$, corresponding to complex pairs (λ, λ^*). 5. With $\mathcal{X}_2$ thus extended to $\mathcal{X}_{2e} = \mathcal{X}_2 \oplus \mathcal{X}_2'$ (say), by inspection enlarge A_3, D_2 to A'_{3e}, D_{2e} in the obvious way, to achieve

$$A_{3e}|\mathcal{X}_2 = A_3, \qquad A'_{3e}\mathcal{X}_2' = 0$$

$$D_{2e}|\mathcal{X}_2 = D_2, \qquad D_{2e}\mathcal{X}_2' = 0.$$

6. Replace A'_{3e} by A_{3e}, where $A_{3e}|\mathcal{X}_2 = A_3$ and $A_{3e}|\mathcal{X}_{2a}$ is selected 'randomly': then (66) will almost surely hold for the extended pair (D_e, A_e). Alternatively a systematic selection rule can be developed (Ex. 8.6). Revising notation, start afresh from (8) with the assurance that now (33) and (34) are true.

Step 4. Compute $F = [0, F_2]$ such that $\mathcal{X}^+(A + BF) \subset \operatorname{Ker} D$. With A_2 in real Jordan form select $\lambda \in \sigma(A_2)$, λ real (say) and of multiplicity $k(\lambda) = k$ in each of q blocks. If $g_i \in \mathcal{X}_2$ $(i \in \underline{q})$ are the corresponding cyclic generators then

$$\operatorname{Ker}(A_2 - \lambda)^k = \operatorname{Span}\left\{(A_2 - \lambda)^{j-1} g_i, \ i \in \underline{q}, \ j \in \underline{k}\right\};$$

and for suitable $h_{ij} \in \mathcal{X}_1$,

$$\operatorname{Ker}(A + BF - \lambda)^k = \operatorname{Span}\left\{h_{ij} \oplus (A_2 - \lambda)^{j-1} g_i, \ i \in \underline{q}, \ j \in \underline{k}\right\}.$$

The vectors h_{ij} and $F_2(A_2 - \lambda)^{j-1} g_i$ are now determined recursively ($j \downarrow$) by the relations

$$\begin{bmatrix} A_1 - \lambda & B_1 \\ D_1 & 0 \end{bmatrix} \begin{bmatrix} h_{ij} \\ F_2(A_2 - \lambda)^{j-1} g_i \end{bmatrix} = \begin{bmatrix} -A_3(A_2 - \lambda)^{j-1} g_i + h_{i,j+1} \\ -D_2(A_2 - \lambda)^{j-1} g_i \end{bmatrix} \tag{67}$$

for $i \in \underline{q}$, $j \in \underline{k}$ and with $h_{i,k+1} \triangleq 0$ ($i \in \underline{q}$). By well-posedness the first-written matrix in (67) is right-invertible and solvability is clear. Complex eigenvalue pairs are handled in a similar way (cf. the proof of Theorem 8.3, and Section 0.11). Finally F_2 itself is determined by an evident matrix inversion.

Step 5. Design a standard minimal-order z-observer to implement the control $v = F_2 x_2$. This will have the form

$$\dot{w} = Tw + Kz$$
$$v = F'w + F''z ,$$

where $w \in \mathcal{W}$, $d(\mathcal{W}) \leq n - q$. It is easily shown (Ex. 8.2) that, just as with the full-order observer (Section 8.4), T can be structured as in (21) with $T_3 = 0$.

Step 6. Synthesize the system according to the signal flow graph, Fig. 8.4. The design is structurally stable (preserves loop stability and z-regulation) in the presence of sufficiently small, but arbitrary, perturbations of the parameters:

$$A_1, A_3, B_1, G', G'', R, H, F_1', F_2', F'', T_1, K_1, K_2 .$$

It is assumed that A_2 (in both locations) together with C_1, C_2, D_1, D_2, remain fixed.

In conclusion we emphasize again that our design requirements have been strictly qualitative: any complete approach must grapple with quantitative features we have left entirely out of account, and these will strongly depend on the application at hand. But little could be hoped from any procedure which did not meet the minimal goals we have actually achieved.

8.10 The Internal Model Principle

To recapitulate, the fundamental properties of our structurally stable synthesis are the following.

1. The controller is of feedback type.
2. The feedback loop incorporates a model of the dynamic system which generates the exogenous signals to be processed.
3. This model is generally richer in structure than the exogenous model adopted a priori.

The design of controllers with the first two features is certainly not new. It is very well known that feedback can reduce sensitivity to parameter variations or uncertainties, this (together with stability) being the major focus of classical feedback control theory. In regard to the second feature, various authors have suggested (not always with supporting evidence) that regulators contain isomorphs of whatever they are regulating against. More concretely, O.J.M. Smith developed a design "philosophy ... that feedback systems contain both linear and nonlinear predictors of several types, and that the construction of these will include models of the mechanisms of generation of the various signals being predicted." Recently, Davison tacitly includes an internal model in his 'robust' feedback controller.

On the other hand, the exploitation of redundancy appears as a less familiar idea in controller design. The concept is closely related to structural reliability, in the achievement of which redundancy plays a long-established role. Intuitively, if a regulator is to operate reliably in response to external stimuli, then its internal model of external reality must be rich enough for it to distinguish these stimuli from the otherwise confusing effects of minor internal disruptions.

It can be shown that these are necessary features of any controller which is structurally stable in the strong sense we have required. This principle of the internal model deserves much broader study than it has hitherto received.

8.11 Exercises

8.1 For Example 1, Section 8.7, find the complete class of perturbations in (A_1, A_3, B_1) for which solvability of RPIS fails.

8.2 In the general discussion, full-order observers were employed only for simplicity of exposition. Show that minimal-order observers (Section 3.4) will serve as well. Does this affect the order of the internal model (of A_2)?

8.3 Investigate how the compensation technique of Section 3.8 might be exploited in the present context.

8.4 For the ill-posed but solvable RPIS of Section 8.7, design a standard feedback controller (e.g., just as illustrated in Section 7.8) which implements a solution of RPIS. Now introduce the perturbation specified by (59). What goes wrong?

8.5 Consider the system (1) with regulated output $z = Dx + Eu$. As indicated in Section 0.16, replace this output equation with

$$\epsilon\dot{v} = -v + u, \qquad z = Dx + Ev.$$

Show that, under suitable assumptions, the corresponding RPIS is well-posed for all $\epsilon > 0$ sufficiently small, if and only if

$$\operatorname{Rank}\begin{bmatrix} A_1 - \lambda & B_1 \\ D_1 & E \end{bmatrix} = n_1 + q, \qquad \lambda \in \sigma(A_2).$$

Show that the same result holds if, alternatively, the 'regularized' RPIS is defined by retaining the original output equation, but taking the control to be $v = \dot{u}$.

8.6 Develop a selection rule for A_3 in Step 3.6, Section 8.9.

8.7 Show in detail how to handle complex eigenvalue pairs in Step 4, Section 8.9.

8.8 Work through the procedure of Section 8.9 with a numerical example. HINT: The following is transparent from its signal flow graph. Let

$$A = \begin{bmatrix} 1 & 1 & 0 & 0 & 0 & 0 & 0 \\ 0 & 0 & 0 & 0 & 0 & 0 & 0 \\ 0 & 0 & 1 & 1 & 0 & 0 & 0 \\ 0 & 0 & 0 & -2 & 0 & 0 & 1 \\ 0 & 0 & 0 & 0 & 0 & 1 & 0 \\ 0 & 0 & 0 & 0 & 0 & 0 & 0 \\ 0 & 0 & 0 & 0 & 0 & 0 & 0 \end{bmatrix}, \qquad B = \begin{bmatrix} 0 & 0 \\ 1 & 0 \\ 0 & 0 \\ 0 & 1 \\ 0 & 0 \\ 0 & 0 \\ 0 & 0 \end{bmatrix},$$

$$C = D = \begin{bmatrix} 1 & 0 & 0 & 0 & 0 & 0 & 0 \\ 0 & 0 & -1 & 0 & 1 & 0 & 0 \end{bmatrix}.$$

For plant pre-stabilizer (64) take, for instance,

$$R = \begin{bmatrix} -4 & 0 \\ 0 & -2 \end{bmatrix}, \quad H = \begin{bmatrix} 1 & 0 \\ 0 & 1 \end{bmatrix}, \quad G' = \begin{bmatrix} 27 & 0 \\ 0 & -1 \end{bmatrix}, \quad G'' = \begin{bmatrix} -7 & 0 \\ 0 & 3 \end{bmatrix}.$$

All plant poles are then assigned to $s = -1$. The composite system involves state variables $(x_1, \ldots, x_7, q_1, q_2)$. Projection mod $\mathcal{N}_D \cap \mathcal{X}^+(A)$ can be accomplished just by deleting x_7 from all equations and reducing the system matrices accordingly. Then at Step 3 one has

$$A_2 = \begin{bmatrix} 0 & 1 \\ 0 & 0 \end{bmatrix}, \qquad A_3 = 0 .$$

Since $q = 2$, A_2 must be augmented to comprise two cyclic blocks with m.p. λ^2, namely

$$A_{2,\text{new}} = \begin{bmatrix} A_2 & 0 \\ 0 & A_2 \end{bmatrix}.$$

To achieve z-detectability let, for instance,

$$A_{3,\text{new}} = \begin{bmatrix} 0 & 0 & 0 & 0 \\ 0 & 0 & 1 & 0 \\ & 0^{7\times 4} & & \end{bmatrix},$$

a choice again quite obvious from the signal flow graph. At Step 4 one has, by inspection,

$$g_1 = \begin{bmatrix} 0 \\ 1 \\ 0 \\ 0 \end{bmatrix}, \qquad g_2 = \begin{bmatrix} 0 \\ 0 \\ 0 \\ 1 \end{bmatrix}.$$

Then (67) yields, in turn,

$$F_2 A_2 g_1 = \begin{bmatrix} -1 \\ 0 \end{bmatrix}, \qquad F_2 g_1 = \begin{bmatrix} 0 \\ 0 \end{bmatrix},$$

$$F_2 A_2 g_2 = \begin{bmatrix} 0 \\ \frac{1}{2} \end{bmatrix}, \qquad F_2 g_2 = \begin{bmatrix} 0 \\ \frac{5}{4} \end{bmatrix}.$$

From this

$$F_2 = \begin{bmatrix} -1 & 0 & 0 & 0 \\ 0 & 0 & \frac{1}{2} & \frac{5}{4} \end{bmatrix},$$

and Step 5 may be left to the reader.

8.9 Develop a computer-aided design program based on the procedure of Section 8.9.

8.12 Notes and References

The exposition in this chapter is based on Francis, Sebakhy and Wonham [1] and Sebakhy [1]. The 'classical' pole-zero approach to linear feedback controller design is thoroughly developed by Horowitz [1]. For a heuristic discussion of what we call the internal model principle see Conant [1] and Conant and Ashby [1], although the formal setup there may seem, to some, jejune and unconvincing. Exploitation of internal models in control engineering design is basic to the methods of Smith [1] and also Davison [1], [2]. In parallel with the present approach, see Pearson and Staats [1]. On the role of redundancy in reliable structures von Neumann's paper [1] is classic. A brief account of structural stability of differential equations can be found in Lefschetz [1] and Hale [1]. A proof that the reduplicated internal model, and feedback, are really demanded by structural stability is given in the setting of this chapter by Francis and Wonham [1]. Further details of computation and numerical examples are reported by Sebakhy and Wonham [1] and Sebakhy [1].

CHAPTER 9

NONINTERACTING CONTROL: BASIC PRINCIPLES

Consider a multivariable system whose scalar outputs z_{ij} have been grouped in disjoint subsets, each having a physical significance to distinguish it from the remaining subsets. Represent the output subsets by vectors

$$z_i = \text{col}\left(z_{i1}, \ldots, z_{ip_i}\right), \qquad i \in \underline{k} .$$

For instance, with $k = 3$ and each $p_i = 2$, z_i could represent angular position and velocity of a rigid body relative to the $i^{\underline{th}}$ axis of rotation. Next suppose the system is controlled by scalar inputs $u_1, \ldots, u_m$, where $m \geq k$. In many applications it is desirable to partition the input set into k disjoint subsets $\underline{U}_1, \ldots, \underline{U}_k$ such that for each $i \in \underline{k}$ the inputs of $\underline{U}_i$ control the output vector z_i completely, without affecting the behavior of the remaining z_j, $j \neq i$. Such a control action is <u>noninteracting</u>, and the system is <u>decoupled</u>. From an input-output viewpoint decoupling splits the system into k independent subsystems. Considerable advantages may result of simplicity and reliability, especially if control is partially to be executed by a human operator.

In general, decoupling in the manner described is impossible: sometimes, however, noninteraction is achievable by introducing state feedback, possibly with auxiliary integrating elements, and by regrouping the input control variables in suitable functional combinations. The objective is to cancel or compensate for inherent cross-couplings, and also to achieve satisfactory dynamic response.

For our linear multivariable system there exists an extensive theory of noninteraction based on the structural concepts we have already developed. In this chapter we introduce the main ideas, in Chapter 10 develop more fully the technique of dynamic compensation, and in Chapter 11 discuss generic solvability. As usual, we shall initially formulate the systems problem in terms of state equations, then extract the underlying algebraic structure.

9.1 <u>Decoupling: Systems Formulation</u>

Let

$$\begin{aligned} \dot{x}(t) &= A\,x(t) + B\,u(t) \\ z_i(t) &= D_i\,x(t)\,, \qquad i \in \underline{k}\,, \quad k \geq 2\,. \end{aligned} \tag{1}$$

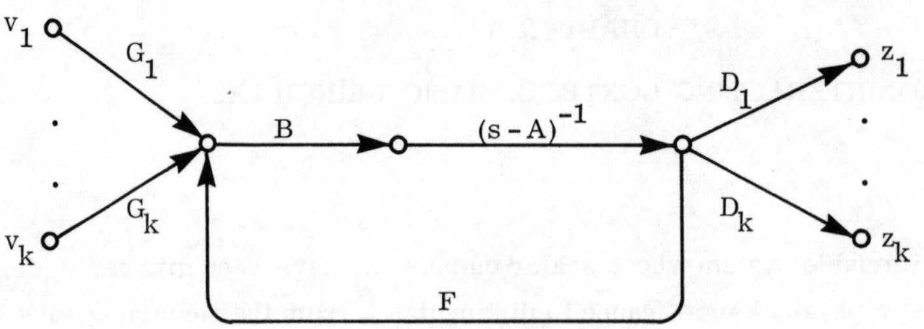

Fig. 9.1.

Signal Flow: Solution of RDP

$$D_j(s - A - BF)^{-1} BG_i = 0 , \qquad j \neq i ;$$

v_i completely controls z_i.

Here, as usual, A: $\mathcal{X} \to \mathcal{X}$, B: $\mathcal{U} \to \mathcal{X}$, and D_i: $\mathcal{X} \to \mathcal{Z}_i$. For the space of output vectors we adopt the external direct sum

$$\mathcal{Z} = \mathcal{Z}_1 \oplus \cdots \oplus \mathcal{Z}_k .$$

We assume that state feedback is allowed with an arbitrary feedback map F, and that arbitrary 'gain' maps G_i can be introduced at the input. Thus the admissible controls are of the form

$$u(t) = F x(t) + \sum_{i=1}^{k} G_i v_i(t) ,$$

where F: $\mathcal{X} \to \mathcal{U}$, G_i: $\mathcal{U} \to \mathcal{U}$ and $v_i(t) \in \mathcal{U}$. The $v_i(\cdot)$ are the new external inputs. The resulting signal flow graph is shown in Fig. 9.1.

The c.s. generated by the control $v_i(\cdot)$ is

$$\mathcal{R}_i = \langle A + BF | \operatorname{Im}(BG_i) \rangle . \tag{2}$$

Our first objective is to arrange that $v_i(\cdot)$ does not affect the outputs $z_j(\cdot)$ for $j \neq i$. Thus we must have

$$D_j \mathcal{R}_i = 0 , \qquad j \neq i , \quad i \in \underline{k} , \quad j \in \underline{k} . \tag{3}$$

Secondly, if $v_i(\cdot)$ is to control the output z_i completely, we must be able to reach each vector in the image of D_i by suitable choice of $v_i(\cdot)$, which means that

$$D_i \mathcal{R}_i = \operatorname{Im} D_i , \qquad i \in \underline{k} . \tag{4}$$

Thus our problem can be initially stated as follows. <u>Given</u> A, B <u>and</u> D_i ($i \in \underline{k}$), <u>find (if possible)</u> F <u>and</u> G_i ($i \in \underline{k}$) <u>such that (3) and (4) are true for the</u> $\mathcal{R}_i$ <u>defined by (2).</u>

9.2 Restricted Decoupling Problem (RDP)

Recalling Proposition 5.3 we see that (2) can be written

$$\mathcal{R}_i = \langle A + BF | \mathcal{B} \cap \mathcal{R}_i \rangle , \qquad i \in \underline{k} . \tag{5}$$

Write $\mathcal{K}_i \triangleq \operatorname{Ker} D_i$ ($i \in \underline{k}$). Then (3) becomes

$$\mathcal{R}_i \subset \bigcap_{j \neq i} \mathcal{K}_j , \qquad i \in \underline{k} . \tag{6}$$

Finally, it is easily verified that (4) is equivalent to

$$\mathcal{R}_i + \mathcal{K}_i = \mathcal{X}, \qquad i \in \underline{k}. \tag{7}$$

Thus the algebraic Restricted Decoupling Problem (RDP) can be stated: Given A, B and subspaces $\mathcal{K}_i \subset \mathcal{X}$ ($i \in \underline{k}$), find (if possible) a map $F: \mathcal{X} \to \mathcal{U}$ and c.s. $\mathcal{R}_i$ ($i \in \underline{k}$) such that (5), (6) and (7) are true. The problem is 'restricted' in the sense that only state feedback is to be utilized, with no augmentation of system dynamic order.

Condition (5) will be referred to as the compatibility condition. In general, if $\mathcal{V}_i \subset \mathcal{X}$ are subspaces such that

$$\underline{F}(\mathcal{V}_i) \neq \emptyset, \qquad i \in \underline{k}, \tag{8}$$

it by no means follows that

$$\bigcap_{i=1}^{k} \underline{F}(\mathcal{V}_i) \neq \emptyset. \tag{9}$$

That is, although there exist F_i ($i \in \underline{k}$) such that

$$(A + BF_i)\mathcal{V}_i \subset \mathcal{V}_i, \qquad i \in \underline{k},$$

it need not be true that some F exists such that

$$(A + BF)\mathcal{V}_i \subset \mathcal{V}_i$$

for all $i \in \underline{k}$ simultaneously. If (9) does hold, the family $\mathcal{V}_i$ ($i \in \underline{k}$) is compatible relative to the pair (A, B). A simple sufficient (but not necessary) condition for compatibility is that (8) hold and the $\mathcal{V}_i$ be independent.

Recalling Proposition 5.3 we see that (5) states that the $\mathcal{R}_i$ are compatible in the sense just defined.

Conditions (6) are the noninteraction conditions and (7) are the output controllability conditions. In these terms, RDP amounts to seeking compatible c.s. which are small enough to guarantee noninteraction, yet large enough to ensure output controllability.

No special restrictions have been placed on the subspaces $\mathcal{K}_i$. However, we may as well assume that

$$\mathcal{K}_i \neq \mathcal{X}, \qquad i \in \underline{k};$$

otherwise $D_i = 0$, i.e., the ith output is identically zero, and we may take $\mathcal{R}_i = 0$ in (2). Next, if RDP is solvable, it is clearly necessary that the subspaces $\mathcal{K}_i^{\perp} \subset \mathcal{X}'$ be independent (i.e., the row spaces of arbitrary matrix representations of the D_i be independent). For if independence fails, then for some $\ell \in \underline{k}$,

$$\mathcal{K}_\ell^\perp \cap \left(\sum_{j \neq \ell} \mathcal{K}_j^\perp \right) \neq 0 ,$$

or

$$\mathcal{K}_\ell + \bigcap_{j \neq \ell} \mathcal{K}_j \neq \mathcal{X} ,$$

and (7) must fail at $i = \ell$. Intuitively, we are attempting to control a variable in the $\ell^{\underline{th}}$ output 'block' which also appears as a linear combination of variables in the remaining output blocks, and if the controls are noninteracting, this is clearly impossible.

Finally, we may as well assume that the pair (A, B) is controllable. Otherwise, we may structure the system as in Ex. 1.1, picking out the controllable subspace $\langle A | \mathcal{B} \rangle$. If the induced map $\bar{A}$ on $\mathcal{X}/\langle A | \mathcal{B} \rangle$ is unstable, the decoupling problem itself is unrealistic. If $\bar{A}$ is stable, then the coset $\bar{x}(t) \to 0$ as $t \to \infty$, and we shall assume that convergence is fast enough for us to neglect the corresponding transient component of $x(\cdot)$ in $\langle A | \mathcal{B} \rangle$.

Returning to RDP, write

$$\hat{\mathcal{K}}_i \triangleq \bigcap_{j \neq i} \mathcal{K}_j , \qquad i \in \underline{k} . \tag{10}$$

On heuristic grounds, it is plausible to attack the problem as follows: find

$$\mathcal{R}_i^* \triangleq \sup \underline{\mathcal{C}}(\hat{\mathcal{K}}_i) , \qquad i \in \underline{k} . \tag{11}$$

The $\mathcal{R}_i^*$ will then satisfy (6). If for some i, $\mathcal{R}_i^*$ fails to satisfy (7), then clearly RDP is not solvable, since $\mathcal{R}_i^*$ is supremal. Suppose, then, that $\mathcal{R}_i^*$ satisfies (7) for each $i \in \underline{k}$. It remains to determine whether the $\mathcal{R}_i^*$ are compatible. If they are, we are done. If they are not, the problem remains unsettled, as there might exist a family of c.s. $\mathcal{R}_1, \ldots, \mathcal{R}_k$ for which $\mathcal{R}_i \subset \mathcal{R}_i^*$ with strict inclusion for some i, with the $\mathcal{R}_i$ all large enough to satisfy (7); and this set of smaller $\mathcal{R}_i$ might now be compatible. As we lack a systematic procedure for scanning over all families of compatible $\mathcal{R}_i$, necessary and sufficient conditions for the solvability of RDP, in the general case, are not yet known.

Luckily, the suggested method works in a special case, and later we shall see that it can be made to work in general, if we allow extension of the state space through dynamic compensation.

9.3 Solution of RDP: Outputs Complete

Let us make the additional assumption that

$$\bigcap_{i=1}^{k} \mathcal{K}_i = 0 . \tag{12}$$

This means simply that if $D_i x = 0$ for all $i \in \underline{k}$ then $x = 0$, i.e., the map $D: \mathcal{X} \to \mathcal{Z}$ defined by

$$Dx \triangleq D_1 x + \cdots + D_k x \tag{13}$$

is monic. In this sense the set of outputs is 'complete'.

THEOREM 9.1. <u>Subject to assumption (12), RDP is solvable if and only if</u>

$$\mathcal{R}_i^* + \mathcal{K}_i = \mathcal{X}, \qquad i \in \underline{k}, \tag{14}$$

<u>where the $\mathcal{R}_i^*$ are defined by (10) and (11).</u>

PROOF: If (14) holds, then (6) and (7) are true for the $\mathcal{R}_i^*$. We show next that the $\hat{\mathcal{K}}_i$ are independent. Indeed

$$\hat{\mathcal{K}}_i \cap \sum_{j \neq i} \hat{\mathcal{K}}_j = \left(\bigcap_{r \neq i} \mathcal{K}_r \right) \cap \sum_{j \neq i} \left(\bigcap_{s \neq j} \mathcal{K}_s \right)$$

$$\subset \left(\bigcap_{r \neq i} \mathcal{K}_r \right) \cap \mathcal{K}_i = \bigcap_r \mathcal{K}_r = 0 .$$

Since $\mathcal{R}_i^* \subset \hat{\mathcal{K}}_i$ $(i \in \underline{k})$ it follows that the $\mathcal{R}_i^*$ are independent, hence compatible.

Conversely, from the fact that the $\mathcal{R}_i^*$ are supremal relative to the condition (6), it follows that (14) is necessary. ∎

Independence of the $\mathcal{R}_i^*$ implies not only compatibility but also that the spectrum of $A + BF$ can be assigned to a suitable region $\mathbb{C}_g$ of the complex plane. For a precise statement, write

$$\rho_i \triangleq d(\mathcal{R}_i^*), \qquad i \in \underline{k}; \qquad \rho_0 \triangleq n - \sum_{i=1}^{k} \rho_i .$$

We have

THEOREM 9.2. <u>Let</u> (A, B) <u>be controllable and assume that (12) holds. Let</u> Λ_j $(j = 0, 1, \ldots, k)$ <u>be a symmetric set of</u> ρ_j <u>complex numbers. There exists</u>

$$F \in \bigcap_{i=1}^{k} \underline{F}(\mathcal{R}_i^*)$$

<u>such that</u>

$$\sigma\left[(A + BF) | \mathcal{R}_i^*\right] = \Lambda_i , \qquad i \in \underline{k} ,$$

and

$$\sigma(A + BF) = \dot{\bigcup_{j=0}^{k}} \Lambda_j .$$

PROOF: By Theorem 5.1 there exist $F_i : \mathcal{X} \to \mathcal{U}$ such that

$$\sigma\left[(A + BF_i) | \mathcal{R}_i^*\right] = \Lambda_i , \qquad i \in \underline{k} .$$

Since (12) holds it follows as in the proof of Theorem 9.1 that the $\mathcal{R}_i^*$ ($i \in \underline{k}$) are independent, hence there exists $F_0 : \mathcal{X} \to \mathcal{U}$ such that

$$F_0 | \mathcal{R}_i^* = F_i | \mathcal{R}_i^* , \qquad i \in \underline{k} .$$

Clearly

$$F_0 \in \bigcap_{i=1}^{k} \underline{F}(\mathcal{R}_i^*) .$$

Write

$$\mathcal{R} \triangleq \mathcal{R}_1^* \oplus \cdots \oplus \mathcal{R}_k^* .$$

Then $F_0 \in \underline{F}(\mathcal{R})$ and by Proposition 4.1 there exists $F : \mathcal{X} \to \mathcal{U}$ such that

$$F | \mathcal{R} = F_0 | \mathcal{R}$$

and

$$\sigma(A + BF) = \Lambda_0 \,\dot{\cup}\, \sigma[(A + BF) | \mathcal{R}] = \Lambda_0 \,\dot{\cup}\, \dot{\bigcup_{j=1}^{k}} \Lambda_j . \blacksquare$$

Our success in solving RDP under the condition (12) depended strongly, of course, on the fact that (12) made the $\mathcal{R}_i^*$ independent. Although in general the $\mathcal{R}_i^*$ will not be independent, they can be transformed into new c.s. which are, by suitable imbedding in an extended state space, as we now establish.

9.4 Extended Decoupling Problem (EDP)

Suppose the system equations (1) are augmented by the equations of n_a auxiliary integrators with scalar inputs u_{ai} and outputs x_{ai}:

$$\dot{x}_{ai} = u_{ai} , \qquad i \in \underline{n}_a . \tag{15}$$

For notational convenience, rewrite (15) as

$$\dot{x}_a = B_a u_a ,$$

where $x_a \in \mathcal{X}_a$, $u_a \in \mathcal{U}_a$ and $B_a: \mathcal{U}_a \approx \mathcal{X}_a$. Thus

$$d(\mathcal{X}_a) = d(\mathcal{U}_a) = n_a .$$

It is convenient to imbed (1) and (15) in common state and input spaces. For this, construct an extended state space as the external direct sum

$$\mathcal{X}_e = \mathcal{X} \oplus \mathcal{X}_a .$$

Similarly, define the extended input space

$$\mathcal{U}_e = \mathcal{U} \oplus \mathcal{U}_a .$$

The maps A, B, B_a have natural extensions defined as follows:

$$A_e: \mathcal{X}_e \to \mathcal{X}_e, \qquad x + x_a \mapsto Ax$$

$$B_e: \mathcal{U}_e \to \mathcal{X}_e, \qquad u + u_a \mapsto Bu$$

$$B_{ae}: \mathcal{U}_e \to \mathcal{X}_e, \qquad u + u_a \mapsto B_a u_a .$$

For simplicity we shall omit the subscript e on these maps, so that from now on

$$A\mathcal{X}_a = B\mathcal{U}_a = B_a\mathcal{U} = 0$$

and

$$\mathcal{B}_a = \operatorname{Im} B_a = \mathcal{X}_a .$$

Let $P: \mathcal{X}_e \to \mathcal{X}_e$ be the projection on $\mathcal{X}$ along $\mathcal{X}_a$:

$$P|\mathcal{X} = 1_{\mathcal{X}}, \qquad P|\mathcal{X}_a = 0 .$$

Thus

$$PA = AP = A, \qquad PB = B, \qquad PB_a = 0 .$$

We now define an <u>extended controllability subspace</u> (e.c.s.) to be a c.s. for the extended pair $(A, B + B_a)$. If $\mathcal{V} \subset \mathcal{X}_e$, write $\underline{F}_e(\mathcal{V})$ for the family of maps $F: \mathcal{X}_e \to \mathcal{U}_e$ such that

$$[A + (B + B_a) F] \mathcal{V} \subset \mathcal{V} .$$

It is now natural to introduce the

Extended Decoupling Problem (EDP):

Given the original maps A: $\mathcal{X} \to \mathcal{X}$, B: $\mathcal{U} \to \mathcal{X}$ and subspaces $\mathcal{K}_i \subset \mathcal{X}$ ($i \in \underline{k}$), find (if possible) $\mathcal{X}_a$ (i.e., n_a) and e.c.s. $\mathcal{S}_i$ ($i \in \underline{k}$) such that

$$\bigcap_{i=1}^{k} \underline{F}_e(\mathcal{S}_i) \neq \emptyset \,, \tag{16}$$

$$\mathcal{S}_i \subset \bigcap_{j \neq i} (\mathcal{K}_j \oplus \mathcal{X}_a) \,, \qquad i \in \underline{k} \,, \tag{17}$$

and

$$\mathcal{S}_i + (\mathcal{K}_i \oplus \mathcal{X}_a) = \mathcal{X} \oplus \mathcal{X}_a \,, \qquad i \in \underline{k} \,. \tag{18}$$

Conditions (16) – (18) express the requirements, respectively, of compatibility, noninteraction and output controllability for the extended problem. Thus EDP has the same formal appearance as RDP, but valuable flexibility is gained from the special structure of the extended pair $(A, B + B_a)$ and the extended output kernels $\mathcal{K}_i \oplus \mathcal{X}_a$.

We can easily justify EDP as the 'correct' description of decoupling by dynamic compensation: the output relations $z_i = D_i x$ ($i \in \underline{k}$) of the original system are preserved on replacing $\mathcal{K}_i$ by $\mathcal{K}_i \oplus \mathcal{X}_a$, or equivalently by defining extensions D_{ia} of the D_i to vanish on $\mathcal{X}_a$; no additional inputs (vectors in $\mathcal{B}$) to the original system (1) are postulated; and, subject to the latter constraint, full linear coupling is allowed between the two systems (1) and (15). The corresponding, more elaborate signal flow is shown in Fig. 9.2, where the extended control has matrix representation

$$\begin{bmatrix} u \\ u_a \end{bmatrix} = \begin{bmatrix} F_{11} & F_{12} \\ F_{21} & F_{22} \end{bmatrix} \begin{bmatrix} x \\ x_a \end{bmatrix} + \begin{bmatrix} G_{11} & \cdots & G_{1k} \\ G_{21} & \cdots & G_{2k} \end{bmatrix} \begin{bmatrix} v_1 \\ \vdots \\ v_k \end{bmatrix} .$$

9.5 Solution of EDP

The fundamental result of decoupling theory is the following.

THEOREM 9.3. For the RDP defined in Section 9.2 let

$$\mathcal{R}_i^* \triangleq \sup \underline{\mathcal{C}}\left(\bigcap_{j \neq i} \mathcal{K}_j \right) , \qquad i \in \underline{k} \,,$$

Then the corresponding EDP of Section 9.4 is solvable if and only if

$$\mathcal{R}_i^* + \mathcal{K}_i = \mathcal{X} \,, \qquad i \in \underline{k} \,. \tag{19}$$

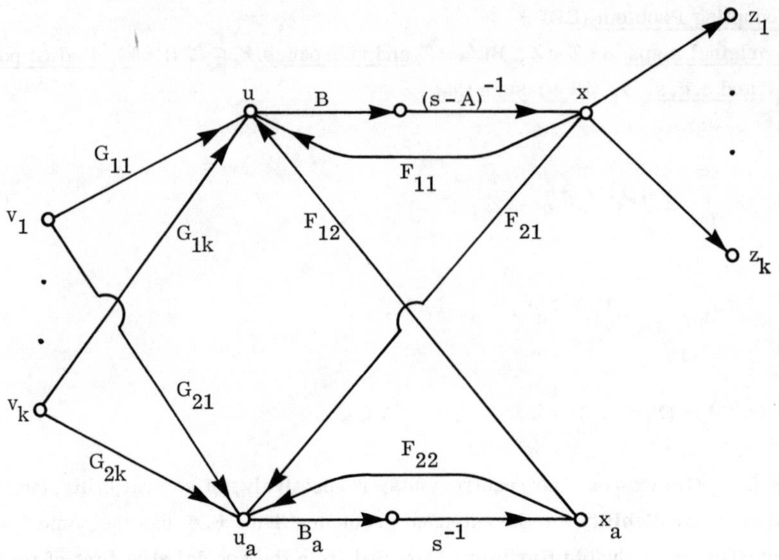

Fig. 9.2.

Signal Flow: Solution of EDP.

Informally, the theorem states that decoupling can be achieved by dynamic compensation if and only if the largest noninteracting c.s. of RDP satisfy merely the output controllability conditions of RDP. The crucial fact is that dynamic compensation makes it possible to satisfy the compatibility condition of EDP.

To prove Theorem 9.3 we need two preliminary results which relate c.s. to their extensions.

LEMMA 9.1. *If $\mathscr{S}$ is an e.c.s. then $P\mathscr{S}$ is a c.s.*

PROOF: We shall apply to $\mathscr{S}$ the results of Chapter 5. Since $\mathscr{S}$ is an e.c.s., $A\mathscr{S} \subset \mathscr{S} + \mathscr{B} + \mathscr{B}_a$. Therefore

$$A(P\mathscr{S}) = PA\mathscr{S} = P\mathscr{S} + \mathscr{B},$$

so that $\underline{F}(P\mathscr{S}) \neq \emptyset$. Also, by Theorem 5.3, $\mathscr{S}^{\mu} \uparrow \mathscr{S}$, where

$$\mathscr{S}^0 = 0 ; \qquad \mathscr{S}^{\mu} = \mathscr{S} \cap \left(A\mathscr{S}^{\mu-1} + \mathscr{B} + \mathscr{B}_a\right), \qquad \mu \in \underline{n+n_a} . \tag{20}$$

Since $\operatorname{Ker} P = \mathscr{X}_a = \mathscr{B}_a$ we have

$$\left(\mathscr{S} + A\mathscr{S}^{\mu-1} + \mathscr{B} + \mathscr{B}_a\right) \cap \operatorname{Ker} P$$

$$= \mathscr{X}_a$$

$$= \mathscr{S} \cap \operatorname{Ker} P + \left(A\mathscr{S}^{\mu-1} + \mathscr{B} + \mathscr{B}_a\right) \cap \operatorname{Ker} P .$$

Hence we can apply (0.7), (0.8) to (20) to obtain

$$P\mathscr{S}^{\mu} = P\mathscr{S} \cap P\left(A\mathscr{S}^{\mu-1} + \mathscr{B} + \mathscr{B}_a\right)$$

$$= P\mathscr{S} \cap (AP\mathscr{S}^{\mu-1} + \mathscr{B}) .$$

Since $P\mathscr{S}^{\mu} \uparrow P\mathscr{S}$, Theorem 5.3 implies that $P\mathscr{S}$ is a c.s. ▮

LEMMA 9.2. *Let $\mathscr{R}$ be a c.s. and let $E: \mathscr{X} \oplus \mathscr{X}_a \to \mathscr{X} \oplus \mathscr{X}_a$ be an arbitrary map with $\operatorname{Im} E \subset \mathscr{X}_a$. Then $\mathscr{S} \triangleq (P+E)\mathscr{R}$ is an e.c.s.*

PROOF: Since

$$A\mathscr{S} = A\mathscr{R} \subset \mathscr{R} + \mathscr{B} = P\mathscr{S} + \mathscr{B} \subset \mathscr{S} + \mathscr{B} + \operatorname{Ker} P = \mathscr{S} + \mathscr{B} + \mathscr{B}_a ,$$

we have $\underline{F}_e(\mathscr{S}) \neq \emptyset$. Also, $\mathcal{R}^\mu \uparrow \mathcal{R}$, where

$$\mathcal{R}^0 = 0\,; \qquad \mathcal{R}^\mu = \mathcal{R} \cap (A\mathcal{R}^{\mu-1} + \mathcal{B})\,, \qquad \mu \in \underline{n}\,.$$

Define

$$\mathscr{S}^0 = 0\,; \qquad \mathscr{S}^\mu = \mathscr{S} \cap \left(A\mathscr{S}^{\mu-1} + \mathcal{B} + \mathcal{B}_a\right), \qquad \mu \in \underline{n+n_a}\,. \tag{21}$$

Then $\mathscr{S}^0 \supset (P+E)\mathcal{R}^0$, and if $\mathscr{S}^{\mu-1} \supset (P+E)\mathcal{R}^{\mu-1}$, (21) yields

$$\begin{aligned}
\mathscr{S}^\mu &\supset [(P+E)\mathcal{R}] \cap \left[A(P+E)\mathcal{R}^{\mu-1} + \mathcal{B} + \mathcal{X}_a\right] \\
&= [(P+E)\mathcal{R}] \cap \left[A\mathcal{R}^{\mu-1} + \mathcal{B} + \mathcal{X}_a\right] \\
&\supset [(P+E)\mathcal{R}] \cap \left[(P+E)\left(A\mathcal{R}^{\mu-1} + \mathcal{B} + \mathcal{X}_a\right)\right] \\
&\supset (P+E)\left[\mathcal{R} \cap \left(A\mathcal{R}^{\mu-1} + \mathcal{B} + \mathcal{X}_a\right)\right] \\
&= (P+E)\left[\mathcal{R} \cap \left(A\mathcal{R}^{\mu-1} + \mathcal{B}\right)\right] \\
&= (P+E)\mathcal{R}^\mu\,.
\end{aligned}$$

Thus for all μ,

$$\mathscr{S} \supset \mathscr{S}^\mu \supset (P+E)\mathcal{R}^\mu \uparrow (P+E)\mathcal{R} = \mathscr{S}\,,$$

hence $\mathscr{S}^\mu \uparrow \mathscr{S}$, so $\mathscr{S}$ is an e.c.s., as claimed. ▮

PROOF of Theorem 9.3. (Only if) Suppose $\mathscr{S}_i$ ($i \in \underline{k}$) is a solution of EDP. By (17),

$$P\mathscr{S}_i \subset P\left[\bigcap_{j\neq i}\left(\mathcal{K}_j \oplus \mathcal{X}_a\right)\right] = \bigcap_{j\neq i} \mathcal{K}_j\,, \tag{22}$$

and by (18),

$$P\mathscr{S}_i + \mathcal{K}_i = \mathcal{X}\,. \tag{23}$$

By Lemma 9.1 and (22)

$$P\mathscr{S}_i \in \underline{\mathcal{C}}\left(\bigcap_{j\neq i} \mathcal{K}_j\right).$$

Therefore $P\mathscr{S}_i \subset \mathcal{R}_i^*$ ($i \in \underline{k}$), and (19) follows from (23).

(If) Suppose (19) is true. Let $\mathcal{X}_{ai}$ be a linear space over $\mathbb{R}$ with $\mathcal{X}_{ai} \approx \mathcal{R}_i^*$ ($i \in \underline{k}$), and introduce the external direct sum

$$\mathcal{X}_a \triangleq \bigoplus_{i=1}^{k} \mathcal{X}_{ai} .$$

Let $E_i : \mathcal{X} \oplus \mathcal{X}_a \to \mathcal{X} \oplus \mathcal{X}_a$ be a map with the properties

$$\mathcal{R}_i^* \cap \operatorname{Ker} E_i = 0 , \qquad i \in \underline{k} ,$$

and

$$\operatorname{Im} E_i = E_i \mathcal{R}_i^* = \mathcal{X}_{ai} , \qquad i \in \underline{k} .$$

Thus E_i is monic on $\mathcal{R}_i^*$ and zero on a complement of $\mathcal{R}_i^*$ in $\mathcal{X} \oplus \mathcal{X}_a$. Define

$$\mathcal{J}_i = (P + E_i) \mathcal{R}_i^* , \qquad i \in \underline{k} . \tag{24}$$

By Lemma 9.2, $\mathcal{J}_i$ is an e.c.s. It is easily checked as well that the $\mathcal{J}_i$ ($i \in \underline{k}$) are independent, hence compatible. Next, from

$$\mathcal{R}_i^* \subset \bigcap_{j \neq i} \mathcal{K}_j , \qquad i \in \underline{k} ,$$

there follows

$$\mathcal{J}_i \subset (P + E_i) \bigcap_{j \neq i} \mathcal{K}_j \subset \left(\bigcap_{j \neq i} \mathcal{K}_j \right) \oplus \mathcal{X}_a$$

$$= \bigcap_{j \neq i} \left(\mathcal{K}_j \oplus \mathcal{X}_a \right) , \qquad i \in \underline{k} ,$$

which verifies (17). From (19) and (24) we have

$$\mathcal{J}_i + (P + E_i) \mathcal{K}_i = (P + E_i) \mathcal{X} . \tag{25}$$

Because

$$(P + E_i) \mathcal{K}_i + \mathcal{X}_a = \mathcal{K}_i \oplus \mathcal{X}_a$$

and

$$(P + E_i) \mathcal{X} + \mathcal{X}_a = \mathcal{X} \oplus \mathcal{X}_a ,$$

(18) results on adding $\mathcal{X}_a$ to both sides of (25). ∎

Since the e.c.s. $\mathscr{S}_i$ constructed in the proof of Theorem 9.3 are independent it follows, as in the proof of Theorem 9.2, that

$$F \in \bigcap_{i=1}^{k} \underline{F}_e(\mathscr{S}_i)$$

can be chosen such that, for each $i \in \underline{k}$,

$$\sigma[(A + (B+B_a)F) | \mathscr{S}_i]$$

is a given symmetric set of $d(\mathscr{S}_i)$ complex numbers.

9.6 Naive Extension

The order of dynamic compensation introduced in the proof of Theorem 9.3, namely

$$n_a = \sum_{i=1}^{k} d(\mathscr{R}_i^*), \tag{26}$$

is unnecessarily large. On grounds of reliability, economy or esthetics it may be desirable to keep the dynamic order of compensation small. While determination of the strictly minimal number of auxiliary integrators required is apparently quite difficult, it is nevertheless easy to improve 'naively' on the bound (26). We have the following.

THEOREM 9.4. If EDP is solvable, the order of dynamic compensation required is no greater than

$$n_a \triangleq \sum_{i=1}^{k} d(\mathscr{R}_i^*) - d\left(\sum_{i=1}^{k} \mathscr{R}_i^*\right). \tag{27}$$

For the proof we need

LEMMA 9.3. Let $\mathscr{R}_1, \ldots, \mathscr{R}_k$ be arbitrary subspaces of $\mathscr{X}$. Define

$$n_a \triangleq \sum_{i=1}^{k} d(\mathscr{R}_i) - d\left(\sum_{i=1}^{k} \mathscr{R}_i\right).$$

Then if $d(\mathscr{X}_a) = n_a$ and $\mathscr{X}_e = \mathscr{X} \oplus \mathscr{X}_a$, there exist maps $E_i: \mathscr{X}_e \rightarrow \mathscr{X}_e$ $(i \in \underline{k})$ such that

$$\text{Im } E_i \subset \mathcal{X}_a, \qquad i \in \underline{k},$$

<u>and the subspaces</u> $\mathcal{S}_i \triangleq (1+E_i)\mathcal{R}_i \ (i \in \underline{k})$ <u>are independent</u>.

PROOF: Write $\mathcal{T}_1 = 0$ and

$$\mathcal{T}_i = \mathcal{R}_i \cap \sum_{j=1}^{i-1} \mathcal{R}_j, \qquad i = 2, \ldots, k.$$

Then

$$\sum_{i=1}^{k} d(\mathcal{T}_i) = \sum_{i=2}^{k} \left[d(\mathcal{R}_i) + d\left(\sum_{j=1}^{i-1} \mathcal{R}_j\right) - d\left(\sum_{j=1}^{i} \mathcal{R}_j\right)\right]$$

$$= \sum_{i=1}^{k} d(\mathcal{R}_i) - d\left(\sum_{i=1}^{k} \mathcal{R}_i\right) = d(\mathcal{X}_a). \tag{28}$$

By (28) there exist maps $E_i: \mathcal{X}_e \to \mathcal{X}_e$ such that

$$\mathcal{T}_i \approx E_i \mathcal{T}_i = \text{Im } E_i \subset \mathcal{X}_a, \qquad i \in \underline{k},$$

and the subspaces $\text{Im } E_i \ (i \in \underline{k})$ are independent. Suppose, contrary to what is claimed, that the $\mathcal{S}_i = (1+E_i)\mathcal{R}_i$ are not independent. Let $i \geq 2$ be the greatest integer such that

$$\mathcal{S}_i \cap \sum_{j \neq i} \mathcal{S}_j \neq 0.$$

There is $x \neq 0$ such that

$$x = (1+E_i)\, r_i = \sum_{j=1}^{i-1} (1+E_j)\, r_j,$$

where $r_j \in \mathcal{R}_j \ (j \in \underline{i})$; so

$$r_i = \sum_{j=1}^{i-1} r_j$$

and therefore $r_i \in \mathcal{T}_i$. By independence of the $\text{Im } E_i$ and the fact that $\text{Im } E_i \subset \mathcal{X}_a$, there follows $E_i r_i = 0$, and as $\text{Ker } E_i \cap \mathcal{T}_i = 0$, there results $r_i = 0$, hence $x = 0$, a contradiction. ▌

PROOF of Theorem 9.4. With E_i and $\mathscr{S}_i$ as in Lemma 9.3 (with $\mathcal{R}_i^*$ in place of $\mathcal{R}_i$) we have that the $\mathscr{S}_i$ $(i \in \underline{k})$ are independent. This with Lemma 9.2 implies that the $\mathscr{S}_i$ are compatible e.c.s. That the $\mathscr{S}_i$ also satisfy (17) and (18) follows exactly as in the proof of Theorem 9.3. That is, the $\mathscr{S}_i$ $(i \in \underline{k})$ provide a solution of EDP, with n_a given by (27). ▮

Just as before, independence of the $\mathscr{S}_i$ implies that the spectra of the maps

$$[A + (B + B_a) F] \,|\, \mathscr{S}_i$$

can be assigned arbitrarily and independently by suitable choice of F.

9.7 Example

Let $n = 5$ and

$$A = \begin{bmatrix} 0 & 1 & 0 & 0 & 0 \\ 0 & 0 & 0 & 0 & 0 \\ 0 & 0 & 1 & 1 & 0 \\ 1 & 0 & 0 & 0 & 1 \\ 0 & 0 & 0 & 0 & 0 \end{bmatrix}, \qquad B = \begin{bmatrix} 0 & 1 \\ 1 & 0 \\ 0 & 0 \\ 0 & 0 \\ 0 & 1 \end{bmatrix},$$

$$D_1 = \begin{bmatrix} 1 & 0 & 0 & 0 & 0 \end{bmatrix}, \qquad D_2 = \begin{bmatrix} 0 & 0 & 0 & 0 & 1 \end{bmatrix}.$$

It is easily checked that

$$\mathcal{R}_1^* = \mathcal{K}_2, \qquad \mathcal{R}_2^* = \mathcal{K}_1.$$

Since

$$\mathcal{R}_1^* \cap \mathcal{R}_2^* = \operatorname{Im} \begin{bmatrix} 0 & 0 & 0 \\ 1 & 0 & 0 \\ 0 & 1 & 0 \\ 0 & 0 & 1 \\ 0 & 0 & 0 \end{bmatrix}$$

is not (A, B)-invariant, the subspaces $\mathcal{R}_1^*$ and $\mathcal{R}_2^*$ are certainly not compatible. Nevertheless, by Theorem 9.3 EDP is solvable, and by Theorem 9.4 we may take

$$n_a = d(\mathcal{R}_1^*) + d(\mathcal{R}_2^*) - d(\mathcal{R}_1^* + \mathcal{R}_2^*)$$

$$= d(\mathcal{R}_1^* \cap \mathcal{R}_2^*) = 3.$$

In the notation of the proof of Lemma 9.3 we have $\mathcal{T}_1 = 0$ and $\mathcal{T}_2 = \mathcal{R}_1^* \cap \mathcal{R}_2^*$. Thus we may define

$$\mathscr{S}_1 = \mathrm{Im}\begin{bmatrix}1&0&0&0\\0&1&0&0\\0&0&1&0\\0&0&0&1\\0&0&0&0\\0&0&0&0\\0&0&0&0\\0&0&0&0\end{bmatrix}, \qquad \mathscr{S}_2 = \mathrm{Im}\begin{bmatrix}0&0&0&0\\1&0&0&0\\0&1&0&0\\0&0&1&0\\0&0&0&1\\1&0&0&0\\0&1&0&0\\0&0&1&0\end{bmatrix}.$$

The design can now be completed by choosing $F \in \underline{F}_e(\mathscr{S}_1) \cap \underline{F}_e(\mathscr{S}_2)$ such that $A+(B+B_a)F$ has a suitable spectrum.

9.8 Partial Decoupling

In certain applications it may be appropriate to replace the stringent requirement of complete dynamic noninteraction by a weaker constraint under which the outputs z_i are only partially decoupled. Suppose, for instance, that the z_i $(i \in \underline{k})$ are to be controlled sequentially rather than simultaneously. First z_1 is controlled by v_1, possibly changing the values of $z_2, \ldots, z_k$; then z_2 is controlled by v_2, with the requirement that the action of v_2 on z_1 be nil, but possibly changing the values of $z_3, \ldots, z_k$; and so forth, with z_k controlled by v_k without influencing $z_1, \ldots, z_{k-1}$. It is easy to see that this situation can be formalized, in our previous notation, as the

Triangular Decoupling Problem (TDP):

Given A, B and $D_1, \ldots, D_k$, find F and c.s. $\mathscr{R}_1, \ldots, \mathscr{R}_k$ such that

$$\mathscr{R}_i = \langle A + BF \mid \mathscr{B} \cap \mathscr{R}_i \rangle, \qquad i \in \underline{k},$$

$$\mathscr{R}_i \subset \bigcap_{j=1}^{i-1} \operatorname{Ker} D_j, \qquad i \in \underline{k}, \tag{29}$$

and

$$\mathscr{R}_i + \operatorname{Ker} D_i = \mathscr{X}, \qquad i \in \underline{k}.$$

In (29) the vacuous condition at $i = 1$ just says $\mathscr{R}_1 \subset \mathscr{X}$. Proof of the following easy result is left to the reader.

THEOREM 9.5. TDP is solvable if and only if

$$\mathscr{R}_i^* + \operatorname{Ker} D_i = \mathscr{X}, \qquad i \in \underline{k},$$

where $\mathcal{R}_i^*$ is the supremal c.s. subject to (29). Furthermore, if $\Lambda_i \subset \mathbb{C}$ ($i \in \underline{k}$) is symmetric with $|\Lambda_i| = d(\mathcal{R}_i^*/\mathcal{R}_{i+1}^*)$ ($i \in \underline{k-1}$), $|\Lambda_k| = d(\mathcal{R}_k^*)$, there exists

$$F \in \bigcap_{i=1}^{k} \underline{F}(\mathcal{R}_i^*)$$

such that

$$\sigma\left[(A+BF) \,\middle|\, \sum_{i=1}^{k} \mathcal{R}_i^*\right] = \dot{\bigcup_{i=1}^{k}} \Lambda_i .$$

Noninteraction constraints other than the 'triangular' are also readily treated; in general one must exploit extension. In this direction we are led finally to the

General Extended Decoupling Problem (GEDP)*

Given A, B and subspaces $\mathcal{K}_i \subset \mathcal{X}$, $\hat{\mathcal{K}}_i \subset \mathcal{X}$ ($i \in \underline{k}$), find $n_a = d(\mathcal{X}_a) = d(\mathcal{U}_a)$, a map

$$F: \mathcal{X} \oplus \mathcal{X}_a \to \mathcal{U} \oplus \mathcal{U}_a ,$$

and e.c.s. $\mathcal{S}_i$ ($i \in \underline{k}$), such that

$$\mathcal{S}_i = \langle A + (B + B_a) F \,|\, (\mathcal{B} \oplus \mathcal{B}_a) \cap \mathcal{S}_i \rangle , \qquad i \in \underline{k} ,$$

$$\mathcal{S}_i \subset \hat{\mathcal{K}}_i \oplus \mathcal{X}_a , \qquad i \in \underline{k} ,$$

and

$$\mathcal{S}_i + (\mathcal{K}_i \oplus \mathcal{X}_a) = \mathcal{X} \oplus \mathcal{X}_a , \qquad i \in \underline{k} .$$

Here no special relation is postulated among the $\mathcal{K}_i$ and $\hat{\mathcal{K}}_i$, although it is clear that GEDP is solvable only if $\mathcal{K}_i + \hat{\mathcal{K}}_i = \mathcal{X}$ ($i \in \underline{k}$). We have

THEOREM 9.6. GEDP is solvable if and only if

$$\mathcal{R}_i^* + \mathcal{K}_i = \mathcal{X} , \qquad i \in \underline{k} , \tag{30}$$

where $\mathcal{R}_i^* \triangleq \sup \underline{\mathcal{C}}(\hat{\mathcal{K}}_i)$. Furthermore, if (30) holds one can take

$$n_a \le \sum_i d(\mathcal{R}_i^*) - d\left(\sum_i \mathcal{R}_i^*\right) .$$

---

* The notation is again that of Section 9.4.

The proof is straightforward mimicry of that of Theorem 9.3, combined with the result of Theorem 9.4, and is left to the reader.

9.9 Exercises

9.1 Compatibility of a family of subspaces

(i) Let $\mathcal{V}_1, \mathcal{V}_2$ be (A, B)-invariant. Show that $\mathcal{V}_1, \mathcal{V}_2$ are compatible if and only if $\mathcal{V}_1 \cap \mathcal{V}_2$ is (A, B)-invariant.

(ii) Show that the family $\{\mathcal{V}_i, i \in \underline{k}\}$ is compatible if and only if the set of linear matrix equations

$$W_i B F V_i = -W_i A V_i, \qquad i \in \underline{k},$$

has an $m \times n$ solution matrix F, for suitably chosen matrices W_i, V_i $(i \in \underline{k})$.

(iii) Let $\underline{\mathcal{V}} = \{\mathcal{V}_i, i \in \underline{k}\}$ be an arbitrary family of subspaces of $\mathcal{X}$. Let $\underline{\mathcal{L}}(\underline{\mathcal{V}}) = \underline{\mathcal{L}}$ be the smallest family of subspaces of $\mathcal{X}$ which contains each $\mathcal{V}_i$ $(i \in \underline{k})$ and is closed under subspace addition and intersection (it should be verified that $\underline{\mathcal{L}}$ exists and is unique!). $\underline{\mathcal{L}}$ is the <u>enveloping lattice</u> of the $\mathcal{V}_i$. Show that if $\underline{\mathcal{L}}$ is a distributive lattice (i.e., the intersection operation distributes over <u>arbitrary</u> sums), then $\underline{\mathcal{V}}$ is decomposable in the following sense: there exist an independent family $\mathcal{W}_j \subset \mathcal{X}$ $(j \in \underline{\ell})$ and index subsets $J_i \subset \underline{\ell}$ $(i \in \underline{k})$ such that

$$\mathcal{V}_i = \bigoplus_{j \in J_i} \mathcal{W}_j, \qquad i \in \underline{k}.$$

NOTE: It is not claimed that the $\mathcal{W}_j$ are unique or that they all belong to $\underline{\mathcal{L}}$.
HINT: Recall the usual Boolean decomposition of an arbitrary union of k subsets into a union of $2^k - 1$ disjoint subsets; first do the problem for $k = 3$, then generalize.

(iv) Show that a family $\{\mathcal{V}_i, i \in \underline{k}\}$ of (A, B)-invariant subspaces is compatible if each $\mathcal{V} \in \underline{\mathcal{L}}(\underline{\mathcal{V}})$ is (A, B)-invariant and $\underline{\mathcal{L}}(\underline{\mathcal{V}})$ is distributive. Show that the first of these conditions is necessary for compatibility, but not sufficient if $k \geq 3$. Show, however, that distributivity of $\underline{\mathcal{L}}(\underline{\mathcal{V}})$ is not necessary.

9.2 Show that conditions (4) and (7) are equivalent.

9.3 Prove the following converse to Lemma 9.3: Let $\mathcal{R}_i \subset \mathcal{X}$ $(i \in \underline{k})$ and suppose there exist $\mathcal{S}_i \subset \mathcal{X} \oplus \mathcal{X}_a$ $(i \in \underline{k})$ such that $P\mathcal{S}_i = \mathcal{R}_i$ $(i \in \underline{k})$ and the $\mathcal{S}_i$ are independent. Then

$$d(\mathcal{X}_a) \geq \sum_i d(\mathcal{R}_i) - d\left(\sum_i \mathcal{R}_i\right).$$

9.4 Show that the following decoupling problem is solvable, possibly with dynamic compensation. Design the decoupled system so that its poles all lie in the region

$$-3 \leq \mathcal{R}e\,\lambda \leq -1, \qquad |\mathcal{I}m\,\lambda| \leq 1$$

and give the signal flow graph for the final result.

$$A = \begin{bmatrix} 0 & 0 & 0 & 0 & 0 & 0 & 1 & 0 \\ 0 & 0 & 0 & 1 & 0 & 0 & 0 & 0 \\ 0 & 1 & 0 & -1 & 1 & -1 & 3 & 2 \\ 0 & 0 & 1 & 0 & 0 & 0 & 0 & 0 \\ 1 & 0 & 0 & 0 & 0 & 0 & 0 & 0 \\ 1 & -1 & 1 & 2 & 2 & 2 & 0 & -1 \\ -1 & 2 & -3 & 1 & 3 & 1 & 0 & -2 \\ 0 & 0 & 0 & 0 & 0 & 1 & 0 & 0 \end{bmatrix}, \quad B = \begin{bmatrix} 0 & 0 & 0 \\ 0 & 0 & 0 \\ 1 & 2 & -1 \\ 0 & 0 & 0 \\ 0 & 0 & 0 \\ 2 & 3 & 1 \\ -1 & 1 & 1 \\ 0 & 0 & 0 \end{bmatrix}$$

$$D_1 = \begin{bmatrix} 1 & 0 & -1 & 0 & 0 & 0 & 0 & 0 \\ 1 & 0 & 0 & 1 & -1 & 0 & 0 & 0 \\ 0 & 1 & 0 & 0 & 0 & 0 & -1 & 0 \end{bmatrix}$$

$$D_2 = \begin{bmatrix} 1 & 0 & 0 & 0 & -1 & 1 & 0 & -1 \\ 1 & 0 & 0 & 0 & 2 & -2 & 3 & -1 \end{bmatrix}.$$

9.5 Prove Theorem 9.5.

9.6 Decoupling by output feedback. With D defined as in (13), assume (D, A) is observable. Consider the constraint on RDP that $\operatorname{Ker} F \supset \operatorname{Ker} D$, i.e., $F = \tilde{F}D$ for some $\tilde{F}$. Show that if $\{\mathcal{R}_i,\ i \in \underline{k}\}$ are c.s. which satisfy (6) and (7), they furnish a solution of the constrained RDP if and only if (i) the $\mathcal{R}_i$ $(i \in \underline{k})$ are independent, and (ii) $A(\mathcal{R}_i \cap \operatorname{Ker} D) \subset \mathcal{R}_i$ $(i \in \underline{k})$. HINT: For (i), show that dependence and (constrained) compatibility contradict observability.

9.10 Notes and References

Noninteraction is a long-established topic in control theory, dating back at least to Voznesenskii [1]: for reviews of early work with transfer matrices see Tsien [1] and

Kavanagh [1]. The state space approach to decoupling was initiated by Morgan [1] and Rekasius [1], and developed further by Falb and Wolovich [1], Gilbert [2] and Gilbert and Pivnichny [1]; these authors confined their investigation to the case of scalar output blocks, with an equal number of scalar inputs. The more general problems discussed in this chapter were formulated and solved by Wonham and Morse [1] and Morse and Wonham [1]; see also Wonham [6], and Morse and Wonham [2], [3]. A significant alternative approach has been developed by Silverman and Payne [1]. For complementary details see in addition Silverman [1], Cremer [1] and Mufti [1], [2]. The result of Ex. 9.6 is due to Denham [2].

CHAPTER 10

NONINTERACTING CONTROL II: EFFICIENT COMPENSATION

In this chapter we continue the discussion in Chapter 9 on solution of EDP by dynamic compensation. A refinement of the construction used to prove Theorem 9.4 permits a further reduction of the bound (9.27) on dynamic order. The reduced bound turns out to be strictly minimal if the number of independent control inputs is equal to the number of output blocks to be decoupled. As these results are somewhat specialized and their proofs are intricate, the reader interested only in the main features of the theory is advised to skip to Chapter 11.

10.1 The Radical

We have seen that the geometric role of dynamic compensation is to supply an auxiliary component of state space. This allows untangling of the $\mathcal{R}_i^*$ in the sense that their extensions can be made independent, hence compatible. To achieve compatibility more efficiently, we first introduce a construction which 'localizes' the mutual dependence of an arbitrary collection of subspaces.

Let $\mathcal{V}_1, \ldots, \mathcal{V}_k$ be a family of subspaces of $\mathcal{X}$. The <u>radical</u> of the family, written $\check{\mathcal{V}}$ or $(\mathcal{V}_\bullet)^\vee$ ($\bullet$ stands for dummy index), is

$$\check{\mathcal{V}} \triangleq \sum_{i=1}^{k} \left[\mathcal{V}_i \cap \left(\sum_{\substack{j=1 \\ j\neq i}}^{k} \mathcal{V}_j \right) \right]. \tag{1}$$

From the definition, $\check{\mathcal{V}} = 0$ if and only if the $\mathcal{V}_i$ $(i \in \underline{k})$ are independent. As a quantitative measure of mutual dependence among the $\mathcal{V}_i$ we introduce also the function

$$\underset{1 \le i \le k}{\Delta} \mathcal{V}_i \triangleq \sum_{i=1}^{k} d(\mathcal{V}_i) - d\left(\sum_{i=1}^{k} \mathcal{V}_i \right).$$

Thus $\Delta_i \mathcal{V}_i \geq 0$, with equality if and only if the $\mathcal{V}_i$ are independent.

The computation of dimensional relations is often rendered more efficient by use of the following identities.*

LEMMA 10.1. (i) Write

$$\check{\mathcal{V}}_i \triangleq \sum_{j \neq i} \mathcal{V}_j, \qquad i \in \underline{k}. \tag{2}$$

The radical $\check{\mathcal{V}}$ has the following properties.

$$\check{\mathcal{V}} = \bigcap_i \check{\mathcal{V}}_i \tag{3}$$

$$= \sum_{j \neq i} \left(\mathcal{V}_j \cap \check{\mathcal{V}}_j\right), \qquad i \in \underline{k} \tag{4}$$

$$= \sum_{j \neq i} \left(\mathcal{V}_j \cap \check{\mathcal{V}}\right), \qquad i \in \underline{k} \tag{5}$$

$$= \sum_i \left(\mathcal{V}_i \cap \check{\mathcal{V}}\right) \tag{6}$$

$$= \left(\mathcal{V}_\bullet \cap \check{\mathcal{V}}\right)^\vee \tag{7}$$

$$= \left(\mathcal{V}_\bullet \cap \mathcal{V}\right)^\vee, \qquad \text{for all } \mathcal{V} \supset \check{\mathcal{V}} \tag{8}$$

$$= \left(\mathcal{V}_\bullet + \check{\mathcal{V}}\right)^\vee. \tag{9}$$

(ii) If $\mathcal{W} \subset \mathcal{X}$ and $\mathcal{V} \triangleq (\mathcal{V}_\bullet \cap \mathcal{W})^\vee$, then

$$\mathcal{V} = \left(\mathcal{V}_\bullet \cap \mathcal{V}\right)^\vee.$$

(iii)** $\check{\mathcal{V}}$ is the smallest subspace $\mathcal{V}_0 \subset \mathcal{X}$ with the property: the factor spaces $(\mathcal{V}_i + \mathcal{V}_0)/\mathcal{V}_0$ ($i \in \underline{k}$) are independent subspaces of $\mathcal{X}/\mathcal{V}_0$.

(iv) $\underset{i}{\Delta} \mathcal{V}_i = \underset{i}{\Delta} (\mathcal{V}_i \cap \mathcal{V})$ for all $\mathcal{V} \supset \check{\mathcal{V}}$. (10)

---

* In the spirit of high-school trigonometry.

** It is this property which suggested the designation 'radical'.

(v) <u>For all</u> $\mathcal{V} \supset \check{\mathcal{V}}$,

$$\bigtriangleup_i \left(\frac{\mathcal{V}_i + \mathcal{V}}{\mathcal{V}} \right) = d \left[\frac{\mathcal{V} \cap \sum_i \mathcal{V}_i}{\sum_i \left(\mathcal{V} \cap \mathcal{V}_i \right)} \right].$$

PROOF: (i) Write $\mathcal{W} \triangleq \cap_i \check{\mathcal{V}}_i$. By an easy induction,

$$\mathcal{W} = \left(\mathcal{V}_2 \cap \check{\mathcal{V}}_2 + \cdots + \mathcal{V}_r \cap \check{\mathcal{V}}_r + \mathcal{V}_{r+1} + \cdots + \mathcal{V}_k \right) \cap \check{\mathcal{V}}_{r+1} \cap \cdots \cap \check{\mathcal{V}}_k$$

for $r = 2, 3, \ldots$. Setting $r = k$ yields

$$\mathcal{W} = \sum_{j=2}^{k} \left(\mathcal{V}_j \cap \check{\mathcal{V}}_j \right),$$

hence by symmetry

$$\mathcal{W} = \sum_{j \neq i} \left(\mathcal{V}_j \cap \check{\mathcal{V}}_j \right), \qquad i \in \underline{k}, \tag{11}$$
$$\subset \check{\mathcal{V}}.$$

By (11), $\mathcal{W} \supset \mathcal{V}_i \cap \check{\mathcal{V}}_i$ $(i \in \underline{k})$, hence

$$\mathcal{W} \supset \sum_i \left(\mathcal{V}_i \cap \check{\mathcal{V}}_i \right)$$
$$= \check{\mathcal{V}} \qquad \text{(by (1) and (2))},$$

and this proves (3) and (4). Also

$$\mathcal{V}_j \cap \check{\mathcal{V}}_j = \left(\mathcal{V}_j \cap \bigcap_{\ell \neq j} \check{\mathcal{V}}_\ell \right) \cap \check{\mathcal{V}}_j$$

$$= \mathcal{V}_j \cap \bigcap_\ell \check{\mathcal{V}}_\ell$$

$$= \mathcal{V}_j \cap \check{\mathcal{V}} \qquad \text{(by (3))},$$

and summing over $j \neq i$ yields (5). By (5),

$$\check{\mathcal{V}} = \sum_{i} \left(\mathcal{V}_i \cap \check{\mathcal{V}} \right) \tag{6 bis}$$

$$= \sum_{i} \left[\mathcal{V}_i \cap \check{\mathcal{V}} \cap \sum_{j \neq i} \left(\mathcal{V}_j \cap \check{\mathcal{V}} \right) \right] \qquad \text{(by (5))}$$

$$= \left(\mathcal{V}_{\bullet} \cap \check{\mathcal{V}} \right)^{\vee} . \tag{7 bis}$$

If $\check{\mathcal{V}} \subset \mathcal{V}$,

$$\check{\mathcal{V}} \subset \left(\mathcal{V}_{\bullet} \cap \mathcal{V} \right)^{\vee} \qquad \text{(by (7))}$$

$$\subset \left(\mathcal{V}_{\bullet} \right)^{\vee} = \check{\mathcal{V}} ,$$

proving (8). For (9), write $\mathcal{W}_j \triangleq \mathcal{V}_j + \check{\mathcal{V}}$ ($j \in \underline{k}$). By application of (6) to the $\mathcal{W}_j$,

$$\check{\mathcal{W}} = \sum_{j} \left(\mathcal{W}_j \cap \check{\mathcal{W}} \right) = \sum_{j} \left[\left(\mathcal{V}_j + \check{\mathcal{V}}_j \right) \cap \sum_{\ell \neq j} \left(\mathcal{V}_{\ell} + \check{\mathcal{V}} \right) \right]$$

$$= \sum_{j} \left[\left(\mathcal{V}_j + \check{\mathcal{V}}_j \right) \cap \left(\check{\mathcal{V}}_j + \mathcal{V} \right) \right]$$

$$= \sum_{j} \left(\mathcal{V}_j + \check{\mathcal{V}} \right) \cap \check{\mathcal{V}}_j \qquad \text{(since } \check{\mathcal{V}}_j \supset \check{\mathcal{V}} \text{)}$$

$$= \sum_{j} \left(\mathcal{V}_j \cap \check{\mathcal{V}}_j + \check{\mathcal{V}} \right) = \check{\mathcal{V}} .$$

(ii) By application of (6) to the family $\mathcal{V}_j \cap \mathcal{W}$ ($j \in \underline{k}$),

$$\mathcal{V} = \left(\mathcal{V}_{\bullet} \cap \mathcal{W} \right)^{\vee} = \left[\left(\mathcal{V}_{\bullet} \cap \mathcal{W} \right) \cap \left(\mathcal{V}_{\bullet} \cap \mathcal{W} \right)^{\vee} \right]^{\vee} = \left(\mathcal{V}_{\bullet} \cap \mathcal{W} \cap \mathcal{V} \right)^{\vee}$$

$$= \left(\mathcal{V}_{\bullet} \cap \mathcal{V} \right)^{\vee} \qquad \text{(since } \mathcal{V} \subset \mathcal{W} \text{)} .$$

(iii) The subspaces $(\mathcal{V}_i + \mathcal{V}_0)/\mathcal{V}_0 \subset \mathcal{X}/\mathcal{V}_0$ are independent if and only if

$$(\mathcal{V}_i + \mathcal{V}_0) \cap \sum_{j \neq i} (\mathcal{V}_j + \mathcal{V}_0) = \mathcal{V}_0 , \qquad i \in \underline{k} ,$$

or equivalently

$$(\mathcal{V}_i + \mathcal{V}_0) \cap \left(\check{\mathcal{V}}_i + \mathcal{V}_0 \right) = \mathcal{V}_0 , \qquad i \in \underline{k} ,$$

or

$$\sum_i \left[\left(\mathcal{V}_i + \mathcal{V}_0\right) \cap \left(\check{\mathcal{V}}_i + \mathcal{V}_0\right)\right] = \mathcal{V}_0 . \tag{12}$$

Let $\hat{\mathcal{V}} = \lim \mathcal{V}^{\mu}$, where

$$\mathcal{V}^{\mu+1} = \sum_i \left[\left(\mathcal{V}_i + \mathcal{V}^{\mu}\right) \cap \left(\check{\mathcal{V}}_i + \mathcal{V}^{\mu}\right)\right], \qquad \mu = 0, 1, 2, \ldots;$$

$$\mathcal{V}^0 = 0 .$$

Then $\mathcal{V}^{\mu} \uparrow$ as $\mu \uparrow$, hence $\hat{\mathcal{V}}$ exists and is easily seen to be the infimal solution of (12); furthermore

$$\check{\mathcal{V}} = \sum_i \left(\mathcal{V}_i \cap \check{\mathcal{V}}_i\right) = \mathcal{V}^1 \subset \hat{\mathcal{V}} . \tag{13}$$

Finally, $\check{\mathcal{V}}$ is a solution of (12); indeed

$$\sum_i \left[\left(\mathcal{V}_i + \check{\mathcal{V}}\right) \cap \left(\check{\mathcal{V}}_i + \check{\mathcal{V}}\right)\right] = \sum_i \left[\left(\mathcal{V}_i + \check{\mathcal{V}}\right) \cap \check{\mathcal{V}}_i\right]$$

$$= \sum_i \left(\mathcal{V}_i \cap \check{\mathcal{V}}_i + \check{\mathcal{V}}\right) = \check{\mathcal{V}} .$$

Hence $\check{\mathcal{V}} \supset \hat{\mathcal{V}}$ and this with (13) proves $\check{\mathcal{V}} = \hat{\mathcal{V}}$.

(iv) By the independence proved in (iii),

$$\sum_i d\left[\frac{\mathcal{V}_i + \check{\mathcal{V}}}{\check{\mathcal{V}}}\right] = d\left[\sum_i \frac{\mathcal{V}_i + \check{\mathcal{V}}}{\check{\mathcal{V}}}\right],$$

so that

$$\sum_i \left[d(\mathcal{V}_i) - d(\mathcal{V}_i \cap \check{\mathcal{V}})\right] = d\left(\sum_i \mathcal{V}_i\right) - d(\check{\mathcal{V}}) . \tag{14}$$

Since

$$d(\check{\mathcal{V}}) = d\left[\sum_i \left(\mathcal{V}_i \cap \check{\mathcal{V}}\right)\right] \qquad \text{(by (6))},$$

(14) yields (10) for the case $\mathcal{V} = \check{\mathcal{V}}$. Applying this result to the family $\{\mathcal{V}_i \cap \mathcal{V},\ i \in \underline{k}\}$,

$$\mathop{\triangle}_i (\mathcal{V}_i \cap \mathcal{V}) = \mathop{\triangle}_i \left[\mathcal{V}_i \cap \mathcal{V} \cap \left(\mathcal{V}_\bullet \cap \mathcal{V}\right)^{\vee}\right]$$

$$= \mathop{\triangle}_i \left(\mathcal{V}_i \cap \mathcal{V} \cap \check{\mathcal{V}}\right) \qquad \text{(by (8))}$$

$$= \mathop{\triangle}_i \left(\mathcal{V}_i \cap \check{\mathcal{V}}\right) = \mathop{\triangle}_i \mathcal{V}_i ,$$

as claimed.

(v) Write $\mathcal{V}_\sigma \triangleq \sum_i \mathcal{V}_i$. We have

$$\mathop{\triangle}_i \left(\frac{\mathcal{V}_i + \mathcal{V}}{\mathcal{V}}\right) = \sum_i d\left(\frac{\mathcal{V}_i + \mathcal{V}}{\mathcal{V}}\right) - d\left(\frac{\mathcal{V}_\sigma + \mathcal{V}}{\mathcal{V}}\right)$$

$$= \sum_i d\left(\frac{\mathcal{V}_i}{\mathcal{V}_i \cap \mathcal{V}}\right) - d\left(\frac{\mathcal{V}_\sigma}{\mathcal{V}_\sigma \cap \mathcal{V}}\right)$$

$$= \sum_i d(\mathcal{V}_i) - \sum_i d(\mathcal{V}_i \cap \mathcal{V}) - d(\mathcal{V}_\sigma) + d(\mathcal{V}_\sigma \cap \mathcal{V}) .$$

Using (10) to evaluate $\sum_i d(\mathcal{V}_i \cap \mathcal{V})$, we get

$$\mathop{\triangle}_i \left(\frac{\mathcal{V}_i + \mathcal{V}}{\mathcal{V}}\right) = -d\left[\sum_i (\mathcal{V}_i \cap \mathcal{V})\right] + d(\mathcal{V}_\sigma \cap \mathcal{V})$$

$$= d\left[\frac{\mathcal{V}_\sigma \cap \mathcal{V}}{\sum_i (\mathcal{V}_i \cap \mathcal{V})}\right],$$

the required result. ▮

10.2 Efficient Extension

The key to efficient extension (contrast Section 9.6) lies in the property (iii) of the radical stated in Lemma 10.1. The idea will be to reduce the radical of a given family to a smaller subspace having better properties, by means of the following construction.

LEMMA 10.2. Let $\mathcal{R}_1, \ldots, \mathcal{R}_k$ be a family of subspaces of $\mathcal{X}$, let $\mathcal{V} \subset \check{\mathcal{R}}$, and

$$\mathcal{R}_0 \triangleq (\mathcal{R}_\bullet \cap \mathcal{V})^\vee .$$

Let

$$n_a \triangleq \underset{1 \le i \le k}{\Delta} \left[\frac{\mathcal{R}_i + \mathcal{R}_0}{\mathcal{R}_0} \right]$$

and take the extended space $\mathcal{X}_e = \mathcal{X} \oplus \mathcal{X}_a$, with $d(\mathcal{X}_a) = n_a$. Then there exist maps E_i: $\mathcal{X}_e \to \mathcal{X}_e$ ($i \in \underline{k}$) such that

$$\operatorname{Im} E_i \subset \mathcal{X}_a , \qquad \operatorname{Ker} E_i \supset \mathcal{R}_0 , \qquad i \in \underline{k} ,$$

and if

$$\mathcal{V}_i \triangleq (1 + E_i)\mathcal{R}_i , \qquad i \in \underline{k} ,$$

then

$$\check{\mathcal{V}} = \mathcal{R}_0 .$$

PROOF: Let $\bar{\mathcal{X}} \triangleq \mathcal{X}/\mathcal{R}_0$ and $P: \mathcal{X} \to \bar{\mathcal{X}}$ be canonical. By Lemma 9.3 there exist maps

$$\bar{E}_i : \bar{\mathcal{X}} \oplus \mathcal{X}_a \to \bar{\mathcal{X}} \oplus \mathcal{X}_a , \qquad i \in \underline{k} ,$$

(where the direct sum is external) such that $\operatorname{Im} \bar{E}_i \subset \mathcal{X}_a$ and the subspaces $(1 + \bar{E}_i)\bar{\mathcal{R}}_i$ ($i \in \underline{k}$) are independent in $\bar{\mathcal{X}} \oplus \mathcal{X}_a$. Let $E_i \triangleq \bar{E}_i P$ and $\mathcal{V}_i \triangleq (1 + E_i)\mathcal{R}_i$. With $\bar{\mathcal{R}}_i \triangleq P\mathcal{R}_i$ we have that

$$\bar{\mathcal{V}}_i = (1 + \bar{E}_i)\bar{\mathcal{R}}_i = \frac{\mathcal{V}_i + \mathcal{R}_0}{\mathcal{R}_0}$$

are independent in $\mathcal{X}/\mathcal{R}_0$, and by Lemma 10.1 (iii) there follows $\mathcal{R}_0 \supset \check{\mathcal{V}}$. For the reverse inclusion, note

$$\begin{aligned} \mathcal{R}_0 &= \left(\mathcal{R}_\bullet \cap \mathcal{R}_0\right)^\vee \qquad \text{(by Lemma 10.1(ii))} \\ &= \sum_i \left[\mathcal{R}_i \cap \mathcal{R}_0 \cap \sum_{j \ne i} (\mathcal{R}_j \cap \mathcal{R}_0) \right] . \end{aligned}$$

Thus $x \in \mathcal{R}_0$ implies

$$x = \sum_i x_i$$

with $x_i \in \mathcal{R}_i \cap \mathcal{R}_0$, and

$$x_i = \sum_{j \ne i} x_{ij} , \qquad i \in \underline{k} ,$$

with $x_{ij} \in \mathcal{R}_j \cap \mathcal{R}_0$. Since Ker $E_i \supset \mathcal{R}_0$,

$$x_i = (1+E_i)x_i \in \mathcal{V}_i$$

and

$$x_{ij} = (1+E_i)x_{ij} \in \mathcal{V}_j .$$

Therefore

$$x_i \in \mathcal{V}_i \cap \check{\mathcal{V}}_i , \qquad i \in \underline{k} ,$$

hence $x \in \check{\mathcal{V}}$. ∎

Suppose now that the $\mathcal{R}_i$ are (A, B)-invariant. In general it is not true that $\check{\mathcal{R}}$ is (A, B)-invariant. Nevertheless, in the case of interest one can generate a useful class of (A, B)-invariant subspaces contained in $\check{\mathcal{R}}$.

LEMMA 10.3. <u>As in RDP, let</u> $\mathcal{R}_i^*$ ($i \in \underline{k}$) <u>be the supremal c.s. contained in</u>

$$\hat{\mathcal{K}}_i \triangleq \bigcap_{j \neq i} \mathcal{K}_j ,$$

<u>and let</u> $\check{\mathcal{R}}^*$ <u>denote their radical. Then</u>

$$\check{\mathcal{R}}^* \subset \bigcap_i \mathcal{K}_i , \tag{15}$$

<u>and if</u> $\mathcal{V} \subset \check{\mathcal{R}}^*$ <u>is</u> (A, B)<u>-invariant, so is</u>

$$\check{\mathcal{R}}_0(\mathcal{V}) \triangleq \left(\mathcal{R}_\bullet^* \cap \mathcal{V}\right)^{\vee} . \tag{16}$$

PROOF: Dropping the superscript (*), we have

$$\check{\mathcal{R}} = \bigcap_i \sum_{j \neq i} \mathcal{R}_j \qquad \text{(by (3))}$$

$$\subset \bigcap_i \sum_{j \neq i} \bigcap_{\ell \neq j} \mathcal{K}_\ell = \bigcap_i \mathcal{K}_i ,$$

proving (15). Since $\check{\mathcal{R}} \subset \hat{\mathcal{K}}_i$ ($i \in \underline{k}$), there results $\mathcal{V} \subset \hat{\mathcal{K}}_i$, hence $\mathcal{V} \subset \mathcal{V}_i$ ($i \in \underline{k}$), where

$$\mathcal{V}_i \triangleq \sup \underline{\mathcal{I}}(A, B; \hat{\mathcal{K}}_i) .$$

There follows

$$\emptyset \neq \underline{F}(\mathcal{V}_i) \cap \underline{F}(\mathcal{V}) \subset \underline{F}(\mathcal{R}_i) \cap \underline{F}(\mathcal{V}) \subset \underline{F}(\mathcal{R}_i \cap \mathcal{V}) ,$$

i.e., $\mathcal{R}_i \cap \mathcal{V}$ is (A, B)-invariant, hence so is

$$\tilde{\mathcal{V}}_i \triangleq \sum_{j \neq i} (\mathcal{R}_j \cap \mathcal{V}) .$$

Now

$$\tilde{\mathcal{V}}_i \subset \sum_{j \neq i} (\mathcal{R}_j \cap \check{\mathcal{R}})$$

$$= \check{\mathcal{R}} \qquad \text{(by (5))}$$

$$\subset \hat{\mathcal{K}}_i ;$$

so $\tilde{\mathcal{V}}_i \subset \mathcal{V}_i$, and applying the same argument as before we get that $\mathcal{R}_i \cap \tilde{\mathcal{V}}_i$ is (A, B)-invariant. Finally

$$\mathcal{R}_0(\mathcal{V}) = \sum_i \left[\mathcal{R}_i \cap \mathcal{V} \cap \sum_{j \neq i} (\mathcal{R}_j \cap \mathcal{V}) \right]$$

$$= \sum_i \left[\mathcal{R}_i \cap \sum_{j \neq i} (\mathcal{R}_j \cap \mathcal{V}) \right] = \sum_i (\mathcal{R}_i \cap \tilde{\mathcal{V}}_i)$$

must be (A, B)-invariant, as claimed. ∎

Next we relate the radical to the concept of compatibility. Recall that a family $\{\mathcal{J}_i \subset \mathcal{X}, i \in \underline{k}\}$ is <u>compatible</u> relative to (A, B) if

$$\bigcap_{i=1}^{k} \underline{F}(\mathcal{J}_i) \neq \emptyset .$$

LEMMA 10.4. <u>Let $\mathcal{J}_i$ $(i \in \underline{k})$ be (A, B)-invariant. If $\check{\mathcal{J}}$ is (A, B)-invariant, then the family</u>

$$\check{\mathcal{J}}, \mathcal{J}_1 + \check{\mathcal{J}}, \ldots, \mathcal{J}_k + \check{\mathcal{J}}$$

<u>is compatible.</u>

PROOF: Let $P: \mathcal{X} \to \overline{\mathcal{X}} \triangleq \mathcal{X}/\check{\mathcal{J}}$ be canonical, let $F_0 \in \underline{F}(\check{\mathcal{J}})$ and $A_0 \triangleq (A + BF_0)$. By Lemma 10.1 (iii) the subspaces $\overline{\mathcal{J}}_i \triangleq P\mathcal{J}_i$ $(i \in \underline{k})$ are independent, and are clearly $(\overline{A}_0, \overline{B})$-invariant relative to the maps $\overline{A}_0: \overline{\mathcal{X}} \to \overline{\mathcal{X}}$ and $\overline{B}: \mathcal{U} \to \overline{\mathcal{X}}$ induced in $\overline{\mathcal{X}}$. Hence there exists $\overline{F}_1: \overline{\mathcal{X}} \to \mathcal{U}$ such that $(\overline{A}_0 + \overline{B}\overline{F}_1)\overline{\mathcal{J}}_i \subset \overline{\mathcal{J}}_i$ $(i \in \underline{k})$. With $F \triangleq F_0 + \overline{F}_1 P$ we have $\overline{A + BF}\, \overline{\mathcal{J}}_i \subset \overline{\mathcal{J}}_i$ $(i \in \underline{k})$ and so

$$(A+BF)\mathcal{J}_i \subset \mathcal{J}_i + \check{\mathcal{J}}, \qquad i \in \underline{k}.$$

Since also

$$(A+BF)\check{\mathcal{J}} = A_0\check{\mathcal{J}} \subset \check{\mathcal{J}},$$

the lemma follows. ∎

Combining results we now show how to exploit extension to construct a compatible family with compatible radical. In the following the notation is that of Section 9.4 for the extended spaces $\mathcal{X}_a, \mathcal{X}_e$, and extended maps A, B, B_a, introduced in EDP.

LEMMA 10.5. Under the assumptions of Lemma 10.3, take

$$d(\mathcal{X}_a) \geq n_0 \triangleq \bigtriangleup_i \left(\frac{\mathcal{R}_i^* + \mathcal{R}_0}{\mathcal{R}_0} \right), \tag{17}$$

where $\mathcal{R}_0 \triangleq \check{\mathcal{R}}_0(\mathcal{V})$ is defined by (16). Then there exist maps $E_i\colon \mathcal{X}_e \to \mathcal{X}_e$ $(i \in \underline{k})$ with the properties:

$$\operatorname{Im} E_i \subset \mathcal{X}_a, \qquad i \in \underline{k}, \tag{18}$$

$$\operatorname{Ker} E_i \supset \mathcal{R}_0, \qquad i \in \underline{k}; \tag{19}$$

the subspaces

$$\mathcal{V}_i \triangleq (1+E_i)\mathcal{R}_i^*, \qquad i \in \underline{k}, \tag{20}$$

are such that

$$\check{\mathcal{V}} = \mathcal{R}_0 \tag{21}$$

$$\subset \bigcap_i \mathcal{K}_i; \tag{22}$$

and the family

$$\check{\mathcal{V}}, \mathcal{V}_1 + \check{\mathcal{V}}, \ldots, \mathcal{V}_k + \check{\mathcal{V}}$$

is compatible relative to $(A, B+B_a)$.

PROOF: Lemma 10.2 provides E_i and $\mathcal{V}_i$ with the properties (18)–(21), and (22) follows by Lemma 10.3 and the fact that $\mathcal{R}_0 \subset \check{\mathcal{R}}^*$. Again by Lemma 10.3, $\mathcal{R}_0$ is (A, B)-invariant, hence $(A, B+B_a)$-invariant. Thus $\check{\mathcal{V}}$ and the $\mathcal{V}_i$ $(i \in \underline{k})$ are $(A, B+B_a)$-invariant, and the result follows by application of Lemma 10.4 with $\mathcal{V}_i$ in place of $\mathcal{J}_i$ and $(A, B+B_a)$ in place of (A, B). ∎

Remark

By Lemma 9.2, the $\mathcal{V}_i$ defined by (20) are extended controllability subspaces (e.c.s.) contained in $\hat{\mathcal{K}}_i \oplus \mathcal{X}_a$. They need not, however, be $(A, B+B_a)$-compatible. This difficulty will be treated next.

10.3 Efficient Decoupling

Assume EDP is solvable, i.e.,

$$\mathcal{R}_i^* + \mathcal{K}_i = \mathcal{X}, \qquad i \in \underline{k}. \tag{23}$$

With $d(\mathcal{X}_a)$ subject to (17) it will be shown how to construct in $\mathcal{X}_e$ a compatible family of e.c.s. which solves EDP, and also permits assignment of closed-loop eigenvalues to a 'good' subset $\mathbb{C}_g \subset \mathbb{C}$. Let $\mathcal{V} \subset \mathcal{X}_e \triangleq \mathcal{X} \oplus \mathcal{X}_a$. Then $\underline{F}(\mathcal{V})$ (resp. $\underline{F}_e(\mathcal{V})$) will denote the set of maps $F: \mathcal{X}_e \to \mathcal{U}_e$ such that $(A+BF)\mathcal{V} \subset \mathcal{V}$ [resp. $(A+(B+B_a)F)\mathcal{V} \subset \mathcal{V}$]. Now according to Lemma 10.5, where the $\mathcal{V}_i$ $(i \in \underline{k})$ are defined, there exists

$$F \in \underline{F}_e(\check{\mathcal{V}}) \cap \bigcap_{i=1}^{k} \underline{F}_e(\mathcal{V}_i + \check{\mathcal{V}}). \tag{24}$$

We define e.c.s. $\mathcal{J}_i$ $(i \in \underline{k})$ by means of

$$\mathcal{J}_i = \langle A + (B+B_a)F \,|\, (\mathcal{B} + \mathcal{B}_a) \cap (\mathcal{V}_i + \check{\mathcal{V}}) \rangle, \tag{25}$$

i.e., $\mathcal{J}_i$ is the supremal e.c.s. in $\mathcal{V}_i + \check{\mathcal{V}}$.

It will be shown that the $\mathcal{J}_i$ solve EDP, namely

$$\mathcal{J}_i + \mathcal{K}_i + \mathcal{X}_a = \mathcal{X} \oplus \mathcal{X}_a, \qquad i \in \underline{k}, \tag{26}$$

and

$$\mathcal{J}_i \subset \hat{\mathcal{K}}_i \oplus \mathcal{X}_a, \qquad i \in \underline{k}. \tag{27}$$

By the remark after Lemma 10.5, the $\mathcal{V}_i$ are themselves e.c.s., and clearly satisfy

$$\begin{aligned} \mathcal{V}_i + \mathcal{K}_i + \mathcal{X}_a &= \mathcal{R}_i^* + \mathcal{K}_i + \mathcal{X}_a \qquad \text{(by (20))} \\ &= \mathcal{X} \oplus \mathcal{X}_a \qquad \text{(by (23))}. \end{aligned} \tag{28}$$

Since $\mathcal{V}_i \subset \mathcal{V}_i + \check{\mathcal{V}}$ and $\mathcal{J}_i$ is supremal, (26) now follows from (28). Finally, as

$$\mathcal{V}_i \subset \mathcal{R}_i^* + \mathcal{X}_a \subset \hat{\mathcal{K}}_i + \mathcal{X}_a \tag{29}$$

we have

$$\mathscr{S}_i \subset \mathscr{V}_i + \check{\mathscr{V}} \qquad \text{(by (25))}$$

$$\subset \hat{\mathscr{K}}_i + \mathscr{X}_a + \bigcap_j \mathscr{K}_j \qquad \text{(by (22), (29))}$$

$$= \hat{\mathscr{K}}_i \oplus \mathscr{X}_a, \qquad i \in \underline{k},$$

proving (27).

It remains to describe our freedom to assign $\sigma[A + (B + B_a) F]$. This is controlled by the choice of $\mathscr{V} \subset \check{\mathscr{R}}^*$, which serves to fix the subspace

$$\mathscr{R}_0 \triangleq \check{\mathscr{R}}_0(\mathscr{V}) \triangleq \left(\mathscr{R}^*_\bullet \cap \mathscr{V}\right)^{\vee}. \tag{16 bis}$$

Starting with a symmetric partition $\mathbb{C} = \mathbb{C}_g \dot{\cup} \mathbb{C}_b$, take $\mathscr{V} = \mathscr{V}_g$ to be the supremal (A, B)-invariant subspace in $\check{\mathscr{R}}^*$ with the property: there is $\tilde{F} \in \underline{F}(\mathscr{V})$ such that

$$\sigma[(A + B\tilde{F}) \mid \mathscr{V}] \subset \mathbb{C}_g .$$

That $\mathscr{V}_g$ exists as just defined was proved in Lemma 5.7. Indeed, let

$$\mathscr{W} \triangleq \sup \underline{\mathscr{I}}(A, B; \check{\mathscr{R}}^*) . \tag{30}$$

If $\mathscr{R} \triangleq \sup \underline{\mathscr{C}}(A, B; \check{\mathscr{R}}^*)$, then

$$\mathscr{R} \subset \mathscr{V}_g \subset \mathscr{W} \subset \check{\mathscr{R}}^* ;$$

taking arbitrary $\hat{F} \in \underline{F}(\mathscr{W})$ and with $P: \mathscr{X} \to \mathscr{X}/\mathscr{R}$ canonical, we have explicitly

$$\mathscr{V}_g = P^{-1}\left[P\mathscr{X}_g(A + B\hat{F}) \cap P\mathscr{W}\right]. \tag{31}$$

Now setting $\mathscr{V} = \mathscr{V}_g$ in (16) we obtain

$$\mathscr{R}_0 = \left(\mathscr{R}^*_\bullet \cap \mathscr{V}_g\right)^{\vee}. \tag{32}$$

We claim there is $F_0 \in \underline{F}(\mathscr{R}_0)$ such that

$$\sigma[(A + BF_0) \mid \mathscr{R}_0] \subset \mathbb{C}_g . \tag{33}$$

As $\mathscr{V}_g$ is (A, B)-invariant so, by Lemma 10.3, is $\mathscr{R}_0$. Furthermore, $\mathscr{R}_0 \supset \mathscr{R}$: indeed $\mathscr{R}$ is a c.s. such that

$$\mathscr{R} \subset \check{\mathscr{R}}^* \subset \hat{\mathscr{K}}_i, \qquad i \in \underline{k} \qquad \text{(by (15))},$$

and as the $\mathcal{R}_i^*$ are supremal in $\hat{\mathcal{K}}_i$ we have $\mathcal{R} \subset \mathcal{R}_i^*$ ($i \in \underline{k}$), hence $\mathcal{R} \subset \mathcal{R}_i^* \cap \mathcal{V}_g$ ($i \in \underline{k}$), and by (32), $\mathcal{R} \subset \mathcal{R}_0$. Choose $F_1 \in \underline{F}(\mathcal{R}) \cap \underline{F}(\mathcal{R}_0)$ with the property

$$\sigma[(A + BF_1)|\mathcal{R}] \subset \mathbb{C}_g .$$

Such F_1 certainly exists, and $F_1|\mathcal{R}_0$ clearly has an extension $F_0 \in \underline{F}(\mathcal{W})$. Now

$$\underline{F}(\mathcal{W}) \subset \underline{F}(\mathcal{R}) \cap \underline{F}(\mathcal{V}_g)$$

so that

$$F_0 \in \underline{F}(\mathcal{R}) \cap \underline{F}(\mathcal{R}_0) \cap \underline{F}(\mathcal{V}_g) \cap \underline{F}(\mathcal{W}) .$$

For the induced map $\overline{A + BF_0}$ on $\mathcal{X}/\mathcal{R}$,

$$\sigma\left[\overline{A + BF_0}\,\middle|\,\frac{\mathcal{V}_g}{\mathcal{R}}\right] \subset \mathbb{C}_g ;$$

and finally

$$\sigma[(A + BF_0)|\mathcal{R}_0] \subset \sigma[(A + BF_0)|\mathcal{R}] \mathbin{\dot{\cup}} \sigma\left[\overline{(A + BF_0)}\,\middle|\,\frac{\mathcal{V}_g}{\mathcal{R}}\right]$$

$$\subset \mathbb{C}_g ,$$

as claimed in (33).

The next step is to construct $F_1 \in \underline{F}_e(\check{\mathcal{V}})$ such that

$$\sigma[(A + (B + B_a) F_1)|\check{\mathcal{V}}] \subset \mathbb{C}_g . \tag{34}$$

As $\check{\mathcal{V}} = \mathcal{R}_0$ we arrange that

$$F_1|\check{\mathcal{V}} = F_0|\mathcal{R}_0 , \qquad F_1\check{\mathcal{V}} \subset \mathcal{U}, \tag{35a, b}$$

with F_0 as in (33); here (35b) ensures that $(B + B_a)F_1 = BF_1$, hence $F_1 \in \underline{F}_e(\check{\mathcal{V}})$, and (34) is true.

Set $A_1 \triangleq A + (B + B_a)F_1$. To complete the definition of F, recall that the $(\mathcal{V}_i + \check{\mathcal{V}})/\check{\mathcal{V}}$ are independent c.s. for the pair induced by $(A_1, B + B_a)$ in $(\mathcal{X} \oplus \mathcal{X}_a)/\check{\mathcal{V}}$, and so there exists $F_2: \mathcal{X} \oplus \mathcal{X}_a \to \mathcal{U} \oplus \mathcal{U}_a$ such that

$$\operatorname{Ker} F_2 \supset \check{\mathcal{V}} \tag{36a}$$

and

$$\sigma[(A_1 + (B + B_a) F_2)|\mathcal{V}_i + \check{\mathcal{V}}] \subset \mathbb{C}_g , \qquad i \in \underline{k} . \tag{36b}$$

Setting $F \triangleq F_1 + F_2$ we obtain that (24) is true and

$$\sigma\left[(A + (B + B_a) F)|\check{\mathcal{V}} + \sum_i \mathcal{V}_i\right] \subset \mathbb{C}_g ,$$

so

$$\sigma\left[\left(A + (B+B_a)F\right)\Big|\sum_i \mathscr{S}_i\right] \subset \mathbb{C}_g .$$

Finally we shall assume that $\langle A|\mathscr{B}\rangle = \mathscr{X}$, hence $(A, B+B_a)$ is controllable. Projecting modulo $\sum_i \mathscr{S}_i$ we proceed, in the standard way, to modify F to get

$$\sigma[A + (B+B_a)F] \subset \mathbb{C}_g ,$$

the desired result.

Summarizing, we have

THEOREM 10.1. For the RDP of Section 9.2, let (A, B) be controllable, and $\mathscr{R}_i^*$ be the supremal c.s. in $\hat{\mathscr{K}}_i$, with radical $\check{\mathscr{R}}^*$. Assume EDP is solvable, i.e., $\mathscr{R}_i^* + \mathscr{K}_i = \mathscr{X}$ $(i \in \underline{k})$. Let $\mathbb{C} = \mathbb{C}_g \dot{\cup} \mathbb{C}_b$ be a symmetric partition. Define

$$\mathscr{V}_g \triangleq \sup\{\mathscr{V}: \mathscr{V} \subset \check{\mathscr{R}}^* \ \&\ \exists F \in \underline{F}(\mathscr{V}),$$

$$\sigma[(A+BF)|\mathscr{V}] \subset \mathbb{C}_g\}, \tag{37a}$$

and

$$\mathscr{R}_0 \triangleq \left(\mathscr{R}_\bullet^* \cap \mathscr{V}_g\right)^{\vee} . \tag{37b}$$

Then EDP is solvable with extension bound

$$d(\mathscr{X}_a) \le \mathop{\triangle}_i \left(\frac{\mathscr{R}_i^* + \mathscr{R}_0}{\mathscr{R}_0}\right). \tag{38}$$

Furthermore the extended feedback map $F: \mathscr{X} \oplus \mathscr{X}_a \to \mathscr{U} \oplus \mathscr{U}_a$ can be chosen so that

$$\sigma[A + (B+B_a)F] \subset \mathbb{C}_g .$$

We remark that the bound (38) is in general lower than the bound

$$d(\mathscr{X}_a) \le \mathop{\triangle}_i \mathscr{R}_i^* \tag{39}$$

obtained in Section 9.6. As illustration consider the example of Section 9.7. In the present notation we have

$$\check{\mathcal{R}}^* = \mathcal{R}_1^* \cap \mathcal{R}_2^* = \operatorname{Im}\begin{bmatrix} 0 & 0 & 0 \\ 1 & 0 & 0 \\ 0 & 1 & 0 \\ 0 & 0 & 1 \\ 0 & 0 & 0 \end{bmatrix}.$$

From (30),

$$\mathcal{W} = \operatorname{Im}\begin{bmatrix} 0 & 0 \\ 0 & 0 \\ 1 & 0 \\ 0 & 1 \\ 0 & 0 \end{bmatrix},$$

which yields $A\mathcal{W} \subset \mathcal{W}$ and $\mathcal{R} = 0$. Now

$$\sigma(A|\mathcal{W}) = \{0, 1\}.$$

Suppose $0 \in \mathbb{C}_g$ and $1 \in \mathbb{C}_b$. Then

$$\mathcal{V}_g = \mathcal{W} \cap \operatorname{Ker} A = \operatorname{Im}\begin{bmatrix} 0 \\ 0 \\ 1 \\ -1 \\ 0 \end{bmatrix}$$

and

$$\mathcal{R}_0 = \mathcal{R}_1^* \cap \mathcal{R}_2^* \cap \mathcal{V}_g = \operatorname{Im}\begin{bmatrix} 0 \\ 0 \\ 1 \\ -1 \\ 0 \end{bmatrix}.$$

This gives

$$d\left[\frac{\mathcal{R}_i^* + \mathcal{R}_0}{\mathcal{R}_0}\right] = 3, \qquad i \in \underline{2},$$

and

$$d\left[\frac{\mathcal{R}_1^* + \mathcal{R}_2^*}{\mathcal{R}_0}\right] = 4.$$

Thus (38) yields $d(\mathcal{X}_a) \leq 2$ in contrast to the bound $d(\mathcal{X}_a) \leq 3$ obtained from (39).

Computation of efficient decoupling e.c.s. for this example is completed in Ex. 10.2.

10.4 Minimal Order Compensation: $d(\mathcal{B}) = 2$

The solution of EDP provided by Theorem 10.1, while 'efficient', is not generally 'minimal', in the sense of requiring least possible order of dynamic compensation subject to the constraint that the closed loop spectrum be 'good'. However, if the number of output blocks to be decoupled happens to equal the number of independent scalar controls, i.e.,

$$d(\mathcal{B}) = k , \tag{40}$$

this is actually so: the bound (38) on $d(\mathcal{X}_a)$ cannot be improved. Quickly stated, the reason is the following: (40) means that $d(\mathcal{B})$ has the least value required if EDP is to be solvable at all; then the only nontrivial c.s. in $\hat{\mathcal{K}}_i$ is the supremal c.s. $\mathcal{R}_i^*$; and for the $\mathcal{R}_i^*$ the extension described in Theorem 10.1 is always minimal.

While of marginal practical interest, this result has a modest esthetic appeal. In this section we shall prove it in the simplest case

$$d(\mathcal{B}) = k = 2 , \tag{41}$$

deferring the generalization to Section 10.5. Actually the central fact required is the following 'projective' property of extensions which in no way depends on decoupling, but is interesting in its own right.

LEMMA 10.6. *Let $\mathcal{W} \subset \mathcal{X} \oplus \mathcal{X}_a$ be $(A, B+B_a)$-invariant, $\mathcal{S}$ the supremal e.c.s. in $\mathcal{W}$, $P: \mathcal{X} \oplus \mathcal{X}_a \to \mathcal{X} \oplus \mathcal{X}_a$ the projection on $\mathcal{X}$ along $\mathcal{X}_a$, and write*

$$\mathcal{V} \triangleq P\mathcal{W}, \qquad \mathcal{R} \triangleq P\mathcal{S} .$$

Then (i) $\mathcal{V}$ is (A, B)-invariant and $\mathcal{R}$ is the supremal c.s. in $\mathcal{V}$; (ii) $\mathcal{V}/\mathcal{R} \approx \mathcal{W}/\mathcal{S}$; and (iii) for all $F \in \underline{F}_e(\mathcal{W})$ and $F_0 \in \underline{F}(\mathcal{V})$, the induced map $\overline{A+BF_0}$ in $\mathcal{V}/\mathcal{R}$ is similar to the induced map $\overline{A+(B+B_a)F}$ in $\mathcal{W}/\mathcal{S}$.

PROOF: (i) Recall that $PA = AP$ and $\mathrm{Im}(B+B_a) = \mathcal{B} \oplus \mathcal{B}_a$, so $A\mathcal{W} \subset \mathcal{W} + \mathcal{B} + \mathcal{B}_a$ implies $A\mathcal{V} \subset \mathcal{V} + \mathcal{B}$. By Theorem 5.6, $\mathcal{S} = \lim \mathcal{S}^\mu$ $(\mu\uparrow)$, where $\mathcal{S}^0 = 0$ and

$$\mathcal{S}^\mu \triangleq \mathcal{W} \cap \left(A\mathcal{S}^{\mu-1} + \mathcal{B} + \mathcal{B}_a\right), \qquad \mu = 1, 2, \ldots .$$

Since $\mathrm{Ker}\,P = \mathcal{X}_a = \mathcal{B}_a$ there follows

$$P\mathcal{S}^\mu = \mathcal{V} \cap (AP\mathcal{R}^{\mu-1} + \mathcal{B}) .$$

Again by Theorem 5.6, $\lim P\mathcal{S}^\mu$ is the supremal c.s. in $\mathcal{V}$, and

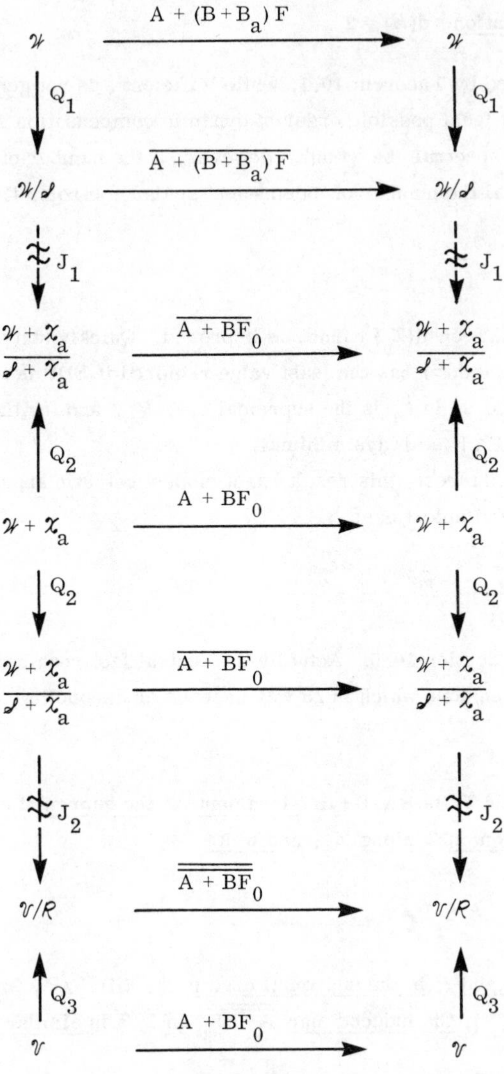

Fig. 10.1.

Commutative Diagram for Proof of Lemma 10.6.

$$\lim P\mathscr{S}^{\mu} = P \lim \mathscr{S}^{\mu} = P\mathscr{S} = \mathscr{R} .$$

(ii) Let $F \in \underline{F}_e(\mathscr{W})$, and write

$$\mathscr{W} = \mathscr{W} \cap (\mathscr{S} + \mathscr{X}_a) \oplus \mathscr{T} .$$

Since $\mathscr{W} \cap \mathscr{X}_a \subset \mathscr{S}$ we have

$$\mathscr{W} \cap (\mathscr{S} + \mathscr{X}_a) = \mathscr{S}, \tag{42}$$

hence

$$\mathscr{W} = \mathscr{S} \oplus \mathscr{T} \tag{43}$$

and

$$\mathscr{W} + \mathscr{X}_a = (\mathscr{S} + \mathscr{X}_a) \oplus \mathscr{T} .$$

As $\mathscr{B}_a = \mathscr{X}_a$, $\mathscr{S} + \mathscr{X}_a$ is (A, B)-invariant, so we take $F_0 \colon \mathscr{X} \oplus \mathscr{X}_a \to \mathscr{U} \oplus \mathscr{U}_a$ such that $F_0 \in \underline{F}(\mathscr{S} + \mathscr{X}_a)$ and $F_0 | \mathscr{T} = F | \mathscr{T}$. Then by (43)

$$\Big[(A + BF_0) - \Big(A + (B + B_a) F\Big)\Big]\mathscr{W}$$

$$\subset (A + BF_0)\mathscr{S} + \Big(A + (B + B_a) F\Big) \mathscr{S} + B_a F \mathscr{T} \subset \mathscr{S} + \mathscr{X}_a . \tag{44}$$

Also

$$(A + BF_0)(\mathscr{W} + \mathscr{X}_a) = (A + BF_0)(\mathscr{S} + \mathscr{T} + \mathscr{X}_a) \subset (A + BF_0)\mathscr{T} + \mathscr{S} + \mathscr{X}_a$$

$$= [A + (B + B_a) F_0] \mathscr{T} + \mathscr{S} + \mathscr{X}_a$$

$$= [A + (B + B_a) F] \mathscr{T} + \mathscr{S} + \mathscr{X}_a \subset \mathscr{W} + \mathscr{X}_a ;$$

and as $\mathscr{V} \subset \mathscr{W} + \mathscr{X}_a$,

$$(A + BF_0)\mathscr{V} = P(A + BF_0)\mathscr{V} \subset P(\mathscr{W} + \mathscr{X}_a) = \mathscr{V} ;$$

so that finally

$$F_0 \in \underline{F}(\mathscr{S} + \mathscr{X}_a) \cap \underline{F}(\mathscr{W} + \mathscr{X}_a) \cap \underline{F}(\mathscr{V}) . \tag{45}$$

By (45), with the inclusions $\underline{F}_e(\mathscr{W}) \subset \underline{F}_e(\mathscr{S})$ and $\underline{F}(\mathscr{V}) \subset \underline{F}(\mathscr{R})$, the first, third, fourth and sixth squares of the diagram (Fig. 10.1) commute (here the Q_i are canonical projections and bars as usual denote the induced maps). We claim that isomorphisms J_1, J_2 exist as shown.

For J_1, let $1 \colon \mathscr{W} \to \mathscr{W} + \mathscr{X}_a$ be the insertion map and define J_1 according to

$$J_1 Q_1 = Q_2 1 ;$$

as

$$\begin{aligned}\mathrm{Ker}\, Q_1 &= \mathscr{S} \\ &= (\mathscr{S} + \mathscr{X}_a) \cap \mathscr{W} \qquad \text{(by (42))} \\ &= \mathrm{Ker}\, Q_2 \cap \mathscr{W} = \mathrm{Ker}(Q_2 1)\,,\end{aligned}$$

J_1 exists and is unique. With $x \in \mathscr{W}$, $J_1(Q_1 x) = 0$ implies $x \in \mathrm{Ker}\, Q_2 1 = \mathscr{S}$, so $Q_1 x = 0$ and J_1 is monic; also

$$Q_2 1\mathscr{W} = Q_2 \mathscr{W} = Q_2(\mathscr{W} + \mathscr{X}_a) = \frac{\mathscr{W} + \mathscr{X}_a}{\mathscr{S} + \mathscr{X}_a}\,,$$

hence J_1 is epic. For the second square, with $x \in \mathscr{W}$,

$$\begin{aligned}\overline{(A + BF_0)}\, J_1(Q_1 x) &= \overline{(A + BF_0)}(Q_2 1 x) \\ &= Q_2(A + BF_0)\, 1x \\ &= Q_2 1[A + (B + B_a)\, F]\, x \qquad \text{(by (44))} \\ &= J_1 Q_1[A + (B + B_a)\, F]\, x = J_1\overline{[A + (B + B_a)\, F]}(Q_1 x)\,,\end{aligned}$$

as claimed.

Define J_2 according to

$$J_2 Q_2 = Q_3 P\,;$$

since

$$\begin{aligned}\mathrm{Ker}\, Q_2 &= \mathscr{S} + \mathscr{X}_a = \mathscr{S} + \mathrm{Ker}\, P = P^{-1}(P\mathscr{S}) \\ &= P^{-1}(\mathscr{X} \cap \mathscr{R}) = P^{-1}(\mathrm{Im}\, P \cap \mathrm{Ker}\, Q_3) = \mathrm{Ker}(Q_3 P)\,,\end{aligned}$$

J_2 exists and is unique; with $x \in \mathscr{W} + \mathscr{X}_a$, $J_2(Q_2 x) = 0$ implies

$$x \in \mathrm{Ker}(Q_3 P) = \mathscr{S} + \mathscr{X}_a = \mathrm{Ker}\, Q_2\,,$$

so $Q_2 x = 0$, and J_2 is monic; as $Q_3 P$ is epic, J_2 is epic too. For the fifth square, with $x \in \mathscr{W} + \mathscr{X}_a$,

$$\begin{aligned}\overline{\overline{(A + BF_0)}}\, J_2(Q_2 x) &= \overline{\overline{(A + BF_0)}}\, Q_3 P x = Q_3(A + BF_0)\, P x \\ &= Q_3 P(A + BF_0)\, P x \quad [\text{since } (A + BF_0)\, P x \in \mathscr{V}] \\ &= J_2 Q_2(A + BF_0)\, P x \quad [\text{since } \mathscr{V} \subset \mathscr{W} + \mathscr{X}_a]\end{aligned}$$

$$= J_2\overline{(A + BF_0)}Q_2 Px$$

$$= J_2\overline{(A + BF_0)}(Q_2 x) \quad [\text{since } x - Px \in \mathcal{X}_a \subset \operatorname{Ker} Q_2] ,$$

and the fifth square commutes, as claimed.

(iii) Cut out the second and fifth squares. Attach the top edge of the fifth to the bottom edge of the second. Then appeal to Theorem 5.7. ▌

Returning to the decoupling problem, we have on the assumption (41),

$$\check{\mathcal{R}}^* = \mathcal{R}_1^* \cap \mathcal{R}_2^* ,$$

$$\mathcal{R}_0 = \mathcal{V}_g , \tag{46}$$

and the bound (38) becomes

$$n_0 = d\left(\mathcal{R}_1^* \cap \mathcal{R}_2^*\right) - d(\mathcal{R}_0) . \tag{47}$$

Our aim is to show that for any solution of EDP such that

$$\sigma[A + (B + B_a) F] \subset \mathbb{C}_g \tag{48}$$

we must have

$$d(\mathcal{X}_a) \geq n_0 . \tag{49}$$

The proof depends on Lemma 10.6 together with some easier relations which we establish next. It will be assumed throughout that (41) holds and $\langle A \mid \mathcal{B} \rangle = \mathcal{X}$.

LEMMA 10.7. Let $\mathcal{R}_1, \mathcal{R}_2$ be c.s. such that

$$\begin{aligned} &\mathcal{R}_1 \subset \mathcal{K}_2 , \qquad \mathcal{R}_1 + \mathcal{K}_1 = \mathcal{X} \\ &\mathcal{R}_2 \subset \mathcal{K}_1 , \qquad \mathcal{R}_2 + \mathcal{K}_2 = \mathcal{X} , \end{aligned} \tag{50}$$

where $0 \neq \mathcal{K}_i \neq \mathcal{X}$ $(i \in \underline{2})$. Then

$$\mathcal{R}_i = \mathcal{R}_i^* \qquad (i \in \underline{2}) .$$

PROOF: By (41) we must have

$$d(\mathcal{B} \cap \mathcal{R}_i) = 0, 1 \text{ or } 2 , \qquad i \in \underline{2} ,$$

and the first and third possibilities are ruled out by (50). Then $\mathcal{B} \cap \mathcal{R}_i = \mathcal{B} \cap \mathcal{R}_i^*$, and choosing $F_i \in \underline{F}(\mathcal{R}_i) \cap \underline{F}(\mathcal{R}_i^*)$, we get

$$\mathcal{R}_i = \langle A + BF_i | \mathcal{B} \cap \mathcal{R}_i \rangle = \langle A + BF_i | \mathcal{B} \cap \mathcal{R}_i^* \rangle = \mathcal{R}_i^* ,$$

as claimed. ▮

LEMMA 10.8. Let $\mathcal{T}_i \subset \mathcal{X}$ ($i \in \underline{2}$), $\mathcal{G} \subset \mathcal{X}$, and Q: $\mathcal{X} \to \mathcal{X}/\mathcal{G}$ the canonical projection. Then

$$d(\mathcal{G}) \geq d\left[\frac{Q\mathcal{T}_1 \cap Q\mathcal{T}_2}{Q(\mathcal{T}_1 \cap \mathcal{T}_2)}\right].$$

PROOF:

$$d\left[\frac{Q\mathcal{T}_1 \cap Q\mathcal{T}_2}{Q(\mathcal{T}_1 \cap \mathcal{T}_2)}\right] = d\left[\frac{(\mathcal{T}_1 + \mathcal{T}_2) \cap \mathcal{G}}{\mathcal{T}_1 \cap \mathcal{G} + \mathcal{T}_2 \cap \mathcal{G}}\right] \quad \text{(by Ex. 0.12(ix))}$$

$$\leq d(\mathcal{G}) . \ ▮$$

As an immediate application we obtain

LEMMA 10.9. Let P be the projection on $\mathcal{X}$ along $\mathcal{X}_a$. Let $\mathcal{S}_i \subset \mathcal{X} \oplus \mathcal{X}_a$ ($i \in \underline{2}$) and $\mathcal{R}_i \triangleq P\mathcal{S}_i$ ($i \in \underline{2}$). If $\mathcal{R}_0$ is such that

$$P(\mathcal{S}_1 \cap \mathcal{S}_2) \subset \mathcal{R}_0 \subset \mathcal{R}_1 \cap \mathcal{R}_2$$

then

$$d(\mathcal{X}_a) \geq d\left[\frac{\mathcal{R}_1 \cap \mathcal{R}_2}{\mathcal{R}_0}\right].$$

PROOF: Apply Lemma 10.8 with $\mathcal{S}_i$, $\mathcal{X} \oplus \mathcal{X}_a$, $\mathcal{X}_a$ and P in place of $\mathcal{T}_i$, $\mathcal{X}$, $\mathcal{G}$ and Q. ▮

As our last preliminary result we have

LEMMA 10.10. If e.c.s. $\mathcal{S}_i$ ($i \in \underline{2}$) provide a solution of EDP such that (48) is true, then

$$P(\mathcal{S}_1 \cap \mathcal{S}_2) \subset \mathcal{R}_0 ,$$

where $\mathcal{R}_0$ is given by (46).

PROOF: By (48) there exists $F \in \underline{F}_e(\mathcal{J}_1 \cap \mathcal{J}_2)$ such that

$$\sigma[(A + (B+B_a) F) \,|\, \mathcal{J}_1 \cap \mathcal{J}_2] \subset \mathbb{C}_g . \tag{51}$$

Writing $\mathcal{J}^*$ for the supremal e.c.s. in $\mathcal{J}_1 \cap \mathcal{J}_2$, and $\mathcal{R}^*$ for the supremal c.s. in $P(\mathcal{J}_1 \cap \mathcal{J}_2)$ we have by Lemma 10.6 that (in our usual notation)

$$\sigma\left[\overline{A + (B+B_a) F} \,\middle|\, \frac{\mathcal{J}_1 \cap \mathcal{J}_2}{\mathcal{J}^*}\right] = \sigma\left[\overline{\overline{A + BF_0}} \,\middle|\, \frac{P(\mathcal{J}_1 \cap \mathcal{J}_2)}{\mathcal{R}^*}\right] \tag{52}$$

for all $F_0 \in \underline{F}[P(\mathcal{J}_1 \cap \mathcal{J}_2)]$. By (51) and (52) there exists $F_0 \in \underline{F}[P(\mathcal{J}_1 \cap \mathcal{J}_2)]$ such that

$$\sigma[(A + BF) \,|\, P(\mathcal{J}_1 \cap \mathcal{J}_2)] \subset \mathbb{C}_g . \tag{53}$$

But as the $\mathcal{J}_i$ solve EDP we have $P\mathcal{J}_i \subset \mathcal{R}_i^*$ $(i \in \underline{2})$, so that

$$P(\mathcal{J}_1 \cap \mathcal{J}_2) \subset \mathcal{R}_1^* \cap \mathcal{R}_2^* . \tag{54}$$

Noting again that $\mathcal{R}_1^* \cap \mathcal{R}_2^* = \check{\mathcal{R}}^*$, and recalling the supremal property (37a) of $\mathcal{V}_g$, we see from (53) and (54) that

$$\begin{aligned} P(\mathcal{J}_1 \cap \mathcal{J}_2) &\subset \mathcal{V}_g \\ &= \mathcal{R}_0 \qquad \text{(by (46))} , \end{aligned}$$

as asserted. ▮

It is now easy to prove our main result, the inequality (49). Assuming $\mathcal{J}_i$ $(i \in \underline{2})$ solve EDP, we have that $P\mathcal{J}_i$ satisfy (50), hence by Lemma 10.7, $P\mathcal{J}_i = \mathcal{R}_i^*$ $(i \in \underline{2})$. By Lemmas 10.9 and 10.10 there results finally

$$\begin{aligned} d(\mathcal{X}_a) &\geq d\left[\frac{\mathcal{R}_1^* \cap \mathcal{R}_2^*}{\mathcal{R}_0}\right] \\ &= n_0 \qquad \text{(by (47))}, \end{aligned}$$

as we set out to show.

10.5 <u>Minimal Order Compensation:</u> $d(\mathcal{B}) = k$

In this section we prove that the bound (38) on $d(\mathcal{X}_a)$ is best possible when $d(\mathcal{B}) = k$, $k \geq 2$ arbitrary. The argument follows the same lines as in Section 10.4, but with $\mathcal{R}_1^* \cap \mathcal{R}_2^*$ now replaced by the radical $\check{\mathcal{R}}^* \triangleq \{\mathcal{R}_i^*, i \in \underline{k}\}^{\vee}$. The first step is to generalize Lemma 10.7.

LEMMA 10.11. Let $\mathcal{R}_i$, $i \in \underline{k}$ be c.s. such that

$$\mathcal{R}_i \subset \hat{\mathcal{K}}_i, \qquad \mathcal{R}_i + \mathcal{K}_i = \mathcal{X}, \qquad i \in \underline{k}, \tag{55}$$

where $0 \neq \mathcal{K}_i \neq \mathcal{X}$, $i \in \underline{k}$. Then

$$\mathcal{R}_i = \mathcal{R}_i^*, \qquad i \in \underline{k}.$$

PROOF: Just as in the proof of Lemma 10.7, it is enough to show that

$$d(\mathcal{B} \cap \mathcal{R}_i^*) = 1, \qquad i \in \underline{k}. \tag{56}$$

To verify (56) start from

$$d\left(\mathcal{B} \cap \sum_{i=1}^{j} \mathcal{R}_i^*\right) \leq d\left(\mathcal{B} \cap \sum_{i=1}^{j+1} \mathcal{R}_i^*\right), \qquad j \in \underline{k-1}. \tag{57}$$

If (57) holds with equality for $j = \ell$, then

$$\mathcal{B} \cap \sum_{i=1}^{\ell} \mathcal{R}_i^* = \mathcal{B} \cap \sum_{i=1}^{\ell+1} \mathcal{R}_i^*. \tag{58}$$

Write $\mathcal{S} \triangleq \sum_{i=1}^{\ell} \mathcal{R}_i^*$. By (58), trivially,

$$\mathcal{B} \cap \left(\mathcal{S} + \mathcal{R}_{\ell+1}^*\right) = \mathcal{B} \cap \mathcal{S} + \mathcal{B} \cap \mathcal{R}_{\ell+1}^*$$

and so, by (0.3)–(0.4),

$$\mathcal{S} \cap \left(\mathcal{B} + \mathcal{R}_{\ell+1}^*\right) = \mathcal{S} \cap \mathcal{B} + \mathcal{S} \cap \mathcal{R}_{\ell+1}^*.$$

Then

$$A\left(\mathcal{S} \cap \mathcal{R}_{\ell+1}^*\right) \subset (\mathcal{B} + \mathcal{S}) \cap \left(\mathcal{B} + \mathcal{R}_{\ell+1}^*\right) \subset \mathcal{B} + \mathcal{S} \cap \mathcal{R}_{\ell+1}^*. \tag{59}$$

By (59), $\underline{F}(\mathcal{S} \cap \mathcal{R}_{\ell+1}^*) \neq \emptyset$, hence there exists $F \in \underline{F}(\mathcal{S}) \cap \underline{F}(\mathcal{R}_{\ell+1}^*)$, and for such F,

$$\begin{aligned}\mathcal{R}_{\ell+1}^* &= \langle A + BF \mid \mathcal{B} \cap \mathcal{R}_{\ell+1}^* \rangle \subset \langle A + BF \mid \mathcal{S} \rangle \\ &\subset \mathcal{S} \subset \sum_{i=1}^{\ell} \bigcap_{j \neq i} \mathcal{K}_j \subset \mathcal{K}_{\ell+1},\end{aligned}$$

which is ruled out by (55). Therefore (57) holds with strict inequality at each $j \in \underline{k-1}$. Since

$$d\left(\mathcal{B} \cap \sum_{i=1}^{k} \mathcal{R}_i^*\right) \le d(\mathcal{B}) = k ,$$

and since, again by (55), $d(\mathcal{B} \cap \mathcal{R}_i^*) \ge 1$ $(i \in \underline{k})$, the result follows. ▮

The remaining task is to generalize the dimensional inequality of Lemma 10.8.

LEMMA 10.12. Let $\mathcal{T}_i$ $(i \in \underline{k})$ and $\mathcal{S}$ be subspaces of $\mathcal{X}$, and let $\mathcal{T}_0 \subset \mathcal{X}$ be any subspace with the properties

$$\check{\mathcal{T}} + \mathcal{S} \subset \mathcal{T}_0 = [(\mathcal{T}_\bullet + \mathcal{S}) \cap \mathcal{T}_0]^{\vee} . \tag{60}$$

Then

$$\triangle_i \left(\frac{\mathcal{T}_i + \mathcal{T}_0}{\mathcal{T}_0}\right) = d\left[\frac{\mathcal{S} + \sum_i (\mathcal{T}_i \cap \mathcal{T}_0)}{\sum_i (\mathcal{T}_i \cap \mathcal{T}_0)}\right] - d\left[\frac{\mathcal{T}_0 + \sum_i \mathcal{T}_i}{\sum_i \mathcal{T}_i}\right] \tag{61}$$

$$\le d(\mathcal{S}) . \tag{62}$$

PROOF: Write $\mathcal{T}_\sigma \triangleq \sum_i \mathcal{T}_i$. By Lemma 10.1(v),

$$\begin{aligned} \triangle_i \left(\frac{\mathcal{T}_i + \mathcal{T}_0}{\mathcal{T}_0}\right) &= d\left[\frac{\mathcal{T}_0 \cap \mathcal{T}_\sigma}{\sum_i (\mathcal{T}_0 \cap \mathcal{T}_i)}\right] \\ &= d\left[\frac{\mathcal{T}_0}{\sum_i (\mathcal{T}_0 \cap \mathcal{T}_i)}\right] - d\left[\frac{\mathcal{T}_0}{\mathcal{T}_0 \cap \mathcal{T}_\sigma}\right] \\ &= d\left[\frac{\mathcal{T}_0}{\sum_i (\mathcal{T}_0 \cap \mathcal{T}_i)}\right] - d\left[\frac{\mathcal{T}_0 + \mathcal{T}_\sigma}{\mathcal{T}_\sigma}\right] . \end{aligned} \tag{63}$$

Now

$$\mathscr{T}_0 = \mathscr{T}_0 + \mathscr{S} = [(\mathscr{T}_\bullet + \mathscr{S}) \cap \mathscr{T}_0]^\vee + \mathscr{S}$$

$$= \sum_i \{[(\mathscr{T}_i + \mathscr{S}) \cap \mathscr{T}_0] \cap [(\mathscr{T}_\bullet + \mathscr{S}) \cap \mathscr{T}_0]^\vee + \mathscr{S} \qquad \text{(by (6))}$$

$$= \sum_i [(\mathscr{T}_i + \mathscr{S}) \cap \mathscr{T}_0] + \mathscr{S} \qquad \text{(by (60))}$$

$$= \sum_i (\mathscr{T}_i \cap \mathscr{T}_0) + \mathscr{S}\,. \tag{64}$$

By (64), trivially,

$$d\left[\frac{\mathscr{T}_0}{\sum_i (\mathscr{T}_0 \cap \mathscr{T}_i)}\right] = d\left[\frac{\mathscr{S} + \sum_i (\mathscr{T}_i \cap \mathscr{T}_0)}{\sum_i (\mathscr{T}_0 \cap \mathscr{T}_i)}\right];$$

substitution of this in (63) yields (61), and (62) is then obvious. ▮

Applying this result in the context of EDP we obtain

LEMMA 10.13. <u>Let</u> P <u>be the projection on</u> $\mathscr{X}$ <u>along</u> $\mathscr{X}_a$. <u>Let</u> $\mathscr{J}_i \subset \mathscr{X} \oplus \mathscr{X}_a$ $(i \in \underline{k})$ <u>and</u> $\mathscr{R}_i \triangleq P\mathscr{J}_i$ $(i \in \underline{k})$. <u>Suppose</u> $\mathscr{R}_0 \subset \mathscr{X}$ <u>and</u> $\mathscr{V} \subset \mathscr{X}$ <u>are such that</u>

$$P\check{\mathscr{J}} \subset \mathscr{R}_0 \triangleq (\mathscr{R}_\bullet \cap \mathscr{V})^\vee\,.$$

<u>Then</u>

$$d(\mathscr{X}_a) \geq \bigtriangleup_i \left(\frac{\mathscr{R}_i + \mathscr{R}_0}{\mathscr{R}_0}\right).$$

PROOF: In Lemma 10.12 replace $(\mathscr{T}_i, \mathscr{S}, \mathscr{X})$ by $(\mathscr{J}_i, \mathscr{X}_a, \mathscr{X} \oplus \mathscr{X}_a)$ and define

$$\mathscr{J}_0 \triangleq [(\mathscr{J}_\bullet + \mathscr{X}_a) \cap (\mathscr{V} + \mathscr{X}_a)]^\vee\,.$$

Since $P\check{\mathscr{J}} \subset \mathscr{V}$ we have $\check{\mathscr{J}} \subset \mathscr{V} + \mathscr{X}_a$, so

$$\mathscr{J}_0 \supset \left[\left(\mathscr{J}_\bullet + \mathscr{X}_a\right) \cap \check{\mathscr{J}}\right]^\vee \supset \left(\mathscr{J}_\bullet \cap \check{\mathscr{J}}\right)^\vee$$

$$= \check{\mathscr{J}} \qquad \text{(by (7))},$$

hence $\mathscr{I}_0 \supset \check{\mathscr{I}} + \mathscr{X}_a$. Also, by Lemma 10.1(ii), applied to the family $\{\mathscr{I}_i + \mathscr{X}_a,\ i \in \underline{k}\}$,

$$\mathscr{I}_0 = [(\mathscr{I}_\bullet + \mathscr{X}_a) \cap \mathscr{I}_0]^\vee .$$

Thus $\mathscr{I}_0$ has the properties required of $\mathscr{T}_0$ in (60), and (62) yields

$$d(\mathscr{X}_a) \geq \bigtriangleup_i \left(\frac{\mathscr{I}_i + \mathscr{I}_0}{\mathscr{I}_0}\right) = \bigtriangleup_i \left(\frac{\mathscr{I}_i + \mathscr{I}_0 + \mathscr{X}_a}{\mathscr{I}_0 + \mathscr{X}_a}\right)$$

$$= \bigtriangleup_i \left[\frac{(\mathscr{I}_i + \mathscr{I}_0 + \mathscr{X}_a)/\mathscr{X}_a}{(\mathscr{I}_0 + \mathscr{X}_a)/\mathscr{X}_a}\right] = \bigtriangleup_i \left[\frac{P\mathscr{I}_i + P\mathscr{I}_0}{P\mathscr{I}_0}\right]$$

$$= \bigtriangleup_i \left(\frac{\mathscr{R}_i + \mathscr{R}_0}{\mathscr{R}_0}\right) . \blacksquare$$

To prove our main result, that the bound (38) is minimal, it now suffices to check the hypotheses of Lemma 10.13 (with $\mathscr{R}_i$ replaced by $\mathscr{R}_i^*$) for any solution $\{\mathscr{I}_i,\ i \in \underline{k}\}$ of EDP which satisfies the additional requirement

$$\sigma[A + (B + B_a)F] \subset \mathbb{C}_g . \qquad \text{(48 bis)}$$

By exactly the same argument as in the proof of Lemma 10.10 (with $\mathscr{I}_1 \cap \mathscr{I}_2$ replaced by $\check{\mathscr{I}}$), (48) implies $P\check{\mathscr{I}} \subset \mathscr{V}_g$. But

$$\check{\mathscr{I}} = (\mathscr{I}_\bullet \cap \check{\mathscr{I}})^\vee \qquad \text{(by (7))}$$

$$= \bigcap_i \sum_{j \neq i} (\mathscr{I}_j \cap \check{\mathscr{I}}) \qquad \text{(by (3))} ;$$

also, Lemma 10.11 applied to $\mathscr{R}_i = P\mathscr{I}_i$ yields $P\mathscr{I}_i = \mathscr{R}_i^*$ $(i \in \underline{k})$; and so

$$P\check{\mathscr{I}} \subset \bigcap_i \sum_{j \neq i} (\mathscr{R}_j^* \cap \mathscr{V}_g)$$

$$= (\mathscr{R}_\bullet^* \cap \mathscr{V}_g)^\vee \qquad \text{(by (3))}$$

$$= \mathscr{R}_0 ,$$

by the definition (37b). The main result is proved.

10.6 Exercises

10.1 Develop a computational procedure for decoupling with efficient compensation. HINT: Given A, B, D_i ($i \in \underline{k}$) and $\mathbb{C} = \mathbb{C}_g \dot{\cup} \mathbb{C}_b$, compute in the following order: $\mathcal{K}_i$, $\hat{\mathcal{K}}_i$, $\mathcal{R}_i^*$ ($i \in \underline{k}$); solvability verification of EDP, (23); $\check{\mathcal{R}}^*$ by (1); $\mathcal{V} \triangleq \sup \underline{\mathcal{I}}(A, B; \check{\mathcal{R}}^*)$, $\mathcal{R} \triangleq \sup \underline{\mathcal{C}}(A, B; \mathcal{V})$; $\hat{F} \in \underline{F}(\mathcal{V})$; P: $\mathcal{X} \to \mathcal{X}/\mathcal{R}$; $\mathcal{X}_g(A + B\hat{F})$; $\mathcal{V}_g$ by (31); $\mathcal{R}_0 \triangleq \check{\mathcal{R}}_0(\mathcal{V}_g)$ by (16); $d(\mathcal{X}_a) = n_0$ by (17); E_i ($i \in \underline{k}$) by Lemma 10.5; $\mathcal{V}_i$ ($i \in \underline{k}$) by (20); F by (24); $\mathcal{J}_i$ ($i \in \underline{k}$) by (25). To assign the spectrum to $\mathbb{C}_g$, modify F by the procedure starting with (33).

10.2 Construct a numerical example to illustrate the procedure of Ex. 10.1. HINT: The example at the end of Section 10.3 illustrates the procedure up to the computation of $n_0 = 2$. To compute the E_i by Lemma 10.5, it is easiest first to pick a basis for $\mathcal{R}_1^* + \mathcal{R}_2^*$ which exhibits $\mathcal{R}_0$ and $\mathcal{R}_1^* \cap \mathcal{R}_2^*$; thus

$$\mathcal{R}_1^* = \operatorname{Im}\begin{bmatrix} 1 & 0 & 0 & 0 \\ 0 & 1 & 0 & 0 \\ 0 & 0 & 1 & 1 \\ 0 & 0 & 0 & -1 \\ 0 & 0 & 0 & 0 \end{bmatrix}, \qquad \mathcal{R}_2^* = \operatorname{Im}\begin{bmatrix} 0 & 0 & 0 & 0 \\ 1 & 0 & 0 & 0 \\ 0 & 1 & 0 & 1 \\ 0 & 0 & 0 & -1 \\ 0 & 0 & 1 & 0 \end{bmatrix}.$$

According to Lemma 10.5, one may pick $E_1 = 0$, and define E_2 such that $E_2\mathcal{R}_0 = 0$ and E_2 maps the complement of $\mathcal{R}_0$, in $\mathcal{R}_1^* \cap \mathcal{R}_2^*$, onto $\mathcal{X}_a$: e.g.,

$$\begin{bmatrix} 0 & 0 \\ 1 & 0 \\ 0 & 1 \\ 0 & 0 \\ 0 & 0 \end{bmatrix} \longmapsto \begin{bmatrix} 0 & 0 \\ 0 & 0 \\ 0 & 0 \\ 0 & 0 \\ 0 & 0 \\ \hline 1 & 0 \\ 0 & 1 \end{bmatrix}.$$

The subspaces $\mathcal{V}_i = (1 + E_i)\mathcal{R}_i^* \subset \mathcal{X} \oplus \mathcal{X}_a$ are then

$$\mathcal{V}_1 = \operatorname{Im}\begin{bmatrix} 1 & 0 & 0 & 0 \\ 0 & 1 & 0 & 0 \\ 0 & 0 & 1 & 1 \\ 0 & 0 & 0 & -1 \\ 0 & 0 & 0 & 0 \\ \hline 0 & 0 & 0 & 0 \\ 0 & 0 & 0 & 0 \end{bmatrix}, \qquad \mathcal{V}_2 = \operatorname{Im}\begin{bmatrix} 0 & 0 & 0 & 0 \\ 1 & 0 & 0 & 0 \\ 0 & 1 & 0 & 1 \\ 0 & 0 & 0 & -1 \\ 0 & 0 & 1 & 0 \\ \hline 1 & 0 & 0 & 0 \\ 0 & 1 & 0 & 0 \end{bmatrix}.$$

It is a routine matter to select B_a, and then compute an F to satisfy (28); one choice yields

$$B + B_a = \left[\begin{array}{cccc} 0 & 1 & 0 & 0 \\ 1 & 0 & 0 & 0 \\ 0 & 0 & 0 & 0 \\ 0 & 0 & 0 & 0 \\ 0 & 1 & 0 & 0 \\ \hline 0 & 0 & 1 & 0 \\ 0 & 0 & 0 & 1 \end{array}\right], \qquad F = \left[\begin{array}{c|ccc} & 0 & 0 & 0 \\ 0_{4\times 4} & 0 & -1 & 0 \\ & 0 & 0 & 0 \\ & 1 & 0 & 1 \end{array}\right].$$

From this there follows

$$A + (B + B_a)F = \left[\begin{array}{ccccc|cc} 0 & 1 & 0 & 0 & 0 & -1 & 0 \\ 0 & 0 & 0 & 0 & 0 & 0 & 0 \\ 0 & 0 & 1 & 1 & 0 & 0 & 0 \\ 1 & 0 & 0 & 0 & 1 & 0 & 0 \\ 0 & 0 & 0 & 0 & 0 & -1 & 0 \\ \hline 0 & 0 & 0 & 0 & 0 & 0 & 0 \\ 0 & 0 & 0 & 0 & 1 & 0 & 1 \end{array}\right],$$

which leaves $\mathcal{V}_1, \mathcal{V}_2$ invariant. Computing the $\mathcal{S}_i$ by (25) we find that $\mathcal{S}_i = \mathcal{V}_i$ $(i \in \underline{2})$ and that

$$\mathcal{S}_1 \cap \mathcal{S}_2 = \operatorname{Im} \operatorname{col}[0 \quad 0 \quad 1 \; -1 \quad 0 \quad 0 \quad 0].$$

While in this synthesis the action of $A + (B+B_a)F$ on $\mathcal{S}_1 \cap \mathcal{S}_2$ is fixed (and is 'good', since $0 \in \mathbb{C}_g$ by definition) one may, of course, assign at will the spectrum of the induced maps on $\mathcal{S}_i/(\mathcal{S}_1 \cap \mathcal{S}_2)$, and also, by controllability of $(A, B+B_a)$, the spectrum on $(\mathcal{X} \oplus \mathcal{X}_a)/(\mathcal{S}_1 + \mathcal{S}_2)$. This is achieved by pole assignment procedures with which the reader will at this stage be familiar.

10.3 Develop an example to show that efficient decoupling in the sense of Section 10.3 need not be minimal in the sense of Section 10.4.

10.4 For some concrete examples, compare the sensitivity (suitably defined) of decoupling controllers designed 'naively' and 'efficiently'.

10.7 Notes and References

The material in this chapter is adapted from Morse and Wonham [1]. The concept of 'radical' of a family of vector spaces was exploited there, but without being named as such;

the term is suggested by vaguely analogous usage in ring theory. The treatment in Section 10.1 is more systematic than in the article cited, and some of the results here are new.

CHAPTER 11

NONINTERACTING CONTROL III: GENERIC SOLVABILITY

In this chapter we discuss solvability of the noninteraction problem from the viewpoint of genericity, in the parameter space of the matrices A, B and the D_i ($i \in \underline{k}$). It turns out that noninteraction is possible for almost all data sets $(A, B, D_1, \ldots, D_k)$ if and only if the array dimensions of the given matrices satisfy appropriate constraints. When these conditions fail decoupling is possible, if at all, only for system structures which are rather special. Finally, in the generically solvable case we determine the generic bounds on dynamic order of a decoupling compensator, corresponding to the 'naive' and 'efficient' extension procedures of Chapters 9 and 10, respectively.

11.1 Generic Solvability of EDP

Consider as usual the system

$$\dot{x} = Ax + Bu \; ; \qquad z_i = D_i x \, , \qquad i \in \underline{k} \, .$$

To discuss genericity we regard A, B and the D_i as real matrix representations of the corresponding maps, computed relative to fixed bases in $\mathcal{U}$, $\mathcal{X}$ and $\mathcal{Z}_i$ ($i \in \underline{k}$). We take A: $n \times n$, B: $n \times m$ and D_i: $q_i \times n$, with $n \geq 1$, $1 \leq m \leq n$, $1 \leq q_i \leq n$ and $k \geq 2$. Listing the matrix elements in arbitrary order we introduce the data point

$$\underline{p} \triangleq (A, B, D_1, \ldots, D_k)$$

in $\mathbb{R}^N$, with $N = n^2 + nm + (q_1 + \cdots + q_k)n$.

By Theorem 9.3 the extended decoupling problem (EDP) is solvable if and only if

$$\mathcal{R}_i^* + \mathcal{K}_i = \mathcal{X} \, , \qquad i \in \underline{k} \, , \tag{1}$$

where

$$\mathcal{K}_i \triangleq \operatorname{Ker} D_i \, , \qquad i \in \underline{k} \, ,$$

$$\mathcal{R}_i^* \triangleq \sup \underline{\mathfrak{C}}(\hat{\mathcal{K}}_i) \, , \qquad i \in \underline{k} \, , \tag{2}$$

and

$$\hat{\mathcal{K}}_i \triangleq \bigcap_{j \neq i} \mathcal{K}_j \, , \qquad i \in \underline{k} \, .$$

Solvability of EDP is thus a property $\Pi: \mathbb{R}^N \to \{0,1\}$; that is, $\Pi(\underline{p}) = 1$ (or 0) according as (1) does (or does not) hold at $\underline{p}$. Our first result is a criterion for generic solvability.

THEOREM 11.1. Π is generic if and only if

$$\sum_{i=1}^{k} q_i \leq n \tag{3}$$

and

$$m \geq 1 + \sum_{i=1}^{k} q_i - \min_{1 \leq i \leq k} q_i . \tag{4}$$

It will be clear from the proof that (3) states simply that the row spaces of the D_i are generically independent, while (4) means that, generically, the number of independent controls is large enough to ensure that

$$\mathcal{B} \cap \hat{\mathcal{K}}_i \neq 0 , \qquad i \in \underline{k} .$$

By the discussion in Chapter 9 it should be obvious that the first condition is necessary for noninteraction while the second is necessary for output controllability.

As an example, if $n = 15$, $k = 2$, $q_1 = 3$ and $q_2 = 5$, then EDP is generically solvable if and only if $m \geq 6$. In general, since $q_i \geq 1$ we always need $m \geq k$; and if, for instance, $m = k$ we can only have $q_i = 1$ for all i.

The following notation will be used in the proof. A prime denotes matrix transpose, dual linear transformation or dual space. If n, m are integers,

$$n \vee m \triangleq \max(n, m) , \qquad n \wedge m \triangleq \min(n, m) .$$

If for each $\underline{p} \in \mathbb{R}^N$, $\mathcal{R}(\underline{p}) \subset \mathcal{X}$ is a linear subspace, we write

$$d(\mathcal{R}) = r \quad (g)$$

to mean that the generic dimension of $\mathcal{R}$ is r, i.e., that $d(\mathcal{R}(\underline{p})) \neq r$ only for $\underline{p}$ in some fixed proper variety $\underline{V} \subset \mathbb{R}^N$ depending on the function $\mathcal{R}(\cdot)$. Subspace inclusions written $\mathcal{R} \subset \mathcal{S}$ (g) are to be interpreted in the same fashion. We observe that a finite union of proper varieties is a proper variety, hence if a finite set of propositions each holds (g), the entire set holds simultaneously (g).

PROOF of Theorem 11.1. 1. Preliminaries. It is clear that

$$d(\mathcal{K}_i) = n - q_i \quad (g) , \qquad i \in \underline{k} ,$$

and

$$d(\mathrm{Im}\, D_i') = q_i \quad (g), \qquad i \in \underline{k}, \tag{5}$$

since the dimensional evaluations fail at $\underline{p}$ only if all $q_i \times q_i$ minors of the $q_i \times n$ matrix D_i vanish. Similarly

$$d\left(\sum_{j \neq i} \mathrm{Im}\, D_j'\right) = n \wedge \sum_{j \neq i} q_j \quad (g), \qquad i \in \underline{k},$$

and

$$d(\hat{\mathcal{K}}_i) = n - d(\hat{\mathcal{K}}_i^{\perp}) = n - n \wedge \sum_{j \neq i} q_j \quad (g), \qquad i \in \underline{k}. \tag{6}$$

By the same reasoning

$$d(\mathcal{B}) = m \quad (g) \tag{7}$$

and

$$\begin{aligned} d(\mathcal{B} \cap \hat{\mathcal{K}}_i) &= d(\mathcal{B}) + d(\hat{\mathcal{K}}_i) - d(\mathcal{B} + \hat{\mathcal{K}}_i) \\ &= m + \left(n - n \wedge \sum_{j \neq i} q_j\right) - n \wedge \left[m + \left(n - n \wedge \sum_{j \neq i} q_j\right)\right] \quad (g) \\ &= 0 \vee \left(m - n \wedge \sum_{j \neq i} q_j\right) \quad (g), \qquad i \in \underline{k}. \end{aligned} \tag{8}$$

2. <u>Necessity.</u> Suppose EDP is solvable at $\underline{p}$. By (1) and (2)

$$\mathcal{K}_i + \hat{\mathcal{K}}_i = \mathcal{X}, \qquad i \in \underline{k},$$

or

$$\left(\sum_{j \neq i} \mathrm{Im}\, D_j'\right) \cap \mathrm{Im}\, D_i' = 0, \qquad i \in \underline{k},$$

that is, the subspaces $\mathrm{Im}\, D_i' \subset \mathcal{X}'$ are independent. It follows from this and (5) that EDP is generically solvable only if

$$\sum_{i=1}^{k} q_i \leq n, \tag{9}$$

as claimed in (3). By (6) and (9),

$$d(\hat{\mathcal{K}}_i) = n - \sum_{j \neq i} q_j \quad (g), \qquad i \in \underline{k};$$

and by (8) and (9),

$$d(\mathcal{B} \cap \hat{\mathcal{K}}_i) = 0 \vee \left(m - \sum_{j \neq i} q_j\right) \quad (g) . \tag{10}$$

Now if $D_i \neq 0$, (1) implies $\mathcal{R}_i^* \neq 0$ and therefore $\mathcal{B} \cap \hat{\mathcal{K}}_i \neq 0$. Thus by (10) generic solvability of EDP implies

$$m - \sum_{j \neq i} q_j \geq 1 , \qquad i \in \underline{k} ,$$

which is equivalent to (4).

3. Sufficiency. Suppose (3) and (4) hold. Write $q_i' \triangleq \sum_{j \neq i} q_j$. By (3) and (6)

$$d(\hat{\mathcal{K}}_i) = n - q_i' \quad (g) . \tag{11}$$

Using (6), (7) and (11), we have

$$\begin{aligned} d(\hat{\mathcal{K}}_i + \mathcal{B}) &= n \wedge (n - q_i' + m) \\ &\geq n \wedge (n+1) \qquad \text{(by (4))} \\ &= n . \end{aligned}$$

It follows that $\hat{\mathcal{K}}_i + \mathcal{B} = \mathcal{X}$ (g) and thus

$$A\hat{\mathcal{K}}_i \subset \hat{\mathcal{K}}_i + \mathcal{B} \quad (g) , \qquad i \in \underline{k} .$$

By Theorem 5.6 we have

$$\mathcal{R}_i^* = \mathcal{R}_i^n \quad (g) ,$$

where

$$\mathcal{R}_i^{\mu+1} = \hat{\mathcal{K}}_i \cap \left(A\mathcal{R}_i^{\mu} + \mathcal{B}\right), \qquad \mu = 0, 1, \ldots, n \tag{12a}$$

and

$$\mathcal{R}_i^0 = 0 . \tag{12b}$$

It will be shown that $\mathcal{R}_i^n = \hat{\mathcal{K}}_i$ (g). For this it is convenient to use a more refined method than heretofore. Replace $\underline{p} \in \mathbb{R}^N$ by the indeterminate $\underline{\lambda} = (\lambda_1, \ldots, \lambda_N)$: i.e., $\underline{\lambda}$ is simply a list representing the N entries of the matrices $A, B, D_1, \ldots, D_k$ regarded as literal variables. We shall consider $A, \ldots, D_k$ as matrices over the integral domain $\mathbb{R}[\lambda]$ or, more properly, its fraction field $\mathbb{R}(\lambda)$ (cf. Section 0.9). We then regard the $\mathcal{R}_i^{\mu}$ defined by (12) as subspaces of the vector space $\mathbb{R}^n(\lambda)$. Let $r_{i\mu}$ (resp. $s_{i\mu}$) be the dimension of $\mathcal{R}_i^\mu$ $\left(\text{resp. } \mathcal{S}_i^\mu \triangleq A\mathcal{R}_i^\mu + \mathcal{B}\right)$ over $\mathbb{R}(\lambda)$. We now compute the $r_{i\mu}$ and $s_{i\mu}$, dropping the subscript i for convenience.

LEMMA 11.1. In the vector space $\mathbb{R}^n(\lambda)$ just described, let

$$\mathcal{S}^\mu = A\mathcal{R}^\mu + \mathcal{B},$$

$$\mathcal{R}^{\mu+1} = \hat{\mathcal{K}} \cap \mathcal{S}^\mu, \qquad \mu = 0,1,\ldots,n; \tag{13}$$

$$\mathcal{R}^0 = 0.$$

Then

$$s_\mu = n \wedge (r_\mu + m),$$

$$r_{\mu+1} = n - n \wedge (n - s_\mu + q'), \qquad \mu = 0,1,\ldots,n; \tag{14}$$

$$r_0 = 0.$$

Furthermore, if the subspaces $\mathcal{R}^\mu(p)$ are computed by (12) with $\lambda = p$, then

$$d[\mathcal{R}^\mu(p)] = r_\mu \text{ (g)}. \tag{15}$$

PROOF: Let R_μ be an $n \times r_\mu$ matrix over $\mathbb{R}(\lambda)$ whose columns are a basis of $\mathcal{R}^\mu$, introduce the $n \times (r_\mu + m)$ matrix

$$\hat{S}_\mu = [AR_\mu, B], \tag{16}$$

let S_μ be an $n \times s_\mu$ matrix such that $\operatorname{Im} S_\mu = \operatorname{Im} \hat{S}_\mu$, and let $S_\mu^\perp$ be an $(n - s_\mu) \times n$ matrix such that $\operatorname{Ker} S_\mu^\perp = \operatorname{Im} S_\mu$. Let $\hat{D}$ be a $q' \times n$ matrix such that $\operatorname{Ker} \hat{D} = \hat{\mathcal{K}}$, and write

$$T_\mu \triangleq \begin{bmatrix} S_\mu^\perp \\ \hat{D} \end{bmatrix}. \tag{17}$$

Then by (13)

$$\mathcal{R}^{\mu+1} = \operatorname{Ker} T_\mu. \tag{18}$$

We define the rank polynomial $\psi(M)$ of a matrix M over $\mathbb{R}(\lambda)$ to be the sum of squares of the minors of M having maximal dimension. Thus M is of full (i.e., maximal) rank if and only if $\psi(M) \neq 0$. By (16),

$$s_\mu = n \wedge (r_\mu + m)$$

if and only if $\psi(\hat{S}_\mu) \neq 0$. By (17),

$$\text{Rank } T_\mu = n \wedge (n - s_\mu + q') \tag{19}$$

if and only if $\psi(T_\mu) \neq 0$; hence by (18) and (19),

$$r_{\mu+1} = n - n \wedge (n - s_\mu + q')$$

if and only if $\psi(T_\mu) \neq 0$. Since $r_0 = 0$ trivially, it follows that (14) is true if and only if

$$\psi(T_{n-1})\, \psi(\hat{S}_{n-1}) \cdots \psi(T_0)\, \psi(\hat{S}_0) \neq 0 \,. \tag{20}$$

A simple inductive argument on μ shows that the rational matrices $\hat{S}_\mu(\underline{\lambda})$ and $T_\mu(\underline{\lambda})$ have the following properties:

(i) Their evaluations $\hat{S}_\mu(\underline{p})$ and $T_\mu(\underline{p})$ are defined (g) for $\underline{p} \in \mathbb{R}^N$.

(ii) If $\mathcal{R}^\mu(\underline{p})$, $\mathcal{S}^\mu(\underline{p})$ are computed by (13) with $\underline{\lambda} = \underline{p}$, then

$$\mathcal{S}^\mu(\underline{p}) = \text{Im } \hat{S}_\mu(\underline{p}) \quad (g) \tag{21a}$$

and

$$\mathcal{R}^{\mu+1}(\underline{p}) = \text{Ker } T_\mu(\underline{p}) \quad (g) \,. \tag{21b}$$

Therefore, to prove (20) it is enough to replace $\underline{\lambda}$ by any $\underline{p} \in \mathbb{R}^N$ for which the asserted dimensional evaluations (14) can be verified. For this let $e_1, \ldots, e_n$ be the unit vectors in $\mathbb{R}^n$, put $e_\nu = 0$ if $\nu > n$, and define

$$Ae_j = 0 \,, \qquad j = 1, \ldots, q' \tag{22a}$$

$$Ae_{q'+r} = e_{m+r} \,, \qquad r = 1, \ldots, n - q' \,; \tag{22b}$$

$$\hat{D} = [\, I_{q'} \;\; 0 \,] \,, \qquad B = \begin{bmatrix} I_m \\ 0 \end{bmatrix} . \tag{22c}$$

Easy computations establish that the $\mathcal{R}^\mu$ and $\mathcal{S}^\mu \subset \mathcal{X}$ generated by (13) with (22) indeed have dimensions r_μ and s_μ given by (14). Hence the polynomial in (20) cannot vanish, (14) follows, and then (15) results from (21). The lemma is proved.

We now show that

$$r_{in} = n - q_i' \,, \qquad i \in \underline{k} \,, \tag{23}$$

and hence that

$$\mathcal{R}_i^n = \hat{\mathcal{K}}_i \quad (g) \,, \qquad i \in \underline{k} \,, \tag{24}$$

as claimed. Dropping the subscript i we have from (14)

$$r_{\mu+1} = n - n \wedge [n - n \wedge (r_\mu + m) + q'] = 0 \vee [n \wedge (r_\mu + m) - q']$$

$$\geq n \wedge (r_\mu + m) - q'$$

$$\geq n \wedge (r_\mu + 1 + q') - q' \qquad \text{(by (4))} .$$

If $r_\mu < n-q'$ then $r_\mu + 1 + q' \leq n$, so

$$r_{\mu+1} \geq (r_\mu + 1 + q') - q' = r_\mu + 1 .$$

Since the $\mathcal{R}^\mu$ defined by (13) are nondecreasing, and since $d(\mathcal{R}^\mu) \leq d(\mathcal{K}) = n - q'$, it follows that $r_\mu \uparrow n - q'$ with convergence in at most $n - q' < n$ steps, and the claim (23) is proved.

Finally, (3) implies that

$$\text{Rank} \begin{bmatrix} D_1 \\ \vdots \\ D_k \end{bmatrix} = \sum_{i=1}^{k} q_i \quad (g) = \sum_{i=1}^{k} \text{Rank } D_i \quad (g) \ ;$$

hence that

$$\left(\sum_{j \neq i} \text{Im } D_j' \right) \cap \text{Im } D_i' = 0 \quad (g) , \qquad i \in \underline{k} \ ;$$

and so

$$\mathcal{K}_i + \hat{\mathcal{K}}_i = \mathcal{X} \quad (g) , \qquad i \in \underline{k} .$$

This combined with (24) shows that (1) is true generically. ▌

Remark 1.

We recall from Section 0.15 the definition that a property Π is well-posed at $\underline{p} \in \mathbb{R}^N$ (or $\underline{p}$ is well-posed relative to Π) if $\Pi(\underline{p}') = 1$ at all $\underline{p}'$ in some open neighborhood of $\underline{p}$. It is clear from the proof of Theorem 11.1 that if either one of conditions (3) or (4) fails, the solvability set for ERP, namely

$$\{\underline{p} : \Pi(\underline{p}) = 1\} \subset \mathbb{R}^N$$

is a subset of some (possibly trivial) proper variety in $\mathbb{R}^N$. It follows that no data point $\underline{p}$ can be well-posed in the sense of our definition. Of course, in a concrete application it may happen that not all perturbations of a given data point $\underline{p}$ are admissible, possibly because of constraints arising from definitional relations among certain state variables. It may then be true that $\underline{p}$ is well-posed in a restricted sense, namely in the topology determined by the class of admissible perturbations. Such cases require separate investigation.

Remark 2.

From the proof of Theorem 11.1 we note that, if (3) and (4) are true, then

$$\mathcal{R}_i^* = \hat{\mathcal{K}}_i \text{ (g)} . \tag{25}$$

Thus (25) holds at almost all p, and the computational effort at such p is reduced accordingly.

11.2 State Space Extension Bounds

We shall now calculate the generic order of a dynamic compensator which achieves decoupling by state space extension. Our first result applies to the 'naive' extension described in Section 9.6, with the corresponding bound n_a provided by Theorem 9.4:

$$n_a \triangleq \sum_{i=1}^{k} d(\mathcal{R}_i^*) - d\left(\sum_{i=1}^{k} \mathcal{R}_i^*\right). \tag{26}$$

THEOREM 11.2. Under the conditions of Theorem 11.1, and by use of the 'naive' extension technique of Section 9.6, EDP is generically solvable by dynamic compensation of order no greater than

$$n_a = (k-1)\left(n - \sum_{i=1}^{k} q_i\right) \text{ (g)} . \tag{27}$$

Thus if $n = 15$, $k = 2$, $q_1 = 3$, $q_2 = 5$ and $m \geq 6$, we have $n_a = 7$ (g). From now on we write

$$q \triangleq \sum_{i=1}^{k} q_i .$$

PROOF: We have

$$n_a = \sum_i d(\hat{\mathcal{K}}_i) - d\left(\sum_i \hat{\mathcal{K}}_i\right) \text{(g)} \qquad \text{(by (25) and (26))}$$

$$= \sum_i d(\hat{\mathcal{K}}_i) - n \wedge \sum_i d(\hat{\mathcal{K}}_i) \text{ (g)} ;$$

and

$$\sum_i d(\hat{\mathcal{K}}_i) = \sum_i \left(n - n \wedge \sum_{j \neq i} q_j \right) \text{ (g)} \qquad \text{(by (6))}$$

$$= \sum_i \left(n - \sum_{j \neq i} q_j \right) \qquad \text{(by (4))}$$

$$= kn - (k-1)\, q \,.$$

Thus

$$n \wedge \sum_i d(\hat{\mathcal{K}}_i) = n \wedge \big(kn - (k-1)\, q \big) \text{ (g)}$$

$$= n \,,$$

and therefore $n_a = (k-1)(n-q)$ (g), as claimed. ▮

The bound (27) can be improved by exploiting the 'efficient' extension technique described in Chapter 10. For this we have the bound given by Theorem 10.1, namely

$$n_a^* \triangleq \sum_{i=1}^{k} d\left(\frac{\mathcal{R}_i^* + \mathcal{R}_0}{\mathcal{R}_0} \right) - d\left(\sum_{i=1}^{k} \frac{\mathcal{R}_i^* + \mathcal{R}_0}{\mathcal{R}_0} \right). \tag{28}$$

Here, in the notation of Chapter 10,

$$\mathcal{R}_0 \triangleq (\mathcal{R}_\bullet^* \cap \mathcal{V}_g)^\vee \,, \tag{29}$$

$$\mathcal{V}_g \triangleq \sup \{ \mathcal{V} : \mathcal{V} \subset \check{\mathcal{R}}^* \;\&\; \exists F \in \underline{F}(\mathcal{V}),\; \sigma[(A+BF) \,|\, \mathcal{V}] \subset \mathbb{C}_g \} \tag{30}$$

and

$$\check{\mathcal{R}}^* \triangleq (\mathcal{R}_\bullet^*)^\vee \,. \tag{30}$$

To compute the generic value of n_a^* under the conditions of Theorem 11.1, we start by noting that

$$\check{\mathcal{R}}^* = (\hat{\mathcal{K}}_\bullet)^\vee \text{ (g)} \qquad \text{(by (25))}$$

$$= \bigcap_{i=1}^{k} \sum_{j \neq i} \hat{\mathcal{K}}_j \qquad \text{(by (10.3))}$$

$$= \bigcap_i \sum_{j \neq i} \bigcap_{\ell \neq j} \mathcal{K}_\ell = \bigcap_i \mathcal{K}_i \,, \tag{31}$$

and thus

$$d(\check{\mathcal{R}}^*) = n - q \ \ (g) .$$

We shall treat separately the cases $m < q$, $m = q$ and $m > q$.

Case 1. $m < q$.

Let

$$\mathcal{V}^* \triangleq \sup \underline{\mathcal{I}}(\check{\mathcal{R}}^*) .$$

Then $\mathcal{V}^* = \lim_\mu \mathcal{V}^\mu$, where

$$\mathcal{V}^0 = \check{\mathcal{R}}^* ; \qquad \mathcal{V}^{\mu+1} = \check{\mathcal{R}}^* \cap A^{-1}(\mathcal{V}^\mu + \mathcal{B}) , \qquad \mu \in \underline{n} .$$

Let $\nu_\mu \triangleq d(\mathcal{V}^\mu)$. By the same technique as in the proof of Theorem 11.1, we get that

$$\nu_{\mu+1} = 0 \vee [(n-q) + n \wedge (\nu_\mu + m) - n] \ \ (g) . \tag{32}$$

By iteration of (32) with $\nu_0 = n - q$, there follows

$$\nu_\mu = 0 \vee (n - m - 2^\mu(q - m)) \ \ (g) ,$$

and therefore $\mathcal{V}^* = 0$ (g). From this and (30), $\mathcal{V}_g = 0$ (g), hence by (29), $\mathcal{R}_0 = 0$ (g). Then (28) yields

$$n_a^* = \sum_i d(\mathcal{R}_i^*) - d\left(\sum_i \mathcal{R}_i^*\right) \ \ (g)$$

$$= (k-1)(n-q) \ \ (g) ,$$

just as in the proof of Theorem 11.2.

Case 2. $m = q$.

We have

$$d(\check{\mathcal{R}}^* + \mathcal{B}) = n \wedge (n - q + m) \ \ (g)$$
$$= n ,$$

and therefore $\check{\mathcal{R}}^* \in \underline{\mathcal{I}}(\mathcal{X})$ (g). Also

$$d(\check{\mathcal{R}}^* \cap \mathcal{B}) = 0 \vee \big((n-q) + m - n\big) \quad (g)$$
$$= 0 ,$$

and so $\check{\mathcal{R}}^*$ contains, generically, no c.s. other than zero. It follows that $\mathcal{V}_g$ is simply the 'good' modal subspace of the map

$$(A + BF) | \check{\mathcal{R}}^* ,$$

computed with any $F \in \underline{F}(\check{\mathcal{R}}^*)$.

Now $\nu_g \triangleq d(\mathcal{V}_g)$ does not possess a generic value. To reckon with its dependence on $\underline{p}$ we shall refine the definition of 'generic' in a way which is ad hoc but suited to our purpose. Let

$$\underline{S} \triangleq \{\underline{p}:\ \underline{p} \in \mathbb{R}^N, d(\mathcal{B}(\underline{p})) = m \ \&\ \check{\mathcal{R}}^*(\underline{p}) \oplus \mathcal{B}(\underline{p}) = \mathcal{X}\} .$$

For $\underline{p} \in \underline{S}$, $\nu_g = \nu_g(\underline{p})$ is well defined and takes values $0 \le \nu_g \le n-q$. By the preceding discussion, there is some proper variety $\underline{V} \subset \mathbb{R}^N$ for which $\underline{V}^c \subset \underline{S}$. Now let

$$\underline{S}_\nu \triangleq \underline{S} \cap \{\underline{p}:\ \nu_g(\underline{p}) = \nu\} .$$

Thus

$$\underline{S} = \bigcup_{\nu=0}^{n-q} \underline{S}_\nu$$

and

$$\underline{V}^c = \bigcup_{\nu=0}^{n-q} (\underline{V}^c \cap \underline{S}_\nu) .$$

If now ψ is a function on the integers, we write

$$n_a^*(\underline{p}) = \psi(\nu_g(\underline{p})) \quad (g) \tag{33}$$

to mean the following: there exists a proper variety $\tilde{\underline{V}} \subset \mathbb{R}^N$ such that, at each $\underline{p} \in \underline{V}^c \cap \tilde{\underline{V}}^c$, we have $n_a^*(\underline{p}) = \psi(\nu)$ for some ν, $0 \le \nu \le n-q$.

We shall not explore in detail the structure of the component subsets $\underline{V}^c \cap \underline{S}_\nu$. However, if we assume that in the usual topology of the complex plane, $\mathbb{C}_g^0 \cap \mathbb{R} \ne \emptyset$ and $\mathbb{C}_b^0 \ne \emptyset$ (where $(^0)$ denotes interior) then it can be shown (Ex. 11.2) that for each ν the interior of $\underline{V}^c \cap \tilde{\underline{V}}^c \cap \underline{S}_\nu$ is nonempty. At an interior point the value of n_a^* given by (35), below, is locally constant.

Proceeding on this basis we have, by (25) and (31),

$$\check{\mathcal{R}}^* \subset \bigcap_i \mathcal{R}_i^* , \qquad i \in \underline{k} \quad (g)$$

so

$$\mathcal{V}_g \cap \mathcal{R}_i^* = \mathcal{V}_g , \qquad i \in \underline{k} \ \ (g)$$

and then

$$\mathcal{R}_0 = \mathcal{V}_g \ \ (g) \ . \tag{34}$$

It follows by (6), (25) and (34) that

$$d\left(\frac{\mathcal{R}_i^*}{\mathcal{R}_0}\right) = \left(n - \sum_{j \neq i} q_j\right) - \nu_g \ \ (g)$$

and therefore

$$\sum_i d\left(\frac{\mathcal{R}_i^*}{\mathcal{R}_0}\right) = k(n - \nu_g) - (k-1)\, q \ \ (g) \ .$$

Finally,

$$\begin{aligned} n_a^* &= \sum_i d\left(\frac{\mathcal{R}_i^*}{\mathcal{R}_0}\right) - d\left(\sum_i \frac{\mathcal{R}_i^*}{\mathcal{R}_0}\right) \\ &= \sum_i d\left(\frac{\mathcal{R}_i^*}{\mathcal{R}_0}\right) - n \wedge \sum_i d\left(\frac{\mathcal{R}_i^*}{\mathcal{R}_0}\right) \ \ (g) \\ &= 0 \vee \left(\sum_i d\left(\frac{\mathcal{R}_i^*}{\mathcal{R}_0}\right) - n\right) \\ &= 0 \vee \left((k-1)(n-q) - k\nu_g\right) \ \ (g) \ . \end{aligned} \tag{35}$$

Case 3. $\quad m > q$.

We have

$$d(\check{\mathcal{R}}^* \cap \mathcal{B}) = m - q > 0 \ \ (g) \ ,$$

and we shall show that $\check{\mathcal{R}}^*$ is generically a c.s. As in Case 2, $\check{\mathcal{R}}^* + \mathcal{B} = \mathcal{X}$ (g), so $\check{\mathcal{R}}^* \in \underline{\mathfrak{I}}(\mathcal{X})$ (g). Thus $\check{\mathcal{R}}^* \in \underline{\mathfrak{C}}(\mathcal{X})$ if and only if $\check{\mathcal{R}}^* = \lim_\mu \mathcal{R}^\mu$, where

$$\mathcal{R}^0 = 0 \ ; \qquad \mathcal{R}^{\mu+1} = \check{\mathcal{R}}^* \cap (A\mathcal{R}^\mu + \mathcal{B}) \ , \qquad \mu \in \underline{n} \ .$$

Let $d(\mathcal{R}^\mu) = \rho_\mu$ (g). Then, as in the proof of Theorem 11.1,

$$\rho_0 = 0 \ , \qquad \rho_{\mu+1} = 0 \vee [(n-q) + n \wedge (\rho_\mu + m) - n] \ ,$$

from which it follows that $\rho_\mu \uparrow n-q$, and the assertion follows. But now $\mathcal{V}_g = \check{\mathcal{R}}^*(g)$, and we need only set $\nu_g = n-q$ in (35) to obtain

$$n_a^* = 0 \ (g) .$$

We summarize results as

THEOREM 11.3. Under the conditions of Theorem 11.1, and by use of the 'efficient' decoupling technique of Section 10.3, EDP is generically solvable by dynamic compensation of order no greater than

$$n_a^* = \begin{cases} (k-1)(n-q) , & m < q \\ 0 \vee [(k-1)(n-q) - k\nu_g] , & m = q \\ 0 , & m > q . \end{cases}$$

Here the result for $m = q$ is interpreted as in (33).

Efficient extension may be generically more economical than naive extension, but only if $m \geq q$. By the conditions for generic solvability, $m \geq q$ must hold when, in particular, the decoupled outputs z_i ($i \in \underline{k}$) are all scalars.

As an example, again let $m = 15$, $k = 2$, $q_1 = 3$ and $q_2 = 5$. We must have $m \geq 6$ and then, generically,

$$n_a^* = 7 \qquad \text{if } m = 6 \text{ or } 7$$

$$= \begin{pmatrix} 7 , & \nu_g = 0 \\ 5 , & \nu_g = 1 \\ 3 , & \nu_g = 2 \\ 1 , & \nu_g = 3 \\ 0 , & 4 \leq \nu_g \leq 7 \end{pmatrix} \qquad \text{if } m = 8$$

$$= 0 \qquad \text{if } m \geq 9 .$$

11.3 Significance of Generic Solvability

The results in this chapter are a guide in identifying practical situations where dynamic decoupling is likely, in principle, to be feasible. Of course, the notions of 'generic solvability' and 'well-posedness' are purely qualitative. They furnish no information about how well conditioned the computations may be which determine a solution (F_e, G_e in Fig. 9.2) at a well-posed data point, or about the sensitivity of a solution in a neighborhood of such a point.

A solution of EDP typically depends critically on the parameters of A and B: with F_e, G_e fixed, decoupling will in general break down if these parameters undergo small variations from the values employed in design. The solution is thus 'finely tuned' and must be maintained by a supervisory control with the capability of adaptive readjustment. The real significance of our results is that they point to exactly this possibility, at least when the conditions of generic solvability are met. Adaptive decoupling poses challenging problems of numerical conditioning and stability of which the study has only just begun.

11.4 Exercises

11.1 Supply the omitted (computational) details in the proof of Lemma 11.1.

11.2 With reference to Remark 1 after Theorem 11.1, develop a plausible example where EDP is well-posed only in a 'restricted' sense. Study the sensitivity of F_e, G_e with respect to the admissible variations of A and B.

11.3 With reference to the discussion of Case 2 of Theorem 11.3 show that, under the assumptions stated and for suitable V and $\tilde{V}$, the set $\underline{V}^c \cap \underline{\tilde{V}}^c \cap \underline{S}_\nu$ has nonempty interior. HINT: Exploit the fact that if A: $n \times n$, B: $n \times m$ and R: $n \times (n-m)$, then with $\mathcal{R} = \text{Im } R$, there follows $\mathcal{R} \oplus \mathcal{B} = \mathcal{X}$ (g) in the parameter space of points $\underline{p} = (A, B, R)$. Given $\nu\ (0 \le \nu \le n-m)$ construct A, together with B, R of maximal rank and $F \in \underline{F}(\mathcal{R})$ such that, if

$$\sigma_1 \triangleq \sigma[(A + BF)\,|\,\mathcal{R}]\,, \qquad \sigma \triangleq \sigma(A+BF)\,,$$

one has $|\sigma_1 \cap \mathbb{C}_g^0| = \nu$ and $|\sigma \cap \mathbb{C}_b^0| = n-\nu$. Finally show that the last two relations hold locally at $\underline{p} = (A, B, R)$.

11.4 From the viewpoint of genericity discuss the partial decoupling problems of Section 9.8

11.5 Notes and References

The material in this chapter is based largely on Fabian and Wonham [1]. For additional applications of the genericity concept, to the combined problem of decoupling and disturbance rejection, see Fabian [1].

CHAPTER 12

QUADRATIC OPTIMIZATION I: EXISTENCE AND UNIQUENESS

In previous chapters our criteria of system design have been almost entirely qualitative: we have indeed imposed requirements like stability on the system spectrum, but in the main have sought to realize very general properties of signal flow, as in tracking or noninteraction. By contrast, in this chapter and the next we take a somewhat more quantitative approach to realizing good dynamic response. We describe a systematic way of computing linear state feedback which ensures 'optimal' recovery from an impulsive disturbance acting at the system input. It will later be clear how to incorporate the method into the framework of design techniques already presented.

Optimality will be understood as the minimization of a positive quadratic functional of system output. It is the quadratic structure which guarantees that the optimal feedback control is linear, hence relatively simple to analyze and implement. In addition the optimal control is fairly easily calculated. Finally, experience has shown that good dynamic response is usually achievable if the quadratic functional is suitably chosen. For these three reasons, rather than any specific interpretation of quadratic cost as such, the method of quadratic optimization has been widely adopted.

12.1 Quadratic Optimization

We begin with the standard system

$$\dot{x}(t) = Ax(t) + Bu(t), \qquad t \geq 0, \tag{1}$$

$$z(t) = Dx(t), \qquad t \geq 0, \tag{2}$$

and regard $\mathcal{U}$, $\mathcal{X}$ and $\mathcal{Z}$ as inner product spaces over $\mathbb{R}$. Suppose

$$x(0+) = x_0 .$$

We may interpret this initial condition as arising from an external disturbance of form $x_0\delta(t)$ appearing implicitly on the right side of (1). Stated loosely, our problem is to choose $u(t)$, $t \geq 0$, such that the system output $z(\cdot)$ is steered from its initial 'disturbed' value $z(0+) = Dx_0$ to its 'desired' regulated value $z = 0$, over a suitable recovery interval $[0, T)$, which may be infinite. To define the optimization problem we must further specify the class of admissible control functions $u(\cdot): [0, T) \rightarrow \mathcal{U}$, and the cost attached to any particular $u(\cdot)$.

In our formulation we shall set $T = +\infty$; admit a priori controls which are essentially arbitrary; and attach to $u(\cdot)$ the cost

$$J(u) \triangleq \int_0^\infty [z(t)' z(t) + u(t)' Nu(t)]\, dt ,$$

where $N \geq 0$ and $z(\cdot)$ is determined by (1) and (2). In fact these are the only known conditions which, subject to mild technicalities, guarantee the following desirable result: the optimal (minimal cost) control can be implemented by linear time-invariant state feedback

$$u(t) = Fx(t) , \qquad t > 0 ,$$

such that the closed-loop system map $A + BF$ is stable. Here F is independent of x_0.

As our final goal is an optimal feedback control we shall rigorously define, in Section 12.2, an optimization problem in which the admissible controls are (possibly nonlinear) state feedback laws. Meanwhile there is something to be gained from a heuristic treatment which leads quickly to our main analytic tool, the functional equation of dynamic programming.

12.2 Dynamic Programming - Heuristics

Write

$$M \triangleq D'D ,$$
$$L(x, u) \triangleq x'Mx + u'Nu . \tag{3}$$

Assuming an optimal control exists, introduce the value function

$$V(x) \triangleq \min_{u(\cdot)} \int_0^\infty L[x(t), u(t)]\, dt , \qquad x(0) = x . \tag{4}$$

Thus $V(x)$ is the minimal cost expressed as a function of the initial state $x(0) = x$. Write

$$x(t) = \xi(t; x, u(\cdot))$$

for the solution of (1) with control $u(\cdot)$ and initial condition $x(0) = x$. Fix x, suppose $u^0(\cdot)$ is optimal on $[0, \infty)$, and let $\tau > 0$. We claim that the control function

$$u^0(t) , \qquad \tau \leq t < \infty , \tag{5}$$

is also optimal, relative to the state $\xi(\tau; x, u^0(\cdot))$ from which we depart at time τ. Indeed for any $u(\cdot)$,

$$J(u) = \left(\int_0^{\tau} + \int_{\tau}^{\infty}\right) L[\xi(t;\ x, u(\cdot)), u(t)]\, dt\ . \tag{6}$$

The first integral depends only on u(t) for $0 \le t \le \tau$, and the second only on $x(\tau)$ together with u(t) for $t > \tau$. Suppose we know $u^0(t)$ for $0 \le t \le \tau$: $x(\tau)$ is now determined. The second integral must then be a minimum when evaluated at the function (5), or we reach a contradiction. Now, because the dynamic equation (1) and the function $L(\cdot,\cdot)$ are invariant under shift of origin of time, we have

$$\min_{\substack{u(t)\\ \tau \le t < \infty}} \int_{\tau}^{\infty} L[x(t), u(t)]\, dt = V[x(\tau)]\ . \tag{7}$$

Combining (4), (6) and (7), and expanding notation a little for clarity, we can write

$$V(x) = \min_{\substack{u(t)\\ 0 \le t \le \tau}} \Bigg[\int_0^{\tau} L[\xi(t;\ x, u(s),\ 0 \le s \le t), u(t)]\, dt$$

$$+ V[\xi(\tau;\ x\ ,\ u(s)\ ,\ 0 \le s \le \tau)]\Bigg]\ . \tag{8}$$

Equation (8) expresses the celebrated, 'intuitively obvious' principle of optimality. We get a very convenient version of (8) in differential form by letting $\tau \downarrow 0$. For this, assume $u(\cdot)$ and $V(\cdot)$ are smooth and write $u \triangleq u(0)$. Then

$$\xi(\tau;\ x, u(\cdot)) = x + \tau(Ax + Bu) + o(\tau)\ ,$$

$$\int_0^{\tau} L[\xi(t;\ x, u(\cdot))\ , u(t)]\, dt = \tau L(x,u) + o(\tau)\ ,$$

and

$$V[\xi(\tau;\ x, u(\cdot))] = V(x) + \tau(Ax+Bu)' V_x(x) + o(\tau)\ ,$$

where V_x is the first partial derivative of V. With these substitutions in (8) a formal passage to the limit yields

$$\min_u [(Ax + Bu)' V_x(x) + L(x,u)] = 0\ . \tag{9}$$

We refer to (9) as Bellman's equation. It says, in effect, to minimize the expression bracketed, regarded as a function of the variable u, with x and V_x as parameters. Suppose the minimizing u is

$$u = \omega(x, V_x)\ . \tag{10}$$

Substituting (10) in (9), we obtain a first-order partial differential equation for V:

$$[Ax + B\omega(x, V_x)]' V_x + L[x, \omega(x, V_x)] = 0 . \tag{11}$$

Now solve (11) for $V = V(x)$, compute $V_x(x)$, and finally obtain from (10) the optimal feedback control law

$$\varphi^0(x) = \omega[x, V_x(x)] . \tag{12}$$

The beauty of this approach lies in its intuitive directness, and the fact that it leads to a feedback control. In addition, it suggests a computational procedure, though as yet (11) is innocent of boundary conditions to render the solution (if any) unique. But rather than try to rigorize these matters directly, we shall redefine the problem precisely, show that (9) and (10) are sufficient conditions for optimality, and compute a reasonably explicit solution. This program will satisfy better the demands of logic.

12.3 Dynamic Programming: Rigor

From now on we confine attention to (possibly nonlinear) state feedback controls

$$u(t) = \varphi[x(t)] .$$

Then (1) becomes

$$\dot{x}(t) = Ax(t) + B\varphi[x(t)] . \tag{13}$$

Introduce the class Φ of admissible controls φ, characterized by the following properties:

(i) The function $\varphi: \mathcal{X} \to \mathcal{U}$ is continuous.

(ii) For every initial state $x(0) \in \mathcal{X}$ the differential equation (13) has a unique solution $x(\cdot)$ defined (and continuously differentiable) for $0 \le t < \infty$.

(iii) For every initial state $x(0)$, the solution $x(\cdot)$ of (13) has the property

$$x(t) \to 0 , \qquad t \to \infty .$$

Observe that if $F: \mathcal{X} \to \mathcal{U}$ is such that $A + BF$ is stable, the linear control $\varphi(x) = Fx$ belongs to Φ.

Existence and uniqueness of the solution of (13) are guaranteed if, for instance, $|\varphi(x)|$ grows no faster than $|x|$ as $|x| \to \infty$ and satisfies a uniform Lipschitz condition in every ball $|x| \le r$ $(r > 0)$; however, we shall not need such conditions explicitly. The stability condition (iii) is formally stronger than the condition of output regulation, namely

$$z(t) = Dx(t) \to 0 , \qquad t \to \infty ;$$

but it is technically convenient, and natural in the applications we shall make of the optimization technique.

Next we introduce the cost functional

$$J: \mathcal{X} \times \Phi \to [0, \infty] ,$$

defined by

$$J(x,\varphi) \triangleq \int_0^\infty L[x(t), \varphi(x(t))] \, dt . \tag{14}$$

In the integrand, $x(\cdot)$ is the solution of (13) with $x(0) = x$. A control $\varphi^0 \in \Phi$ is optimal if $J(x,\varphi^0) < \infty$ for all $x \in \mathcal{X}$ and if

$$J(x,\varphi^0) \le J(x,\varphi) , \qquad x \in \mathcal{X}, \quad \varphi \in \Phi . \tag{15}$$

Our first technical assumption guarantees that Φ is nonempty and that $\varphi \in \Phi$ exists such that $J(x,\varphi) < \infty$ for all x.

A.1 The pair (A, B) is stabilizable.

In fact if $A + BF$ is stable and $\varphi(x) = Fx$,

$$J(x,\varphi) = \int_0^\infty x' e^{t(A+BF)'} (M + F'NF) \, e^{t(A+BF)} x \, dt$$

$$\le c|x|^2 , \qquad x \in \mathcal{X}, \tag{16}$$

for some constant c. Thus we can now (rigorously) define the value function

$$V^0(x) \triangleq \inf \{ J(x,\varphi) \colon \varphi \in \Phi \} . \tag{17}$$

Clearly

$$0 \le V^0(x) \le c|x|^2 .$$

Next we shall demonstrate a sufficient condition for optimality of an admissible control.

THEOREM 12.1 (Optimality Criterion). Suppose there exist a control $\varphi^0 \in \Phi$ and a function $V: \mathcal{X} \to \mathbb{R}$ with the properties:

(i) $V(\cdot)$ is continuously differentiable for $x \in \mathcal{X}$. (18)

(ii) For some constant c,

$$0 \le V(x) \le c|x|^2 , \qquad x \in \mathcal{X} . \tag{19}$$

(iii) $[Ax + B\varphi^0(x)]' V_x(x) + L[x, \varphi^0(x)] = 0, \qquad x \in \mathcal{X}.$ (20)

(iv) $(Ax + Bu)' V_x(x) + L(x,u) \geq 0, \qquad x \in \mathcal{X}, \quad u \in \mathcal{U}.$ (21)

<u>Then</u>

$$V(x) = V^0(x) \tag{22}$$

<u>and φ^0 is optimal.</u>

PROOF: Write $\xi(t; x, \varphi)$ for the solution of (13) with $x(0) = x$. Then (18) and (20) imply

$$-\frac{d}{dt}\{V[\xi(t; x, \varphi^0)]\} = L[\xi(t; x, \varphi^0), \varphi^0(\xi(t; x, \varphi^0))], \qquad t \geq 0.$$

Since $\xi(\cdot; x, \varphi^0)$ satisfies (13), and $\varphi^0(\cdot)$ is continuous, we can integrate to obtain

$$V(x) = V[\xi(t; x, \varphi^0)] + \int_0^t L[\xi(s; x, \varphi^0), \varphi^0(\xi(s; x, \varphi^0))]\, ds.$$

Since $\xi(t; x, \varphi^0) \to 0$ $(t \to \infty)$, we have from (19) and the definition (14) of J,

$$V(x) = J(x, \varphi^0), \qquad x \in \mathcal{X}. \tag{23}$$

Let $\varphi \in \Phi$. Setting $u = \varphi(x)$ in (21) and integrating along the path $\xi(\cdot; x, \varphi)$ we get similarly

$$V(x) \leq V[\xi(t; x, \varphi)] + \int_0^t L[\xi(s; x, \varphi), \varphi(\xi(s; x, \varphi))]\, ds.$$

Letting $t \to \infty$,

$$V(x) \leq J(x, \varphi). \tag{24}$$

Inequality (15) follows by (23) and (24), so that φ^0 is optimal and (22) is true. ▮

Observe that conditions (20) and (21) are equivalent to Bellman's equation (9) or explicitly (10) and (11). We shall compute a solution of (9) with properties (18) and (19), and such that the corresponding control φ^0 given by (10) is admissible. Then Theorem 12.1 will establish that φ^0 is optimal. Let us assume

A.2 $\qquad N > 0.$ (25)

Recalling (3), we find from (9) and (10)

$$\omega(x, V_x) = -\frac{1}{2} N^{-1} B' V_x \tag{26}$$

and then (11) becomes

$$(Ax)' V_x - \frac{1}{4} V_x' BN^{-1} B' V_x + x' Mx = 0 . \tag{27}$$

We now make the inspired guess that optimal control is linear and note from (16) that V must necessarily be quadratic. Put

$$V(x) = x'Px , \qquad x \in \mathcal{X} ,$$

where P is symmetric. Substitution in (27) yields the matrix quadratic equation

$$A'P + PA - PBN^{-1}B'P + M = 0 . \tag{28}$$

To solve (28) we need

A.3 __The pair__ (D, A) __is detectable.__ Then we have

THEOREM 12.2. __Under assumptions A.1, A.2 and A.3, the matrix quadratic equation (28) has a unique solution__ P^0 __in the class of symmetric, positive semidefinite maps. Furthermore, the map__

$$A - BN^{-1}B'P^0$$

__is stable.__

The proof will be deferred to Section 12.4. Assuming this result, it is clear that

$$V(x) = x'P^0 x \tag{29}$$

satisfies conditions (i) and (ii) of Theorem 12.1. On the basis of (12) and (26) define

$$\varphi^0(x) \triangleq -N^{-1}B'P^0 x . \tag{30}$$

By Theorem 12.2 the control (30) yields a stable system map, and therefore φ^0 is admissible. By (26), φ^0 and V satisfy conditions (iii) and (iv) of Theorem 12.1, so $V = V^0$, the value function, and φ^0 is optimal.

We shall demonstrate that optimal control is even unique. By (29), (30) and a short computation,

$$(Ax + Bu)' V_x^0(x) + L(x,u) - [Ax + B\varphi^0(x)]' V_x^0(x) - L[x,\varphi^0(x)]$$

$$= (u + N^{-1} B' P^0 x)' N(u + N^{-1} B' P^0 x) \tag{31}$$

for all $x \in \mathcal{X}$ and $u \in \mathcal{U}$. Denote the right side of (31) by $\Delta(u - \varphi^0(x))$. Clearly $\Delta \geq 0$, and $\Delta = 0$ if and only if $u = \varphi^0(x)$. Let $\varphi \in \Phi$. If $\varphi \neq \varphi^0$ there is a state $x_0 \in \mathcal{X}$ and, by continuity, a neighborhood $\mathfrak{N}$ of x_0 such that $\varphi(x) \neq \varphi^0(x)$ for $x \in \mathfrak{N}$. By (20) and (31)

$$[Ax + B\varphi(x)]' V_x^0(x) + L[x,\varphi(x)] = \Delta[\varphi(x) - \varphi^0(x)] . \tag{32}$$

Put $x = \xi(t; x_0,\varphi)$ in (32) and integrate on $[0,\infty)$. The result is

$$J(x_0,\varphi) = \int_0^\infty L[\xi(t; x_0,\varphi),\varphi(\xi(t; x_0,\varphi))]\, dt$$

$$= V^0(x_0) + \int_0^\infty \Delta[\varphi(\xi(t; x_0,\varphi)) - \varphi^0(\xi(t; x_0,\varphi))]\, dt . \tag{33}$$

By continuity of $\xi(\cdot; x_0,\varphi)$ there exists $\delta > 0$ such that $\xi(t; x_0,\varphi) \in \mathfrak{N}$ for $0 \leq t \leq \delta$, hence the integrand in (33) is strictly positive on $[0,\delta]$. Therefore $J(x_0,\varphi) > V^0(x_0)$ and so φ cannot be optimal.

Summarizing results we have

THEOREM 12.3. *If (A, B) is stabilizable, (D, A) is detectable and $N > 0$, an optimal feedback control φ^0 exists and is unique in the class of admissible controls. In addition, $\varphi^0(x)$ is linear in x, and the corresponding closed loop system matrix is stable.*

We turn finally to a constructive proof of Theorem 12.2 which yields an algorithm for computing P^0 and thus φ^0.

12.4 Matrix Quadratic Equation

To prove Theorem 12.2 we recall Proposition 0.6 on the convergence of a bounded monotone sequence of symmetric maps, and the results of Sections 3.6 and 3.10 on detectability. In addition we need three preliminary lemmas.

LEMMA 12.1. *If $Q \geq 0$ and A is stable, the linear equation*

$$A'P + PA + Q = 0$$

has a unique solution P, and $P \geq 0$.

PROOF: If P is a solution

$$-\frac{d}{dt}(e^{tA'}Pe^{tA}) = -e^{tA'}(A'P + PA)e^{tA} = e^{tA'}Qe^{tA}$$

for all t. Integrating and using stability of A,

$$P = \int_0^\infty e^{tA'}Qe^{tA}\,dt \geq 0 . \tag{34}$$

On the other hand the integral in (34) is clearly a solution. ∎

LEMMA 12.2 (Lyapunov Criterion). Suppose $P \geq 0$, $Q \geq 0$, $(\sqrt{Q}, A)$ is detectable and

$$A'P + PA + Q = 0 . \tag{35}$$

Then A is stable. If $(\sqrt{Q}, A)$ is observable, then actually $P > 0$.

PROOF: From (35) there results the identity

$$P = e^{tA'}Pe^{tA} + \int_0^t e^{sA'}Qe^{sA}\,ds , \qquad t \geq 0 .$$

Since $(\sqrt{Q}, A)$ is detectable, Proposition 3.2 asserts that the integral

$$Q(t) = \int_0^t e^{sA'}Qe^{sA}\,ds , \qquad t \geq 0$$

is bounded only if A is stable. Since

$$0 \leq Q(t) \leq P$$

the first conclusion follows. For the second we recall from Lemma 3.1 that $Q(t) > 0$ if $t > 0$. ∎

LEMMA 12.3. Let P be symmetric, $N > 0$ and $F^0 = -N^{-1}B'P$. Write

$$\psi(F) \triangleq (A + BF)'P + P(A + BF) + F'NF .$$

Then

$$\psi(F) - \psi(F^0) = (F - F^0)'N(F - F^0) ,$$

i.e., F^0 minimizes $\psi(F)$.

The proof is a simple computation.

PROOF of Theorem 12.2. We rewrite (28) in the form of two simultaneous equations for P and the state feedback F determined by (30):

$$(A + BF)'P + P(A + BF) + M + F'NF = 0\,, \tag{36}$$

$$F = -N^{-1}B'P\,. \tag{37}$$

The point of this maneuver is that (36) is <u>linear</u> in P for fixed F. This suggests that we construct a sequence $\{F_k, P_k;\ k = 1, 2, \dots\}$ as follows.

1. Choose F_1 so that $A + BF_1$ is stable.
2. Having chosen $F_1, \dots, F_k$ obtain P_k from

$$(A + BF_k)'P_k + P_k(A + BF_k) + M + F_k'NF_k = 0\,. \tag{36$_k$}$$

3. Define

$$F_{k+1} \triangleq -N^{-1}B'P_k\,. \tag{37$_k$}$$

It will be shown that the sequence P_k is well-defined, $P_k \geq 0$ and $P_k \downarrow$. By Lemma 12.1, P_1 is uniquely determined by $(36)_1$ and $P_1 \geq 0$. Suppose $P_1, \dots, P_k$ are defined and non-negative. Then F_{k+1} is determined by $(37)_k$. By Lemma 12.3,

$$\begin{aligned}
(A + BF_{k+1})'P_k &+ P_k(A + BF_{k+1}) + M + F_{k+1}'NF_{k+1} \\
&= (A + BF_k)P_k + P_k(A + BF_k) + M + F_k'NF_k \\
&\quad - (F_k - F_{k+1})'N(F_k - F_{k+1}) \\
&= -(F_k - F_{k+1})'N(F_k - F_{k+1}) \qquad \text{by } (37)_k \\
&= -Q_k, \text{ say,}
\end{aligned}$$

where $Q_k \geq 0$. Thus

$$(A + BF_{k+1})'P_k + P_k(A + BF_{k+1}) + M + Q_k + F_{k+1}'NF_{k+1} = 0\,. \tag{38}$$

By Theorem 3.6 (ii), the pair

$$\left(\sqrt{M + Q_k + F_{k+1}'NF_{k+1}}\,,\ A + BF_{k+1}\right)$$

is detectable. Since $P_k \geq 0$ by assumption, Lemma 12.2 asserts that $A + BF_{k+1}$ is stable. Then Lemma 12.1 ensures that $P_{k+1} \geq 0$ is determined by $(36)_{k+1}$.

Subtracting $(36)_{k+1}$ from (38) we get

$$(A + BF_{k+1})'(P_k - P_{k+1}) + (P_k - P_{k+1})(A + BF_{k+1}) + Q_k = 0$$

and again by Lemma 12.1, $P_k - P_{k+1} \geq 0$. Thus $0 \leq P_k \downarrow$, and by Proposition 0.6,

$$P^0 \triangleq \lim P_k, \qquad k \uparrow \infty,$$

exists. Then

$$F^0 \triangleq \lim F_{k+1} = -N^{-1}B'P^0$$

exists as well. Taking the limit in $(36)_k$ we have that F^0, P^0 satisfy (36) and (37). By Theorem 3.6. (ii), the pair

$$\left(\sqrt{M + F^{0\prime}NF^0},\ A + BF^0\right)$$

is detectable. Then by Lemma 12.2, $A + BF^0$ is stable.

It remains to show uniqueness. Suppose $\tilde{P}, \tilde{F}$ satisfy (36), (37) and $\tilde{P} \geq 0$. Write

$$\tilde{A} = A + B\tilde{F}, \qquad A^0 = A + BF^0.$$

By Lemma 12.3

$$A^{0\prime}\tilde{P} + \tilde{P}A^0 + M - Q + F^{0\prime}NF^0 = 0, \tag{39}$$

where

$$Q = (\tilde{F} - F^0)'N(\tilde{F} - F^0) \geq 0.$$

Also

$$A^{0\prime}P^0 + P^0A^0 + M + F^{0\prime}NF^0 = 0. \tag{40}$$

Subtracting (39) from (40) yields

$$A^{0\prime}(P^0 - \tilde{P}) + (P^0 - \tilde{P})A^0 + Q = 0. \tag{41}$$

Since A^0 is stable, Lemma 12.1 implies $P^0 \geq \tilde{P}$. Also, (36) for $\tilde{P}, \tilde{F}$, together with Theorem 3.6 (ii) and Lemma 12.2, implies that the pair

$$\left(\sqrt{M + \tilde{F}'N\tilde{F}},\ \tilde{A}\right)$$

is detectable and $\tilde{A}$ is stable. By an argument symmetric to the one leading to (41) we conclude that $\tilde{P} \geq P^0$, and thus finally $\tilde{P} = P^0$. ▮

It is interesting to see what happens if we drop the assumption that (D, A) be detectable. Suppose the optimization problem is given by

$$\dot{x} = u\,, \qquad \int_0^\infty u(t)^2\, dt = \min.\,,$$

where x and u are scalars. Then (28) becomes $P^2 = 0$, so $P^0 = 0$, and $\varphi^0(x) = -P^0x = 0$. Of course, the resulting system is not stable, and φ^0 is not admissible. On the other hand the admissible controls

$$\varphi_\epsilon(x) = -\epsilon x\,, \qquad \epsilon > 0$$

yield

$$J(x, \varphi_\epsilon) = \frac{\epsilon x^2}{2}$$

so that

$$V^0(x) = \inf_{\varphi} J(x, \varphi) = 0\,.$$

Thus an optimal control does not exist.

Again, consider the problem

$$\dot{x} = x + u\,, \qquad \int_0^\infty u(t)^2\, dt = \min.$$

From (28), $2P - P^2 = 0$, and we have two nonnegative solutions $P_1^0 = 0$, $P_2^0 = 2$, giving controls

$$\varphi_1^0(x) = 0\,, \qquad \varphi_2^0(x) = -2x\,.$$

Clearly $J\left(x, \varphi_1^0\right) = 0$, but φ_1^0 is not admissible. On the other hand φ_2^0 is admissible and so by Theorem 12.1 it is optimal.

We conclude that detectability is not necessary for the existence of an optimal control, but if detectability is absent existence may fail; and the same can be said about uniqueness of a nonnegative solution of (28). On the other hand, it can be shown (Ex. 12.5) that $(\sqrt{M}, A)$ is necessarily detectable if (28) has exactly one nonnegative solution P^0, where P^0 has the property that $A - BN^{-1}B'P^0$ is stable.

12.5 Exercises

12.1 Consider the linear regulator problem with cost functional

$$\int_0^\infty e^{2\alpha t}\, L[x(t), u(t)]\, dt \tag{42}$$

where α is a real constant and L is defined as in the text. Reasoning as in Section 12.1, show formally that the value function satisfies

$$(Ax)'V_x - \frac{1}{4}V_x' BN^{-1}B'V_x + 2\alpha V + x'Mx = 0 .$$

Find the corresponding matrix quadratic equation and obtain the counterparts of Theorems 12.2 and 12.3.

12.2 Show that if (A, B) is stabilizable and (D, A) is detectable, the same is true with A replaced by $A - \alpha I$, $\alpha > 0$; but the converse is false.

12.3 Show that if the regulator problem of Ex. 12.1 is solvable for some α, then it is solvable for any $\alpha' < \alpha$, in the sense that linear state feedback exists such that (42), with exponent α', is minimized. But is it necessarily true that the closed loop system matrix is stable?

12.4 For the scalar system

$$\dot{x} = ax + u$$

$$\int_0^\infty (mx^2 + u^2)\, dt = \min. \qquad (m > 0) ,$$

solve the quadratic equation (28) explicitly, and also by successive approximation as in the proof of Theorem 12.2. Show that the latter technique is simply Newton's method. What can be said about the rate of convergence? Extend your discussion to the general case.

12.5 Verify the last assertion of Section 12.5 by showing that if $(\sqrt{M}, A)$ is not detectable, there exists a solution $P \geq 0$ of (28) such that

$$A - BN^{-1}B'P$$

is not stable. HINT: Write

$$\mathcal{N} \triangleq \bigcap_{i=1}^{n} \operatorname{Ker}(DA^{i-1})$$

for the unobservable subspace of (D, A), and $\mathcal{X}^+$ for the subspace of unstable modes of A. Show that if $(\sqrt{M}, A)$ is not detectable then

$$\mathcal{N}^+ \triangleq \mathcal{N} \cap \mathcal{X}^+ \neq 0 .$$

Check that $\mathcal{N}^+$ is A-invariant and that $\overline{D}$ exists such that the diagram commutes:

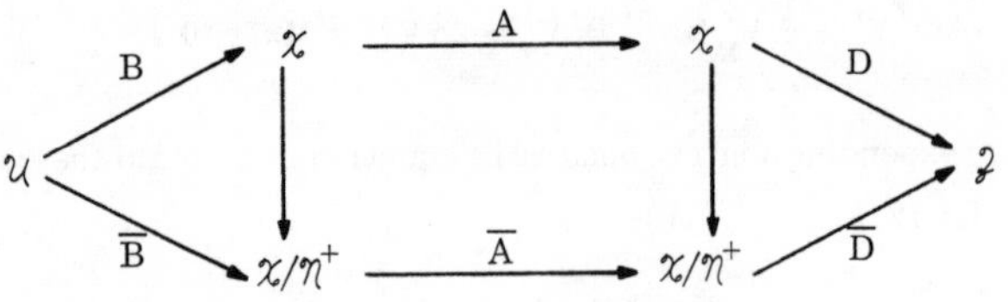

Verify that the triple $(\bar{D}, \bar{A}, \bar{B})$ is detectable and stabilizable if (A, B) is stabilizable. Next write

$$\mathcal{X} = \mathcal{N}^+ \oplus \hat{\mathcal{X}}$$

and show that the corresponding matrices have the form

$$A = \begin{bmatrix} A_1 & A_3 \\ 0 & A_2 \end{bmatrix}, \qquad B = \begin{bmatrix} B_1 \\ B_2 \end{bmatrix}, \qquad D = [\,0\,,\ D_2\,]\,.$$

It is now easy to verify that (28) has a solution P with the stated properties.

12.6 Show that if the hypothesis of detectability in Theorem 12.2 is strengthened to observability then P^0 is positive definite.

12.6 Notes and References

The 'linear-quadratic' regulator has been a topic of longstanding interest in control theory (cf. Newton, Gould and Kaiser [1], Kalman [2]), both for the reasons mentioned at the beginning of this chapter and because the problem can often be solved in more general settings: as with partial differential equations (Lions [1]) or with account taken of random noise (e.g., Wonham [4]). In accordance with the scope of this book we have restricted attention to the infinite process time interval, as it is this which leads to a time-invariant control. For a more general treatment see especially Lee and Markus [1], Bellman [2] and Anderson and Moore [1].

The proof of Theorem 12.2 follows Wonham [2]; the method used there, sometimes called 'quasilinearization' or 'approximation in policy space', had been extensively discussed by Bellman [1], Kalaba [1] and Kleinman [1]. An alternative approach to the matrix quadratic equation was developed by Potter [1], who expresses P in terms of the eigenvectors of the 'Hamiltonian' matrix

$$\begin{bmatrix} A & -BN^{-1}B' \\ -D'D & -A' \end{bmatrix}$$

discussed in Chapter 13. A variety of results are known which relate stabilizability of (A, B), detectability or observability of (D, A), and properties of the Hamiltonian matrix: see

Martensson [1] and Kučera [1]. In particular, the remark that Theorem 12.2 is true with (D, A) merely detectable (rather than observable) is due to Kučera [1], as is the result of Ex. 12.5.

CHAPTER 13

QUADRATIC OPTIMIZATION II: DYNAMIC RESPONSE

The approach to linear regulator design described in the previous chapter has been widely advertised as a systematic technique to achieve good transient response with reasonable computational effort. This claim is based on practical experience rather than compelling theoretical arguments. Actually, little has been rigorously established about the qualitative behavior of the closed loop system as a function of the weighting matrices M and N of the cost functional (12.3). In this chapter we present a catalog of fragmentary results, incomplete but suggestive, as a point of departure in future research.

13.1 Dynamic Response: Generalities

We recall from Theorem 12.3 that the optimization problem was posed in such a way that the optimal system is necessarily stable, so that

$$z(t) = Dx(t) \to 0 , \qquad t \to \infty . \tag{1}$$

On intuitive grounds we might expect that if the weighting matrix N is diminished (thus attaching a lower penalty to large values of $|u(t)|^2$) convergence in (1) would be speeded up. This is only broadly true: as N decreases, some eigenvalues of A + BF may actually move to the right in the complex plane. Furthermore, attempts to improve convergence in (1) may lead to impracticably large values of the elements of F as well as large amplitude peaks in $|z(\cdot)|$. Very roughly, the problem is to arrange that A + BF is such that convergence in (1) is rapid, and damped to avoid excessive overshoot and oscillation, while keeping the norm of F small. The last requirement is needed to prevent saturation of actuating elements by the control signals, in response to initial disturbances (values of $x(0+)$) which the system would normally encounter. A systematic procedure taking all these constraints into account is not yet available.

13.2 Example 1: First-Order System

Let $n = 1$ and A, B, M, N be scalars, which we write with lower case letters. Solving the quadratic equation (12.28), we get

$$p^0 = \frac{\sqrt{a^2 + n^{-1}b^2m} + a}{n^{-1}b^2},$$

$$f^0 = -\frac{\sqrt{a^2 + n^{-1}b^2m} + a}{b},$$

$$a + bf^0 = -\sqrt{a^2 + n^{-1}b^2m}\,.$$

As the control weighting n decreases to zero the value function p^0x^2 does the same, i.e., performance becomes perfect; the optimal gain f^0 increases in magnitude to $+\infty$, as does speed of response as measured by the eigenvalue $a + bf^0$. Conversely, heavy control weighting (large n) may result in sluggish response. Obviously the influence of m is reciprocal to that of n.

13.3 Example 2: Second-Order System

Let

$$\dot{x}_1 = x_2, \qquad \dot{x}_2 = u, \qquad z = \left(x_1, \sqrt{m_2}\,x_2\right),$$

$$L(x,u) = x_1^2 + m_2x_2^2 + nu^2\,.$$

Thus

$$A = \begin{bmatrix} 0 & 1 \\ 0 & 0 \end{bmatrix}, \qquad B = \begin{bmatrix} 0 \\ 1 \end{bmatrix},$$

$$M = \begin{bmatrix} 1 & 0 \\ 0 & m_2 \end{bmatrix}, \qquad N = n\,.$$

Let

$$P^0 = \begin{bmatrix} p_1 & p_3 \\ p_3 & p_2 \end{bmatrix}.$$

Solving (12.28) we get

$$p_1 = \sqrt{m_2 + 2\sqrt{n}}$$

$$p_2 = \sqrt{n(m_2 + 2\sqrt{n})}\,,$$

$$p_3 = \sqrt{n}\,,$$

$$F^0 = -N^{-1}B'P^0 = -\left(\frac{1}{\sqrt{n}}, \sqrt{\frac{m_2 + 2\sqrt{n}}{n}}\right).$$

From this,

$$\sigma(A + BF) = -\sqrt{\frac{m_2 + 2\sqrt{n}}{4n}} \pm \sqrt{\frac{m_2 - 2\sqrt{n}}{4n}}.$$

If $m_2 > 0$, P^0 does not vanish as $n \downarrow 0$, and only one eigenvalue λ of $A + BF$ is unbounded:

$$\lambda \sim -\frac{1}{\sqrt{m_2}}, \ -\sqrt{\frac{m_2}{n}}.$$

The feedback gains become large:

$$F^0 \sim -\left(\frac{1}{\sqrt{n}}, \sqrt{\frac{m_2}{n}}\right);$$

nevertheless, as $n \downarrow 0$ the 'peaking index'

$$\sup_{t \geq 0} |\exp t(A + BF^0)| \tag{2}$$

remains bounded, showing that $|z(t)|$ is bounded as $n \downarrow 0$, uniformly for $t \geq 0$ and $|x(0)| = 1$. It is clear that the weighting factor m_2 attached to the derivative $x_2 = \dot{x}_1$ inhibits very fast response, as this would call for nearly impulsive velocities, and the square of a unit Dirac impulse has (formally) infinite integral.

If $m_2 = 0$, we have

$$\lambda = \sqrt{\frac{1}{2\sqrt{n}}}\,(-1 \pm i)\,.$$

As $n \downarrow 0$ response becomes arbitrarily fast, necessarily at the expense of a high peaking index (2), which can be shown to behave unboundedly as $n^{-1/4}$. On the other hand, the 'damping ratio', defined for a second order system as

$$\zeta = -\frac{(\lambda_1 + \lambda_2)}{2|\lambda_1 \lambda_2|^{1/2}},$$

satisfies the inequality $\zeta \geq 1/\sqrt{2}$ for all $m_2 \geq 0$ and $n > 0$. It follows that $\sigma(A + BF^0)$ is confined to the left-plane sector enclosed by the rays

$$\arg\lambda = \frac{3\pi}{4}, \frac{5\pi}{4};$$

and this is a standard specification restricting 'overshoot' associated with rapid oscillation.

13.4 Hamiltonian Matrix

Let $\lambda_0 \in \sigma(A + BF^0)$, with eigenvector ξ. Recalling (12.28) and (12.37) we have

$$\lambda_0\xi = (A + BF^0)\xi = A\xi - BN^{-1}B'\eta, \tag{3}$$

where $\eta = P^0\xi$. Thus

$$\lambda_0\eta = P^0(A + BF^0)\xi = (P^0A - P^0BN^{-1}B'P^0)\xi$$

$$= (-M - A'P^0)\xi = -M\xi - A'\eta. \tag{4}$$

From (3) and (4) there results

$$H\begin{bmatrix}\xi\\ \eta\end{bmatrix} = \lambda_0\begin{bmatrix}\xi\\ \eta\end{bmatrix},$$

where H is the Hamiltonian matrix

$$H \triangleq \begin{bmatrix} A & -BN^{-1}B' \\ -M & -A' \end{bmatrix}. \tag{5}$$

Write $A^0 \triangleq A + BF^0$. From (12.28) and (12.37) it is quickly verified that H satisfies the identity

$$\begin{bmatrix} I & 0 \\ P & -I \end{bmatrix}(\lambda - H)\begin{bmatrix} I & 0 \\ P & I \end{bmatrix} = \begin{bmatrix} \lambda - A^0 & BN^{-1}B' \\ 0 & -\lambda - A^{0\prime} \end{bmatrix}. \tag{6}$$

Taking determinants on both sides of (6) we get

$$\det(\lambda I - H) = \det(\lambda I - A^0)\det(\lambda I + A^0). \tag{7}$$

From (7) there follows

$$\sigma(H) = \sigma(A^0) \dot{\cup} \sigma(-A^0) = \sigma(A^0) \dot{\cup} (-\sigma(A^0)).$$

Thus $\sigma(H)$ is symmetric about the imaginary, as well as the real, axis of $\mathbb{C}$, and the characteristic polynomial of H can be written as a polynomial in λ^2. Since A^0 is stable, $\sigma(A^0)$ is that half of $\sigma(H)$ which lies in the open left-half complex plane.

To exploit this observation we compute $\det(\lambda - H)$ in terms of the open-loop transfer matrix

$$G(\lambda) \triangleq D(\lambda I - A)^{-1} BN^{-1/2}, \tag{8}$$

where $D'D = M$. Set

$$\pi(\lambda) \triangleq \det(\lambda I - A), \qquad \pi^0(\lambda) \triangleq \det(\lambda I - A^0).$$

From (5), (7) and standard determinantal manipulations (Ex. 13.10) there results

$$\begin{aligned} \pi^0(\lambda)\, \pi^0(-\lambda) &= (-1)^n \det(\lambda I - H) \\ &= \pi(\lambda)\, \pi(-\lambda) \det[I + G(\lambda)\, G(-\lambda)'] . \end{aligned} \tag{9}$$

Thus if $M \downarrow 0$, or if $N \geq \nu I$ and $\nu \uparrow \infty$, the closed-loop poles tend, by (Rouché's) Theorem 0.3, to the roots of $\pi(\lambda)\, \pi(-\lambda)$ in $\mathcal{R}e\, \lambda \leq 0$, that is, to the open-loop poles reflected, if necessary, in the imaginary axis. The behavior of the closed-loop poles as $N \downarrow 0$ is more complicated and will be described in the two sections to follow.

13.5 Asymptotic Root Locus: Single Input System

Suppose $B = b$ and set $N = \epsilon^2$. For simplicity we assume as well that (A, b) is controllable. By a similarity transformation, we can arrange that the matrices of A, b are in standard canonical form (1.7). It is then easy to compute the characteristic polynomial of H directly from (5). The result is

$$(-1)^n \det|\lambda - H| = \epsilon^{-2}\theta(\lambda)' M \theta(-\lambda) + \pi(\lambda)\, \pi(-\lambda), \tag{10}$$

where $\pi(\lambda)$ is the ch.p. of A and

$$\theta(\lambda) \triangleq \mathrm{col}[1, \lambda, \ldots, \lambda^{n-1}].$$

Write $\pi^0(\lambda)$ for the ch.p. of A^0. From (7) and (10) there follows

$$\epsilon^2 \pi^0(\lambda)\, \pi^0(-\lambda) = \theta(\lambda)' M \theta(-\lambda) + \epsilon^2 \pi(\lambda)\, \pi(-\lambda). \tag{11}$$

We are interested in the behavior of the roots of $\pi^0(\lambda)$ as $\epsilon \downarrow 0$, since this condition is equivalent to light weighting of the control and thus would be expected to encourage fast dynamic response. In this direction we have the following asymptotic result.

THEOREM 13.1. Let

$$\theta(\lambda)' M\theta(-\lambda) = \varphi(\lambda)\varphi(-\lambda), \tag{12}$$

where the roots s_i of $\varphi(\lambda)$ belong to the closed left-half complex s-plane. If $\deg \varphi = k$, then as $\epsilon \downarrow 0$, k of the roots of $\pi^0(\lambda)$ approach the fixed values s_i ($i \in \underline{k}$), while the remaining $n-k$ roots tend to infinity with asymptotic values

$$\epsilon^{-1/(n-k)} \exp\left[\frac{i\pi}{2(n-k)}(n-k+1+2\nu)\right], \qquad \nu = 0, 1, \dots, n-k-1. \tag{13}$$

A proof is given at the end of this section.

The quantities (13) are simply the left-half plane roots of the equation

$$(-1)^{n-k}\lambda^{2(n-k)} + \epsilon^{-2} = 0.$$

The theorem says that for small ϵ the roots of $\pi^0(\lambda)$ (i.e., the closed loop poles) are nearly independent of the roots of $\pi(\lambda)$ (i.e., the eigenvalues of A), being determined essentially by the choice of the state weighting matrix M. The number k ($0 \le k \le n-1$) of asymptotically finite closed loop poles is simply the highest order of derivative $x_1^{(k)} = x_{k+1}$ which is assigned positive weight in the cost functional. Next, (13) shows that the remaining $n-k$ closed loop poles are asymptotically uniformly distributed along a circular arc which terminates on rays at an angle $(n-k)^{-1}\pi/2$ with the imaginary axis. The corresponding factor in the squared real frequency response is

$$\left(\omega^{2(n-k)} + \epsilon^{-2}\right)^{-1},$$

called in circuit theory a Butterworth characteristic. The time response of a Butterworth filter to an impulse is known to be well damped, and if ϵ is small, response is fast. However, there is no assurance that the asymptotically finite poles (roots of φ) are well damped. Indeed if $n = 8$, $k = 6$ and

$$L(x, u) = \mu^2\left(x_1^2 + x_7^2\right) + u^2,$$

then

$$\theta(\lambda)' M\theta(-\lambda) = 1 + \lambda^{12},$$

which yields an unpleasantly oscillatory pole pair

$$\exp i\left(-\pi \pm \frac{5\pi}{12}\right).$$

To investigate output behavior in more detail, suppose

$$z(t) = \sum_{i=1}^{k+1} d_i x_i(t) = \sum_{i=1}^{k+1} d_i x_1^{(i-1)}(t) ,$$

so that $M = dd'$, where

$$d \triangleq \mathrm{col}[d_1, \ldots, d_{k+1}, 0, \ldots, 0] .$$

Write

$$\psi(\lambda) \triangleq \sum_{i=1}^{k+1} d_i \lambda^{i-1} . \tag{14}$$

From (12) and (14)

$$\psi(\lambda)\,\psi(-\lambda) = \varphi(\lambda)\,\varphi(-\lambda) .$$

If $\psi(\lambda)$ happens to be stable then we have $\psi(\lambda) = \varphi(\lambda)$, the so-called minimum phase relation, and the transfer function from u to z is

$$\frac{\hat{z}}{\hat{u}} \triangleq d'\left(\lambda - A^0\right)^{-1} b = \frac{\psi(\lambda)}{\pi^0(\lambda)} = \frac{\varphi(\lambda)}{\pi^0(\lambda)} .$$

According to Theorem 13.1, for small ϵ $\varphi(\lambda)$ is approximately cancelled from $\pi^0(\lambda)$, and the transfer function is nearly Butterworth, as already noted. On the other hand, if $\psi(\lambda)$ has a factor

$$\lambda - \sigma,\ \sigma > 0 ; \qquad \text{or} \qquad (\lambda - \sigma)^2 + \omega^2 ,\ \sigma > 0 ,$$

then for small ϵ, $\hat{z}/\hat{u}$ will contain a factor close to

$$\frac{\lambda - \sigma}{\lambda + \sigma} \qquad \text{or} \qquad \frac{(\lambda - \sigma)^2 + \omega^2}{(\lambda + \sigma)^2 + \omega^2} ,$$

respectively. The component this factor adds to time response might well be slow or lightly damped.

The conclusion is that light weighting of the control may often yield but cannot guarantee good dynamic behavior of an arbitrarily chosen scalar output, in response to an initial perturbation of this output and its derivatives. Our analysis of the single-input single-output situation has revealed that the approach works best if the output to be quadratically minimized is in a minimum phase relation with the system state.

It is clear that a similar analysis applies in the dual situation where the regulated output is a scalar, i.e., rank(M) = 1 and rank(B) is arbitrary.

We conclude this section with a proof of Theorem 13.1. For this we need two preliminary results.

LEMMA 13.1. Let $\alpha(\lambda), \beta(\lambda) \in \mathbb{R}[\lambda]$. There exists $\varphi(\lambda) \in \mathbb{R}[\lambda]$ such that

$$\alpha(\lambda)\,\alpha(-\lambda) + \beta(\lambda)\,\beta(-\lambda) = \varphi(\lambda)\,\varphi(-\lambda)\,.$$

Furthermore, if $0 \le M \in \mathbb{R}^{n \times n}$, with M symmetric and if $\theta(\lambda) \in \mathbb{R}^n[\lambda]$, there exists $\varphi(\lambda) \in \mathbb{R}[\lambda]$ such that

$$\theta(\lambda)' M \theta(-\lambda) = \varphi(\lambda)\,\varphi(-\lambda)\,.$$

PROOF: Write

$$\omega(\lambda) \triangleq \alpha(\lambda)\,\alpha(-\lambda) + \beta(\lambda)\,\beta(-\lambda)\,.$$

Since $\omega(-\lambda) = \omega(\lambda)$ and $\omega(s) \ge 0$ for $\mathcal{Re}\ s = 0$, the prime factors of ω must be of form $\pi(\lambda)\,\pi(-\lambda)$ with $\pi(\lambda) \in \mathbb{R}[\lambda]$. The first statement is now clear, and the second follows by induction on the number of summands in the scalar product $(\sqrt{M}\,\theta(\lambda))'\sqrt{M}\,\theta(-\lambda)$. ∎

Remark.

By swapping over prime factors if necessary it is clear that we can always arrange that the complex roots of $\varphi(\lambda)$ lie in $\mathcal{Re}\ \lambda \le 0$.

LEMMA 13.2. Let $\xi(\lambda), \eta(\lambda)$ be monic polynomials in $\mathbb{R}[\lambda]$, with

$$n = \deg \xi > \deg \eta = m\,.$$

For $s \in \mathbb{C}$ and $\epsilon \ge 0$ let

$$\zeta(s, \epsilon) \triangleq \epsilon\, \xi(s) + \eta(s)\,.$$

Then as $\epsilon \downarrow 0$, m of the roots of $\zeta(\cdot, \epsilon)$ tend to the roots of η, while the remaining $n - m$ roots tend asymptotically to

$$\epsilon^{-1/(n-m)} \times \{\text{roots of } t^{n-m} + 1 = 0\}\,.$$

PROOF: Let s_0 be a root of η, and pick $\delta > 0$ such that no root of η other than s_0 lies in the disk $|s - s_0| \le \delta$. Write $\mathfrak{S} \triangleq \{s\colon |s - s_0| = \delta\}$ and

$$q \triangleq \min_{s \in \mathfrak{S}} |\eta(s)| .$$

If $\epsilon_0 > 0$ is chosen such that

$$\epsilon_0 \max_{s \in \mathfrak{S}} |\xi(s)| < q$$

then for all $|\epsilon| < \epsilon_0$ we have

$$|\epsilon\xi(s)| < q \le |\eta(s)| , \qquad s \in \mathfrak{S} .$$

It follows by Rouché's Theorem that $\eta(s)$ and $\epsilon\xi(s) + \eta(s)$ have the same number of roots within $\mathfrak{S}$, i.e., if s_0 is of multiplicity σ, then for all ϵ sufficiently small, $\zeta(s, \epsilon)$ has exactly σ roots within $\mathfrak{S}$. Taking $\delta > 0$ arbitrarily small, we get that m roots of $\zeta(\cdot, \epsilon)$ approach the m roots of η as $\epsilon \to 0$. Next let t^* be a fixed root of $t^{n-m} + 1 = 0$. It will be shown that $\zeta(\cdot, \epsilon)$ has a root $s(\epsilon)$ such that

$$\frac{s(\epsilon)}{\epsilon^{-1/(n-m)} t^*} \to 1 \qquad \text{as} \qquad \epsilon \downarrow 0 .$$

For this let

$$\xi(s) = \mu(s)\, \eta(s) + \nu(s) ,$$

where $\deg \mu = n - m$, $\deg \nu \le n - m - 1$. Then

$$\zeta(s, \epsilon) = [\, \epsilon\mu(s) + 1\,]\, \eta(s) + \epsilon\nu(s)$$

so that

$$\hat{\zeta}(s, \epsilon) \triangleq \frac{\zeta(s, \epsilon)}{\eta(s)} = \epsilon\mu(s) + 1 + \frac{\epsilon\nu(s)}{\eta(s)} .$$

Put $t = \epsilon^{1/(n-m)} s$. Then simple computations verify that

$$\epsilon\mu(s) = t^{n-m} + O(\epsilon^{1/(n-m)}) ,$$

and

$$\frac{\epsilon\nu(s)}{\eta(s)} = O(\epsilon^{(m+1)/(n-m)}) ,$$

as $\epsilon \downarrow 0$, uniformly for $1/2 \le |t| \le 3/2$. It follows that

$$\tilde{\zeta}(t, \epsilon) \triangleq \hat{\zeta}(\epsilon^{-1/(n-m)} t, \epsilon) = t^{n-m} + 1 + O(\epsilon^{1/(n-m)})$$

under the same conditions. Now $|t^*| = 1$, and so for $\delta > 0$ small and fixed, there exists $\epsilon_0 > 0$ such that

$$|\tilde{\zeta}(t, \epsilon) - (t^{n-m} + 1)| < |t^{n-m} + 1|$$

for all t with $|t-t^*| = \delta$ and all ϵ, $0 \le \epsilon < \epsilon_0$. By Rouché's Theorem, $\tilde{\zeta}(t,\epsilon)$ has exactly one root, say $t^*(\epsilon)$, in $|t-t^*| < \delta$. Then

$$s^*(\epsilon) \triangleq \epsilon^{-1/(n-m)} t^*(\epsilon)$$

satisfies

$$\hat{\zeta}(s^*(\epsilon),\epsilon) = \tilde{\zeta}(t^*(\epsilon),\epsilon) = 0 ,$$

and also

$$|t^*(\epsilon) - t^*| = |\epsilon^{1/(n-m)} s^*(\epsilon) - t^*| < \delta ,$$

so that

$$\left| \frac{s^*(\epsilon)}{\epsilon^{-1/(n-m)} t^*} - 1 \right| < \frac{\delta}{|t^*|} = \delta ,$$

as we had to show. ∎

PROOF of Theorem 13.1. Apply Lemma 13.1 to the polynomial $\theta(\lambda)' M \theta(\lambda)$ and then Lemma 13.2 to the polynomial on the right side of (11). ∎

13.6 Asymptotic Root Locus: Multivariable System

We retain the definition (8) of $G(\lambda)$, but effectively multiply N by ϵ^2 by replacing $G(\lambda)\,G(-\lambda)'$ by $\epsilon^{-2} G(\lambda)\,G(-\lambda)'$ in (9). Our objective is to describe the behavior of the roots of $\pi^0(\lambda)$ as $\epsilon \downarrow 0$. For this let ρ be the rank of the rational matrix $G(\lambda)$ over the field $\mathbb{R}(\lambda)$ of rational functions of λ. For $\sigma \in \underline{\rho}$ define

$$\hat{\gamma}_\sigma(\lambda^2) \triangleq \sum \{\sigma \times \sigma \text{ principal minors of } G(\lambda)\,G(-\lambda)'\} . \tag{15}$$

It can be shown (Ex. 13.13) that none of the rational functions $\hat{\gamma}_\sigma(\lambda^2)$ is identically zero. Fix $\sigma \in \underline{\rho}$, and write $i \triangleq (i_1, \dots, i_\sigma)$ etc. for the multi-index having $1 \le i_1 < i_2 < \cdots < i_\sigma \le n$, subject to dimensional compatibility with the matrices involved. Finally write $G^i_j(\lambda)$ etc. for the minor of $G(\lambda)$ formed by selecting the entries having row index in the list i and column index in j.

Starting with the modified factor in (9), we have

$$\det [I + \epsilon^{-2} G(\lambda)\,G(-\lambda)'] = 1 + \sum_{\sigma=1}^{\rho} \epsilon^{-2\sigma} \hat{\gamma}_\sigma(\lambda^2) . \tag{16}$$

By (8), (15) and the Cauchy-Binet formula for minors,

$$\hat{\gamma}_\sigma(\lambda^2) = \sum_i \left[G(\lambda)\, G(-\lambda)'\right]_i^i = \sum_{i,j} G_j^i(\lambda) \left[G(-\lambda)'\right]_i^j$$

$$= \sum_{i,j} G_j^i(\lambda)\, G_j^i(-\lambda)\,.$$

Similarly, and by the rule for evaluating the minors of a matrix inverse,

$$G_j^i(\lambda) = \sum_{k,\ell} D_k^i \left[(\lambda I - A)^{-1}\right]_\ell^k \left(BN^{-1/2}\right)_j^\ell$$

$$= \pi(\lambda)^{-1} \sum_{k,\ell} (-1)^{|k|+|\ell|}\, D_k^i (\lambda I - A)_{k'}^{\ell'} \left(BN^{-1/2}\right)_j^\ell, \tag{17}$$

where $|k| \triangleq k_1 + \cdots + k_\sigma$ and k' denotes the list of $n-\sigma$ indices complementary to k. By (17),

$$\gamma_j^i(\lambda) \triangleq \pi(\lambda)\, G_j^i(\lambda)$$

is a polynomial in $\mathbb{R}[\lambda]$. Thus

$$\gamma_\sigma(\lambda^2) \triangleq \pi(\lambda)\, \pi(-\lambda)\, \hat{\gamma}_c(\lambda^2) \in \mathbb{R}[\lambda^2]\,. \tag{18}$$

Now by (17), $G_j^i(\lambda)$ is of the form

$$G_j^i(\lambda) = \pi(\lambda)^{-1}\left[g_{ij}\, \lambda^{n-\sigma} + \cdots\right],$$

where the leading term $g_{ij}\, \lambda^{n-\sigma}$ is contributed by those terms in the double sum having $\ell' = k'$, i.e., $\ell = k$:

$$g_{ij} \triangleq \sum_k D_k^i \left(BN^{-1/2}\right)_j^k = \left(DBN^{-1/2}\right)_j^i. \tag{19}$$

Thus, formally

$$\gamma_\sigma(\lambda^2) = (-1)^{n-\sigma} \left(\sum_{i,j} g_{ij}^2\right) \left(\lambda^2\right)^{n-\sigma} + \cdots,$$

the remainder denoting terms of lower degree in λ^2. We shall write this as

$$\gamma_\sigma(\lambda^2) = g_\sigma \left(-\lambda^2\right)^{n-\sigma} + \cdots, \tag{20}$$

where

$$g_\sigma \triangleq \sum_{i,j} g_{ij}^2 . \tag{21}$$

Collecting results, we have by (9), (16), (18) and (20) that

$$\pi^0(\lambda)\,\pi^0(-\lambda) = \pi(\lambda)\,\pi(-\lambda) + \sum_{\sigma=1}^{\rho} \epsilon^{-2\sigma}\left[g_\sigma\left(-\lambda^2\right)^{n-\sigma} + \cdots\right]. \tag{22}$$

To describe the asymptotic root locus as $\epsilon \downarrow 0$ we shall content ourselves with the case where the above formal analysis matches the actual situation, namely all the numbers g_σ are nonvanishing. By (19) and (21) this means simply that $\operatorname{rank}(DB) \geq \rho$, hence (Ex. 13.16) $\operatorname{rank}(DB) = \rho$. Our assumption is a priori plausible and is in fact valid for 'generic' choices of the $q \times n$ matrix D and $n \times m$ matrix B, inasmuch as $\rho \leq \min(q, m)$. Of course, it may cease to hold for structures which in some sense are 'special'. In any event, we have

THEOREM 13.2. Let the rank of $G(\lambda)$ over $\mathbb{R}(\lambda)$ be ρ and assume that $\operatorname{rank}(DB) = \rho$. Then as $\epsilon \downarrow 0$, $n - \rho$ of the closed-loop poles tend to the stable roots of

$$\gamma_\rho(\lambda^2) = 0,$$

where

$$\gamma_\rho(\lambda^2) \triangleq \pi(\lambda)\,\pi(-\lambda) \sum_i [G(\lambda)\,G(-\lambda)']_i^i$$

and the sum is taken over all the $\rho \times \rho$ principal minors of $G(\lambda)\,G(-\lambda)'$. The remaining ρ closed-loop poles tend asymptotically to $\epsilon^{-1}\mu_r$ $(r \in \underline{\rho})$, where $\mu_1, \ldots, \mu_\rho$ are the stable roots of the polynomial

$$\mu^{2\rho} + \sum_{\sigma=1}^{\rho} (-1)^\sigma g_\sigma \mu^{2(\rho-\sigma)}, \tag{23}$$

determined by

$$g_\sigma \triangleq \sum_{i,j} \left[\left(DBN^{-1/2}\right)_j^i\right]^2, \qquad \sigma \in \underline{\rho},$$

the sum being taken over all $\sigma \times \sigma$ minors of $DBN^{-1/2}$.

PROOF: The proof follows the same lines as that of Theorem 13.1, and so need only be sketched. For the fixed poles, multiply through (22) by $\epsilon^{2\rho}$ and let $\epsilon \downarrow 0$. The only term remaining is

$$g_\rho\left(-\lambda^2\right)^{n-\rho} + \cdots = \gamma_\rho(\lambda^2) .$$

By Rouché's theorem it follows that $\pi^0(\lambda)\,\pi^0(-\lambda)$ has exactly one root in any fixed, small neighborhood of each root λ of γ_ρ, for all $\epsilon > 0$ sufficiently small. For the ρ remaining roots, multiply through (22) by $\lambda^{-2n}(\epsilon\lambda)^{2\rho}$, set $\mu \triangleq \epsilon\lambda$, let $\epsilon \downarrow 0$ and note that what remains is the polynomial (23). Another appeal to Rouché finishes the proof. ▮

The foregoing result reduces to that of Theorem 13.1 if $\rho = 1$ and, in (12), $\deg \varphi = n-1$. Roughly stated, our condition on rank(DB) means that a 'maximal' number of state variables are weighted in the performance index (for a given value of ρ), thus minimizing the number of asymptotically infinite poles. It is worth noting that the asymptotic pole pattern determined by (23) will in general not be of Butterworth type, or even decomposable into sub-patterns of Butterworth type.

13.7 Upper and Lower Bounds on P^0

By use of Lemmas 12.1 and 12.3 it is easy to see that an upper bound for P^0 can be calculated by choosing any F such that $A + BF$ is stable and computing the corresponding matrix P from (12.36). As shown in Section 12.4 such upper bounds can be successively improved to yield P^0 in the limit.

It is interesting that a lower bound on P^0 can be computed provided we strengthen stabilizability of (A, B) to controllability, and detectability of (D, A) to observability. Under the latter condition it is easily verified (Ex. 12.6) that $P^0 > 0$, so that $P^{0\,-1}$ exists. The following lemma shows that it suffices to compute an upper bound for $P^{0\,-1}$.

LEMMA 13.3. *Let* $0 < Q^0 \le Q$. *Then* $Q^{0\,-1} \ge Q^{-1}$.

PROOF: Choose T orthogonal such that

$$T'Q^0T = \operatorname{diag} \Lambda ;$$

then

$$\Lambda^{-1/2}T'Q^0T\Lambda^{-1/2} = I .$$

Write

$$R \triangleq \Lambda^{-1/2}T'QT\Lambda^{-1/2}$$

and choose S orthogonal such that $S'RS = \operatorname{diag} M$. Then $M \ge S'IS = I$; clearly $M^{-1} \le I$; and the result follows by a simple computation. ▮

Now let $Q \triangleq P^{-1}$ and multiply both sides of (12.28) by Q to obtain

$$(-A')'Q + Q(-A') - QMQ + BN^{-1}B' = 0 . \tag{24}$$

By Theorem 12.2 and Ex. 12.6, (24) has a unique solution $Q^0 > 0$ in the class of positive semidefinite matrices, provided $(-A', \sqrt{M})$ is stabilizable and $(\sqrt{BN^{-1}B'}, -A')$ is observable. As these properties follow by the assumptions stated above, we conclude that $Q^0 = P^{0\,-1}$. Choosing K so that $-A' + \sqrt{M}K$ is stable, we solve for Q the linear equation obtained from (24), namely

$$(-A' + \sqrt{M}K)'Q + Q(-A' + \sqrt{M}K) + BN^{-1}B' + K'NK = 0 .$$

Then $0 < Q^0 \le Q$ and by Lemma 13.3,

$$P^0 \ge Q^{-1} .$$

Although these bounding procedures per se offer little insight into the behavior of the solution as a function of the parameters, they are useful in computation and, as will be shown next, help to provide information on the stability margin of $A + BF^0$.

13.8 Stability Margin

If $A: \mathcal{X} \to \mathcal{X}$ is stable we define the stability margin α of A as the distance of $\sigma(A)$ from the imaginary axis:

$$\alpha \triangleq -\max\{\mathrm{Re}\ \lambda : \lambda \in \sigma(A)\} .$$

A simple estimate of α is provided by the following.

PROPOSITION 13.1. *If A is stable, $Q > 0$, P is symmetric, and*

$$A'P + PA + Q = 0 , \tag{25}$$

then

$$\alpha \ge \frac{1}{2}\,|P|^{-1}\,|Q^{-1}|^{-1} .$$

PROOF: By Lemma 12.2, $P > 0$. From (25)

$$(A + \beta I)'P + P(A + \beta I) + Q - 2\beta P = 0 .$$

Again by Lemma 12.2, $A + \beta I$ is stable if $Q - 2\beta P > 0$, that is, if (in obvious notation)

$$2\beta < \frac{\min \sigma(Q)}{\max \sigma(P)} = \left[\max \sigma(Q^{-1}) \max \sigma(P)\right]^{-1} = \left(|Q^{-1}||P|\right)^{-1} . \blacksquare$$

Applying this result to (12.36) and (12.37) we get for the stability margin α^0 of $A + BF^0$:

$$\alpha^0 \geq \frac{1}{2} |P^0|^{-1} \left| \left(M + P^0 B N^{-1} B' P^0\right)^{-1} \right|^{-1} .$$

The result may be useful if an upper bound for P^0 is known; thus $P^0 \leq pI$ implies

$$\alpha^0 \geq \frac{1}{2} p^{-1} \min \sigma(M) . \tag{26}$$

13.9 Return Difference Relations

In this section we derive an identity involving the frequency response of an optimal system. This will be interpreted, albeit artificially, as an indication of the insensitivity of system response to a perturbation of the open loop system matrix A.

Consider (12.28), written as

$$-A'P - PA + PBN^{-1}B'P - M = 0 . \tag{27}$$

For simplicity of notation replace B by $B\sqrt{N}$ (or set $N = I$). Recall

$$M = D'D , \qquad F = -B'P ,$$

and write $R(\lambda) \triangleq (\lambda - A)^{-1}$. Then from (27) we obtain by successive manipulations:

$$(-\lambda - A)'P + P(\lambda - A) + PBB'P = M ;$$

$$B'PR(\lambda)B + B'R(-\lambda)'PB + B'R(-\lambda)'PBB'PR(\lambda)B$$

$$= B'R(-\lambda)'MR(\lambda)B ;$$

$$[I - FR(-\lambda)B]'[I - FR(\lambda)B]$$

$$= I + [DR(-\lambda)B]'[DR(\lambda)B] . \tag{28}$$

Define the return ratio

$$T(\lambda) \triangleq -FR(\lambda)B$$

and the return difference

$$\Phi(\lambda) \triangleq I - FR(\lambda)B\,. \tag{29}$$

Then from (28)

$$\Phi(-\lambda)'\Phi(\lambda) = I + H(-\lambda)'H(\lambda)\,, \tag{30}$$

where

$$H(\lambda) \triangleq DR(\lambda)B$$

is the open loop transfer matrix from u to z. Set $\lambda = i\omega$ in (30) and note that a matrix of the form $\Phi^{*\prime}\Phi\colon \mathbb{C}^m \to \mathbb{C}^m$ is positive semidefinite relative to the complex inner product. There follows

$$\Phi^{*\prime}(i\omega)\Phi(i\omega) \geq I\,, \qquad \omega \in \mathbb{R}\,. \tag{31}$$

Equation (30) is the <u>return difference identity</u> and (31) is the <u>return difference inequality</u>. The term 'return difference' originates in circuit theory; its use here is prompted by the signal flow graph, Fig. 13.1, where we put $u = Fx + v$.

From the flow graph we see that formally

$$\hat{x} = (I - R(\lambda)BF)^{-1}R(\lambda)B\hat{v}\,.$$

Introduce the <u>sensitivity matrix</u>

$$S(\lambda) \triangleq (I - R(\lambda)BF)^{-1}\,. \tag{32}$$

It is easily checked that the rational matrix inversion is legal. By (29) and (32), the (trivial) identity

$$[I - F'B'R(-\lambda)']F'F[I - R(\lambda)BF]$$

$$= F'[I - B'R(-\lambda)'F'][I - FR(\lambda)B]F$$

can be written

$$\left[S(-\lambda)^{-1}\right]'F'FS(\lambda)^{-1} = F'\Phi(-\lambda)'\Phi(\lambda)F\,,$$

and then by (31) there follows

$$F'F = S^{*\prime}(i\omega)F'\Phi^{*\prime}(i\omega)\Phi(i\omega)FS(i\omega) \geq S^{*\prime}(i\omega)F'FS(i\omega)\,. \tag{33}$$

It will be shown that (33) implies a qualitative distinction between the 'closed loop' graph, Fig. 13.1, and the 'open loop' graph, Fig. 13.2. In Fig. 13.2 the open loop control u_0 is defined by

$$\hat{u}_0(\lambda) = FS(\lambda)R(\lambda)x(0+)\,, \tag{34}$$

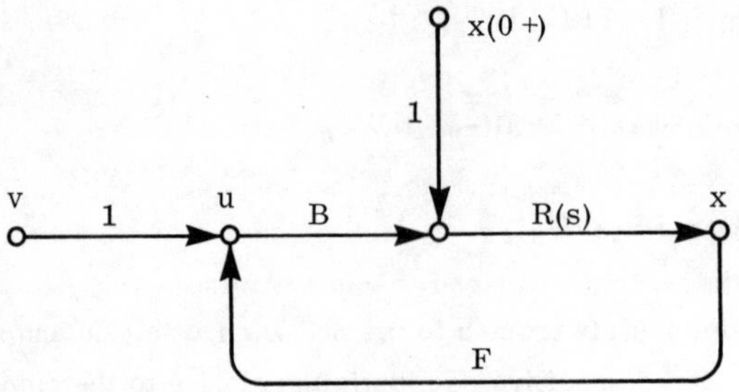

Fig. 13.1.

Closed-loop Graph.

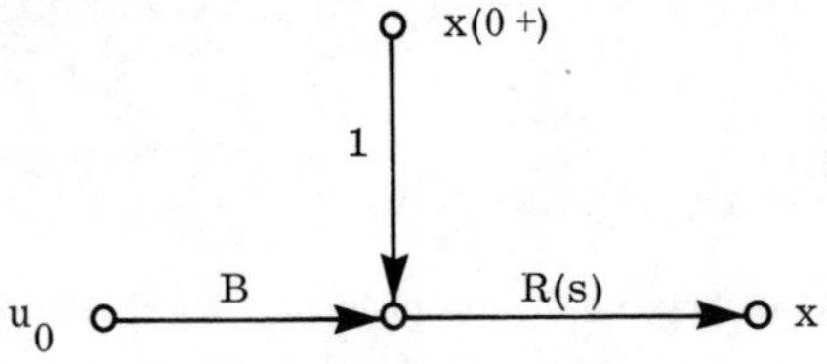

Fig. 13.2.

Open-loop Graph.

so that for both graphs

$$\hat{x}(\lambda) = S(\lambda)\, R(\lambda)\, x(0+)\ .$$

Suppose now that the system matrix A depends on a real parameter θ, with $A = A(\theta)$ continuously differentiable in a neighborhood of some nominal parameter value, say $\theta = 0$. Then $R = R(\lambda, \theta)$, $S = S(\lambda, \theta)$ and

$$\frac{\partial S(\lambda, 0)}{\partial \theta} = S(\lambda, 0)\,\frac{\partial R(\lambda, 0)}{\partial \theta}\,BFS(\lambda, 0)\ .$$

For the closed loop graph, $\hat{x}(\lambda) = \hat{x}_c(\lambda, \theta)$ say, and

$$\frac{\partial \hat{x}_c(\lambda, 0)}{\partial \theta} = \frac{\partial\,[S(\lambda, 0)\,R(\lambda, 0)]}{\partial \theta}\,x(0+)$$

$$= S(\lambda, 0)\,\frac{\partial R(\lambda, 0)}{\partial \theta}\,[BFS(\lambda, 0)\,R(\lambda, 0) + I]\,x(0+)\ . \tag{35}$$

For the open loop graph, let $\hat{x}(\lambda) = \hat{x}_0(\lambda, \theta)$. The derivative will be computed on the assumption that the open loop control (34) does not depend on θ:

$$\frac{\partial \hat{x}_0(\lambda, 0)}{\partial \theta} = \frac{\partial R(\lambda, 0)}{\partial \theta}\,[x(0+) + B\hat{u}_0(\lambda)]\ . \tag{36}$$

Comparison of (34) – (36) yields

$$\frac{\partial \hat{x}_c(\lambda, 0)}{\partial \theta} = S(\lambda, 0)\,\frac{\partial \hat{x}_0(\lambda, 0)}{\partial \theta}\ . \tag{37}$$

To exploit (37) we proceed formally. For θ small,

$$\delta x_c(t, \theta) = x_c(t, \theta) - x_c(t, 0) \simeq \theta\,\frac{\partial x_c(t, 0)}{\partial \theta}\ ,$$

$$\delta x_0(t, \theta) = x_0(t, \theta) - x_0(t, 0) \simeq \theta\,\frac{\partial x_0(t, 0)}{\partial \theta}$$

Applying Parseval's theorem and using (33) and (37), we get for the first order variations

$$2\pi \int_0^\infty \left| F\delta x_0(t, \theta) \right|^2 dt = \int_{-\infty}^\infty \left| F\delta\hat{x}_0(i\omega, \theta) \right|^2 d\omega$$

$$\simeq \theta^2 \int_{-\infty}^\infty \left| F\,\frac{\partial \hat{x}_0(i\omega, 0)}{\partial \theta} \right|^2 d\omega \geq \theta^2 \int_{-\infty}^\infty \left| FS(i\omega)\,\frac{\partial \hat{x}_0(i\omega, 0)}{\partial \theta} \right|^2 d\omega$$

$$= \theta^2 \int_{-\infty}^\infty \left| F\,\frac{\partial \hat{x}_c(i\omega, 0)}{\partial \theta} \right|^2 d\omega \simeq 2\pi \int_0^\infty \left| F\delta x_c(t, \theta) \right|^2 dt\ . \tag{38}$$

The inequality (38) reveals that the closed loop graph (Fig. 13.1) is less 'sensitive' (or no more so) than the open loop graph (Fig. 13.2), with respect to a small parameter change in A, and when sensitivities are measured by the indicated quadratic integral. Inasmuch as the latter measure was carefully selected to make the indicated inequality come out, not much can be claimed for the practical significance of the result. In any event, the calculation (easy) and the conclusion (fashionable) have a modicum of intrinsic interest.

13.10 Applicability of Quadratic Optimization

It should be clear from this chapter and the preceding that quadratic optimization is simply one technique for computing a feedback map F such that $A + BF$ is stable, given a stabilizable pair (A, B). As such, it does not by itself solve any of the basic structural problems of system synthesis. Indeed we have seen in our study of noninteraction, and of regulation, that considerable algebraic preparation of a synthesis problem may be necessary before the issue of pole assignment in general, or stabilization in particular, can be properly dealt with. After such preparation has been carried out, we are typically in a position to stabilize several pairs (A, B), which arise as the system matrices for suitable independent sub-problems of the main problem we started with. It is at this stage that the quadratic optimization algorithm may prove useful, but only in competition with alternative stabilization techniques. Indices of performance based on more direct descriptions of transient response, explored with efficient algorithms for parameter optimization, may well supersede the quadratic optimization technique in practical design.

13.11 Exercises

13.1 Using a computer, solve the regulator problem for a system of fourth or fifth order, and explore the effect on dynamic response of varying M and N.

13.2 Regard the Hamiltonian matrix (5) as a map $H: \mathcal{X} \oplus \mathcal{X}' \to \mathcal{X} \oplus \mathcal{X}'$. Under the conditions of Theorem 12.2, the polynomials $\pi^0(\lambda), \pi^0(-\lambda)$ are coprime, so that

$$\mathcal{X} \oplus \mathcal{X}' = \operatorname{Ker} \pi^0(H) \oplus \operatorname{Ker} \pi^0(-H) .$$

Show that if

$$\begin{bmatrix} \xi_i \\ \eta_i \end{bmatrix}, \qquad i \in \underline{n},$$

is a basis for $\operatorname{Ker} \pi^0(H)$, then P^0 can be represented as the $n \times n$ matrix

$$P^0 = \left[\eta_1, \ldots, \eta_n\right]\left[\xi_1, \ldots, \xi_n\right]^{-1} .$$

13.3 Referring to the Hamilton-Jacobi theory of first-order partial differential equations, show that the characteristic strips of (12.27) satisfy the ordinary differential system

$$\frac{d}{dt}\begin{bmatrix}\xi\\ \eta\end{bmatrix} = H\begin{bmatrix}\xi\\ \eta\end{bmatrix}. \tag{39}$$

13.4 Referring to the theory of the Bolza problem in the calculus of variations, consider the variational problem

$$\int_0^T [x(t)'Mx(t) + u(t)'Nu(t)]\, dt = \min.,$$

with T free, and side condition

$$\dot{x}(t) = Ax(t) + Bu(t).$$

Show formally that the Euler equations for this problem are equivalent to (39).

13.5* Obtain a generalization of Theorem 13.2 with no special assumption on rank(DB).

13.6* Obtain a significant improvement of the inequality (26).

13.7* A relation not well understood is the quantitative dependence of the sensitivity of a system on the topology of its signal flow graph. A major reason for synthesizing feedback configurations is that one <u>may</u> thereby achieve superior sensitivity performance as compared to open-loop configurations with the same nominal transmission (cf. Chapter 8). Investigate quantitatively.

13.8* Find a good estimate of the 'peaking index'

$$\sup_{t \geq 0} \left| \exp[t(A + BF^0)] \right|$$

and relate it effectively to M and N.

13.9 Using the fact that $A(\theta) + BF$ is stable for θ small, introduce appropriate extra hypotheses to rigorize the application of Parseval's theorem in deriving (38). Does the comparison of open and closed loop graphs make sense if $A(0)$ is unstable?

---

* Research problem.

13.10 Verify the representation (9) using the general determinantal relations:

$$\det \begin{bmatrix} A & B \\ C & D \end{bmatrix} = \det A \cdot \det(D - CA^{-1}B) , \qquad \det A \neq 0 , \tag{40}$$

and

$$\det(I + EF) = \det(I + FE) , \tag{41}$$

for arbitrary matrices of compatible dimension. HINT: For (40) multiply $\begin{bmatrix} A & B \\ C & D \end{bmatrix}$ on the left by

$$\begin{bmatrix} I & 0 \\ -CA^{-1} & I \end{bmatrix} .$$

For (41) note that

$$\begin{bmatrix} I & E \\ -F & I \end{bmatrix} \approx \begin{bmatrix} I & -F \\ E & I \end{bmatrix} \tag{42}$$

under the orthogonal transformation $\begin{bmatrix} 0 & I \\ I & 0 \end{bmatrix}$, and apply (40) to both sides of (42).

13.11 It is known that the rank of a Hermitian matrix (over $\mathbb{C}$) is the size of its largest nonvanishing principal minor. Prove that the same is true for the rank of $G(\lambda)\, G(-\lambda)'$ over $\mathbb{R}(\lambda)$. HINT: note that $G(i\omega)\, G(-i\omega)'$ is Hermitian for all real ω where $G(i\omega)$ is defined, and exploit analyticity.

13.12 Supply the details in the proof of Theorem 13.2.

13.13 Taking $\rho = 3$, verify by an example the final remark in Section 13.6. HINT: Having selected the array sizes, assign numerical entries randomly.

13.14 If ρ is the rank of $D(\lambda I - A)^{-1}B$ over $\mathbb{R}(\lambda)$, show that $\rho \geq \operatorname{rank}(DB)$.

13.12 Notes and References

Algebraic properties of the Hamiltonian matrix are discussed by Potter [1], Martensson [1] and Kučera [1]; the result in Ex. 13.2 was first proved (in somewhat less generality) by Potter. Theorem 13.1 is due essentially to Chang [1]; see also Kalman [3]; and, in the direction of a multivariable generalization, Tyler and Tuteur [1], and Kwakernaak and Sivan [1]. Theorem 13.2 is new. The determinantal relations used in Sections 13.4 and 13.6 can be found in Gantmakher [1]: for the Cauchy-Binet Theorem, p. 9; the rule for minors of an inverse matrix, p. 21; the identity (40), p. 45; and the formula for the coefficients of the ch.p., p. 70. The trick in Section 13.7 for obtaining a lower bound for P^0 is due to Bellman [3]; an alternative and neat proof of Lemma 13.3 is given by Beckenbach and Bellman [1]. The return difference relations (30) and (31) are simple extensions of results of Kalman [3].

A general discussion of return difference and sensitivity in multivariable systems can be found in Cruz and Perkins [1], Perkins and Cruz [1], and Cruz [1]; see also Pagurek [1]. For insight into Ex. 13.7 consult Wierzbicki [1].

REFERENCES

B.D.O. ANDERSON, J.B. MOORE

[1] Linear Optimal Control. Prentice-Hall, Englewood Cliffs, N.J., 1971.

G. BASILE, G. MARRO

[1] Luoghi caratteristici dello spazio degli stati relativi al controllo dei sistemi lineari. L'Elettrotecnica 55 (12), 1968, pp. 1-7.

[2] Controlled and conditioned invariant subspaces in linear system theory. J. Opt. Th. & Appl. 3 (5), 1969, pp. 306-315.

[3] On the observability of linear time-invariant systems with unknown inputs. J. Opt. Th. & Appl. 3 (6), 1969, pp. 410-415.

E. BECKENBACH, R. BELLMAN

[1] Inequalities. Springer-Verlag, Berlin, 1961.

R. BELLMAN

[1] Dynamic Programming. Princeton University Press, Princeton, N.J., 1957.

[2] Introduction to the Mathematical Theory of Control Processes. Vol. 1, Linear Equations and Quadratic Criteria. Academic Press, New York, 1967.

[3] Upper and lower bounds for the solutions of the matrix Riccati equation. J. Math. Anal. & Appl. 17, 1967, pp. 373-379.

S.P. BHATTACHARYYA

[1] Output regulation with bounded energy. IEEE Trans. Aut. Control AC-18 (4), 1973, pp. 381-383.

S.P. BHATTACHARYYA, J.B. PEARSON, W.M. WONHAM

[1] On zeroing the output of a linear system. Information and Control 20 (2), 1972, pp. 135-142.

F.M. BRASCH, JR., J.B. PEARSON

[1] Pole placement using dynamic compensators. IEEE Trans. Aut. Control AC-15 (1), 1970, pp. 34-43.

P. BRUNOVSKY

[1] A classification of linear controllable systems. Kybernetika 6 (3), 1970, pp. 173-188.